THE POLITICS OF POLITICAL SCIENCE

In this thought-provoking book, Paulo Ravecca presents a series of interlocking studies on the politics of political science in the Americas.

Focusing mainly on the cases of Chile and Uruguay, Ravecca employs different strands of critical theory to challenge the mainstream narrative about the development of the discipline in the region, emphasizing its ideological aspects and demonstrating how the discipline itself has been shaped by power relations. Ravecca metaphorically charts the (non-linear) transit from "cold" to "warm" to "hot" intellectual temperatures to illustrate his—alternative—narrative. Beginning with a detailed quantitative study of three regional academic journals, moving to the analysis of the role of subjectivity (and political trauma) in academia and its discourse in relation to the dictatorships in Chile and Uruguay, and arriving finally at an intimate meditation on the experience of being a queer scholar in the Latin American academy of the 21st century, Ravecca guides his readers through differing explorations, languages, and methods.

The Politics of Political Science: Re-Writing Latin American Experiences offers an essential reflection on both the relationship between knowledges and politics and the political and ethical role of the scholar today, demonstrating how the study of the politics of knowledge deepens our understanding of the politics of our times.

Paulo Ravecca is Assistant Professor in the Department of Political Science at the Universidad de la República, Uruguay, where he researches epistemology and the history of political science; critical theories (queer, neo-Marxist, postcolonial, and poststructural approaches); political economy and international relations; and gender and sexuality. He is an associate editor of the *Journal of Narrative Politics* and *Crítica Contemporánea. Revista de Teoría Política*. He holds a PhD in Political Science from York University.

THE POLITICS OF POLITICAL SCIENCE

Re-Writing Latin American Experiences

Paulo Ravecca

Routledge
Taylor & Francis Group

NEW YORK AND LONDON

First published 2019
by Routledge
52 Vanderbilt Avenue, New York, NY 10017

and by Routledge
2 Park Square, Milton Park, Abingdon, Oxon OX14 4RN

Routledge is an imprint of the Taylor & Francis Group, an informa business

British Library Cataloguing-in-Publication Data
A catalogue record for this book is available from the British Library

Library of Congress Cataloging-in-Publication Data
A catalog record for this book has been requested

ISBN: 978-0-8153-6307-1 (hbk)
ISBN: 978-0-8153-6308-8 (pbk)
ISBN: 978-1-351-11055-6 (ebk)

Typeset in Times New Roman
by Apex CoVantage, LLC

To

my mother, Cristina, and Andrew.

Voyage

from home

to home

from home

CONTENTS

*Complex Relationality at Work: A Radical Alternative
    to Mainstream Tales 219*
*Whose Theory? Sustaining Thinking, Protecting
    (Self-)Reflection 231*

TABLES

FIGURES

ACKNOWLEDGMENTS

This is a book full of people. My gratitude is colossal and ineffable.

For helping me to untangle academia and its powers, I thank my interviewees: Adolfo Garcé, Alberto Mayol, Alfonso Donoso, Alfredo Joignant, Alfredo Rehren, Álvaro Rico, Andreas Feldmann, Anthony Pezzola, Carlos Durán, Carlos Fortín, Carlos Huneeus, Carmen Midaglia, Claudia Heiss, Claudio Fuentes, Daniel Buquet, Daniel Chasquetti, David Altman, Diego Rossello, Eugenio Guzmán, Francisco Díaz, Gerardo Caetano, Hugo Frühling, Jacques Ginesta, Jaime Baeza, Jaime Yaffé, Javier Gallardo, Jorge Landinelli, Jorge Lanzaro, José Miguel Busquets, José Viacava, Juan Andrés Moraes, Juan Carlos Gómez Leyton, Julián González Guyer, Julieta Suárez, Laura Gioscia, Leonardo Letelier, Lorena Oyarzún, Lucía Selios, Luis Senatore, Marcelo Mella, María de los Ángeles Fernández Ramil, María Ester Mancebo, María Francisca Quiroga, Marisa von Bülow, Mónica Tagle, Nicolás Bentancur, Niki Johnson, Óscar Landerretche, Pablo Bulcourf, Patricio Navia, Pedro Narbondo, Roberto Durán, Rodrigo Egaña, Romeo Pérez Antón, Rossana Castiglioni, Stéphanie Alenda, Tomás Chuaqui, and Umut Aydin; also Germán Parula, who shared his views on academia and its political role in Uruguay.

I have so many treasured memories from my years in the Department of Political Science at York University in Toronto. Courses and professors left deep marks in this text: Andil Gosine, Asher Horowitz, Carlota McAllister, Esteve Morera, Hannes Lacher, Liisa North, Shannon Bell, Steven Hellman, as well as Anna Agathangelou and Ananya Mukherjee-Reed, who provided extraordinary support in the first steps of the project. I am grateful to many friends whose presence in Toronto enriched my thinking—and life, among them: Art Babayants, Balca Arda, Carmen Sanchez, Carmen Teeple Hopkins, Cory Jansson, Enrique López de Mesa, Gökbörü Sarp Tanyıldız, Hide Miyagawa, Jan Anderson,

Jessica Parish, Johannah May Black, Jordi Diez, Juan Marsiaj, Karl Dahlquist, Nadia Hasan, Nausheen Quayyum, Nishant Upadhyay, Ruth Felder, Sarah LeBlanc, Sarah Naumes, Shelley Liebembuk, Thomas Chiasson-LeBel, and Vilma Filici. The Church and Wellesley yoga community was a space for healing and joy: the word *yoga* appears twice in a study about knowledge and power because of you. Ana María Araújo, Anabel Rieiro, Carla Álvarez, Cécile Casen, Carmen Dangiolillo, Denisse Rodriguez, Doris Hajer, Fortunato Morales, Gonzalo Ghio, Inés Ksiazenicki, Juan Andrés Bresciano, Leonardo Carrión Eguiguren, Lucía Tiscornia, Marcelo Rossal, María Eugenia Jung, María Gravina, María José Vega, Pablo Liddle, Raquel Lubartowski, Sofía Schuster, Sol Montero, Soledad Morales, Susana Mallo, and Valeria Mura also nurtured, in different moments and ways, the journey of this book.

In addition to my interviewees, several colleagues at the Instituto de Ciencia Política have supported this project: Ana Laura De Giorgi, Camilo López Burián, Cecilia Rocha, Diego Sempol, Florencia Antía, and Marcela Schenck. I will highlight one colleague: Pedro Narbondo, who passed away in 2015, leaving a legacy of critical thinking, a sharp sense of humor, and a suspicion of *neoliberalism* (his emphasis). I am grateful to Federico Traversa, Lucía Selios, and Verónica Pérez, also from my current department, as well as to Diego Hernández and Mariana Mosteiro for their guidance in the construction of the database of academic articles employed in Chapters 2 and 3. Special thanks to Marcos Segantini for (re)teaching me SPSS. Belén Villegas, Camila Zeballos, and Mariana Mancebo helped me with the data analysis. Mariana also provided important support throughout the research phase.

The Research Group on the History of Political Science of the Latin American Political Science Association (ALACIP) and the Research Committee 33: The Study of Political Science as a Discipline of the International Political Science Association (IPSA) have both been good venues to share this research and to get feedback. Special thanks to Arturo Fernández, Bob Reinalda, Cecilia Lesgart, Emily Hauptmann, Enrique Gutiérrez Márquez, Erkki Berndtson, Héctor Zamitiz, João Feres, John E. Trent, Julián Caicedo, Karla Valverde Viesca, Katarzyna Krzywicka, Michael B. Stein, Nastassja Rojas Silva, Nelson Cardozo, Robert Adcock, Sergio Ángel Baquero, Thibaud Boncourt, and Victor Alarcón Olguín. Juan Pablo Luna provided useful comments on previous versions of Chapters 2 and 3.

I thank The Latin American Council of Social Sciences (CLACSO), The Centre for Research on Latin America and the Caribbean (CERLAC) at York University, and the Tokyo Foundation for their support at different stages of this study.

The classroom is my favorite corner of academia. I have the privilege of sharing and discussing my ideas with students in various graduate and undergraduate courses. Agustín Abreu, Diego León Pérez, Gabriel Delacoste, Gastón Mántaras, Mauro Casa, and Sofía Idiarte were among the first participants in my course on critical theory back in 2012. I still keep emails, comments, and notes from those conversations. The exchanges held in a critical theory group in the Instituto de Ciencia Política during the year in 2016 were insightful and helpful. Recently, I was invited to speak at the Second International Meeting of Political Science in Popayán, Colombia, an event entirely conceived of and run by students for students. While there, I had the opportunity to engage in productive dialogue about the discipline and its politics with Aníbal Pérez-Liñán and Porfirio Cardona Restrepo, among other colleagues.

Constanza Moreira was a doula at my academic birth and encouraged the urge that launched this journey. Javier Gallardo embraced this project from its inception, when I wrote a transgressive BA thesis. Eduardo Canel always provided me with precious guidance. In both Canada and Uruguay, we discussed the database as well as Chapter 2 for hours. Naeem Inayatullah was extremely generous with his detailed and insightful feedback on a previous version of Chapter 4. Antonio Torres-Ruiz is a friend with whom I share the dream of (as well as the everyday struggle for) a more self-reflexive academia.

David McNally was my professor and doctoral supervisor. He always shelters the space of reflection and puts into action his theoretical and political convictions in a way that I respect and relish. The generosity of Viviana Patroni, who met with me numerous times to discuss this research in depth, is something that I treasure. Her theoretical insights and expertise on Latin America helped improve many sections of the manuscript. Alan Sears helped me choose effective metaphors to articulate the leading epistemological points of the study, and Fernando Leiva was the most careful, kind, and sharp reader that one could ask for.

The conceptually beautiful cover of the book was designed by a phenomenal artist and poet: Kilby Smith-McGregor. Germán Fernández took stunning pictures that served as raw material for its crafting. Lilian Yap carefully read the entire manuscript, making both editorial and conceptual suggestions; this book and its author have an endless debt to her. Natalja Mortensen, my editor at Routledge, has been incredibly supportive in this process; from the beginning I knew that I was in extremely careful and caring hands. María Landschoot has always been there to patiently answer my questions and orient me through the complexities of putting a book together.

Elizabeth Dauphinee is my frequent coauthor and beloved friend. Our beings merge in the rhythms of awe when we write and think together. Chapter 4 has been possible because of her emotional and intellectual input.

Ana Franco was incredibly supportive in my first few months in Toronto. Paul Soren and Barbara Soren are family and people who carefully listen to others; I just love that—I have the unusual blessing of being able to talk about my research to a very interested mother-in-law. I spent six happy years of walks, conversations, laughter, and critical thought with my friend Robert Kohls. We founded an empire on Church Street: we queered the space and, even though we now live thousands of kilometers apart, we still do!

Amparo Menéndez-Carrión has been a true mentor for me—growth and durability are markers of a pedagogical relationship always on the move. The significance of her feedback to the entire manuscript was unparalleled. Gabriela Mosteiro is my beloved sister and I would not be writing these pages without her support: for giving me Foucault and Freud to read when I was almost a child, and for many other things—thank you. Once, Cristina Barcia said to me that the best destiny of pain and trauma is creation. *En eso estamos*. This book is part of such an in*terminable* existential task.

Marta Fonseca, my mother, embraces me with unconditional love. Her very presence in the world pushes me to be a better person, whatever that means for a post-structural*ized* Marxist scholar—thank you for teaching me solidarity and for reading poems and stories to me when I was little. The thirst for making sense of the world that I absorbed from you is at the basis of this book.

Finally, I thank my intimate reader: Andrew Soren. Our relationship, made by passion, love, and *eudaemonia*, is inscribed in the heart of this book. In contrast to what many writers confess, I do not feel compelled to thank my partner for his "patience," because while I was writing this, you were on your own journey of creation and thinking. I celebrate that, together *and* separately, we strive for beauty and excellence.

Readers will call me on the failures of this book: the hard task of critique and emancipation is always in need of others—my gratitude, then, to the other.

INTRODUCTION

The Politics of Political Science in Latin America

All truth is simple. Is that not a double lie?
—Friedrich Nietzsche (2007, p. 156)

Proclamar la verdad: ¡el supremo ardid de guerra! [Proclaiming the truth: the supreme ruse of war!]
—Antonio Machado (1969, p. 154)

This book is built on two lifelong intellectual obsessions: the relationship between knowledge and power, and the liberating potential of self-reflection. These themes will be unraveled through the critique of a scholarly discipline that has become my academic home. I still remember some of the questions that would keep me awake during my undergraduate years: Why were poetry and literature, so crucial for making sense of the world to me, frequently considered nonpolitical? Why was Marxism, which I found fascinating, contradictory, and complex, usually regarded as dated, useless, or dangerous? Why did my professors viscerally reject the two authors who captivated me for so many years: Nietzsche and Foucault? What force was always pushing me to desperately try to find other vocabularies and other spaces, beyond the walls of political science (PS), to grapple with the existential and *political* questions that tormented me? If psychoanalytical self-reflection was so important for my survival and growth, could epistemological reflection not make a contribution to PS, allowing it to become more sensitive to its own motions of power? The queries evolved over time, reaching far beyond my academic experience in Uruguay. Were there significant connections between dominant conceptions of democracy and the defeat of socialism? Did neoliberalism affect the practice of PS in the region and beyond? What were the political implications of positivism? What should, finally, our role as political scientists—as teachers, in particular—be in this broken and unjust world?

While reading these questions, the reader will probably suspect that this book will not offer full, satisfying answers. And such a mistrust is, I am afraid, not misguided. This study deals with these concerns by situating them on relatively narrow ground: the politics of political science (PPS) in Latin America, with a special focus on Chile and Uruguay.

PPS will be explored through a series of interlocking studies that present detailed empirical analyses of disciplinary trajectories as well as glimpses from personal experience, all of which will be woven together with threads of critical theory.[1] The core argument of this exercise is that PS mutations in the region have been interlinked with broader political transformations and that these mutations—more importantly—are themselves political. Therefore, reading the alleged academic shift from the loud presence of Marxism in the 1960s to the hegemony of liberalism in the 1990s as ascetic scholarly progress, which has become disciplinary common sense, conceals power. In other words, not only are changes in PS political, but the ways in which they have been frequently discussed and framed by the discipline's practitioners—what I call the mainstream narrative—constitute an *internal* moment of the political processes engulfing academia. Framing PS history is an exercise of power itself, and this project is all about uncovering power, particularly through exploring how the latter operates through the ways PS narrates itself in Latin America.

By unraveling the entanglements between PS, politics, and society, the book challenges mainstream PS' pretensions to detachment, neutrality, and objectivity and questions its tale about the virtuous and supposedly necessary link between our discipline and democracy. The ideological changes within social sciences at large, and in political science more specifically, are related, I propose, to a complex set of changes that includes the political defeat of the left, the effects of the 1970s' right-wing dictatorships, and the regional hegemony of the US. PPS shifts from the question of the discipline's institutionalization—a leitmotif of the scholarship about PS development in Latin America—to the problem of *what* has been and is being institutionalized, and its political implications. Thus, this is a book about the politics of knowledge as well as about politics, period: through exploring the politics of knowledge, we will deepen our knowledge of the politics of our times. By looking, for instance, at the different ways the Chilean and Uruguayan dictatorships managed their relationship with PS, we will expand our knowledge about these two regimes.

Such an exploration of PS' trajectory in Chile and Uruguay (including snapshots of other countries in the Americas) illustrates how our ways of knowing are part of the history we are trying to understand. Thus, it points to the *political* relevance of self-reflection in the study of politics, particularly if our intention is to avoid reproducing dominant relations of power through scholarship. To be sure—and this is a leading theoretical argument of the book—that knowledge is political means that its practitioners are politically and ethically accountable.

This book engages with the intersections between epistemology, political science, and politics, and it takes the reader on a journey of different explorations, languages, and methods: from detailed quantitative analyses of three regional scholarly journals to the study of the role of subjectivity (and political trauma) in academia and its discourse; from the dictatorships in Chile and Uruguay to the experience of being queer in the Latin American academia of the 21st century. The very structure of the book, in particular the way in which it displays its variety of methods and epistemological idioms, embodies a third argument: there is a need to know in different ways; knowledge requires pluralization. Epistemological plurality demands, if not to be embraced, then at least to be accepted by mainstream political scientists. In the journey of writing this book, plurality has become another obsession for me.

The themes of knowledge, power, self-reflection, and plurality, then, are the core of this book. They are put into motion through three stories about political scientists and political science that take place in Chile and Uruguay—and Canada. The examination of these experiences, however, transcends their national settings, offering us tools to think about power and knowledge interactions in other parts of Latin America, and even elsewhere. Research for this book included the systematic analysis of 1,194 articles published in the leading journals of the countries under study, 58 semi-structured interviews, an auto-ethnographic narrative, as well as other complementary strategies.

The first story (Chapter 2) will take us to Chile and the PS developed during Pinochet's dictatorship, which I will call authoritarian political science (APS). By showing that important elements of the discipline's infrastructure were created during, and sometimes by, this authoritarian regime, the chapter challenges the dominant PS narrative (Altman, 2005, 2006; Barrientos Del Monte, 2012; Buquet, 2012; Fortou, Leyva Botero, Preciado, & Ramírez, 2013; Huneeus, 2006; Viacava, 2012, among others) that links the institutionalization of the discipline to liberal democracy in a linear fashion. The analysis of APS is theoretically significant because it transforms liberalism from a "hero" into a less attractive creature—a creature deprived of its intrinsic democratic powers. The trinity of liberalism-democracy-PS is scrutinized, and the chapter concludes by suggesting a need for nuanced and empirically and theoretically informed understandings of PS's multiple historical trajectories. The focus will be on how democracy is discussed by APS, and with what consequences.

This chapter is "cold." In a sort of Brechtian tone, APS' story is meant to reach the minds, not the hearts. Detailed empirical data expressed in numbers and historical records will lead the analysis. Social sciences, however, are human activities, and therefore we need to look at the human beings involved in them in order to grasp the "reality" of these disciplines. If the aim is to make sense of the historical trajectories of knowledge and power, then witnessing other stories—and, perhaps more importantly, *other ways of telling stories*—seems warranted.

Chile and Uruguay are typical research material in comparative politics. I will come back to the theoretical status and epistemological role of comparison in this study at the end of this Introduction, but the similarities include relatively robust democratic experiences and *coup d'etats* in 1973, followed by right-wing dictatorships. However, their PS trajectories were different. APS was not developed in Uruguay. The dictatorship there was monolithically repressive *vis-à-vis* the social sciences. Indeed, Uruguayan PS would not be fully institutionalized until after the transition to democracy. This book aims to unpack the *theoretical* significance of such a contrast. What are the implications, for interpretive purposes, of the absence of APS for the politics of the discipline in Uruguay? What does this difference reveal about PS' history and about these two regimes that, in other respects (the use of terror, to begin with), were so similar? To complicate the analysis even more, their divergent disciplinary trajectories did not prevent an overarching commonality between the two cases—the ultimate hegemony of liberalism and the rise of mainstream forms of analysis. How can we make sense of this?

In order to unpack these complex paths of convergence and divergence, Chapter 3 embarks on a comprehensive study of PPS in Uruguay. The chapter proceeds through a problematizing re-description (Shapiro, 2005) of the history of PS from the point of view of power-knowledge dynamics (Foucault, 1991a, 1991b; Marcuse, 1991; Gramsci, 2008) and identifies the conceptual and institutional components that constitute the dominant disciplinary discourse (Foucault, 1991a, 1991b). The emphasis is again on the way democracy is discussed, and the focus is on Uruguay, but a comparative perspective is kept by partially following the previous chapter's structure and analytical strategy. The journey will stop at the various intersections between power and knowledge that reveal meaningful similarities and contrasts with Chile.

In addition to the numbers and the historical records, the inquiry in this chapter makes use of in-depth interviews with Uruguayan political scientists. In contrast with the previous chapter, the discourse analysis here pays attention to the role that the traumatic experience of the dictatorship had on PS' ideological motions. In this way, the book takes an extra step to grasp the role of lived experience and subjectivity in intellectual and political transformations, thus deepening and furthering self-reflection. These theoretical and methodological features make this chapter epistemologically "warmer" than its predecessor.

Self-reflection transforms analysis: Chapter 4 is an auto-ethnographic account that raises the book's temperature to the point of burning, threatening to melt the boundaries between story, subject, and object. The exploration of (my own) subjectivity and personal experience as a young queer scholar serves to deepen *and pluralize* the analysis of PPS (Brigg & Bleiker, 2010; Dauphinee, 2013; Ravecca & Dauphinee, 2018). Concretely, the narrative looks at the discipline as a place of human interaction and shows that what happens "there"—or rather, here—affects its inhabitants and the knowledge that we can or cannot create. It also offers a reflection on how the multilayeredness of knowledge and power seems to always exceed the vocabularies meant to grasp it.

The "I" (i.e., my story) is, in this case, a *tool* for knowledge production and theoretical reflection. It enriches the previous chapters. Yet it also depends on them to fulfill its aims, and this means that the linearity of epistemological temperatures that we have been going through so far (cold, warm, and hot) needs to be questioned and complexified; and it will be, by Chapter 5. What if all the epistemological temperatures were needed and their syncretic mixtures acknowledged? What if our thermostats had to collapse so as to be reimagined by leaving aside epistemic supremacies?

The personal will be allowed into the main chamber of the book—i.e., the philosophical meditation on thinking, as such—in order to destabilize and enrich it. The hidden plot that unfolds throughout this book is the struggle for sustaining reflexive thinking, a genuine human need in the sense of Marcuse, amid power, trauma, and abuse (be it sexual, political, or academic; the difference is, after all, irrelevant). Thinking is threatened by different forms of power that leave traces and marks on the body of thought, and the body of PS is not an exception. This book tries to appropriate such threats and traumas, both personal and collective, to unleash PS' political and intellectual possibilities.

Let me now turn to the broader story woven together by the different chapters of this book. In the 1960s, Marxism was influential in the Latin American social sciences. In the 1990s, this situation changed, and liberalism became dominant. This is particularly salient in the cases of Chile and Uruguay, but it applies, at least to certain degree, to other Latin American countries as well. In the continent that hosted liberation theology, dependency theory, critical pedagogy, and local expressions of socialist thought,[2] the advancement of mainstream forms of social science did imply significant shifts in writing and thinking. The mainstream PS narrative today describes this shift as a process of modernization and improvement, since social scientists would have moved from "activism" to "serious science," "rightly" embracing the principle of academic neutrality.[3] This study proposes an alternative interpretation (Bevir, 2003; Geertz, 1997, 2003) of this process, telling the story of these changes in a different way.

The broader argument here is that changes within PS in the region are related to power relations and contextual transformations at different levels: the rise of the United States, the collapse of the Soviet Union, the traumatizing dictatorships of the 1970s, the democratic transitions, the hegemony of neoliberalism, as well as academic dynamics of conflict and institution-building all impacted PS' discourse and people. Power affects—sometimes limits—thinking: the question is how this has been so in the experiences under study. Furthermore, that PS *is* human activity (Marx, 1978) that has affected and is affecting others necessarily means that it was not only shaped by these dynamics but that it also contributed to shaping them, as we will see in Chapters 2, 3, and 4.

In an effort to make sense of the interplay between the processes referred to above and PPS, I propose an organizing category—*complex relationality*. This notion is informed by different critical theories (see Chapter 1) and attempts to gather together the multiplicity of these registers of knowledge and power to unravel their interconnectedness. This theoretical category will organize the analytical journey.

Why complex, and why relationality? It is *complex* because gathering these diverse processes into a unifying interpretation is challenging, given that they seem to belong to different arenas of social reality (academia, the political, the international, the economic, and so on). In order to navigate this multiplicity, this book needs to look for assemblages (Puar, 2007) or points of porosity (Buck-Morss, 2009) between knowledge production and dissemination, identity, subjectivity, political economy, conventional politics, and the transnational dimension of political change. PPS is also *relational* because in its account all these aspects not only intersect but also dynamically affect, and even mutually constitute, each other.[4] The interpretive exercise shows how apparently disconnected realms of experience are, in effect, intermingled. Displaying the intertwinements between registers of change is a core interest of my reinterpretation of PS' transformations (Bevir, 2003).

The leading premise of this study, from which the notion of complex relationality unfolds, is that knowledge production is a key component of the broader social relations in which it occurs, and therefore, knowing is itself an embedded social process that has no exteriority from the multiple manifestations of power. Conceiving things as relations is to interiorize their interdependence into the thing itself (Ollman, 1971). Consequently, acknowledging PS as a relational field means that PS *is* those relations that constitute it. At odds with a mainstream narrative sustained by a positivist, dualistic, mind-world mindset (Jackson, 2011), this book proposes instead a reflexivist exercise that empirically shows some of the ways that in Chile and Uruguay, politics affected PS, and PS participated in politics (i.e., PPS).

In short, the story of the institutionalization and development of Latin American PS, in particular the consolidation of its mainstream, is a powerful occasion to explore the relationship between knowledge and politics. In order to unpack PPS through the dynamics of complex relationality, this book will need the assistance of critical theory, or better yet, of critical theor*ies* in plural. Before I present the theoretical and methodological "how" of the research in the following chapter, let me conclude this Introduction by referring to two issues: first, what I mean in this book by mainstream PS and mainstream narratives and, second, on what basis this book focuses on Chile and Uruguay as case studies.

Kathryn Sikkink argued in the closing roundtable of the Fifth Congress of the Uruguayan Political Science Association that to delineate "the mainstream" is always a situated and, to some extent, arbitrary exercise (Asuntos Públicos, 2014). Not quite. The controversies around the Perestroika movement within the

American Political Science Association (Monroe, 2005) were not an accident, and it is not simply fortuitous that in the email that started the revolt in 2000, an anonymous Mr. Perestroika asked American political scientists: "Why are all the articles from APSR from the same methodology—statistics or game theory—with a 'symbolic' article in Political Theory. Where is political history, international history, political sociology, interpretative methodology, constructivists, area studies, critical theory and last but not least—post modernism?" (cited in Monroe, 2005, p. 10). There is more than enough empirical evidence to show the existence of a mainstream within American PS that is characterized by empiricism, quantitativism, and rationalist assumptions. In this environment shaped by an obsession with statistics and mathematics (Isaac, 2015; Fujii, 2016; Trent, 2012), political theory is perceived as a "luxury" (Brown, 2011) and, therefore, something that the discipline can live without. Even qualitative research, case studies in particular, has been displaced from the most prestigious US journals. Research, in this context, seems to be driven by methods and not by problems, which according to some observers makes it useless and disconnected from the "real" world. Critics have pointed out the lack of reflection about the epistemological and ideological premises behind all of these choices.[5]

The mainstream is not only liberal and positivist, but also sexist and based on white supremacy (Ahmed, 2012; Fujii, 2016; Rocha Carpiuc, 2016). Critics from inside and outside the discipline have argued that mainstream forms of American PS, both old and new, besides embracing liberal democracy, have been functional to the reproduction of capitalist, patriarchal, and/or racist structures (Ake, 1979; Alexander, 2005; Cox, 1987; Groth, 1998; Marcuse, 1991; Kaufman, 2005; Lowi, 2005).[6]

The influence of continental Europe, the tradition of the public intellectual, as well as the presence of forms of analysis inspired by Marxism have been stronger in Latin America than in North America. Let us notice, for instance, that dependency theory (Cardoso & Faletto, 1979) was written *after* the behavioral revolution consolidated in the US (Berndtson, 1997). Even though the increasing penetration of American academia is quite visible (Bulcourf, Krzywicka, & Ravecca, 2017; Rocha Carpiuc, 2014; Borón, 2007), this sort of heterodoxy in theory *and* methods persists today. What does mainstream mean, then, in this context? The equation that I want to highlight—and unpack—here is between mainstream Latin American PS and the liberal order.[7] By the mainstream narrative about the development of PS, I simply mean the way in which the history of the discipline has been predominantly told in numerous venues such as books, articles, conference presentations, oral traditions, and so on (see the "Methods" section in Chapter 1). The section entitled "Complex Relationality at Work" in Chapter 5 shows how the way PS' story is told by old and new mainstreams exercises epistemic violence by naturalizing positivism, liberalism, and, by extension, capitalism.

As I mentioned above, Chile and Uruguay are often compared. Both countries are located in the Southern Cone, are small, and relatively "developed" within the Latin American context. Additionally, they share similar political trajectories; both had relatively strong democratic institutions that were seriously challenged and broken down around the same time and under similar circumstances. The dictatorships that followed also had plenty of common features. The two countries are frequently equated in terms of the development of PS as well because of the relative youth of the discipline *vis-à-vis* other social sciences (Altman & Policzer, 2013).

Once the similarities and differences of Chile's and Uruguay's PS are addressed, one specific feature of their divergent trajectories comes to light: I refer to the very existence of APS in Chile, and its absence in Uruguay. It was this sharp contrast between the two disciplinary trajectories that triggered the comparative component of this book. This difference will be accounted for by looking at the relationship between the discipline and its political context, in particular the different ways their respective authoritarian regimes exercised power. Moreover, even though some recent analyses have classified their current or recent center-left governments in the same group (Lanzaro, 2007), Chile and Uruguay also differ in terms of their relationship with neoliberalism (Bogliaccini, 2012; Bogliaccini & Filgueira, 2011). I will pay some attention to this because it is a significant aspect of the context of PS.[8] I want to stress the following point, however: the main epistemological role of the study of the experiences of Chile and Uruguay is to empirically *inform* the theoretical reflection that this book offers about the relationship between knowledge and power. The heart of this book belongs to critical theory, and not to comparative politics.

After witnessing, and, of course, being protagonists of the four stories on knowledge and power (the comparison itself being the fourth one), we will breathe deeply and slowly walk from the PPS amphitheater to the (seemingly) more peaceful chamber of philosophical reflection. The temperature will be strangely pleasant now. We will lie down on the old divan placed at the center of the structure. Abruptly, we will be asked if the house should be reformed—again—to become a home, or if it should simply be demolished.

Outline of the Book

Chapter 1 offers a summary of different theories that challenge neopositivism and acknowledge the political nature of knowledge and, by extension, academia. Through this exploration, I craft my own theoretical vocabulary to analyze PPS. I introduce the category of complex relationality, which builds from those critical theories and attempts to capture the complexity of the power-knowledge relationship. The chapter also presents the methodological strategy followed by the book.

Chapter 2 studies the development of political science during Pinochet's dictatorship in Chile. It fully rewrites the history of the discipline in the country by highlighting a side of it that has hitherto been neglected: the fact that the main components of the infrastructure of Chilean political science were created during, *and by*, the dictatorship. The story of the "Chicago Boys" in economics has frequently been told. However, the Chilean dictatorship was also active in the other social sciences, and this is significant to both the study of the history of political science as well as the recent political history of the country.

Chapter 3 explores the Uruguayan case, which is different from the Chilean one in significant respects. The dictatorship there persecuted the social sciences without founding its own sites of knowledge production. This is interesting because it shows how powers with more cultural density are more effective in creating hegemony: in Uruguay, the dictatorship did not produce the same kind of lasting (cultural and institutional) legacy. However, the dictatorship did have strong impacts. For instance, the political trauma it inflicted on the (left-leaning) academic community pushed it in the direction of abandoning all forms of radicalism and to instead naturalize liberal democracy. This chapter begins to deal with the relationship between academic shifts, power, and subjectivity. Ideological-epistemological shifts also "happen" in people's (in this case, scholars') subjectivities.

Chapter 4 is an auto-ethnography that grapples with my experiences as a young gay political scientist in Uruguay and PhD candidate in Canada. The exercise deals with the complexities of acceptance, homophobia, and rejection in Uruguayan and Canadian academia. It theorizes the multiplicity of power and shows how the power-knowledge linkage does not respect the boundaries that we impose on it: it travels from the body to nation-states (and penetrates the discipline that attempts to study politics).

Chapter 5 weaves the previous ones into one consolidated story. It theorizes the findings and offers a meditation on the relationship between knowledges and politics, and on the political and ethical role of the scholar today.

The case studies show how, in both Chile and Uruguay, the discipline has been shaped by power relations (domestic and international, academic and political). This challenges the mainstream narrative about the development of the discipline in the region, which (*a*) does not explore the ideological dimension *of* or *within* political science; and (*b*) contradictorily, highlights the virtuous relationship between political science and democracy. Chapter 4 approaches the issue from an entirely different perspective: that of personal experience in Latin America and Canada.

There is a progression from Chapter 2 to 4 in terms of the integration of subjectivity and self-reflection into the analysis of the discipline and its politics. Chapter 2 is cold and distant, full of quantitative and qualitative data. Chapter 3 approaches the issue by including the subjectivity of the scholars who were interviewed: the transition from Marxism to liberalism was also an affective process. Finally, the auto-ethnography fully deals with the relationship between the personal, the academic, and the political. Chapters 1 and 5 provide the framework of PPS: Chapter 1 explores a range of critical theories that tackle the political dimension of knowledge production (and, thus, craft the theoretical language and approach to PPS that is mobilized in the following chapters), and Chapter 5 offers the general story that results from putting all of the previous chapters together, including my own meditation on the political responsibility of the critical scholar. Chapter 5 also problematizes the very structure of the book from "cold" (hard data) to "hot" (subjectivity), showing how these different epistemological moments of making sense of reality need each other. In other words, the very progression that the book deploys (cold-warm-hot) will be challenged at the end.

Notes

1. The expression "the politics of political science" is not mine. It is employed by other authors; for instance, by Morris-Jones (1983). However, in this case the same name does not mean the same thing: the specificity of this study lies at the intersection between the literature on the development of PS and critical theory.
2. The Marxist intellectual José Carlos Mariátegui (1979) and the pedagogue Paulo Freire (1970) are icons of this saga of Latin American critical thought while writers such as Eduardo Galeano (1973), Pablo Neruda (1960), and Gabriel García Márquez (1967) are examples of the frequent interpenetration between literature and politics in the region. Meanwhile, the composers, musicians, and singers Violeta Parra, Alfredo Zitarrosa, and Silvio Rodríguez, well known in Latin America for their politically engaged lyrics, marked generations of activists. Numerous critical intellectual projects are being developed outside of mainstream PS today. A recent example from Ecuador is the *buen vivir* or *sumak kawsay* [to live well]. This notion, understood as being of indigenous origins, attempts to overcome not just capitalism, but a civilizational crisis. This crisis is understood as resulting from what is usually identified as "Western" ontology, which as the narratives goes, separates reason from body, and thus culture from nature. The *buen vivir* proposes an integrated view where human beings are part of nature, and not opposed to it, which would thus prevent us from perpetuating the instrumental relationship with nature that has led to the environmental crisis that we are facing. The *buen vivir*, finally, would have implications for thinking/practicing politics in Latin America and the Caribbean and anywhere else, and also for scholars and their understanding of the analytical endeavor (Carpio Benalcázar, 2009; Ceceña, 2010; Lander, 2010; León, 2009; Ramírez, 2010).
3. For instance, Bejarano and Wills (2005), Garcé (2005), Lanzaro (2000), Amorim Neto and Santos (2005), Mejía Acosta, Freidenberg, and Pachano (2005), and Loaeza (2005), among many others, embody such a view.
4. PPS is not completely structuralist: this mutual constitution is full of accidents and can only be comprehended by looking at concrete *histories*.
5. See Andrews (2010); Bennett, Barth, and Rutherford (2003); Caterino (2010); Schram and Caterino (2006); Green and Shapiro (1994, 1996); Kasza (2005); Luke and McGovern (2010); McGovern (2010); Mead (2010); Monroe (2005); Pion-Berlin and Clearly (2005); Sartori (2004); Shapiro (2005); Taagepera (2007); and Trent (2009, 2014).
6. In October 2004, Giovanni Sartori published an article entitled "Where Is Political Science Going?" in which he harshly criticized a discipline that, in the author's own words, he contributed to creating. Sartori argued that even though he had always resisted American PS' influence, he "could not foresee the narrowness that the notion of science would acquire on American soil" (Sartori, 2004, p. 785). Mainstream PS "has adopted an unsuited model of science (drawn from the hard, exact sciences)

and has failed to establish its own identity (as a soft science) by failing to establish its own, distinctive methodology" (p. 785). In other words, PS became crudely neo-positivist. He also suggests that the "technical" aspects of research have displaced all the other dimensions of science. PS does not reflect on the "process of thinking" (and knowing): future political scientists are trained in "research techniques and statistical processing" which "have almost nothing to do with the 'method of logos,' with the method of thinking" (p. 785). Sartori also denounced the extreme quantitativism that "is in fact driving us into a march of either false precision or precise irrelevancy," and thus insisted that "the alternative, or at least, the alternative for which I side, is to resist the quantification of the discipline. Briefly put, *think before counting*; and, also, *use logic* in thinking" (p. 786, emphasis in original). This does not imply the rejection of quantification and formalization as strategies to analyze social reality. What is rejected is the arrogance and narrow-mindedness with which this is usually done. I think that Sartori's critique should be expanded and radicalized. He states that PS "is going nowhere" and explains what he means by that, but the question of why this has happened, and how the mainstream can be confronted, is not fully addressed. Sartori ignores the issue of power. The Italian author offers a "half critique" incapable of deconstructing the deep roots of what bothers him. Furthermore, his "incomplete" account tends to reproduce the patterns under his critical examination. In very simple words, a cup that is half full is not always better than an empty one: Sartori seems oblivious to the fact that, even if we accept that the relationship between PS and poli-tics cannot be understood in terms of simple overlapping—they belong to different logics and realms of human activity—such a relation is also unthinkable in terms of total disconnection; knowledge and power do interact. Therefore, their interpenetra-tion should be explored. To sum up: the main characteristics of PS noted by Sartori are functional to the ideological role that the discipline performs in contemporary societies (Lowi, 2005).

7. This book will identify and describe two generations of mainstream PS practitioners. The first generation actively embraced liberal democracy and liberalism, which came to be a disciplinary consensus in Latin America. The second generation does not rep-resent an ideological shift: they also embrace liberalism. The generational clash has taken the form of a methodological battle around the alleged supremacy of quantifica-tion (Ravecca, 2014; Rocha Carpiuc, 2012). To what extent the second generation of mainstream political scientists has imposed her vision of science is an open question. I will show these tensions through the Uruguayan case. In any case, that articles with descriptive statistics fall into the "quantitative" camp in many Latin American con-versations, while they are classified as "qualitative" in the US (for example by Pion-Berlin & Clearly, 2005 and Kasza, 2005), reveals that differences persist.

8. The story of the Chicago Boys would be unthinkable without Pinochet's government. Furthermore, and at least to some extent, APS as well as its neoliberal model of devel-opment were both forged by the dictatorship in alliance with appropriate elites that were ready to significantly contribute to the regime's decision making in academia and public policy.

Works Cited

Ahmed, S. (2012). *On being included: Racism and diversity in institutional life*. Durham, NC: Duke University Press.

Ake, C. (1979). *Social science as imperialism: A theory of political development*. Ibadan: Ibadan University Press.

Alexander, J. M. (2005). *Pedagogies of crossing: Meditations on feminism, sexual poli-tics, memory, and the sacred*. Durham, NC: Duke University Press.

Altman, D. (2005). La institucionalización de la ciencia política en Chile y América Latina: Una mirada desde el sur. *Revista de Ciencia Política, 25*(1), 3–15.

Altman, D. (2006). From Fukuoka to Santiago: Institutionalization of political science in Latin America. *PS: Political Science & Politics, 39*(1), 196–203.

Altman, D., & Policzer, P. (2013). Comparative politics of Chile and Uruguay. In R. Valelly (Ed.), *Oxford bibliographies in political science*. New York: Oxford University Press.

Amorim Neto, O., & Santos, F. (2005). La ciencia política en Brasil: El desafío de la expansión. *Revista de Ciencia Política, 25*(1), 101–110.

Andrews, C. W. (2010). Esboço de uma disciplina em crisa: A disputa metodológica na ciência política norte-americana. *Perspectivas: Revista de Ciências Sociais, 38*, 171–194.

Asuntos Públicos [Asuntos Públicos]. (2014, November 7). *¿Qué ciencia política para qué democracia? Parte 4: ¿Clima de perestroika?* [Video file]. Retrieved from www.youtube.com/watch?v=CrHCvveeN98

Barrientos Del Monte, F. (2012). La institucionalización de la ciencia política en América Latina. In F. Reveles Vázquez (Ed.), *La ciencia política en México hoy: ¿Qué sabemos?* (pp. 21–48). Mexico City: Plaza y Valdés.

Bejarano, A. M., & Wills, M. E. (2005). La ciencia política en Colombia: De vocación a disciplina. *Revista de Ciencia Política, 25*(1), 111–123.

Bennett, A., Barth, A., & Rutherford, K. R. (2003). Do we preach what we practice? A survey of methods in political science journals and curricula. *PS: Political Science & Politics, 36*(3), 373–378.

Berndtson, E. (1997, August). *Behaviouralism: Origins of the concept*. Paper presented at the World Conference of Political Science, Seoul, Korea. Retrieved from www.mv.helsinki.fi/home/berndtso/behavior.htm

Bevir, M. (2003). Interpretivism: Family resemblances and quarrels. *Qualitative Methods Newsletter of the American Political Science Association, 1*(2), 18–20. doi: 10.5281/zenodo.998729.

Bogliaccini, J. A. (2012). *Small latecomers into the global market: Power conflict and institutional change in Chile and Uruguay* (Doctoral dissertation). Retrieved from https://cdr.lib.unc.edu/indexablecontent/uuid:617a0663-6b00-4469-b798-410f5794141a

Bogliaccini, J. A., & Filgueira, F. (2011). Capitalismo en el Cono Sur de América Latina luego del final del consenso de Washington: ¿Notas sin partitura? *Revista del CLAD Reforma y Democracia, 51*, 1–23.

Borón, A. (2007). Aristóteles en Macondo: Notas sobre el fetichismo democrático en América Latina. In G. Hoyos Vázquez (Ed.), *Filosofía y teorías políticas entre la crítica y la utopía* (pp. 49–67). Buenos Aires: CLACSO.

Brigg, M., & Bleiker, R. (2010). Autoethnographic international relations: Exploring the self as a source of knowledge. *Review of International Studies, 36*, 779–798.

Brown, W. (2011). La teoría política no es un lujo: Una respuesta a "La Teoría Política Como Profesión" de Timothy Kaufman-Osborn. *Crítica Contemporánea: Revista de Teoría Política, 1*, 1–9. Retrieved from http://cienciassociales.edu.uy/institutodeciencia politica/wp-content/uploads/sites/4/2015/09/wendy.pdf

Buck-Morss, S. (2009). *Hegel, Haiti and universal history*. Pittsburgh: University of Pittsburgh Press.

Bulcourf, P., Krzywicka, K., & Ravecca, P. (2017). Reconstruyendo la ciencia política en América Latina. *Anuario Latinoamericano—Ciencias Políticas y Relaciones Internacionales, 5*, 17–31.

Buquet, D. (2012). El desarrollo de la ciencia política en Uruguay. *Política, 50*(1), 5–29.

Cardoso, F. H., & Faletto, E. (1979). *Dependency and development in Latin America.* Berkeley: University of California Press.

Carpio Benalcázar, P. (2009). El buen vivir, más allá del desarrollo: La nueva perspectiva constitucional en Ecuador. In A. Acosta & E. Martínez (Eds.), *El buen vivir: Una vía para el desarrollo* (pp. 115–148). Quito: Ediciones Abya-Yala.

Caterino, B. (2010). Perestroika's last stand. *PS: Political Science & Politics, 43*(4), 753–754.

Ceceña, A. E. (2010). Pensar la vida y el futuro de otra manera. In I. León (Ed.), *Sumak kawsay/buen vivir y cambios civilizatorios* (pp. 73–88). Quito: Fedaeps.

Cox, R. (1987). *Production, power and the world order.* New York: Columbia University Press.

Dauphinee, E. (2013). *The politics of exile.* New York: Routledge.

Fortou, J. A., Leyva Botero, S., Preciado, A. F., & Ramírez, M. F. (2013). Ciencia política en Colombia: Una revisión de la literatura sobre el estado e historia de la disciplina en el país. In S. Botero Leyva (Ed.), *La ciencia política en Colombia: ¿Una disciplina en institucionalización?* (pp. 27–56). Medellín: Colciencias, Asociación Colombiana de Ciencia Política, Centro de Análisis Político—Universidad Eafit.

Foucault, M. (1991a). *Historia de la sexualidad 1: La voluntad de saber.* Madrid: Siglo Veintiuno de España Editores.

Foucault, M. (1991b). *Saber y verdad.* Madrid: Ediciones La Piqueta.

Freire, P. (1970). *Pedagogy of the oppressed.* New York: Herder and Herder.

Fujii, L. A. (2016). The dark side of DA-RT. *Comparative Politics Newsletter, 26*(1), 25–27.

Galeano, E. (1973). *Open veins of Latin America: Five centuries of the pillage of a continent.* New York: Monthly Review Press.

Garcé, A. (2005). La ciencia política en Uruguay: Un desarrollo tardío, intenso y asimétrico. *Revista de Ciencia Política, 25*(1), 232–244.

García Márquez, G. (1967). *Cien años de soledad.* Bogotá: Editorial Sudamericana.

Geertz, C. (1997). *La interpretación de las culturas.* Barcelona: Gedisa.

Geertz, C. (2003). Interview with Clifford Geertz (J. Gerring, Interviewer). *Qualitative Methods Newsletter of the American Political Science Association, 1*(2), 24–28. doi: 10.5281/zenodo.998745.

Gramsci, A. (2008). *Selections from the prison notebooks* (Q. Hoare & G. Nowell, Trans. & Eds.). New York: International Publishers.

Green, D., & Shapiro, I. (1994). *Pathologies of rational choice theory: A critique of applications in political science.* New Haven, CT: Yale University Press.

Green, D., & Shapiro, I. (1996). Pathologies revisited: Reflections on our critics. In J. Friedman (Ed.), *The rational choice controversy* (pp. 235–276). New Haven, CT: Yale University Press.

Groth, T. (1998, September). *Conceptual understandings of state reform.* Paper presented at the annual meeting of the Latin American Studies Association, Chicago, USA.

Huneeus, C. (2006). El lento y tardío desarrollo de la ciencia política en América Latina, 1966–2006. *Estudios Internacionales, 155*, 137–156.

Isaac, J. C. (2015). The parochialism of the universal, or beware of American political scientists bearing gifts. *The Romanian Journal of Society and Politics, 10*(2), 7–25.

Jackson, P. T. (2011). *The conduct of inquiry in international relations: Philosophy of science and its implications for the study of world politics.* London: Routledge.

Kasza, G. J. (2005). Methodological bias in the American journal of political science. In K. R. Monroe (Ed.), *Perestroika! The raucous rebellion in political science* (pp. 343–353). New Haven, CT: Yale University Press.

Kaufman, S. J. (2005). Rational choice, symbolic politics, and pluralism in the study of violent conflict. In K. R. Monroe (Ed.), *Perestroika! The raucous rebellion in political science* (pp. 87–102). New Haven, CT: Yale University Press.

Lander, E. (2010). Crisis civilizatoria: El tiempo se agota. In I. León (Ed.), *Sumak kawsay/buen vivir y cambios civilizatorios* (pp. 27–40). Quito: Fedaeps.

Lanzaro, J. (2000). *La "segunda" transición en el Uruguay*. Montevideo: Fundación de Cultura Universitaria/ICP.

Lanzaro, J. (2007). La "tercera ola" de las izquierdas latinoamericanas: Entre el populismo y la social-democracia. *Encuentros Latinoamericanos, 1*(1), 20–57.

León, M. (2009). Cambiar la economía para cambiar la vida: Desafíos de una economía para la vida. In A. Acosta & E. Martínez (Eds.), *El buen vivir: Una vía para el desarrollo* (pp. 63–74). Quito: Ediciones Abya-Yala.

Loaeza, S. (2005). La ciencia política: El pulso del cambio mexicano. *Revista de Ciencia Política, 25*(1), 192–203.

Lowi, T. J. (2005). Every poet his own Aristotle. In K. R. Monroe (Ed.), *Perestroika! The raucous rebellion in political science* (pp. 45–52). New Haven, CT: Yale University Press.

Luke, T. W., & McGovern, P. J. (2010). The rebels' yell: Mr. Perestroika and the causes of this rebellion in context. *PS: Political Science & Politics, 43*(4), 729–731.

Machado, A. (1969). *Poesías completas*. Madrid: Espasa-Calpe.

Marcuse, H. (1991). *One-dimensional man: Studies in the ideology of advanced industrial society*. Boston: Beacon Press.

Mariátegui, J. C. (1979). *Siete ensayos de la realidad peruana*. Lima: Editorial Aumauta.

Marx, K. (1978). Economic and philosophic manuscripts of 1844. In R. C. Tucker (Ed.), *The Marx-Engels reader* (pp. 66–125). New York: W.W. Norton & Company.

McGovern, P. J. (2010). Perestroika in political science: Past, present, and future. *PS: Political Science & Politics, 43*(4), 725–727.

Mead, L. M. (2010). Scholasticism in political science. *Perspectives on Politics, 8*(2), 453–464.

Mejía Acosta, A., Freidenberg, F., & Pachano, S. (2005). La ciencia política en Ecuador: un reflejo de su fragilidad democrática (1978–2005). *Revista de ciencia política, 25*(1), 147–161.

Monroe, K. R. (Ed.). (2005). *Perestroika! The raucous rebellion in political science*. New Haven, CT: Yale University Press.

Morris-Jones, W. H. (1983). The politics of political science: The case of comparative studies. *Political Studies, 31*, 1–24.

Neruda, P. (1960). *Canción de gesta*. Havana: Imprenta Nacional de Cuba.

Nietzsche, F. (2007). *The antichrist, Ecce homo, Twilight of the idols, and other writings* (A. Ridley & J. Norman, Eds.). Cambridge: Cambridge University Press.

Ollman, B. (1971). *Alienation: Marx's conception of man in capitalist society*. New York: Cambridge University Press.

Pion-Berlin, D., & Clearly, D. (2005). Methodological bias in the APSR. In K. R. Monroe (Ed.), *Perestroika! The raucous rebellion in political science* (pp. 305–329). New Haven, CT: Yale University Press.

Puar, J. (2007). *Terrorist assemblages: Homonationalism in queer times*. Durham, NC: Duke University Press.

Ramírez, R. (2010). La transición ecuatoriana hacia el buen vivir. In I. León (Ed.), *Sumak kawsay/buen vivir y cambios civilizatorios* (pp. 125–142). Quito: Fedaeps.

Ravecca, P. (2014). *La política de la ciencia política en Chile y Uruguay: Ciencia, poder, contexto. Primeros hallazgos de una agenda de investigación* (Working Paper No. 01/14). Montevideo: Instituto de Ciencia Política.

Ravecca, P., & Dauphinee, E. (2018). Narrative and the possibilities for scholarship. *International Political Sociology, 12*(2), 125–138.

Rocha Carpiuc, C. (2012). La ciencia política en Uruguay (1989–2009): Temas, teorías y metodologías. *Revista Uruguaya de Ciencia Política, 21*(2), 97–127.

Rocha Carpiuc, C. (2014). ¿Hacia una hegemonía del 'modelo mainstream norteamericano'? Enfoques de la ciencia política en América Latina (2000–2012). *Revista Latinoamericana de Investigación Crítica (I+C), 1*(1), 131–166.

Rocha Carpiuc, C. (2016). Women and diversity in Latin American political science. *European Political Science, 15*(4), 457–475.

Sartori, G. (2004). Where is political science going? *PS: Political Science & Politics, 37*(4), 785–787.

Schram, S., & Caterino, B. (2006). *Making political science matter: Debating knowledge, research and method.* New York: NYU Press.

Shapiro, I. (2005). Problems, methods, and theories in the study of politics or what's wrong with political science and what to do about it. In K. R. Monroe (Ed.), *Perestroika! The raucous rebellion in political science* (pp. 66–86). New Haven, CT: Yale University Press.

Taagepera, R. (2007). Why political science is not scientific enough: A symposium. *European Political Science, 6*(2), 111–113.

Trent, J. E. (2009, July). *Political science 2010: Out of step with the world? Empirical evidence and commentary.* Paper presented at the 21st International Political Science World Congress, Santiago, Chile. Retrieved from www.johntrent.ca/published-writings/IPSAIsPolSci-0709.html

Trent, J. (2012). Issues and trends in political science at the beginning of the 21st century: Perspectives from the World of Political Science book series. In J. Trent & M. Stein (Eds.), *The world of political science: A critical overview of the development of political studies around the globe: 1990–2012* (pp. 91–153). Toronto: Barbara Budrich Publishers.

Trent, J. (2014, July). *The state of political studies in the world: Thinking about new paradigms.* Paper presented at the World Congress of the International Political Science Association, Montréal, Canada.

Viacava, J. (2012). La ciencia política en Chile: Una carrera en expansión y transformación. *Política, 50*(1), 93–110.

1

POWER, KNOWLEDGE, AND COMPLEX RELATIONALITY

Theory and Method*

> When I am active *scientifically*, etc.,—when I am engaged in activity which
> I can seldom perform in direct community with others—then I am *social*,
> because I am active as a *man*. Not only is the material of my activity given
> to me as a social product (as is even the language in which the thinker is
> active): my *own* existence *is* social activity, and therefore that which I make
> of myself, I make of myself for society and with the consciousness of myself
> as a social being.
>
> —Karl Marx (1978, p. 86)

Knowledge is a battlefield. From Marxism to postcolonial studies, this insight
is shared by every theory self-identified as "critical," and indeed, it may be
regarded as the epistemological heart of critical thinking and emancipatory politics. After all, challenges against *any* form of oppression need to confront the
narratives and knowledges that sustain it—hence the endless discussion about
the ultimate source or cause of oppression. The theoretical point of departure of
this book is, thus, straightforward: *knowledge is political.*

This chapter explores a handful of theories and authors that, in different
ways, show how this is so. I do not pretend to cover all of the relevant material
here. Such an objective would set itself up for failure, not only for the obvious
reason that reading all of the critical theory that has ever been written is humanly
impossible, but also because there surely exist wonderful texts that I do not have
access to because they might be written in languages that I am not familiar with
or because they have not been recognized by academia, among other infinitely
possible circumstances. Consequently, this is a very situated and inherently
incomplete exercise. The objective is to navigate lexicons that allow us to grasp
the political condition of academia.

Once such theoretical vocabularies have been gathered, the building blocks to theorize and empirically grasp the politics of political science (PPS) will be available. Only then is it going to be possible to fully unfold this book's main argument: that power relations at different levels (between institutions, people, and countries) are unavoidable when trying to make sense of the social sciences' "institutionalization" or "development" – the two apparently politically neutral terms used by the Latin American literature on the history of political science (PS) (for example, Altman, 2005; Buquet, 2012; Bulcourf, 2012; Garcé, 2005; Huneeus, 2006; Sepúlveda, 1996; among others)—and that, complementarily, conceptually situating the social sciences as political sheds analytical light on politics as a whole. The pages that follow explore some theorists that are instrumental in delineating a critical epistemology of knowledge and power.

Marxism has thus far been the main language for confronting injustice (Keucheyan, 2016), so it is a good place to start. For Marx, human beings cannot escape the fact that we live our lives among others, and the scientist is no exception: like any other subject who is active in the world, the knowledge producer practices his or her activity as a social being. Science and thinking are human activity (Marx, 1978) and, therefore, they are necessarily affected by historical conditions while taking part in the battles of history. For Marx, the dominant narratives and knowledges about the world—such as religion or political economy—sustain the injustice of capitalist exploitation. When liberal thinkers and political economists pose the constitution of the individual as untouched by social ties and imagine the scientist as an objective bearer of knowledge—locating both personhood and science outside of the human relations in which they are embedded—they actively contribute to the impossibility of thinking through clearly how certain relationships among people, for instance that between capitalists and laborers, can become a vehicle through which laborers' lives become less than human as a result of actions taken by capitalists in the pursuit of economic profit. The impossibility of intellectually grasping the inherently exploitative nature of this relationship reinforces the reproduction of capital.

Marx burdened himself with the arduous task of confronting capitalism on the terrain of knowledge production—how else can *Capital* be read and thought of? In Marxism, epistemology and political economy go together, and I find the intersection powerful because it is both analytically productive as well as profoundly political. Knowledge and knowing are not only imbricated in social life; they *are* social life. Thus, they are, as human existence itself, conflictingly constituted by both creativity and apodictic determination at the same time. In other words, for Marx, knowing becomes a worldly—even sensuous— enterprise, a battlefield with consequences in the "real" world. Knowledge participates in both alienation and emancipation. Knowledge is part of everything that is human, be it tragedy or comedy. It is part and parcel of any social transformation, regardless of its direction or result.[1] The implications of this are significant: if human activity can be alienated by the wage relationship, the activity of academic thinking (which is not ontologically different from other human activities) can also be alienated.

Turning our attention to the dismal circumstances of contemporary academia, writing paper after paper after paper just for the sake of producing papers resonates with the torture that Marx described as work under capitalism and the dehumanizing reign of exchange value and violent abstraction. This makes me think about what happens when critical theory itself becomes the commodity we try to sell. Can the industry of critical theory, with all of its layers of inequality (most critical scholars we read produce from privileged positions in the Global North) be alienated and alienating? Neoliberalism (Amadae, 2016; Brown, 2015) complicates this landscape even more through the production of new subjectivities centered on self-promotion and success, which affects both activism and critical academia. I will come back to this point at the very end of the book. But, for now, the exploration of voices and authors that are instrumental to creating a vocabulary to grasp PPS shall continue.[2]

There are two names that cannot be absent in a reflection about the intersection between knowledge and power: Friedrich Nietzsche and his student par excellence, Michel Foucault. How to read Nietzsche is, in itself, an engaging question. Going through his books has been, for me, an existential journey of exploration. His is a writing subjectivity, a transient thinking that moves through writing and affects the reader. Despite their rough surface, his texts are incredibly open and hospitable to the plurality of experience and meaning—the opposite of academic "fortress writing" (Ravecca & Dauphinee, 2018). Nietzsche's nudity is not obscene, but it is a provocation that calls for a response. Such a response is the business of the reader—it is her problem. Everyone will have her own Nietzsche, the one that she wants or is able to have. This form of writing that *asks* even as it screams arbitrary truths at the reader's face can be conceptually situated as liberating because it defies the structures—including the moral ones—that mummify imagination. Such a lively style of writing and thinking, particularly its spirit of intellectual transgression, is something that this book appreciates and capitalizes from.

Nietzsche is well-known for having devoted considerable attention to the question of the role of religion and morality in human history. He argued that what he called the ascetic ideal (in short, the Judeo-Christian set of moral beliefs) had made Europe a place of weakness and decay. I will bypass the tale of the weak and the strong and other aspects of his *oeuvre* here, but his recurring point that those who represent the good frequently build the gallows of history is significant: projecting an evil other is a devastating operation of power. In other words—a second point fully endorsed by this study—morality is immanent *vis-à-vis* power relations. Here, however, I want to particularly focus on how his critique of religion and morality translated into the way he thought about knowledge.

It is not frequently mentioned that, for Nietzsche, positivism was the epistemological expression of the ascetic ideal. His attack against moral conventions ends up in a critique of scientific neutrality and objectivity, which is the translation of Christianity into epistemology (Nietzsche, 1989; see in particular the third essay, "What Is the Meaning of Ascetic Ideals?"). This is so because god dwarfs man, and truth is the god of modern science; therefore, the twilight of the idols points toward a critique of the very notion of scientific truth, which paradoxically represents another chapter of history marked by man's heteronomy and disempowerment. We could even say that, for Nietzsche, objective science is the opium of knowledge: it takes away its strength and its vitality.

Nietzsche has a conception of knowledge as violence and of power as a creative force. Righteousness and true knowledge are for him incompatible. In *Beyond Good and Evil* (1990), he states: "Pity has an almost ludicrous effect on a man of knowledge, like tender hands on a Cyclops" (p. 105). In other words (and relocating an expression used by Hannah Arendt in her analyses of revolutions), violence is part of the *anatomy*, not the pathology, of knowing. The third Nietzschean aspect of this book, therefore, is its embrace of this way of conceptualizing truth production as power and knowledge as dystopian. Nietzsche's insights about the power of language and interpretation[3] and about the relationship between knowledge, morality, and oppression are crucial for the present study on the history of political science and its critique of liberalism, which seems to play the incarnation of good and virtue in politics today. However, perhaps taking distance from Nietzsche, or maybe radicalizing some of his insights, in Chapters 4 and 5 I follow Edward Said's plea to untangle the node between knowledge and harm.

To sum up this brief commentary on the conceptualization of knowledge of two intellectual giants, if Marx theorizes the intersection between capitalism, struggle, and knowledge production, then Nietzsche locates deontology and epistemology in a common space of problematization; his insights on the opacity of morality, language, and knowledge are fundamental for critical theory.

Foucault (1980, 1989, 1991a, 1991b, 1992, 1993, 2006) expanded Nietzsche's insight that everything is an interpretation into the notion of discourse as the site where truth is constructed and regulated. The Foucauldian notion that power and knowledge sustain each other in complex ways—in *any* political system or situation—debunks the commonsensical idea that power represses knowledge production. Discourses on truth are not located outside the mechanisms of power: truth is in itself power (Foucault, 1992, p. 200). However, if all knowledges participate in power dynamics, they do so on highly unequal terms (Foucault, 1980). To understand knowledge in the plural means to recognize that there are privileged and unprivileged knowledges.[4] As the case studies of this book show, some knowledges are eliminated by other, more privileged knowledges (De Sousa Santos, 2008). Is knowledge, then, always hurtful? Is it just about power, resistance, and war? As mentioned above, I do not think so, and I come back to this later. One of the many questions that the problem of knowledge and violence opens up is whether narrative approaches (Ravecca & Dauphinee, 2018) might provide a negotiating space between the need to de-essentialize and the humanist search for universality and personalism. Even though I do not fully unfold this *problématique* analytically in this book, I do offer glimpses into this question.

Culture and knowledge were also pivotal to the analyses of Antonio Gramsci and the Frankfurt School, which, by shaking economic reductionisms in different ways, represented a shift within Marxism. The notion of hegemony emphasizes the significance of the cultural terrain for both the analysis of power and the exercise of class struggle (Buttigieg, 1990; Giroux, 1999; Gramsci, 2008; Green & Ives, 2009; Laclau & Mouffe, 2004; Sassoon, 1987). In the same vein, the notion of "materialism imageless" developed by Theodor Adorno in *Negative Dialectics* (2005, p. 205) referred to a kind of materialism that does not conceive of the ideational level as a simple reflection of the so-called economic base. These efforts have critically engaged with the political effects of mainstream social science and its pretensions of objectivity, and have also included the issue of subjectivity into the epistemological reflection in inspiring ways. In Adorno's (2005) words, for instance, "if the subject is bound to mulishly mirror the object—necessarily missing the object, which only opens itself to the subjective surplus in thought—the result is the unpeaceful spiritual silence of integral administration" (p. 205). From this perspective, the denial of subjectivity in knowledge implies the loss of the object and of objectivity, creating the conditions for subjects to be treated as objects (that is, integral administration). In short, attention to culture and subjectivity have enriched Marxism, and the present study belongs to this saga of efforts.

This book conceives of powers and knowledges as immanently inseparable. This interpretive move is an invitation to study them together, which has significant consequences in terms of how we understand academia and our identity as social scientists. If we understand knowledge as political, then epistemological introspection becomes politically relevant, as it may indeed be read as an intervention in the realm of politics. The introspection of knowledge thus becomes *extrospective* social research.

In psychoanalytic terms, the narratives that individuals hold about themselves must be reflectively dived into and critically unpacked if the aim is to develop some sense of autonomy. This self-reflective standpoint may be extended to the social sciences. Pierre Bourdieu (1973) argued that epistemology was for science what psychoanalysis was for the individual. Disciplinary introspection, thus conceived, generates autonomy *vis-à-vis* internal structures of power and also has the potential to challenge academic institutions' ties with broader forms of domination. If, for instance, the university and academia are involved in the reproduction of inequality, it is important to explore how this is so; academic narratives about reality, therefore, become the object of critical analysis. From this perspective, I understand political science as a terrain where the political is represented and where disputes over the configuration of the terrain itself are held. The parallel here between psychoanalytic and academic self-reflection is political. Epistemology might have a politically therapeutic effect. The *divan* (i.e., the therapy couch) and epistemology are sites where the polity is imagined, projected, and built.

I share critical theory's concern with emancipation (Horkheimer, 1978) and its challenge to forms of knowledge that reify power relations at the level of thinking. In that sense, this book is particularly inspired by Herbert Marcuse's explorations of the intersection between Marxism and psychoanalysis. In Marcuse's hands, psychoanalysis' engagement with subjectivity becomes dialectical critical thinking (Horowitz, 1977). This move, on the one hand, pulls Marxism into the kind of introspection that Marx' philosophically textured *Economic and Philosophical Manuscripts* already practiced, for instance, through the notion of alienation; and, on the other hand, pushes psychoanalysis toward extrospection. In *Eros and Civilization* (1974), Marcuse liberates psychoanalysis from Freud's political moods, offering a productive theoretical intervention. Through the distinction between basic repression (civilization, humanization) and surplus repression (alienation, division of labor, neurosis), the author makes the encounter between psychoanalysis and historical emancipation possible while delineating communism as the place where "the pain of separation is no longer experienced as the essence of selfhood" (p. 214). I am less interested in discussing the specifics of this argument (which Marcuse revised in his later work) and more interested in emphasizing that the need to navigate the connections between subjectivity and political economy still stands.

In *One-Dimensional Man* (1991), Marcuse pays special attention to the role of knowledge and language in power relations. The book is particularly relevant for the study of PPS because, in contrast with other theorists of power and knowledge dynamics like Michel Foucault or Edward Said, Marcuse *explicitly* critiques (American) political science. He includes the discipline among the expressions of "technological rationality," understood as "positive" or "conformist" thinking, which contains but transcends positivism, where the given universe of facts (liberal democracy, capitalism) operates as its final context of validation.[5]

For Marcuse, the supposed political neutrality of mainstream PS is highly ideological and is implicated in the erasure of the difference between actuality and potentiality (1991, p. 114). This academic expression of technological rationality reduces "the opposition to the discussion and promotion of alternative policies *within* the status quo" (p. 2). One-dimensionality redraws the boundaries of the possible: while technological advancements give the impression that everything is possible, power is erased from the political conversation, and in fact nothing important can be changed. Marcuse is then a critic of the liberal emptying of democracy, because the "free election of masters does not abolish the masters or the slaves" (p. 7).

It should be noted that there is a significant difference between Marcuse and other fundamental authors for this book, particularly Michel Foucault who, in a Nietzschean move, is highly suspicious of any attempt to totalize. Foucault's rejection of a holistic theory of society is linked to his refusal to enlist his activist and intellectual efforts into a global project of emancipation. However, his decision was not capricious: pretentions to universalism and totality had inhibited local battles and sometimes were blatantly oppressive. Marcuse, in contrast, chose to unpack the wholeness—the interconnection between different moments—of power relations in order to understand how the system of domination works. As long as it remains fiercely self-critical for the reasons just noted, the move toward "totalization" might neutralize the deleterious ideological effects of the fragmentation of social justice struggles as well as of the theoretical reflections sustaining them (Keucheyan, 2013). Between Foucault and Marcuse, the question is perhaps if universalism can be rescued from ethnocentrism and from operating as the locus of other forms of suppression (Buck-Morss, 2010).[6]

Marcuse's work, perhaps underestimated in academic circles, is exceptionally powerful in its exploration of the interconnections between academia and politics. His notes on language and power are fascinating. He elaborates on the transformation of academic, political, and advertising language, expressing concern about the imposition of "a syntax in which the structure of the sentence is abridged and condensed in such way that no tension, no 'space' is left between the parts of the sentences" (1991, p. 86). If language, politics, and political imagination are linked in one-dimensional times, formal reason and tight writing displaces dialectical thinking, and instrumentality displaces reflection:

> Such nouns as "freedom," "equality," "democracy," and "peace" imply, analytically, a specific set of attributes which occur invariably when the noun is spoken or written. In the Western analytical predication, it is in such terms as free enterprise, initiative, elections, individual . . . [that] [t]he ritualized concept is made immune against contradiction.
>
> *(Marcuse, 1991, p. 88)*

This point reminds me of the concerns about the transformation of academic writing that many of us have today, which has been discussed recently from different critical perspectives (Ravecca & Dauphinee, 2018; Holt, 2003). Avoiding complexity and to not think too much seems to be the current—and scary— mandate for both undergraduate and graduate students (I come back to this issue in Chapter 3). Exactly the opposite was advised to students by the Uruguayan thinker Carlos Vaz Ferreira (1957) at the beginning of the 20th century in his *Moral for Intellectuals*. Students had, for him, a mandate to be cultured, to expand their thinking, and to cultivate curiosity. This book embraces and celebrates such a mandate. In any case, and to sum up, positivist PS is, from a Marcusean perspective, a form of writing that undermines (self-) reflection, which is an operation of power at the level of knowledge production: if epistemology and power go together, the way the academic establishment has gathered them together does not deliver freedom and human fulfillment.

More recently, postcolonial studies, queer theory, and post-Marxist strands in political theory have also politicized language and knowledge, arguing that the way in which objects of study—be it sex/gender, madness, the Global South, democracy, etc.—are approached is actually part of the problem to be addressed. From these perspectives, mainstream knowledges are, again, the epistemological face of domination (Kaufman, 2005). Judith Butler, Ernesto Laclau, and Edward Said's *oeuvres*, in particular, were instrumental to me as an undergraduate student to explore politics from its cultural and discursive dimensions (see Ravecca, 2007). In sharp contrast to the notions of political culture (Almond & Verba, 1963) or social capital (Putnam, 1993), which force the complex notion of culture into a conceptual straitjacket and into analytical strategies that entomologize nations (classifying them into narrow boxes as one might do to insects), these alternative critical theories allowed me to perform two complementary operations: on the one hand, to challenge orthodox Marxism's economism and, on the other, to politicize epistemological self-reflection. Concretely, in my BA thesis, where the first seeds of this project were sown, I argued that if culture and discourse are political, then PS frameworks and narratives—which are a part of culture—are also political. A language-discourse sensitive approach to power illuminates the political productivity of epistemological self-reflection. I have argued this, in these exact terms, since my early conversations with my undergraduate professors. These authors provided me with some intellectual fresh air (as well as with effective weapons) in the rather mainstream academic environment where I was trained. None of them were introduced to me by school; I had to find and appropriate them by my own means. I theorize the significance of this in Chapter 4.

This study of PPS requires self-decolonization. Up to now, the authors I have referred to are, on the whole, dead white men. Political science remains white and Western, whatever the latter term means, but so is most of academic critical theory. My own intellectual background reveals the coloniality of knowledge: while there is no need to essentialize geography and skin color, we also cannot ignore them. As Gayatri Spivak has suggested, we must first attempt critique with the materials and tools that we have at hand: a critical exploration of the implications and limitations of our own education—of who we are—is always part of the permanent effort of unlearning oppression. In the following lines, I briefly outline the contributions of postcolonial theorizing to this book.

I discovered *Orientalism* and *Nuevas Crónicas Palestinas* [New Palestinian Chronicles][7] in my early 20s, after years of reading Nietzsche, Marquis de Sade, Marx, Foucault, Freud, and other continental critical thinkers. I still find Said's (1979) main argument convincing and relevant: the representations of "the Orient" dominant in the so-called West are functional to a political project of domination. Many followed Said's legacy of critiquing orientalism. Yet others like Enrique Dussel (2000) chose a different direction, showing instead the fluidity of the notion of Europe, which implies de-essentializing both East and West (Aristotle, the author notes, was considered oriental in the Middle Ages). In this way, given that it critiques, but paradoxically also reinforces, the East-West divide, the category of orientalism may be considered both a gain and a limit for critical thinking and analysis.[8] This tension between, on the one hand, forms of critique that reify identities and, on the other, perspectives that deconstruct them, is both conceptually and politically significant. I come back to this in Chapters 4 and 5. In any case, postcolonial and decolonial efforts reveal the imperialistic condition of academia, a very relevant fact in this study given that the very emergence of political science has been related to how power has been, and is being, exercised in the era of European and American dominance (Ake, 1979).

The complicated paths of power and resistance, along with their social geographies, are inseparable from the paths and social geographies of knowledge and theory. Domination is deployed through the regulation of whose—and how—knowledge, writing, thinking, and culture matters (Fanon, 1961, 1967). The displacement, destruction, or appropriation of "native" knowledges has been named as an epistemicide (De Sousa Santos, 2008). And, in postcolonial times (if the prefix *post* really applies), "white" and "Western" subjects still retain a certain ownership of the world (Smith, 1999). Power is exercised at "both explicit and implicit levels" (Smith, 1999, p. 43) and academia, including political science, is no exception. White privilege (Escobar, 2004, p. 216), the hierarchical relation that "has historically privileged white people at the expense of non-European and colored people," affects classrooms and journals. Perhaps, and contrary to the progressive common sense of the Global North, even more so in South American classrooms, where the discourse of inclusion and diversity has not penetrated with the same strength as in North American universities.

Colonialism is part of PPS and part of the politics of the humanities more generally: an African philosopher is an *African* philosopher while a European philosopher is just a philosopher. Regardless of its self-perception as being of European descent, the same applies to Uruguay, my "home" country, and I will elaborate on this more in my discussion of the *Uruguayan* intellectual Carlos Real de Azúa (see Chapters 4 and 5). Universality has been stolen and shipped to the so-called Global North, and a lot of people from the South located in both the North and the South collaborate in the shipping. This stealing is perhaps the only way to produce *any* form of universality (Butler, Laclau, & Zizek, 2003); but the point is perhaps to uncover the precarious grounds on which scholarly prestige and hierarchy are built, in order to undo its most oppressive aspects. Dependency (Cardoso & Faletto, 1979; Dos Santos, 1970; Frank, 1966) does not only operate at the level of political economy: it is also intellectual. Some countries produce highly manufactured theories (critical or not), while others provide the raw materials for academic production, and this troubling observation certainly also applies to political science (I confront this issue in Chapter 5).[9]

The volume edited by King, Lehman Schlozman, & Nie (2009), *The Future of Political Science: 100 Perspectives*, showcases the imperialistic logic that frames the very definition of our discipline. Even though the editors claim that the book debates the future of political science at a global level, almost all of its contributors are academics based in American universities. This is not exceptional: the supposedly progressive Perestroika movement within the American Political Science Association (Monroe, 2005) also ignored power dynamics within the discipline at the transnational scale.[10] This troubling feature is even reproduced by critical scholars, including, paradoxically, postcolonial, and decolonial theorists located in American universities who, in many cases, seem oblivious to the irony of this situation, and by people who—like the writer of this text—have emigrated to places such as Canada, the UK, and of course the US in order to move their academic careers forward.[11] As Razmig Keucheyan has argued (2013), "the Americanization of critical thinking contains the seeds of its political neutralization" (p. 255). This thought pushes me to believe that critical scholars need to embark on a *political economy of the self* to complete the critical task of self-reflection.

In this sense, postcolonial studies symptomatize the moving intersections between knowledge and power; even critical scholarship may be part of the same colonial and neocolonial dynamics it tries to resist and problematize. Moreover, indigenous perspectives, both old and new, destabilize the very notion of post-coloniality, showing that this framework erases the fact that colonialism is still ongoing (Byrd & Rothberg, 2011; Jackman & Upadhyay, 2014). This is an interesting twist within the critique of critical knowledge production.

This book is also inspired by queer theory's critique of the reification of cultural arrangements (Butler, 1990). This critique not only denaturalized gender but also reached the stubborn terrain of sexuality, sex, and the body, showing how gender indeed produces bodies.[12] By showing how something as allegedly natural and factual as the body is constituted by culture—even shaping its materiality—queer theory has become one of the most powerful tools available to challenge dominant narratives about any identity. If we accept that discourses on nature (about, for instance, such fundamental things as what it means to be a man or a woman) work to naturalize arbitrary arrangements, then political and academic views' pretension to solidity, stability, and dominance becomes immanently precarious. The queering of identity troubles empiricism and the illusion of the neutrality of knowledge.

Queer theory informs this book's argument that narratives about how political science came to be and their concomitant search for disciplinary identity have a political dimension and, therefore, need to be self-critical if they do not want to become oppressive. *Vis-à-vis* the narratives of mainstream PS, my approach to PPS is queer because it reflectively opens up PS selfhood by, among other operations, exploring the anxiety among Latin American political scientists regarding the discipline's status and unpacking their contempt with sociologists. Chapters 3 and 4 appropriate queer insights to explore the power implications of different ways of delineating PS identity.

"Queer," however, does not mean innocent. Sharp critiques of western feminism (Alexander, 2005; Mohanty, Russo, & Torres, 1991; Wekker, 2006) have revealed that both the dominant feminist agenda as well as the "global gay" (Alexander, 2005; Manalansan, 1995) may be colonized and colonizing. Furthermore, even radical strands of queerness can be implicated in oppression. Besides the serious issue of post-structuralism's (debatable) ultimate denial of the materiality of power relations (McNally, 2002; Ciriza, 2010), the relationships between modernity, statehood, neoliberalism, and queerness are extremely complex (Puar, 2007; Morgensen, 2010; among others).

The "post-" something theories lack innocence in another sense. Political science is trapped within the capitalist political economy. Capitalism frames democracy in theory and practice, and this needs to be critically analyzed and challenged. After the collapse of the Soviet Union and amid the consolidation of the US as the virtually uncontested global power, Marxism—the most effective critique of capitalism ever proposed—has been the object of a ferocious discrediting campaign. The liberal representation of Marxism and neo-Marxism as a dated and useless theory within PS and beyond has been brutal. And some forms of post-structuralism, in a strange assemblage (Puar, 2007) with the neoliberal discourse, have been functional to this form of othering (Ahmad, 1992).[13] Indeed, the ideational turn within critical theory can be seen as politically problematic (McNally, 2002). It is not by chance that the obsession with language became dominant within critical academia when Marxism and socialism were defeated both academically and politically. This means that the "post-" theories can be, and to some extent have been, functional to global neoliberalism (Harvey, 2005; Wood, 2002; Borón, 2007), as they sometimes end up trafficking in the naturalization of capitalism under the cover of difference. It seems unfeasible to confront the dynamics of power and knowledge, both analytically and politically, without the aid of Marxist political economy. Capitalism, and within it, neoliberalism, has produced a particular set of knowledge dynamics, and transformations within PS are among them.[14] Luckily, Marxist and neo-Marxist critics have persisted in studying the relationships between capitalism, neoliberalism, and knowledge production (Anderson, 2010; Harvey, 2003; McNally, 2002, 2006, 2011 are only a few recent examples).[15]

What are *all* of these voices saying? From the point of view of this book, willingly or not, they stand as a reminder that knowledges belong to history and play a crucial political role in it. How, then, can we try to grapple with the question of historical change without paying a modicum of attention to the knowledges that talk about it? And, complementarily, how can we really make sense of the history of PS without critically examining the conditions and political contexts within which it unfolds? In short, for our purposes here, the voices explored above share the idea with which this chapter began: *knowledge is political*, a simple (and empowering) concept that tends to be conveniently overlooked or disingenuously dismissed by upholders of the discipline's mainstream, their devotion to knowledge notwithstanding.

At this point, an additional reminder about the function of critical thinking is in order: capitalism, patriarchy, (neo)colonialism, and neoliberalism are all rubrics for power structures that also "happen" in knowing and knowledge; critical thinking attempts to name and challenge the knowledges that sustain these forms of injustice.

The different theories alluded to above share a conception of knowledge production as political, and they challenge different forms of oppression. Yet despite their common social justice orientation, they seem either uncomfortable or at odds with each other. Alternatively, we could reason that, *because* they are political, conflicts between them are unavoidable (it is widely known, by the way, that internal quarrels seem to be a permanent feature of the left). Each of them highlights an important moment of power (be it gender, colonialism, or capitalism, and so on) but forgets others that are equally relevant. In other words, each of these forms of critique has its own political economy of conceptual violence, and thus may be liberating and oppressive at the same time (Ravecca, 2010a; Ravecca & Upadhyay, 2013). After all, all theoretical approaches inevitably organize perception in a way that hurts, excludes, or orientalizes (exoticizes, reduces, etc.) someone. For instance, Marxists neglected the racialized and gendered processes that were key to understanding the dynamics of capitalism (Eley, 2002), while some versions of post-structuralism deny the materiality of oppression (McNally, 2002). Thus, we are talking about contrasting ways of conceptualizing power relations where language, the economy, race, and other artifacts operate in different ways, and with varied implications. More tragically put, critical theories may oppress each other, which somehow mirrors the situation of subalterns oppressing subalterns (I am consciously distorting Spivak's notion of subalternity here). Granted, this internal violence imprinted in the ways theories or approaches are organized is also external. It goes far beyond books: it is linked to extra-theoretical and extra-academic power dynamics. This is thus not a post-structuralist lament only: I am in fact thinking of the linkage between any academic discourse to very concrete power dynamics that are cultural and material.

It seems appropriate now to go back to the most abstract level of my project. Academia, *critical or not*, is *structurally* implicated in power relations (and domination) in many ways—again, good intentions, when uninformed, are counterproductive and even dangerous. It seems warranted to ponder whether or not the way in which we engage in theoretical and cross-paradigmatic conversations may somehow be connected to the logic of capitalist competition between self-centered egos that neoliberalism has exacerbated. Critical theories sold as luxury commodities and star academics (first-class-flights-only) and even "big name" public intellectuals perhaps are not the most appropriate formulas for liberation. I am talking not only about the theory that we produce, but also about the *mechanics* of academia (and maybe some forms of global activism as well). The material and subjective conditions in which we operate reinforces, among other problematic tendencies, fortress writing and what I would call "selfie" forms of criticality, which is more about cultivating an ego ideal rather than about a service to others.[16]

In the preceding pages, I have presented conceptual vocabularies that point to the theoretical and practical productivity of exploring the politics of knowledge and, more particularly, the politics of the knowledge of politics; in short, the politics of political science. The tensions among these different theories remain unresolved. I will come back to this issue in Chapters 4 and 5.

PPS—the approach to the politics of political science developed by this book—builds from these tensions and understands power as a *complex relationality* between knowledge production and dissemination, identity, subjectivity, political economy, conventional politics, and the transnational dimension of the political. In my perspective, all of these aspects dynamically affect (or mutually constitute) each other. I have already stated that knowledge production is a key component of the broader social relations in which it occurs, but the theoretical emphasis is on *relations* here, relations that are complex and mobile. Given that knowledge and theory do not lie outside power, it follows that any conception or assessment of the political has political implications, which alerts us to the perils of reproducing the asymmetries we see "out there" (and which we seek to denounce) within our own analysis. But the implications go further: if defining the political is a political act and if researching politics has political impacts, then investigating our discipline is an apt point of entry to the political in our times. Epistemology, thus understood, *is* political science.

Complex relationality does not follow the additive logic of piling up "dimensions." On the contrary, it explores *the friction* between and within experiences and critical approaches. Each story told by PPS—Chapters 2, 3 and 4— performs different analytical tasks and narrates PS in one internally plural way. The ensemble of these stories constitutes a unified intellectual *and political* effort to productively navigate these theories and experiences. But such an effort or series of interconnected efforts does not cohere into a fictional synthesis that resolves the contradictions and incompleteness of PPS. My approach to PPS negotiates the immanent impossibility of grasping everything that is going on in and around our research questions and objects of analysis. Concretely, through complex relationality, PPS does not account for the wholeness of PS and the constellations of power it is involved in, neither in Latin America nor in the specific national cases under study. What it does offer is the interpretive opening of the plurality and multilayeredness of PS' experiences.

PPS brings different voices and experiences into a rather syncretic conversation (Buck-Morss, 2009). This porosity in ways of writing and praxis makes this project part of Jasbir Puar's (2007) unhomed interdisciplinarity or at least part of Mattei Dogan's (1997) hybrid research. PPS advances through making connections between apparently unrelated situations and concepts, and by using different methods and even varied epistemologies.[17] This feature makes the result potentially interesting and fragile at the same time. This is a book about political science written by a political scientist (whose three postsecondary degrees are in political science), yet which, paradoxically, does not fully belong to the discipline, a fact that is not necessarily convenient (see Chapter 5). However, as John Trent (2012) points out, "restrictiveness within disciplinary boundaries inhibits us from comprehending the broader context of politics" (p. 170) and, I would add, also of PS' experience. I would like to think with Trent that hybrids can contribute to the collective enterprise of the flourishing of knowledge (p. 161).

Through the perspectives, characters, scenarios, and stories that it hosts, PPS' aim remains consistent: to understand power and knowledge dynamics around PS' history. As shown in the next section, this theoretical meditation on knowledge is firmly anchored in detailed empirical research. It comes to conclusions and presents concrete findings: after all, contingency and mobility should be acknowledged but not totalized. Narrative approaches (Ravecca & Dauphinee, 2018), the last critical voice that PPS brings into the conversation, analytically negotiate durability and change; in other words, they bind the instability of identity through the recognition of its integrity.[18] Concretely, though they are not stable, peoples and academic disciplines *do* have identities. The issue is how these identities are naturalized or discussed, policed or expanded. A solid subjectivity or academic community is that which enables change, diversity, dialogue, and learning. Critical self-reflection lends to the integrity of the subject, in this case, of political science. This is a study that celebrates political science.

Another aspect in which narrative approaches are invaluable to this book is the way they do analysis. The complex relationality approach is simple and straightforward: it simply tries to navigate the relations between different moments of human experience, in this case of the PS experience, abandoning the notion of primacy (of the economy, of subjectivity, of culture, of language, and so on). Narrative gathers all these aspects of the human experience, which are separated by standard academic forms of analysis, and weaves them into a story (see Chapter 4).

We can learn a great deal about a society and its power relations by analyzing the ways in which it studies itself. Epistemology should thus be prioritized for the purposes of collective self-clarification. By studying PS, this book studies, and hopefully tells a compelling story about, politics as such.

PPS' Strategy for (Disciplinary) Self-Reflection

In this book, mainstream approaches to the study of politics and PS institutions become objects of analysis. PPS' introspective exercise is of a specific kind: it applies critical theory to disciplinary self-reflection, therefore practicing a *political* self-analysis in the realm of PS. Or, in other words, the discipline and its theory are brought into the realm of politics. Hence, the study also offers a theoretical reflection on the political as such through an exploration of knowledge and power dynamics within a specific area of human activity called political science. The following pages present how I intend to fulfill these aims.

A move toward introspection has become common among political scientists in the past few decades. The efforts to make PS more self-reflexive are illustrated by the creation of the International Political Science Association Research Committee 33—The Study of Political Science as a Discipline in 1989, and the debates around the Perestroika movement at the American Political Science Association, among others.[19] Reflections and debates about the discipline have brought to the fore issues such as the specificity of PS, its relationship to other social sciences, the problem of hyperspecialization, the alleged hegemony of rational choice theory and its consequences, the quantitative/qualitative divide, and the professional associations and university departments' internal politics of academic divisions, hiring policies, and career development.

This study is not interested in addressing the issues above. Nor is PPS particularly interested in the contributions that our discipline can potentially make to improve public policy, the topic of how liberal democracy propitiates the development of the discipline, or the question of the impact that state policies have on research agendas. My main concern is not how to make the academic market niche of PS somehow better. Rather—and bearing in mind that prior to being disciplines, social sciences *are* human activity (Marx, 1978) and that it is in human activity where the shape of our (collective) lives and the political is at play and at stake—PPS is interested in framing these issues in an entirely different way. The same can be said about the innovative scholarship on PS and sexuality (Brettschneider, 1997, 2011; Smith, 2011; Rocha Carpiuc, 2016). Although this book does not study gender and diversity within the discipline, I will reframe the issue by addressing relevant questions that queer theory may open up about PS' identity (see Chapters 3 and 4).

By locating the discipline as a manifestation of wider social relations of power and knowledge though recognizing its internal density and relative autonomy,[20] PPS critically antagonizes the strategies for introspection currently practiced by mainstream PS in Latin America. In other words, PPS proposes a critical *meta*-self-reflection. But why should this particular kind of meta-introspection be considered pertinent at all?[21]

Different bodies of literature have shown that self-reflection is desirable: looking at oneself helps one to see better; and probably observing one's own sight helps to recalibrate it. I take it as a premise that self-reflection is necessary for science and for narratives about science. While thinking about our own thinking may improve our capacity to critically engage with the world, the absence of self-reflection brings about the impossibility of self-critique along with an incapacity to change our ways of thinking (Foucault, 1991a; Butler et al., 2003). Self-reflection operates, then, as the opposite of the obliteration of critical thinking (Butler et al., 2003).[22] In this sense, the PPS project belongs to the realm of philosophy as defined by Michel Foucault: the critique of established ways of thinking in order to imagine alternative ones. Interrogating mainstream approaches opens up the possibility of identifying and transcending their violence(s) and limitations (Foucault, 1991a). This implies challenging the established politics of truth (Foucault, 1992) articulated to discursive and institutional forms of dominant power—in this case, that of PS. I thus consider PPS as an opportunity to interrogate the complexities of PS selfhood, and also (fundamentally) as a strategy to question the instrumentalization of our discipline by projects of oppression.[23]

Even though I am skeptical of pristine ways of linking knowing and ethics[24] (see Chapter 5), PPS accepts the challenge of unpacking the oppressive implications of dominant forms of thought, in both practicing as well as talking *about* PS. This implies an ethical commitment upfront that distances itself from moralist and self-righteous rhetorics, and that is ready to uncover its own miseries (see Chapter 4). What is more, building from psychoanalysis, and mobilizing my own lived experience of psychoanalytic therapy, PPS conceives of transformative introspection *also* as a journey to the outside (i.e. an exploration of those external experiences that substantially contribute to forging the internal world). That internal world (of the scientist, of the discipline) then feeds back into the external one (the discipline *vis-à-vis* the academic, broader social arenas *vis-à-vis* PS), and that articulation, following the point to its logical conclusion, bears consequences, in turn, for understanding and inhabiting the political. Introspection thus conceived becomes social research, and self-reflection, a political enterprise.

This book explores, as it were, PS' disciplinary self. Given that a significant part of my life has taken place and continues to take place in its various spaces (classrooms, conferences, journals, faculty meetings, university hallways, and so on) my personal experience becomes, in this context, relevant research material. PPS explores human groups I belong to, in one way or another; some of the most revealing moments of the so-called fieldwork occurred in situations that transcend "participatory observation," since they were episodes of my own life. As the auto-ethnographic researcher, I investigated myself *as* social material. Indeed, the third story told by this book (Chapter 4) could qualify as an auto-ethnography that practices disciplinary introspection through personal self-reflection. PPS, as an approach to the history of political science, shares common aims with narrative approaches and other forms of reflexivity (Amoureux & Steele, 2016; Jackson, 2011). By mobilizing self-reflection as a form of knowledge production, it seeks to both reconceptualize analytical rigor (Brigg & Bleiker, 2010) and challenge mainstream epistemologies of objectivity and detachment (Ravecca & Dauphinee, 2018).

Theory—and even more so *critical* theory—is about our lives, which are social, which are about others. In the end, academic writing is an intimate endeavor housed in a fortress of references, quotes, numbers, and other artifacts that simulate detachment. My purpose is to unpack this vulnerable dimension within the activity of knowing. In this way, I look for a reflection that helps me grasp the complex relationality that shapes my experience as an academic and as a human being, enhancing awareness of my circumstances, my practices, and their implications. This may sound like postmodern narcissism, but I do not think it necessarily is. My own experience is a point of departure and not a point of arrival for the analysis—perhaps it is a bit of both.[25] This is a book about theory and politics, and I agree with Wendy Brown (2002) that "theory's most important political offering is [the] opening of a breathing space between the world of common meanings and the world of alternative ones, a space of potential renewal for thought, desire, and action" (p. 574). If power relations shape the ways in which we experience the world, if they have an impact on desire, identity, feelings, ways of knowing, etc., then we need to work through those desires, identities, feelings, and ways of knowing in order to grasp those relations that have and continue to forge us to, finally, open breathing space.

Besides narrative, this research extends disciplinary introspection through means that are more convincing to a broader academic audience: statistics, analysis of historical records, and formal interviews (Chapters 2 and 3). I made this choice taking into account that, as Elizabeth Dauphinee once said to me, we are a generation of minds poisoned by objectivist rationality. A previous version of Chapter 2 was able to engage a diverse range of scholars. Its obsession with empirical reconstruction, the deployment of massive amounts of evidence, as well as its adoption of a quantitative strategy in dealing with discourse analysis, seemed appealing. PPS mobilizes idioms that mainstream scholars can relate to in order to enhance the intensity of its critique. This multiplicity, however, is *not* only the result of a rational (in the sense of instrumental) decision. As mentioned in the Introduction, the very architecture of this study expresses my deep conviction in pluralism in the terrain of thinking and social research. In the terms of the epistemological temperatures, hot does not overcome cold. This study does not dismiss "objectivist rationality," as is shown in the following section.

Methods

In broad methodological terms, this study may be described as interpretivist. It grapples with discourses and meanings as well as with their operations in political contexts. In the words of Clifford Geertz (2003): "one is trying to get a story, a meaning frame to provide an understanding of what is going on" (p. 27; see also, Geertz, 1997). In the same vein, Mark Bevir (2003) argues that "our practices are . . . radically contingent in that they lack any fixed essence or logical path of development. This emphasis on the contingency of social life explains why interpretivists denaturalize alternative theories" (p. 19). This book's job is to denaturalize (i.e., politicize) mainstream narratives about the development of political science in Latin America, showing how politics affects the discipline and vice versa. This deconstructive operation is done through a problematizing redescription (Shapiro, 2005) of the discipline's history in Chile and Uruguay through the lens of critical theory.[26] However, in contrast with Bevir's characterization of human behavior, which of course has to include the practice of interpretivism itself, this book *does* have a logical path of development. PPS cares about meanings *and* structures. To put it metaphorically, in this book, Foucault's uneasiness with globalizing abstractions mingles with Marcuse's (1991) general analysis of contemporary society. Thus, it re-*inscribes* the discipline into the social structures in which it is situated (see Chapter 5).

The interpretive analysis is done through a series of interlocking studies that mobilize different theoretical and methodological idioms. The discontinuity between the following chapters is a product of my conception of social science and its emphasis on epistemological plurality in particular. I resort to these ruptures between the chapters as an attempt to capture the complexity of PPS from different angles. The chronological scope of the stories is also multiple. However, the right-wing dictatorships of the 1970s and 1980s and the transition to democracy operate as the constant historical anchor for the analysis of PS trajectories in Chile and Uruguay. In other words, all of the chronologies of the stories that happen in PPS are *conceptually* tied together by the historicity of the experience of authoritarianism and its effects. PPS is furnished with violence, hence the danger of collapse I referred to in the Introduction.

In the final analysis, this study is a political, methodological, and epistemological effort of de-reification. Drawing from two case studies that are useful for the purposes of analytically displaying the complex relationality that engulfs PS trajectories, it proposes a shift within the interpretation of PS history in Latin America and, potentially, beyond. PPS meshes knowledge, personal experience, and politics in a journey that enhances our awareness of the complexity of our identity as people who research and teach renditions of the political.

The basic components of the research strategy are the following:

Analysis of Academic Articles

I conducted a systematic and in-depth analysis of the 1,194 academic articles published by the leading PS journals in Chile and Uruguay since their foundation up until 2012. These included:

- 163 articles in *Revista Uruguaya de Ciencia Política* (RUCP) [Uruguayan Journal of Political Science]; Uruguay, 1987–2012
- 487 articles in *Política* [Politics]; Chile, 1982–2012
- 544 articles in *Revista de Ciencia Política* (RCP) [Journal of Political Science]; Chile, 1979–2012

In the case of Chile, the analysis was particularly systematic for the authoritarian period: this consisted of 188 articles in *Política* from 1982 to 1989, and 122 articles in *RCP* from 1979 to 1989. The procedure was two-fold. Each article was read at least four times. The pieces were assigned values using a database with 89 descriptive and conceptual variables that operationalize PPS' dimensions of analysis.[27]

The most relevant conceptual variables through which the ideological analysis of PS was performed (what I call the PPS variables) included: view of Marxism; view of communism; position toward the US and the USSR; type of democracy promoted (i.e., polyarchy versus "protected democracy"); view of neoliberal reforms; view of the West and Christianity; religion as the article's main topic; spatial conception of politics (from narrow to expansive); theoretical perspective; and presence of alternative topics (within the journal). Appendix A, as well as Chapters 2 and 3, offer a detailed explanation of how the conceptual dimensions were operationalized. The articles were also analyzed in an interpretive fashion by reconstructing the main conceptual components of the discourse used regarding the discipline.

Semi-Structured Interviews

Fifty-eight semi-structured interviews (with 16 primary questions) were conducted with political scientists of varied national origins (Argentina, Brazil, Chile, France, Turkey, United States, Uruguay and Venezuela). They were based in Argentina (1), Chile (35), and Uruguay (22).

A total of 86.7 hours of interviews were transcribed and processed with the same dimensions of analysis employed for the articles database. These transcriptions were also engaged with in interpretive terms. The interviews served different purposes. In the case of Chile (Chapter 2), the statistical data and historical records were cross-checked with, and enriched by, the evidence provided by the scholars' testimonies. This also applies to Uruguay (Chapter 3), but in this case, the analysis included a systematic engagement with the role of subjectivity and trauma within academic and political transformations.

The spectrum of scholars covered by the interviews is comprehensive given the scale of the PS community in these countries. In fact, virtually the whole institutional universe of the discipline has been included. Appendix B contains the complete list of interviewees, questions, details on coding, and institutions covered.[28] Confidentiality has been retained by assigning codes to the interviews, which do not coincide with the order of the names as they appear in the acknowledgments. Additional complementary conversations with activists as well as with political scientists from Asia, Europe, North America, and Latin America were held in the context of a variety of international academic events.

Auto-Ethnographical Self-Reflection

The use of auto-ethnographical writing has already been referred to before, but given that in narrative approaches theory and method are not kept apart, it seems pertinent to come back to this here. PPS' architectural composite has its own intimate structure. Chapter 4 starts by delineating this intimacy and concludes by digging even deeper into the very auto*bio*graphical foundations of this book. The auto-ethnographical exercise tackles the following questions: which affects and experiences sustain PPS' research questions about PS and power? Why is it so important for us, political scientists, to interrogate our discipline as a political object? Why am I doing this exercise of disciplinary self-critique? Why, finally, am I so intellectually and politically invested in the practice of introspection? The analysis will not offer a positivist search for the ultimate causes of the research project. Rather, it will navigate some meaningful life moments in order to engage with the story *inside* the history that this research explores. It locates disciplinary introspection within personal introspection. The issue of trauma will be revisited (see also Introduction and Chapter 5).

Observation In Situ in PS Departments and Seminars

The following are some of the institutions that I visited with ethnographic purposes and where I took part in different academic activities:[29]

Chile

- Instituto de Asuntos Públicos [Institute of Public Affairs], Universidad de Chile [University of Chile]
- Universidad de Chile
- Instituto de Ciencia Política [Institute of Political Science], Pontificia Universidad Católica de Chile [Pontifical Catholic University of Chile]
- Pontificia Universidad Católica de Chile
- Universidad Diego Portales
- Universidad de Santiago de Chile (USACH)
- Instituto de Estudios Internacionales [Institute of International Studies], Universidad de Chile
- Universidad del Desarrollo [University of Development]
- Universidad Andrés Bello
- Escuela de Ciencia Política [School of Political Science], Universidad ARCIS
- Escuela de Historia [School of History], Universidad ARCIS
- Universidad ARCIS
- Fundación Chile 21 [Chile 21 Foundation]

Uruguay

- Instituto de Ciencia Política (ICP) [Institute of Political Science], Universidad de la República (UdelaR) [University of the Republic]
- Departamento de Ciencias Sociales y Políticas [Department of Social Sciences and Politics], Universidad Católica del Uruguay [Catholic University of Uruguay]
- Centro de Estudios Interdisciplinarios Uruguayos [Center of Uruguayan Interdisciplinary Studies], Facultad de Humanidades [Faculty of Humanities], UdelaR
- Centro Latinoamericano de Economía Humana (CLAEH) [Latin American Centre of Human Economy]
- Facultad de Derecho [Faculty of Law], UdelaR
- Facultad de Humanidades, UdelaR

Argentina

- Universidad de Buenos Aires (UBA) [University of Buenos Aires]
- Consejo Latinoamericano de Ciencias Sociales (CLACSO) [Latin American Council of Social Sciences]

Observation In Situ in Conferences

Conferences are an important site in the making of the discipline. Many of my analytical observations were registered during my active participation in academic events such as the following:[30]

- 9th Latin American Conference of Political Science (Montevideo, 2017)
- 24th World Conference of Political Science (Poznań, 2016)
- 8th Latin American Conference of Political Science (Lima, 2015)
- 5th Uruguayan Conference of Political Science (Montevideo, 2015)[31]
- Launch of the *Revista de Ciencia Política*, Volume 35, Issue 1 (8th Latin American Conference of Political Science, Lima, 2015)
- 50th Anniversary Celebration of the BA Program in Political Science and Public Administration, "Challenges for Political Science's Reflection in Mexico" (Mexico City, Universidad Iberoamericana, 2014)
- Roundtables on Mining (Montevideo, ICP, 2014)[32]
- 23rd World Conference of Political Science (Montréal, 2014)
- 11th Argentinian Conference of Political Science (Paraná, 2013)
- 7th Latin American Conference of Political Science (Bogotá, 2013)
- Panel titled "The Study of Public Policy in Uruguay: Evolution, Assessment and Perspectives" at the 12th Research Conference of the School of Social Sciences (Montevideo, UdelaR, 2013)[33]

- 2nd Symposium of Students of Politics and International Relations (Bogotá, Universidad Diego Arboleda, 2013)
- Launch of the *Revista Uruguaya de Ciencia Política* (11th Argentinian Conference of Political Science, Paraná, 2013)
- Roundtable of Research Committee 33, International Political Science Association (Córdoba, 2012)
- 4th Uruguayan Conference of Political Science (Montevideo, 2012)
- "International Symposium on Political Science Today" (Algiers, l'Ecole Nationale Supérieure des sciences politiques, 2012)
- "Carlos Real de Azúa, 1916–1977. Evocation and Colloquium with Tulio Halperin Donghi" (Montevideo, CLAEH, 2007)
- 6th Research Conference of the School of Social Sciences (Montevideo, UdelaR, 2007)
- 1st Uruguayan Conference of Political Science (Montevideo, 2006)
- 5th Research Conference of the School of Social Sciences (Montevideo, UdelaR, 2006)
- Roundtable "Carlos Real de Azúa, Political Science Pioneer in Uruguay (1916–1977). Evocation after 25 years of his death" (Montevideo, 2002)

As part of my fieldwork, I also attended book launches, PhD dissertation defenses, roundtables, seminars on the development of PS, as well as other academic PS activities in Asia, Europe, North America, and Latin America.[34]

A final note on fieldwork: the core of the data collection took place from August 2012 to July 2013. It included teaching Social Sciences, Knowledge Production and Contemporary "Radical" Thinking, a university course based on the theories and reflections that inform PPS, at the Institute of Political Science in Uruguay (ICP). The group of students was wonderful and created a sort of permanent laboratory of (self-)reflection that resulted in an undergraduate seminar with several critical and sharp presentations on knowledge and power within PS. The event was attended by, among others, the Director of ICP at the time, Dr. Pedro Narbondo.[35] Both the course and the seminar that gave closure to the process served as examples of the transformative praxis of self-reflection that PPS aspires to.[36]

My students are part of the environment I research. Our conversations frequently end in a lively self-exploration of PS. Thanks to their stories about their experiences within the discipline, I learn a great deal about the nature of PS in Uruguay and beyond. The encounter between research, teaching, and radical critique seem to be a good place to start unlearning oppression—PPS needs to reach, and be reached by, the classroom. Only through teaching does research become alive.

Notes

1. Thus, *Capital* can be read as an introspective intervention that dismantles political economy as the science that reifies (and reproduces) capitalist relations at the

level of knowledge production. By unpacking this knowledge, we can attain a deeper understanding of the structural dynamics of capitalism as well as of political economy itself, which is both a moment and a symptom of the former. Marxism goes deep into capitalism, as psychoanalysis goes deep into subjectivity: from the surface (exchange/rationalized symptom) to the roots of the troubles human beings deal with. There is no need to agree with the specifics of these theories, which have so many variations and interpretations, in order to appreciate their inclination toward *radical* reflection.

2. Given the extent of penetration of neoliberal logic today (Brown, 2015) the question is unavoidable: What happens when the critique of commodification and oppression becomes a fancy commodity produced in ultra-exclusive settings in the Global North by well-paid workers—regardless of ethnicity—who only travel first class and do not have the time to even respond to an email of colleagues or students from the same Global South that they love to visit?

3. For Nietzsche (1999b), every word is a trap, and language hides a "philosophical mythology."

4. Foucault (1980), for instance, challenged the claims that psychoanalysis and Marxism are "sciences" by asking what kind of power dynamics are deployed through such claims, and what kind of knowledges they disqualify.

5. He invests some time in dealing with his contemporary American political analysts. To illustrate the ideological character of empiricism, Marcuse (1991) suggests taking a look at "a study of political activity in the United States" (p. 114). His example illustrates a form of knowledge production where "the descriptive analysis of facts blocks the apprehension of facts and becomes an element of the ideology that sustains the facts" (p. 119).

6. I do not aim to unpack the (relevant) differences between Foucauldian and Marcusian analyses of power. What I wish to appropriate for my own journey is the analytical move, shared by them, of locating science on a historically grounded theoretical reflection of power and knowledge.

7. A Spanish book that compiles Said's texts on the Palestinian question (2003a).

8. On the one hand, it challenges arbitrary and violent reductionisms (conservative and maybe also progressive exoticizations of imagined others), but on the other hand, as Ahmad (1992) and others have shown, at the end it reproduces the very binary logic of thinking that it pretends to denounce. Orientalism-as-theoretical-framework does not really break with the logic of the orientalist social process: once we seriously try to deal with the *relational* dimension of selfhood and otherness, the simplistic hypothesis that the "West," an invincible and homogeneous agent, "invented" the "East" in ways that are functional to a project of total domination simply does not work. Paradoxically, Said's intervention is one of the practices that constitute orientalism (!) and, therefore, it is part of the orientalist problem. It is not only the two sides of the orientalist dichotomy (i.e., East-West) that need to be questioned, but *the dichotomies themselves* (including the North-South divide) should be radically problematized (Lazarus, 2002). They are simply inappropriate strategies to deal with complex and contradictory human realities. The very notion of the West is, for me, *an act of dispossession* of reason which is somehow perpetuated by Said's notion of orientalism.

9. Even more: in North American universities, professors from the so-called Global South are sometimes treated as regional informants and second-class academics. The international division of labor has manifestations *within* academic departments where liberal and, for the most part, condescending forms of descriptive representation are applied to scholarship.

10. The International Political Science Association's Research Committee 33 has started to think about this issue (Trent, 2012).

11. According to some critics, some leading postcolonial thinkers do not seem to be very sensitive to the materiality of power, including colonialism (see Chapter 5; Ahmad, 1992; Lazarus, 2002).
12. Certainly, Foucault (1991a) already showed how knowledges and theories about sex and sexuality are implicated in government and domination. Not by chance is queer theory sometimes located under the strange label of French theory.
13. Newman (2007) is a good example of this.
14. Neoclassical economics is still the most prestigious social science discipline in many settings, even after the incredibly dire effects of its public policy implications (Bello, 2008; Morelli, 2008).
15. These discussions seem not to have had enough room within the Perestroika movement (Monroe, 2005) which, despite being the most critical faction within American PS, has been criticized for being not political enough (Rudolph, 2005).
16. After all, "intellectuals are not exempt from the general laws governing the social field in which they operate" (Keucheyan, 2013, p. 51). We are also embedded in the competitive environment that neoliberalism has enforced and where new forms of subjectivities have emerged. In such a context, the warning of Sara Ahmed (2012) seems extremely relevant: when criticality becomes an ego ideal, it can participate in not seeing complicity (p. 179).
17. PPS problematizes dichotomist thinking and its reified divisions: object/subject; epistemology/research; inside/outside; identity politics/class struggle; North/South; Western/Eastern; global/local; power/knowledge-morality; internal/external; critical/conservative; and even the trichotomy Marxist/liberal/postmodern (see Chapters 1, 4, and 5). I aim to offer a relational perspective that shows the porosity (Buck-Morss, 2009) between power and knowledge and also between these other spaces and stories.
18. Judith Butler argued decades ago that post-structuralism does not obliterate autobiographic writing, but it complicates such an enterprise.
19. For examples of a move toward introspection in PS in both the North and the South since the 1990s, see Adcock (2014), Almond (1990), Altman (2005), Baer, Malcolm, and Sigelman (1991), Bejarano and Wills (2005), Bulcourf (2012), Bulcourf, Gutiérrez Márquez, and Cardozo (2015), Cansino (2008), Casen and Ravecca (2010), Easton, Gunnell, and Stein (1995), Evans and Moulder (2011), Farr et al. (1999), Fernández Ramil and Grebe (2010), Fowler et al. (2007), Freidenberg (2017), Garcé (2005), Hartlyn (2008), Hix (2004), Huneeus (2006), King et al. (2009), Laitin (2004), Leiras and D'Alessandro (2005), Mejía Acosta, Freidenberg, and Pachano (2005), Monroe (2005), Munck and Snyder (2007), Puello-Socarrás (2010), Ravecca (2010b), Rocha Carpiuc (2016), Rojas Silva and Baquero (2017), Sánchez González (2005), Sartori (2004), Schram and Caterino (2006), Trent (2009, 2012), and Varnoux Garay (2005).
20. In order to study any realm of experience or object we need to acknowledge its own identity or "personality," then proceed to examine its interrelations with its context. Both object and context are conceptual constructs (Bourdieu, 1973). In other words, the analysis does not uncover an essential self-sufficiency of the object but unfolds a situated point of view from which such an object *becomes* relatively autonomous. This study recognizes the relative autonomy of PS and, *because of that*, also looks at its multiple "dependencies." This clarification seems necessary given the absurd belief, which persists in some circles of Latin American PS, in the radical division between "socio-centric" (sociology) and properly "political" (PS) explanations of political processes. In this logic, only the acknowledgment of the autonomy of politics creates room for the autonomy of PS: social disciplines do not embody different points of view but rival hypotheses. The consequences of this sort of fundamentalist, a-epistemological, and primitive way of looking at the very identity

of social disciplines (as enemies!) are certainly significant as well as revealing of power-knowledge dynamics. Paradoxically, liberal PS can have at times a fascist relationship with the sociological other, where there is no room for difference and complementarity.

21. This book is part of a collective and ongoing effort of including the issue of power into the study of PS development in Latin America. Pablo Bulcourf—a leading scholar on the history of the discipline in Latin America—has promoted these new critical developments, including in his own recent work insights from the sociology of knowledge, historiography, as well as other disciplines. For an overview of the current debates about Latin American PS see Cigales (2017).

22. The destruction of the possibility of engaging in reflection about ourselves has taken varied historical forms, all of them connected to some kind of oppression and/ or repression: as neurosis and "surplus-repression" (Horowitz, 1977), as fascism (Gramsci, 2008), as positivism and reified formal reason (Bourdieu, 1973; Marcuse, 1974, 1991), as subjugating knowledge dynamics (Foucault, 1993), and, I add, as neopositivism/(neo)liberalism.

23. Metaphorically speaking, self-reflection is an antidote against, or at least the opposite of, Hannah Arendt's (1999) Eichmann.

24. See, for instance, Marcuse (1991), for whom "epistemology is in itself ethics, and ethics is epistemology" (p. 125), or Gad Horowitz (1977), who argues that any scientific analyst who is not committed to the possibility of emancipation is pledged not to reason, but to the reason of established domination.

25. I find this Gramscian formulation very meaningful: "The starting-point of critical elaboration is the consciousness of what one really is, and is 'knowing thyself' as product of the historical process to date which has deposited in you an infinity of traces, without leaving an inventory" (Gramsci, 2008, p. 324). Thus, for Gramsci, knowing thyself is the starting point, and not the end, of critical elaboration. This leads me in a couple of directions. First, this fits very well with the notion I have just proposed that introspection is about the outside too (and about power) and that genuine self-reflection is always about others. Therefore, exploration of the self is not just a postmodern narcissistic exercise. Second, there is another way of looking at this that perhaps problematizes Gramsci's rigidity or even lack of dialectical thinking. Knowing thyself never ends: Freud argued that the journey that one starts with psychoanalytic therapy was somehow impossible and, therefore, infinite. This means that one is *always* beginning the (self-)critical journey. If Marx's original accumulation may be read as an analytical category instead of as a self-contained historical moment, as Harvey (2010) has pointed out, I believe that knowing thyself is the permanent exercise that sustains critical consciousness, in an always failed attempt to repeal the alienation provoked by the system erected on original accumulation. Linear temporality is not a good container for dialectics. Putting together our "traces" is a life-long personal and collective task, precisely because there is no inventory (as many seem to think).

26. Or, in more radical and perhaps theoretically dense terms, I aim to do a problematizing re-*inscription* of the discipline's story: re-inscribing PS, its texts and materialities, into the society in which it is embedded (see Chapter 5). PPS is interpretivist, but also Marxist.

27. The following are only a few examples: title, language, journal, year, volume, number, keywords (up to five), author's name (up to two), author's sex (up to two), author's nationality (up to two), author's institutional affiliations (up to four), author's position (up to four), author's academic training (up to two), author's country of academic training (up to two), research area (up to two), funding, quantitative component (Ravecca, 2014), and methods (up to two).

28. Shortage of space prevented me from including the analytical tables that summarize the interviewees' perceptions of the following dimensions: dictatorship, democratic

transition, democracy, the United States, Europe, Marxism, *ensayismo*, and political theory. The material can be provided upon request.

29. In some cases, I mention a department as well as the university that hosts it. This means that, even though the highlighted specific academic unit had a particularly important role in the research, I also explored other institutional spaces within the university in question.

30. In some cases, I mention both a conference and a specific activity hosted by the former. This means that I took part in (or at least attended) other panels and events at the conference in question, but I decided to highlight the specific event that is mentioned. I have translated the titles of Latin American events.

31. In this case I had access to the videos of some of the presentations.

32. Shortage of space prevented me from including a case study and in-depth analysis of two 2014 roundtables that the ICP at the University of the Republic in Uruguay organized on "Extractive Industries." The case study highlights the lack of critical distance between Uruguayan PS and political elites (see Appendix D).

33. A research assistant took fieldnotes and recorded the event.

34. The research also included activities such as: (*a*) seminars on the theories employed by PPS; (*b*) systematic analysis of the regional and global literature on the development of PS and other related topics (over 1,000 titles); (c) production of four summary documents on the state of the art of PS' history and development; (*d*) in-depth examination of regional PS journals' earliest issues (with particular attention to Uruguay and Chile), syllabi and curricula of BA, MA, and PhD programs, Program Directors' talks and speeches at relevant events, institutional documents, as well as other materials (see Chapters 2 and 3); (*e*) description of the life trajectory of the early contributors to *RUCP*, *Política*, and *RCP* (see Chapters 2 and 3); (*f*) historical and contextual analysis of the academic units in which these journals are located; (*g*) complete digitalization of the journals and other materials; (*h*) analysis of visual archives and photographic registers (Chapters 2 and 3); (*i*) participatory observation in meetings and PS events in the Americas (Chapters 2, 3, and 4); (*j*) collection, systematization, and analysis of press releases of PS departments; (*k*) collection, systematization, and analysis of faculty performance evaluation criteria employed by academic units of both countries; (*l*) collection and digitalization of MA theses in political science at the University of Chile for the years 1982–2012; and (*m*) writing a Methodological Memory in which the challenging process of the database's construction is described in detail.

35. Dr. Pedro Narbondo (1953–2015) was a critical scholar who became the Director of the ICP. More importantly, he was the most sophisticated analyst of the Uruguayan state and his classes were incredibly intellectually inspiring.

36. Teaching my research as an unfolding, open-ended adventure allowed me to *research my teaching* and my pedagogical views which, in their turn, affect my identity as a scholar and my very conception of PS.

Works Cited

Adcock, R. (2014). *Liberalism and the emergence of American political science: A transatlantic tale*. Oxford: Oxford University Press.

Adorno, T. W. (2005). *Negative dialectics*. New York: Continuum.

Ahmad, A. (1992). Orientalism and after. In A. Ahmad (Ed.), *In theory: Classes, nations, literatures* (pp. 159–220). London: Verso.

Ahmed, S. (2012). *On being included: Racism and diversity in institutional life*. Durham, NC: Duke University Press.

Ake, C. (1979). *Social science as imperialism: A theory of political development*. Ibadan: Ibadan University Press.

Alexander, J. M. (2005). *Pedagogies of crossing: Meditations on feminism, sexual politics, memory, and the sacred.* Durham, NC: Duke University Press.

Almond, G. (1990). *A discipline divided.* Thousand Oaks, CA: Sage Publications.

Almond, G., & Verba, S. (1963). *The civic culture: Political attitudes and democracy in five nations.* Princeton, NJ: Princeton University Press.

Altman, D. (2005). La institucionalización de la ciencia política en Chile y América Latina: Una mirada desde el sur. *Revista de Ciencia Política, 25*(1), 3–15.

Amadae, S. M. (2016). *Prisoners of reason: Game theory and neoliberal political economy.* New York: Cambridge University Press.

Amoureux, J. L., & Steele, B. J. (Eds.). (2016). *Reflexivity and international relations: Positionality, critique, and practice.* New York: Routledge.

Anderson, K. (2010). *Marx at the margins: On nationalism, ethnicity, and non-western societies.* Chicago: University of Chicago Press.

Arendt, H. (1999). *Eichmann en Jerusalén: Un estudio sobre la banalidad del mal.* Barcelona: Lumen.

Baer, M. A., Malcolm, E. J., & Sigelman, L. (1991). *Political science in America: Oral histories of a discipline.* Lexington, KY: University Press of Kentucky.

Bejarano, A. M., & Wills, M. E. (2005). La ciencia política en Colombia: De vocación a disciplina. *Revista de Ciencia Política, 25*(1), 111–123.

Bello, W. (2008, May 16). *How to manufacture a global food crisis: Lessons from the World Bank, IMF and WTO.* Transnational Institute. Retrieved from www.tni.org/en/article/how-to-manufacture-a-global-food-crisis-lessons-from-the-world-bank-imf-and-wto

Bevir, M. (2003). Interpretivism: Family resemblances and quarrels. *Qualitative Methods Newsletter of the American Political Science Association, 1*(2), 18–20. doi: 10.5281/zenodo.998729.

Borón, A. (2007). Aristóteles en Macondo: Notas sobre el fetichismo democrático en América Latina. In G. Hoyos Vázquez (Ed.), *Filosofía y teorías políticas entre la crítica y la utopía* (pp. 49–67). Buenos Aires: CLACSO.

Bourdieu, P. (1973). *El oficio del sociólogo.* Buenos Aires: Siglo Ventiuno.

Brettschneider, M. (1997). *The family flamboyant: Race politics, queer families, Jewish lives.* Albany, NY: State University of New York Press.

Brettschneider, M. (2011). Heterosexual political science. *PS: Political Science & Politics, 44*(1), 23–26.

Brigg, M., & Bleiker, R. (2010). Autoethnographic international relations: Exploring the self as a source of knowledge. *Review of International Studies, 36,* 779–798.

Brown, W. (2002). At the edge. *Political Theory, 30*(4), 556–576.

Brown, W. (2015). *Undoing the demos: Neoliberalism's stealth revolution.* New York: Zone Books.

Buck-Morss, S. (2009). *Hegel, Haiti and universal history.* Pittsburgh: University of Pittsburgh Press.

Buck-Morss, S. (2010). The second time as farce . . . historical pragmatics and the untimely present. In C. Douzinas & S. Žižek (Eds.), *The idea of communism* (pp. 67–80). New York: Verso.

Bulcourf, P. (2012). El desarrollo de la ciencia política en Argentina. *Política, 50*(1), 59–92.

Bulcourf, P., Gutiérrez Márquez, E., & Cardozo, N. (2015). Historia y desarrollo de la ciencia política en América Latina: Reflexiones sobre la constitución del campo de estudios. *Revista de Ciencia Política, 35*(1), 179–199.

Buquet, D. (2012). El desarrollo de la ciencia política en Uruguay. *Política, 50*(1), 5–29.

Butler, J. (1990). *Gender trouble: Feminism and the subversion of identity*. New York: Routledge.

Butler, J., Laclau, E., & Zizek, S. (2003). *Contingencia, hegemonía, universalidad: Diálogos contemporáneos en la izquierda*. Buenos Aires: Fondo de Cultura Económica.

Buttigieg, J. A. (1990). Gramsci's method. *Boundary, 17*(2), 60–81.

Byrd, J. A., & Rothberg, M. (2011). Between subalternity and indigeneity. *Interventions, 13*(1), 1–12.

Cansino, C. (2008). *La muerte de la ciencia política*. Rosario: Espacios políticos.

Cardoso, F. H., & Faletto, E. (1979). *Dependency and development in Latin America*. Berkeley: University of California Press.

Casen, C., & Ravecca, P. (2010, July 18). Le confit égalitaire: Un impensé de la science politique en Amérique Latine. *Contretemps: Revue de Critique Communiste*. Retrieved from www.contretemps.eu/interventions/conflit-egalitaire-impense-science-politique-en-amerique-latine

Cigales, M. (2017). Historia de la ciencia política en América Latina. Uma entrevista con Pablo Bulcourf. *Realis, 7*(01), 234–257.

Ciriza, A. (2010, October 17). A propósito de una controversia feminista: Sobre ambivalencias conceptuales y asuntos de disputa. Las relaciones entre cuerpo y política. *Herramienta: Debate y Crítica Marxista, 45*. Retrieved from www.herramienta.com.ar/revista-herramienta-n-45/proposito-de-una-controversia-feminista-sobre-ambivalencias-conceptuales-y-

De Sousa Santos, B. (2008). *Another knowledge is possible: Beyond northern epistemologies*. London: Verso.

Dogan, M. (1997). The new social sciences: Cracks in the disciplinary walls. *International Social Science Journal, 49*(153), 429–443.

Dos Santos, T. (1970). The structure of dependence. *The American Economic Review, 60*(2), 231–236.

Dussel, E. (2000). Europe, modernity and eurocentrism. *Nepantia: Views from the South, 1*(3), 465–478.

Easton, D., Gunnell, J. G., & Stein, M. B. (1995). *Regime and discipline: Democracy and the development of political science*. Ann Arbor, MI: University of Michigan Press.

Eley, G. (2002). *Forging democracy: The history of the left in Europe, 1850–2000*. New York: Oxford University Press.

Escobar, A. (2004). Beyond the third world: Imperial globality, global coloniality and anti-globalisation social movements. *Third World Quarterly, 25*(1), 207–230.

Evans, H. K., & Moulder, A. (2011). Reflecting on a decade of women's publications in four top political science journals. *PS: Political Science & Politics, 44*(4), 793–798.

Fanon, F. (1961). *The wretched of the earth*. New York: Grove Weidenfeld.

Fanon, F. (1967). *Black skin, white masks*. New York: Grove Press.

Farr, J., Dryzek, J. S., & Stephen, L. T. (1999). *La ciencia política en la historia*. Madrid: Istmo.

Fernández Ramil, M. A., & Grebe, C. (2010). Ciencia política e historia disciplinar: Modelo para armar. *Revista Politeia, 33*(44), 1–30.

Foucault, M. (1980). Two lectures. In C. Gordon (Ed.), *Power/knowledge: Selected interviews and other writings 1972–1977* (pp. 78–109). New York: Pantheon.

Foucault, M. (1989). *Vigilar y castigar*. Mexico City: Siglo Veintiuno Editores.

Foucault, M. (1991a). *Historia de la sexualidad 1: La voluntad de saber*. Madrid: Siglo Veintiuno de España Editores.

Foucault, M. (1991b). *Saber y verdad*. Madrid: Ediciones La Piqueta.

Foucault, M. (1992). *Microfísica del poder*. Madrid: Ediciones La Piqueta.

Foucault, M. (1993). *Genealogía del racismo*. Montevideo: Nordam.

Foucault, M. (2006). *Seguridad, territorio, población: Curso en el Collège de France (1977–1978)*. Buenos Aires: Fondo de Cultura Económica.

Fowler, J. H., Grofman, B., & Masuoka, N. (2007). Social networks in political science: Hiring and placement of PhDs, 1960–2002. *PS: Political Science & Politics, 40*(4), 729–739.

Frank, A. G. (1966). *The development of underdevelopment*. Boston: New England Free Press.

Freidenberg, F. (2017). *La ciencia política sobre América Latina: Docencia e investigación en perspectiva comparada*. Santo Domingo: Funglode.

Garcé, A. (2005). La ciencia política en Uruguay: Un desarrollo tardío, intenso y asimétrico. *Revista de Ciencia Política, 25*(1), 232–244.

Geertz, C. (1997). *La interpretación de las culturas*. Barcelona: Gedisa.

Geertz, C. (2003). Interview with Clifford Geertz (J. Gerring, Interviewer). *Qualitative Methods Newsletter of the American Political Science Association, 1*(2), 24–28. doi: 10.5281/zenodo.998745.

Giroux, H. A. (1999). Rethinking cultural politics and radical pedagogy in the work of Antonio Gramsci. *Educational Theory, 49*(1), 1–19.

Gramsci, A. (2008). *Selections from the prison notebooks* (Q. Hoare & G. Nowell, Trans. & Eds.). New York: International Publishers.

Green, M., & Ives, P. (2009). Subalternity and language: Overcoming the fragmentation of common sense. *Historical Materialism, 17*, 3–30.

Hartlyn, J. (2008). Tendencias de la ciencia política en Norteamérica y diálogos con la ciencia política en América Latina. In S. Pachano (Ed.), *Temas actuales y tendencias en la ciencia política* (pp. 25–33). Quito: FLACSO.

Harvey, D. (2003). *The new imperialism*. Oxford: Oxford University Press.

Harvey, D. (2005). *A brief history of neoliberalism*. Oxford: Oxford University Press.

Harvey, D. (2010). *A companion to Marx's Capital*. New York: Verso.

Hix, S. (2004). A global ranking of political science departments. *American Political Studies Review, 2*(3), 293–313.

Holt, N. L. (2003). Representation, legitimation, and autoethnography: An autoethnographic writing story. *International Journal of Qualitative Methods, 2*(1), 18–58.

Horkheimer, M. (1978). *Théorie critique*. Paris: Payot.

Horowitz, G. (1977). *Basic and surplus repression in psychoanalytic theory: Freud, Reich and Marcuse*. Toronto: University of Toronto Press.

Huneeus, C. (2006). El lento y tardío desarrollo de la ciencia política en América Latina, 1966–2006. *Estudios Internacionales, 155*, 137–156.

Jackman, M. C., & Upadhyay, N. (2014). Pinkwatching Israel, whitewashing Canada: Queer (settler) politics and indigenous colonization in Canada. *WSQ: Women's Studies Quarterly, 42*(3), 195–210.

Jackson, P. T. (2011). *The conduct of inquiry in international relations: Philosophy of science and its implications for the study of world politics*. London: Routledge.

Kaufman, S. J. (2005). Rational choice, symbolic politics, and pluralism in the study of violent conflict. In K. R. Monroe (Ed.), *Perestroika! The raucous rebellion in political science* (pp. 87–102). New Haven, CT: Yale University Press.

Keucheyan, R. (2013). *The left hemisphere: Mapping critical theory today*. New York: Verso.

Keucheyan, R. (2016). Las mutaciones de la teoría crítica: Un mapa del pensamiento radical hoy. *Nueva Sociedad, 261*(enero-febrero), 36–53.

King, G., Lehman Schlozman, K., & Nie, N. (2009). *The future of political science: 100 perspectives*. New York: Routledge.

Laclau, E., & Mouffe, C. (2004). *Hegemonía y estrategia socialista: Hacia una radicalización de la democracia*. Buenos Aires: Fondo de Cultura Económica.

Laitin, D. (2004). ¿Adónde va la ciencia política? Reflexiones sobre la afirmación del profesor Sartori de que "la ciencia política estadounidense no va a ningún lado." *Política y Gobierno, 11*(2), 361–367.

Lazarus, N. (2002). The fetish of "the west" in postcolonial theory. In C. Bartolovich & N. Lazarus (Eds.), *Marxism, modernity and postcolonial studies* (pp. 43–64). Cambridge: Cambridge University Press.

Leiras, M., & D'Alessandro, M. (2005). La ciencia política en Argentina: El camino de la institucionalización dentro y fuera de las aulas universitarias. *Revista de Ciencia Política, 25*(1), 76–91.

Manalansan, M. F. (1995). In the shadows of Stonewall: Examining gay transnational politics and the diasporic dilemma. *GLQ: A Journal of Lesbian and Gay Studies, 2*(4), 425–438.

Marcuse, H. (1974). *Eros and civilization. A philosophical inquiry into Freud*. Boston: Beacon Press.

Marcuse, H. (1991). *One-dimensional man: Studies in the ideology of advanced industrial society*. Boston: Beacon Press.

Marx, K. (1978). Economic and philosophic manuscripts of 1844. In R. C. Tucker (Ed.), *The Marx-Engels reader* (pp. 66–125). New York: W.W. Norton & Company.

McNally, D. (2002). *Bodies of meaning: Studies on language, labor, and liberation*. New York: State University of New York Press.

McNally, D. (2006). *Another world is possible: Globalization and anti-capitalism*. Monmouth: The Merlin Press.

McNally, D. (2011). *Global slump: The economics and politics of crisis and resistance*. Oakland: PM Press.

Mejía Acosta, A., Freidenberg, F., & Pachano, S. (2005). La ciencia política en Ecuador: un reflejo de su fragilidad democrática (1978–2005). *Revista de Ciencia Política, 25*(1), 147–161.

Mohanty, C. T., Russo, A., & Torres, L. (1991). *Third world women and the politics of feminism*. Bloomington: Indiana University Press.

Monroe, K. R. (Ed.). (2005). *Perestroika! The raucous rebellion in political science*. New Haven, CT: Yale University Press.

Morelli, C. (2008, June 24). Behind the world food crisis. *International Socialism, 119*. Retrieved from www.isj.org.uk/index.php4?id=455&issue=119

Morgensen, S. L. (2010). Settler homonationalism: Theorizing settler colonialism within queer modernities. *GLQ: A Journal of Lesbian and Gay Studies, 16*(1–2), 105–131.

Munck, G. L., & Snyder, R. (2007). Who publishes in comparative politics? Studying the world from the United States. *PS: Political Science & Politics, 40*(2), 339–346.

Newman, S. (2007). Anarchism, poststructuralism and the future of radical politics. *SubStance 36*(2), 3–19.

Nietzsche, F. (1989). *Genealogy of morals*. New York: Vintage Books.

Nietzsche, F. (1990). *Beyond good and evil*. London: Penguin Books.

Nietzsche, F. (1999b). *El caminante y su sombra*. Madrid: Edimat Libros.

Puar, J. (2007). *Terrorist assemblages: Homonationalism in queer times*. Durham, NC: Duke University Press.

Puello-Socarrás, J. F. (2010). La miseria de la politología: Trayectoria histórica, perspectivas políticas y proyecciones sociales. *América Latina, 9*, 211–265.

Putnam, R. (1993). *Making democracy work: Civic traditions in modern Italy*. Princeton, NJ: Princeton University Press.

Ravecca, P. (2007). *Política 'flota' si 'cultura' irrumpe: Un ejercicio de interpretación*. Montevideo: Mimeo.

Ravecca, P. (2010a). *Marxism, postcolonial studies and queer theory today: Economies of conceptual violence and horizons beyond the apartheid. An epistemological and political reflection*. Buenos Aires: Fysip Publications.

Ravecca, P. (2010b). La política de la ciencia política: Ensayo de introspección disciplinar desde América Latina hoy. *América Latina, 9*, 173–210.

Ravecca, P. (2014). *La política de la ciencia política en Chile y Uruguay: Ciencia, poder, contexto*. Primeros hallazgos de una agenda de investigación (Working Paper No. 01/14). Montevideo: Instituto de Ciencia Política.

Ravecca, P., & Dauphinee, E. (2018). Narrative and the possibilities for scholarship. *International Political Sociology, 12*(2), 125–138.

Ravecca, P., & Upadhyay, N. (2013). Queering conceptual boundaries: Assembling indigenous, Marxist, postcolonial and queer perspectives. *Jindal Global Law Review, 4*(2), 357–378.

Rocha Carpiuc, C. (2016). Women and diversity in Latin American political science. *European Political Science, 15*(4), 457–475.

Rojas Silva, N., & Baquero, S. Á. (2017). 'Estancamiento paradójico': La ciencia política en los tiempos de la Revolución Bolivariana. *Anuario Latinoamericano—Ciencias Políticas y Relaciones Internacionales, 5*, 157.

Rudolph, S. H. (2005). Perestroika and its other. In K. R. Monroe (Ed.), *Perestroika! The raucous rebellion in political science* (pp. 12–20). New Haven, CT: Yale University Press.

Said, E. (1979). *Orientalism*. New York: Vintage Books.

Said, E. (2003a). *Nuevas crónicas palestinas: El fin del proceso de paz*. Barcelona: Debolsillo.

Sánchez González, S. (2005). La ciencia política en Panamá: Un nuevo punto de partida. *Revista de Ciencia Política, 25*(1), 204–221.

Sartori, G. (2004). Where is political science going? *PS: Political Science & Politics, 37*(4), 785–787.

Sassoon, A. S. (1987). *Gramsci's politics*. London: Hutchinson Education.

Schram, S., & Caterino, B. (2006). *Making political science matter: Debating knowledge, research and method*. New York: NYU Press.

Sepúlveda, A. (1996). El desarrollo de la ciencia política en Chile. *Política, 34*, 135–147.

Shapiro, I. (2005). Problems, methods, and theories in the study of politics or what's wrong with political science and what to do about it. In K. R. Monroe (Ed.), *Perestroika! The raucous rebellion in political science* (pp. 66–86). New Haven, CT: Yale University Press.

Smith, C. A. (2011). Gay, straight, or questioning? Sexuality and political science. *PS: Political Science & Politics, 44*(1), 35–38.

Smith, T. (1999). *Decolonizing methodologies: Research and indigenous peoples*. London: Zed Books.

Trent, J. E. (2009, July). *Political science 2010: Out of step with the world? Empirical evidence and commentary*. Paper presented at the 21st International Political Science World Congress, Santiago, Chile. Retrieved from www.johntrent.ca/published-writings/IPSAIs PolSci-0709.html

Trent, J. (2012). Issues and trends in political science at the beginning of the 21st century: Perspectives from the World of Political Science book series. In J. Trent & M. Stein (Eds.), *The world of political science: A critical overview of the development of political studies around the globe: 1990–2012* (pp. 91–153). Toronto: Barbara Budrich Publishers.

Varnoux Garay, M. (2005). La ciencia política en Bolivia: Entre la reforma política y la crisis de la democracia. *Revista de Ciencia Política, 25*(1), 92–100.

Vaz Ferreira, C. (1957). *Moral para intelectuales*. Montevideo: Cámara de Representantes de la República Oriental del Uruguay.

Wekker, G. (2006). *The politics of passion: Women's sexual culture in the afro-surinamese diaspora*. New York: Columbia University Press.

Wood, E. M. (2002). *The origin of capitalism: A longer view*. New York: Verso.

2

WHEN POLITICAL SCIENCE WAS AUTHORITARIAN

Chile, 1979–1989 (Cold)*

> Game theory is ubiquitous.
>
> —S.M. Amadae (2016, p. 286)

In most mainstream accounts of the discipline, Augusto Pinochet's authoritarian regime has been portrayed as being hostile toward political science (PS) (Altman, 2005, 2006; Barrientos Del Monte, 2012; Beigel, 2014; Buquet, 2012; Fortou, Leyva Botero, Preciado, & Ramírez, 2013; Huneeus, 2006; Puryear, 1994; Viacava, 2012, among others). This chapter destabilizes this understanding by showing that fundamental elements of the discipline's current infrastructure were produced during, *and in some cases by*, the authoritarian regime.[1] It also challenges the more wide-ranging narrative that links the institutionalization of PS in Latin America to liberal democracy in a linear fashion, and suggests the need for a more nuanced, empirically informed, and theoretically dense understanding of PS' multiple historical trajectories.

By examining how PS was produced during the Chilean dictatorship, I identify and characterize an institutional and intellectual space that I will call *authoritarian political science* (APS). Given that the politics of political science (PPS) treats PS as an object of political inquiry, I also highlight the political and intellectual role played by PS during this period. I have already presented the theoretical framework that sustains this perspective (see Chapter 1), but let me briefly revisit theory in order to situate the interpretive exercise proposed here.

The notions of discourse (Foucault, 1991a, 1991b; Said, 1979), hegemony (Cox, 1987; Gramsci, 2008; Laclau & Mouffe, 2004), and even the more mainstream concept of Weberian legitimacy are examples of attempts to grasp the epistemological and cultural dimensions of politics and power. PPS belongs to this intellectual saga and argues that thinking and knowledge are entrenched in power structures and dynamics; thus, academia and the knowledge that it produces are not outside power and the political struggles that they analyze. In other words, there is no exteriority between academia, power, and political economy (Alexander, 2005; Marcuse, 1991).[2] Furthermore, through multiple vocabularies, critical theorists have argued that powers that "think and talk" are more vigorous and effective than a culturally naked power. This theoretical insight is particularly relevant here because the outstanding effectiveness of the dictatorship in reshaping the fabric of Chilean society (Lechner, 1990; Mayol, 2012; Moulián, 2009) may be better understood by paying attention to the regime's engagement with knowledge and academia (Mella, 2011a). Here, I will show that such an engagement included PS, and, critically, the mobilization of the liberal democratic idiom.[3]

The main purpose of this chapter is to present the core features of APS, emphasizing their implications for how we understand the linkage between political science as a discipline and power. Two clarifications should be made at the outset to avoid misunderstandings. First, this chapter does not address what is outside of APS: this includes private and international academic institutions such as the Facultad Latinoamericana de Ciencias Sociales (FLACSO) [Latin American School of Social Sciences], where intellectual opposition to the regime took refuge, as well as scholars in exile. The significance of both has been abundantly documented in the literature (Heine, 2006; Huneeus, 2006). Jeffrey M. Puryear's *Thinking Politics: Intellectuals and Democracy in Chile, 1973–1988* (1994) extensively documented the important academic opposition to the regime. Even though I am less inclined to embrace the celebratory and uncritical view of the academics who, per the author, modernized social science and contributed to the re-building of Chilean democracy, the academic and political significance of this opposition *is taken for granted* here. Second, and in connection with the first, to examine how the dictatorship was involved in knowledge production (PS in this case) does *not* imply forgetting the obvious: that authoritarianism meant the loss of ideas and the shutting down of alternative voices.[4] These two caveats—the acknowledgment of what this study leaves unattended and recognizing that the dictatorship did exercise repression over knowledge production—do not undermine the interest in studying APS, whose academic and political significance has been largely ignored.

The analysis focuses on what is one of the most delicate issues for any political scientist and for politics as such: the democratic question. It relies on a systematic and in-depth analysis of all of the articles published during the dictatorship by the two main PS journals in Chile, *Política* [Politics] (188 pieces, 1982–1989) and *Revista de Ciencia Política* (RCP) [Journal of Political Science] (122 pieces, 1979–1989), along with other relevant historical records.[5] In order to locate APS within the broader chronological context, and especially to compare it with the PS that would come after the transition, a larger data set was used that includes 487 articles published by *Política* (1982–2012) and 544 articles published by *RCP* (1979–2012).

The chapter proceeds in five parts. In the first section, APS will be unpacked by analyzing its discourse (Foucault, 1991a) around the transition to democracy, the Cold War (the perception of the US, the Soviet Union, communism, and Marxism), the notion of *protected democracy*, as well as by exploring the explicit conception of democracy when available in the articles. Given that this is an exploration of how meanings are regulated (Geertz, 1997), the second section will address significant silence(s). The third section will look at the location of neoliberalism and the state's role in the economy in APS' theorizing on democracy. The cultural dimension of politics in a broad sense and the more specific issue of the weight assigned to Christianity and the East-West divide are addressed in the fourth section. Throughout, but particularly in the last two sections, I will show that APS was, indeed, academic and highly internationalized. Both aggregated data and specific illustrative cases are provided as evidence.[6] At all times, I will pay careful attention to the sharp academic and political differences between *Política* and *RCP* and their home institutions. My main aim, however, will be to theorize the different materials they provide to interpretively assemble APS.

A tormenting and fascinating question inspires me to write this, our first PPS story. Augusto Pinochet's dictatorship meant for Chile systematic torture, killing, and forced disappearances. However, *at the same time*, Chilean APS *was thinking* and publishing on issues ranging from the nature of Marxism to the pros and cons of different electoral systems. What does the overlap of these contrasting realities—killing and thinking—reveal about the relationship between knowledge and power? This question, addressed in section five of this chapter from an empirical and situated standpoint, expresses the polyvalence of knowledge and lies at the heart of this book. It will appear once and again in different contexts and forms and with singular existential force in Chapter 4. Exploring the productive aspects of the powers that hurt, or have hurt us individually or collectively, seems necessary if the aim is to know such forces deeply and to resist the engulfment of life by trauma.

My aim here is not to displace previous critical analysis of this painful period. On the contrary, my expectation is that the interrogation of APS' concrete historical experience will *expand* and enrich the kinds of questions that Latin American political scientists ask about the discipline and its politics. With that in mind, I will propose a definition of APS and will advance some reflections about its theoretical implications. The interpretation here does not attempt to dive into the subjective world of the protagonists of this story. What the reader will find in what follows is a dry and cold text uninterested in empathy and understanding that attempts to dissect a political, cultural, and academic phenomenon called authoritarian political science. The people that populate it are just mice in PPS' interpretive laboratory.

Institutionalized Transition: Toward a Protected Democracy

I visited the documentation center of the Institute of Public Affairs (INAP, formerly the Institute of Political Science) at the University of Chile several times in January 2013. Thanks to a generous librarian recruited in the early 1980s, I found out about the *Memoria de Actividades* [Register of Activities], an institutional newsletter published from 1982 to 1992. As the name suggests, these booklets document the memory of the institution.

I was surprised when my interviewee mentioned that Lucía Pinochet, the dictator's daughter, was "a regular" at the Institute's many activities. This minor anecdote revealed to me that Pinochet's regime was different from the Uruguayan dictatorship, which had significant implications for PS' history.[7] However, I was going to see something more interesting and surprising. I remember the scene of the finding very clearly: we were sitting in my interviewee's office. It was a hot afternoon, but the house of INAP was pleasantly cool. While listening to her I was leafing through the pages of these old documents. From one of them, this picture emerged from the shadows of PS' history and the first PPS story began to be written (Figure 2.1).

The ceremony depicted above was held in 1983, when Augusto Pinochet received the first copy of a special issue of *Política*, the official journal of the University of Chile's Institute of Political Science (IPS-CHU). Titled "Chile

FIGURE 2.1   Augusto Pinochet (left) at a ceremony at the Institute of Political Science, University of Chile in 1983

(Instituto de Ciencia Política, Universidad de Chile, 1983)

1973–1983: Perspectives for a Decade," the publication analyzed the first decade of "military government" (as nondetractors call it) (see Figure 2.2).

IPS-CHU was formally founded on November 16, 1981, through Legal Act 14.251, which was signed by Brigadier General Alejandro Medina Lois, then the university's president (see Figure 2.3). *Política* was launched in 1982, the same

FIGURE 2.2 Cover of a November 1983 special edition of *Política*. The title of the special edition reads: "Chile 1973–1983: Perspectives for a Decade."

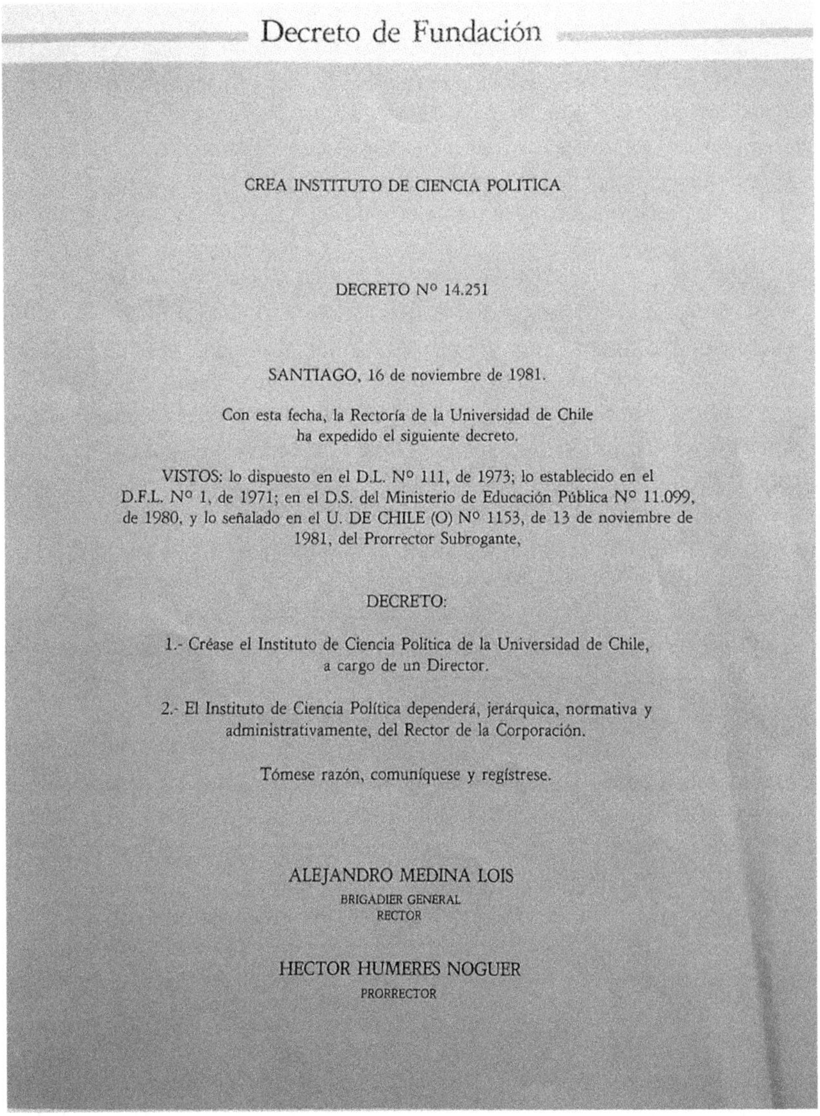

Decreto de Fundación

CREA INSTITUTO DE CIENCIA POLITICA

DECRETO N° 14.251

SANTIAGO, 16 de noviembre de 1981.

Con esta fecha, la Rectoría de la Universidad de Chile
ha expedido el siguiente decreto.

VISTOS: lo dispuesto en el D.L. N° 111, de 1973; lo establecido en el
D.F.L. N° 1, de 1971; en el D.S. del Ministerio de Educación Pública N° 11.099,
de 1980, y lo señalado en el U. DE CHILE (O) N° 1153, de 13 de noviembre de
1981, del Prorrector Subrogante,

DECRETO:

1.- Créase el Instituto de Ciencia Política de la Universidad de Chile,
a cargo de un Director.

2.- El Instituto de Ciencia Política dependerá, jerárquica, normativa y
administrativamente, del Rector de la Corporación.

Tómese razón, comuníquese y regístrese.

ALEJANDRO MEDINA LOIS
BRIGADIER GENERAL
RECTOR

HECTOR HUMERES NOGUER
PRORRECTOR

FIGURE 2.3   Decree 14.251 enacting the creation of IPS-CHU

(Instituto de Ciencia Política, Universidad de Chile, 1982)

year that the Institute's MA Program in PS—with concentrations in government
and political theory—was established. Three years prior, the Pontifical Catholic
University of Chile's (PUC) Institute of Political Science (IPS-CU), established
in 1969, launched the *Revista de Ciencia Política* (*RCP*) in 1979.

These institutional developments happened in the academic epicenter of Chile; that is, at the two major universities of the time—widely regarded, to this day, as the most prestigious institutions of higher education in the country. My interviewee, a non-academic person, understood well something that some academics today seem to have forgotten: "those weren't moments of intellectual darkness, the Institute of Political Science was more productive than today!" (CHL30).[8] Indeed, measuring productivity through output, *Política* published more articles in the period from 1982 to 1990 (47%) than between 1991 and 2000 (30%). Similarly, *RCP* published 24% of its articles in the period between 1979 and 1990 and 18% between 1991 and 2000.

These tangible forms of disciplinary development during Pinochet's rule go against the commonsense narrative that links the expansion of PS to democracy. Yet if facts become meaningful only thanks to theory, we must ask the question: What might that old picture and the events it evokes tell us—political scientists and other intellectuals alike—if theoretically interrogated? Might it be saying something about "us," in the present? What does the establishment of an institute for political science at a major public university and the launching of a journal for the cultivation of political science thinking during Chile's brutal dictatorship tell us about the discipline, liberalism, and politics?

A conceptual examination of the articles published in both journals during the dictatorship reveals a constellation of narratives that gravitated around the institutional development and expansion of what I have called APS. It goes without saying that it would be farfetched to suggest that all of the authors who published in Chile during this period held authoritarian values (in fact many of them did not), or that each analyzed piece fits all of the characteristics attributed to APS. What I offer, rather, consists of an empirically grounded interpretive reconstruction (Geertz, 1997) or a problematizing re-description (Shapiro, 2005) of a set of ideas and views that were *prominent* within our discipline in the period under analysis. Based on aggregated data and specific illustrative cases, I trace APS through a set of dimensions that seek to capture the ideological features of PS at the time. The analysis revolves around one specific question: How is democracy discussed?

One of the key topics addressed by the PS of this period is the importance of strong and durable institution building (Cea Egaña, 1982a; Cuevas Farren, 1979a, 1979b) for the country and for the discipline itself. The voice of Gustavo Cuevas Farren is particularly relevant, for he served as the director, successively, of both the public and the Catholic universities' Institutes of Political Science (between 1975 and 1982 for IPS-CU, and from 1982 to 1994 for IPS-CHU). It should not go unmentioned that Cuevas Farren's discourse shifts over time from a strong authoritarian tone to a liberal democratic or at least quasi-democratic framework.[9] What remains constant in this voice is the notion that the development of PS is his main aim and that the discipline is called to make a crucial contribution to the institutional development of Chile (Cuevas Farren, 1979b, p. 1, 1991, p. 114).

The language employed, centered on the notion of institutions, is familiar to any political scientist. After all, it is *our own, liberal* language. Hence, from the outset, its deployment begs the question of the continuities between APS and liberal PS. Although a few authors explicitly reject political parties and liberal democracy (Rodríguez Grez, 1986, p. 136; Ibáñez, 1985, p. 161), most of them reflect on a possible and even desirable transition to democracy. The transition to democracy was indeed a salient topic in the agenda of both journals—and the institutes that housed them—ever since their foundation; the question was addressed both domestically and in reference to other international contexts of the time.[10]

A main concern was that this process be stable, peaceful, and well organized. In some cases, this concern crystalized in a concrete conceptual category, institutionalized transition (IT) (Benavente Urbina, 1985, 1989; Cuevas Farren, 1989a, 1989b, 1990; Gajardo Lagomarsino, 1989a; Carmona, 1983), which denoted the control that the military government needed to exercise over the process of regime change. For this purpose, a set of institutional tools provided by the 1980 Constitution were mobilized in thematizing the near political future of Chile (see, for instance, Yrarrázaval, 1982, pp. 116–117).

Thus, in *Política*'s and *RCP*'s extensive reflections on the production of a stable democracy, a sort of double movement is at work: the coming back of democracy is welcomed as long as the new system has some crucial differences with the pre-1973 political regime that allowed Unidad Popular [Popular Unity, a political party] and President Allende to polarize Chilean society, eroding order and stability to a point that, in this view, the army had to intervene (Cuevas Farren, 1979a). Thus, a 1985 article argues that IT "corresponds to non-traditional governments that, because of powerful reasons, have disrupted the institutional continuity of a country and are now compelled to establish a new and permanent political order so that the institutional crisis that obliged them to intervene does not occur again" (Benavente Urbina, 1985, p. 46).[11] This argumentative component of APS' discourse is noticeable in *both* journals even though it is more prominent in the University of Chile's *Política* and less so in the Catholic university's *RCP*, where, as it will be shown, a right-wing but polyarchic tone prevailed before the transition.

What kind of democracy should Chile become through IT? And why is IT—i.e., a controlled transition—necessary at all? APS' model of democracy is defined through a number of elements that I explore in the following pages. One of them is the overriding need for "protection" (Cuevas Farren, 1979a, p. 6; Ribera Neumann, 1986, p. 67). The traumatic experience of the Popular Unity government and the threats brought about by the Cold War meant that Chile's new democracy was going to need to be defended against its internal and external enemies—namely, communism and other radical political projects (Yrarrázaval, 1979, 1982).

It is not surprising, then, that 70% of *Política*'s articles and 48% of *RCP*'s hold strong anti-communist views (see Figures 2.4 and 2.5). Democracy and communism are seen as incompatible. Furthermore, communism is understood to mobilize the means offered by democracy to destroy it from the inside.

APS' anti-communist framework was fairly international, adhering to Cold War lines. Both the Soviet Union and the US had an intense presence: 56% of *Política*'s and 40% of *RCP*'s articles depict the USSR in negative terms. Moreover, 23% and 20% of articles from both journals, respectively, are unabashedly aligned with the US. Given that there is not a single article aligned with the USSR, almost none that criticize the US (when they do so, it is usually from a neoconservative perspective), and many that simply do not address international politics, these numbers are significant (see Figures 2.6 and 2.7).

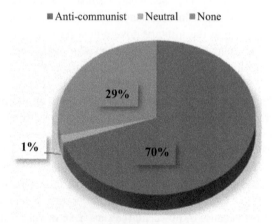

FIGURE 2.4   View of communism in *Política*, 1982–1989

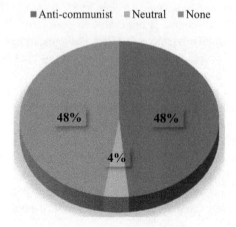

FIGURE 2.5   View of communism in *RCP*, 1979–1989

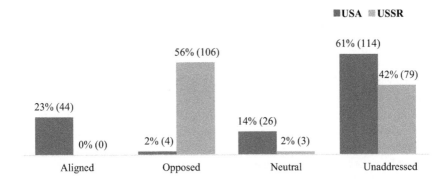

FIGURE 2.6 Position toward the US and the USSR in *Política*, 1982–1989

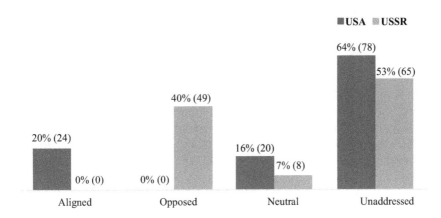

FIGURE 2.7 Position toward the US and the USSR in *RCP*, 1979–1989

The institutional-intellectual collaboration between Chilean and American anti-communism is further illustrated by American contributions to *RCP* (such as Theberge, 1979) and *Política* (such as Tambs & Aker, 1982), the latter being particularly brutal in its language on how to deal with (in fact destroy) the Marxist forces in El Salvador (Ravecca, 2014). This collaborative roster is a telling illustration of the interpenetration between academia and the making of international politics. James Theberge published in both *Política* (1984, 1988) and *RCP* (1979, 1983) before, during, and after he served as Ronald Reagan's ambassador to Chile.[12] He criticizes US pro–human rights policies and what he called the Carter administration's "moralism" (Theberge, 1979, p. 66). In 1988, he received a posthumous tribute by the IPS-CHU (Cuevas Farren, Mac Hale, & Trucco, 1988). Other *RCP* articles that target the Carter administration because of its pro-human rights policies and rhetoric in South America and Africa are, respectively, Wiarda (1985) and Kunert (1979).[13]

Other contributors included Roger Fontaine (1980), Reagan's adviser on Latin American issues and Director of Latin American Studies at Georgetown University's Center for Strategic and International Studies, who subtly supported Pinochet's regime while criticizing Carter's lack of hemispheric perspective, and Howard T. Pittman (1981), introduced as an American "Ex-Colonel" who holds a PhD in the social sciences.

Numerous conversations and interviews with academic and administrative staff working during those years confirmed the intense relationship between *both* IPS-CU and IPS-CHU and the American embassy, as well as some American universities. A very concrete example of this is the IPS-CHU's publication, Estudios Norteamericanos [North American Studies], supported by the US government and printed by the gendarmería, which was and still is part of the Chilean security forces and in charge of prisons. It is even more remarkable that some issues of *Política* were printed by the police (see Figures 2.8 and 2.9).

As the theoretical culprit of communism, Marxism had to be seriously dealt with in academia and in all sorts of public forums, including the media. In contrast to the relative silence and indifference that would predominate in later years, APS produced articles, papers, theses, and books that dealt with Marxism as an intellectual enemy. Marx is confronted on philosophical, theological, ethical, and political grounds. The articles are numerous: 79 in *Política* and 45 in *RCP*. Paradigmatic examples of this trend are Yrarrázaval (1979 and 1982). While engagements with classical liberal authors such as Thomas Hobbes (Miranda, 1984, 1986; Godoy Arcaya, 1987–1988), Immanuel Kant (Miranda, 1986), Adam Smith (Mertz, 1984) and Alexis de Tocqueville (Godoy Arcaya, 1983) have an empathetic tone, Marx's views are systematically dismissed.[14] The following quote is quite representative: "Marxism is an ideological model that simulates the real" (Yrarrázaval, 1979, p. 8).[15] As many as 42% of *Política*'s and 37% of *RCP*'s articles published in the authoritarian period had a negative view of Marxism (see Figures 2.10 and 2.11). Given that there are no articles that embrace any form of Marxism or neo-Marxism and that many of the pieces explore topics unrelated to any ideological debate, these are very high numbers. Even so, aggregated data cannot compete with the revealing capacity of details. The first issue of *Política* published an article entitled "Partisan Programs, Ideologies and Preferences: Anthony Downs' Model" (Wilhelmy, 1982). The topic of the piece decidedly belongs to the mainstream repertoire of our discipline. Therefore, the mention of Marxism-Leninism in a footnote reveals to what extent its presence was conspicuous in APS' conceptual universe.

Marxism is not only identified with concrete political parties, movements, or foreign governments: it is portrayed as an enemy that manifests its influence in the cultural realm, broadly understood, and, therefore, it should also be fought in the muddier terrain of ideas and ideology. This results in an interesting form of political analysis that cares about the cultural dimension of politics and

FIGURE 2.8   Cover of an issue of the *Estudios Norteamericanos* (North American Studies) series published by IPS-CHU (1986)

Impreso en los Talleres Gráficos
de Gendarmería de Chile
Santiago — 1986

FIGURE 2.9   "Printed in the printing works of the *Gendarmería* of Chile. Santiago–1986"

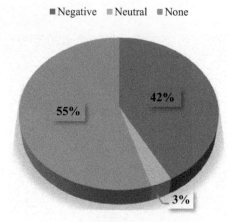

FIGURE 2.10   View of Marxism in *Política*, 1982–1989

academia itself. I will come back to this argument later in the chapter. Communism and Marxism will consistently diminish their presence in both journals after the transition, to the point that they practically disappear in the period between 2001 and 2012.

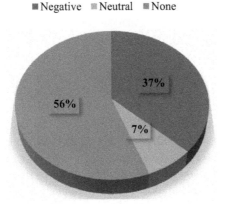

FIGURE 2.11 View of Marxism in *RCP*, 1979–1989

Protecting the Future (of) Democracy

I will now delineate in more detail the notion of protected democracy forged by right-wing Chilean forces within and beyond academia, in which the institutional and discursive constellation of APS plays a significant role.[16] Protection relates to the necessary restriction of political pluralism and to the active role that the army needs to have in the future democracy. A form of tutelage is thus needed in order to make sure that democracy does not destroy itself. In this logic, the political act of limiting the powers of democracy stands as a genuinely democratic procedure. For proponents of protected democracy, "naïve democracy," "artless liberalism," and "ahistorical rationalism" (all terms used by Mario Justo López and appropriated by Teodoro Ribera Neumann) should be avoided. Ribera Neumann (1986, p. 33), following Justo López (1963), calls this paradoxical form of saving democracy "dialectical suicide," i.e., when democracy, in order to avoid the destruction of its essential principle (i.e., freedom), limits the scope of its application. This contrasts with the "factual suicide" that is the consequence of keeping pluralism in the context of polarization and the communist threat. In any case, the point is that democracy must be defended even if that implies a temporary restriction of rights and freedoms.

In the same vein, an article in *Política* argues that "the democratic system allows an unrestrictive pluralism and thus propitiates its own destruction. These are the reasons why the Chilean legislators determined some basic limits to political pluralism. This new conception has been called 'Protected Democracy'" (Zepeda Hernández, 1985, p. 161). Only in this way will Chile be a well-organized and rational democracy (Yrarrázaval, 1979, p. 9).

The way in which the experience of Popular Unity and the coup is understood frames APS' engagement with the transition and the new democracy. In this narrative, the military government is apolitical and nonpartisan; that is, it is beyond politics. It has obediently followed the mandate—given by diverse social groups and sectors—of transcending particular interests and putting the Chilean nation first. That is why the presidential succession process should avoid "the reappearance of the kind of divisions and sectarian behaviors that *forced* the military pronouncement of 1973" (Núñez Tome, 1988, p. 75, emphasis mine). The language with which APS names the *coup d'état* is revealing in itself. The violent overthrow of President Salvador Allende that ended his life is on numerous occasions conveniently called a "pronouncement," while limitations to majority rule are discussed as academic considerations about the trade-off between pluralism and order—a language that is not foreign to mainstream PS and contemporary liberalism.

A strong nationalist language is linked to a kind of right-wing international project. Democracy is said to have external and internal allies as well as external and internal enemies such as the Communist Party and the Revolutionary Left Movement (MIR). These kinds of enemies allegedly coordinate with both external and internal anti-democratic forces, and thus, the need for protecting democracy arises. To illustrate, Andrés Benavente Urbina (1987) depicts the MIR in dramatic terms: they are young people who were and still are incapable of perceiving their own reality (recall that Yrarrázaval (1979) conceptualizes Marxism as a *simulation* of reality). They are always ready to imitate foreign ideas, attracted by a "strange seduction for violence and blood and that is why they cannot understand Chile, its past, and its vocation for integration. They give their backs to History and reality, so their country has ended up looking at them with disdain, as strangers" (Benavente Urbina, 1987, p. 155). For these writers, Marxism and communism are alien (and alienating), insidious enemies that undermine the strength of the Chilean nation.

The fear of judicial retaliation by those persecuted by the military government seems to be an important component of how APS frames the transition to democracy. It goes without saying that such a fear could hardly be explicitly presented in the narrative offered by APS. It had to operate in subtle ways to be effective. In that narrative's logic, the military defeated the enemies of Chile. How could democracy betray its saviors? If protecting democracy is a question of justice and fairness (it could hardly be otherwise), it should also be about protecting its saviors. Hence: "it is desirable that in the immediate future the military-civilian relationship develops in a friendly and harmonious manner according to the framework that follows from the new institutional political framework" (Cuevas Farren, 1989a, p. 56).

The point should be highlighted: mainstream PS' expertise and topics were a fundamental component of Chile's APS. Arturo Marín Vicuña (1986) worked on electoral systems from the point of view of institutionalized transition and protected democracy. His argument goes as follows: between 1963 and 1973, partisan competition pushed the political system toward the left and weakened the right (p. 139). The policy implication: the center should be strengthened by applying the electoral binomial system, while the political presence of the military will guard the new democracy by keeping (leftist) "extremists" at bay.

Between 1982 and 1989, 41% of the articles in *Política* supported protected democracy, while 22% supported polyarchy (see Figure 2.12). In this respect, *RCP*'s situation is almost the inverse of *Política*'s: 17% of its articles promoted protected democracy, and 42% were polyarchic (see Figure 2.13). Clearly, polyarchy prevailed in *RCP*, and this speaks of a sharp and important difference between the two journals. And yet, besides the fact that aggregated data cannot represent the intensity of a discourse well, that almost one in five articles promotes a limited type of democracy is still outstanding. The authoritarian framing of democracy is present in both journals. This conception of democracy literally *disappears* from the Catholic university's *RCP* in the 1990s, and similarly drops off abruptly in the same period in the public university's *Política*. By the 2000s, the narrative of protected democracy was gone from Chilean PS.

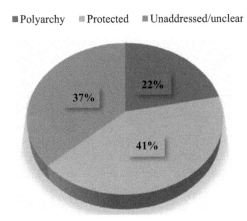

FIGURE 2.12   Type of democracy promoted in *Política*, 1982–1989

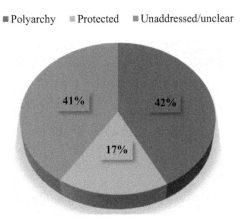

FIGURE 2.13   Type of democracy promoted in *RCP*, 1979–1989

During the dictatorship, IPS-CHU was very active in mobilizing international networks, organizing thematic seminars, and coordinating numerous academic activities (Ravecca, 2014). The institutional newsletters (i.e., *Memoria de Actividades*) published in this period (1982–1992), Cuevas Farren's speeches, *Política* itself and other historical records attest to that. By the second half of the 1980s, many articles focused on the transition. An entire seminar in 1986 supported by the conservative German Hanns Seidel Foundation was dedicated to the fundamentals of democracy at the institutional, geographical-territorial, economic, and even spiritual levels. The interventions were published in two special editions of *Política*. The notion of a protected democracy appeared in these conversations as well as in seminars about "The Subsidiary State" and "Social Communication and Politics," published in Volume 13 of *Política* in 1987, among others. However, APS allowed for *some* dissent. Protected democracy was occasionally contested by some participants of those activities. Thus, Article 8 of the 1980 Constitution that proscribed political groups that threatened the family or promoted class struggle was called a "legal aberration" by Francisco Cumplido Cereceda (Rojas Sánchez, Ribera Neumann, & Cumplido Cereceda, 1987, p. 151).

RCP, or the Meaning of Silence

The dynamics of passive acceptance or discreet resistance within *RCP vis-à-vis* the military government are complex and ambiguous. Indeed, *RCP*'s location and status within APS is more complex than *Política*'s. As already noted, protected democracy is not a dominant narrative on its pages; many of its articles speak the standard and supposedly objective academic idiom. And yet, the case may be made that, overall, *RCP* belongs to the space of APS. The analytical point that I want to make here is that the narrative of protected democracy did not necessarily have to be deployed in order for the articles to fit as a whole within APS. This was achieved through other significant gestures, silence being one of them.

The *RCP* spectrum encompasses different ideological perspectives and positions *vis-à-vis* the military government. Cuevas Farren (1979a) illustrates poignantly one side of this spectrum with his open support for the coup and the military regime. On the other end, we could locate Myers (1989), who addresses forced disappearances in a rather abstruse but evidently critical way: it is the first time that the *desaparecidos* [the disappeared] are mentioned in the journal. Myers (1989) conceptualizes them as a travesty of death and murder (p. 29). Interestingly, the article does not refer to Chile but to Argentina. Standing in the middle, there is a space inhabited by polyarchic, conservative, and authoritarian discourses along with significant silence(s).

Reading silences is always a challenge (Auyero, 2002; Butalia, 2000; Enloe, 2004; Dauphinee, 2013a, 2013b; Jelin, 2011; Spivak, 1988). The problem with aggregated data and numbers is precisely that the subtlety of discourses, powerful details, and relevant silences get lost. If "a scholar who leaves no room for answering is by definition part of the discourse police" (Neumann, 2016, p. 274), dealing with the polyvalence of silence is crucial to any form of reflexivity be it as positionality, as critique or as practice (Amoureux & Steele, 2016). Exploring silences is also part of "an ethos through which [we] strive to keep [our] own thinking mobile and fluid" (Dauphinee, 2016, p. 51). In this case, analytically listening to *RCP*'s silences keeps the possibilities of interpretation open. Overall, silence is an opportunity for curiosity and interpretation (Enloe, 2004). Let me show what I mean by significant silences through a few examples.

Roberto Durán (1980) and María Teresa Infante (1980) approached issues in international relations (IR) from theoretical and public policy perspectives respectively. One could not guess that these articles were written in the midst of a dictatorship. *RCP*'s international relations orientation allows for disconnection with the troubled local political context, which is simply absent in these two texts' discussions about functionalist IR theory and the UN Law of the Sea Convention. However, two articles in the same issue, "The Subversive War as a Method in International Relations" (Sasse, 1980) and "Elements of a Totalitarian Conception" (Rojas Sánchez, 1980), break the silence from a right-wing perspective—a gesture that (re)situates silence.

Meanwhile, María Teresa Miranda (1982) analyzes the Chilean electoral system and its effects. Its updated bibliography, as well as its narrative, belongs to mainstream Anglo-Saxon PS. The piece mentions "the fall of Allende's government" (1982, p. 59) *en passant* and then simply continues its conversation with Duverger and Douglas Rae. Sergio Tuteleers (1982) argues that checks and balances and the separation of state powers is "one of the main guarantees offered by the democratic system to Men in order to defend themselves against an arbitrary government and, therefore, to be able to live in freedom" (p. 97). This piece, written by a Chilean scholar, completely ignores the situation in Chile. Furthermore, the quintessential components of democracy such as universal suffrage and political equality are not mentioned. The reader is left very curious about how to situate this article in the Chile of its time.

The presence of a very professional form of geopolitical analysis, which extends the silence about democracy, is also noteworthy. Pinochet de la Barra (1985) and Riesco (1985), for instance, were originally interventions in a seminar at the IPS-CU in 1984 on the Chile-Argentina territorial controversies. There are many others of this kind, such as Meneses (1979). Durán (1981) documents a 1980 seminar on the relationship between geopolitics and international relations, and offers some interesting theoretical reflections on the topic. The framework is clearly academic. He cites American military official and scholar John Child's (1979)[17] contribution to the *Latin American Research Review* and in endnote 17 acknowledges military official Juan Emilio Cheyre's intervention at the seminar (Durán, 1981, p. 25).[18] How is APS operating here? What is it enabling or precluding? And why should what they enable or preclude be important—considering the rather unremarkable feature of a repressive dictatorship, which is that there are perhaps things that cannot be said? In these concrete cases, the interpretative point is that the way in which these articles frame the national interest of Chile not only, once again, displaces democracy as a topic of conversation, but also actively reinforces the rationale of the government and its military aims.

The *RCP*'s neoliberal (Hayek, 1982; Nishiyama, 1982; Novak, 1983) and right-wing discourses (Bravo Lira, 1987–1988; Cea Egaña, 1982a; Sasse, 1980), which were sometimes framed in religious terms, as we will see later, are juxtaposed to numerous curious and interesting silences that leave the reader with more questions than answers. Cleary, the two institutions under study are different. While IPS-CHU performed the role of the intellectual arm of the dictatorship, within IPS-CU divergent logics coexisted.

A note on complexity is needed here. It is true that comparatively, in *RCP*, the polyarchic discourse was preeminent;[19] however, even *Política*, as aligned with the military government as it was, should not be simplified either. *Política* also contained texts that were in favor of liberal democracy and thus it was also, in its way, a diverse space. On its pages, Uruguayan scholar Héctor Gros Espiell (1983) argued early on for the restoration of the rule of law and pluralism in Uruguay while Álvaro Pezoa Bissieres (1989) explored Guillermo O'Donnell's *oeuvre* in analytical and academic terms. Even more interestingly, a few pages away from Lewis Tambs and Frank Aker's (1982) article, which engaged with the situation in El Salvador from an extreme right-wing perspective, there is a book review of Edward Said's *Orientalism*, a keystone of postcolonial studies.[20]

Ricardo Israel Zipper (1982) not only acknowledges Said's main contribution to contemporary critical thinking but also appropriates the book to advance some reflections about knowledge-power dynamics within area studies. Applying the logic and argument of *Orientalism* to Latin American studies, the author argues that sometimes American scholars easily become the academic authority on a country or region after spending a few weeks in the place. Their perspective is frequently simplistic and superficial. Zipper also refers to academic dependency and how many Latin American scholars learn about their own reality at institutions in Europe or the US. As a result, they end up reproducing problematic accounts of their own political and social reality (I share this view; see Chapter 5). The tone of the author is careful, and he does clarify that this is a general tendency with many exceptions. This is the kind of relevant, self-reflexive epistemological conversation about the geopolitics of academia and knowledge production that mainstream PS seems reluctant to have today. I will advance my point through a question: What does the presence of a review of *Orientalism*, an icon of contemporary critical theory, in *Política* mean? For sure, it implies something quite important: the complexity of APS and, by extension, of the regime that *Política* supported.

A Re-Founding Trilogy: Protected Democracy, Market Economy, and Private Property

Neoliberal capitalism stands as key ideological feature of APS. The market economy and private property rights are posed as indispensable for the (protected) democratic system. In other words, they are seen as key components of what democracy ought to be. It goes without saying that in this schema, the state's limited role in the country's economy is a prerequisite for freedom (Cuevas Farren, 1979a; Nishiyama, 1982; Pazos, 1987). This conflation of democracy and neoliberal capitalism is a fundamental conceptual move with radical material implications. Indeed, APS and the Chicago Boys agree in their public policy recommendations. Here are some illustrations of how that narrative is deployed.[21]

In a seminar at the IPS-CHU in 1986, the "Fundamentals of a Democratic Regime," documented by a special issue of *Política*, the first featured article in the economic section collects two interventions with no disagreement on a crucial point: private property rights are fundamental for democratic stability (Urenda Zegers & Eyzaguirre García de la Huerta, 1987). (The title leaves no doubt about that: "Private Property Rights: The Basis for Democratic Stability.") Carlos Urenda Zegers clarifies that he is particularly referring to private ownership over "the means of production" (p. 16), and defends "the Christian and Western democratic system," where this right guarantees the dispersion of power within society. The intervention closes with references to de Tocqueville and Kant. Meanwhile, José Eyzaguirre García de la Huerta refers to Locke, Montesquieu, and (quite paradoxically) Rousseau. His argument is framed in terms of possessive individualism. The normative linkage between (the "natural right" of) private property and democracy is freedom. The author warns the reader that future governments should not make the same mistakes of Popular Unity if Chilean society is to avoid the collapse of its new democracy. The welfare state undermines democracy. And the state—the "subsidiary state" in the author's words—appears as one among other legal and constitutional provisions necessary for the protection of private property and democracy. The world of ideas and meanings is not absent in this perspective: there should be cultural consensus about the necessity of a private property regime and an ethical framework for the exercise of such a right.

Política also dedicated an entire issue to a seminar titled "The Entrepreneurial State" and to a draft of the Constitutional Organic Law that, by a reinterpretation of the 1980 Constitution, improved the protection of the subsidiarity principle (see Figure 2.14). The introduction to the seminar proceedings is explicitly framed in political terms; its title reads "The Subsidiarity Principle and the Chilean Political Regime" (Cuevas Farren, 1987). Here, the subsidiary state is understood as the opposite of (and as a remedy to) "an absorbent state," and corresponds to a "modern," "efficient," and "free" institutional framework (p. 17). Unsurprisingly, neoliberalism is presented as the best development strategy.

POLITICA

Nº 13   SANTIAGO – SEPTIEMBRE   1987

EL ROL DEL ESTADO EMPRESARIO

Guillermo Bruna, Juan de Dios Carmona,
Modesto Collados, Gustavo Cuevas,
Manuel Feliú, Ricardo García

POLITICA Y COMUNICACION SOCIAL

Guillermo Bruna, José Antonio Cousiño,
Gustavo Cuevas, Francisco Cumplido,
Rigoberto Díaz, Edmundo Eluchans,
Juan Hamilton, Tomás Mac Hale,
Rafael Otero, Roberto Pulido,
Abraham Santibáñez

INSTITUTO DE CIENCIA POLITICA
UNIVERSIDAD DE CHILE

FIGURE 2.14   Cover of a special issue of *Política*: "The Role of the Entrepreneurial State" and "Politics and Social Communication" (1987, Volume 13)

The Minister of Interior, Ricardo García Rodríguez, participated in this seminar. The minister did not fail to mention the importance of holding this gathering at the University of Chile, given the university's paramount role in shaping the nation's future. He also reminded the participants that a private sector-based economy is the path to a free and developed society (García Rodríguez, 1987). His presence in the seminar stands as an official recognition of the importance assigned by the government to the principle of subsidiarity. In the course of his intervention, he mobilized the notion of protection to specifically refer to the threat that "anti-market parties" pose to a political regime. The participants included Juan de Dios Carmona Peralta, a member of the Constitutional Organic Laws Study Commission appointed by the Pinochet government who was invited to speak about the technicalities of the law, as well as Manuel Feliú Justiniano, President of the Production and Commerce Confederation, who celebrated corporations and insisted, following the neoliberal formula, on the need of keeping social policies exclusively focused on the poor.

The following fragment from a professor of PUC who was also a member of the Commission is a telling representation of the explicit linkage between knowledge production and Pinochet's government:

> *Fortunately*, knowledge about the relationship between personal freedom and private property has recently spread. . . . In the new scheme that has emerged after 1973, freedom has become the symbol and aim of the country's new institutional arrangements. Freedom is guaranteed by private property, free economic initiative and by the full adoption of the concept of the subsidiary state. *An abundance of social market economy and neo-conservative thinkers nurture the government officials who are creating a new Constitution in order to put the State into Man's service.*
> *(Bruna Contreras, 1987, pp. 59, 68, emphasis mine)*

The seminar concluded with the words of Modesto Collados Núñez, an ex-Minister of State who quoted Locke and Hobbes to argue that the Chilean state was still a Leviathan that should be reduced as soon as possible and *en passant* referred to Manuel Feliú (the big entrepreneur) as his "great friend" (Collados Núñez, 1987, p. 79). His final remarks were framed in terms of Chile's belonging to Western culture and ethics.

For the most part, the "abundance" of neoliberal and neoconservative thinkers referred to in the quote above were not Chilean. The neoliberal component of APS was embedded in an international project (British and American, in the main) that successfully reshaped power relations during the 1970s and 1980s. This international dimension affected not only Chile but was a product of US hegemony in the region. Guillermo Bruna Contreras (1987) was not the only one to assert that international neoconservative academia nurtured the military government. Many APS authors argued that ideas shaped policy and that concepts and theories were powerful political weapons at the national and international level. The following quote capitalizes on a well-known US scholar, Samuel Huntington, to defend the neoconservative agenda and justify neoliberalism:

> The democratic system should allow and foment individual economic progress, not only for economic reasons but also, as Samuel Huntington has shown, for political ones: a market economy always demands the dispersion

of economic power. This dispersion creates alternatives to the power of the State. . . . In this regard, an interesting phenomenon took place in a country like Chile where political and economic thinking used to have the aim of pointing out how wrong those with a different ideology were. Today, perspectives have changed and this allows us to have hope about the future.

(Gajardo Lagomarsino, 1989b, p. 58)

In this view, democracy has intrinsic limits based on the absolute principle of private property. In other words, democracy cannot decide about everything: protected democracy is meant to protect the market economy. It is revealing that the contours chosen to delineate the limits to democratic power are not the notion of human rights (i.e. the *demos* cannot decide to harm people's dignity, right to live, and so on), but rather the "sacred" principle of private property (democracy shall respect capitalism). The change of perspective alluded to in the quote above implies that Pinochet's regime and its intellectual and social allies were winning the battle not only in the institutional realm, but especially in the cultural terrain. In other words, for them, Chilean culture had changed for the better—neoliberalism had been successfully imposed.

That the pursuit of a free society entails the affirmation of the private property system is elaborated upon in many other articles published throughout the dictatorship (Cuevas Farren, 1979a; Novak, 1983; Pazos, 1987; Sandoz, 1983; Yrarrázaval, 1982, among others), as is the idea that both the reduction of the state and the enforcement of private property are key to achieving development (Pazos, 1987, p. 191). In this light, the Pinochet regime's main aim is to expand freedom (Cuevas Farren, 1979a, p. 17). To be sure, 22% of *Política* and 18% of *RCP* articles promoted neoliberal reforms. This is not a low number taking into account that (*a*) PS journals do not have economic reforms at the center of the conversation, and (*b*) only pieces that in *very* explicit terms support neoliberalism were computed under this category (see Figures 2.15 and 2.16). APS

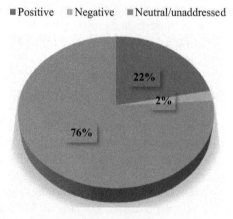

FIGURE 2.15   View of neoliberal reforms in *Política*, 1982–1989

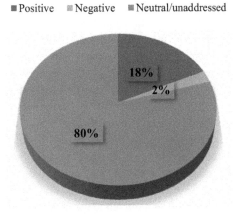

FIGURE 2.16   View of neoliberal reforms in *RCP*, 1979–1989

conceptualizes development and freedom in strictly possessive individualist and liberal terms, excluding the egalitarian dimension of democracy.

Many critical Chilean intellectuals would agree with Patricio Gajardo Lago-marsino in that the subordination of politics to the market economy is one of the most remarkable achievements of Pinochet's regime—an achievement that persisted after the transition (Lechner, 1990; Leiva, 2008; Mayol, 2012; Mella, 2011a; Moulián, 2002). If neoclassical economics arguably successfully colonized politics in post-transition Chile (CHL23), and considering the contributions examined here, the systematic and cultural function of our discipline in such an achievement can hardly be ignored.

Saving the West: Culture, Christianity, and Internationalization

Ideology and the world of culture (Geertz, 1997) are taken seriously by APS. In this regard, there is a (perhaps unexpected) conceptual overlap between APS and contemporary critical approaches to politics informed by Gramsci and Foucault.[22] The realm of culture and of ideas in general is read by APS' authors from the lenses of power relations and the production of hegemony. This cultural density is, in my view, particularly appealing and interesting, and is a pillar of APS' discourse. This feature refers not only to its analytical approach to politics but also to its normative *and political* take on right-wing politics. Several authors of the texts analyzed above did not hide the fact that they are organic intellectuals of the military government.

Protected democracy is, indeed, *also* a cultural and discursive project. In Rojas Sánchez et al.'s (1987) article titled "Defending Democracy," Rojas Sánchez argues that democracy should be circumscribed to a form of government. In other words, the meaning of democracy should not be stretched to the point that it includes an entire way of life and should not be extended to other realms such as the family or the institutions for education. Therefore, democracy for the author should *not* be considered a broader cultural project transcending the institutional realm. Yet, his argument is precisely that fundamental values that *transcend* and sustain democracy are taught in non-democratic institutions, which should be kept that way. It is thought-provoking that the first thing that a piece on defending democracy does is assert the centrality of non-democratic institutions and hierarchy as the substratum of modern democracy (and civilization). The ontological density of both the family and the church, the argument goes, transcends any form of government, including the democratic one. In this regard, they are more fundamental because they incarnate Western civilization, Christianity, and humanism. The author explores the role of the university along with the importance of keeping the purity of political language to capture the truth.[23]

In a 1987 seminar titled "Politics and Social Communication" (see Figure 2.14), Bruna Contreras and Cumplido Cereceda (1987) as well as Díaz Gronow (1987) discussed Articles 8 and 9 of the 1980 Constitution that forbade the proselytism of destabilizing theories that promote class struggle and violence and/or attack the family. In these interventions, there is a clear conceptual awareness about the role of journalism in particular, and culture in general, in power struggles. Roberto Pulido and Abraham Santibañez (1987, p. 175) and Rafael Otero (1987) debated the notion of personal and public honor protected by Article 19 of the 1980 Constitution. Juan Hamilton and Edmundo Eluchans (1987) engaged in a debate about the regulation of television; they disagreed on how much freedom the mass media should enjoy. The clashes between the seminar participants show APS' complexity: as I discuss elsewhere (Ravecca, 2014), this neoconservative formation allowed space for dissent, which was a smart way of navigating the transition. The clashes in these seminars indicate the need to understand APS as a space rather than as a monolithic discourse. The inclusion of power and culture in these debates makes them more interesting than many of those hosted by liberal PS later. APS goes far beyond a narrowly conceived notion of politics.

Suzanne Labin (1983) once argued: "we should not forget this capital lesson of history: powers that philosophize are frequently more evil than those that just administer" (p. 149). According to this logic, the international left operated in the cultural and academic realm; therefore, the retaliation should also be cultural and academic. In an international conference on neoconservative thinking organized by IPS-CHU (see Figure 2.17), the editor-in-chief of *El Mercurio*, the most widely circulated newspaper in Chile, paid attention to Julien Freund (referring to a talk that he gave in the same room five years before; see Figure 2.18), Noberto Bobbio, Carl Schmitt, and Antonio Gramsci—in his view, the last represented a cultural project of destruction of Christian and Western civilization (Antúnez Aldunate, 1987).[24] Jaime Antúnez Aldunate, who was also a professor at IPS-CHU at the time, contended that right-wing politics were still

FIGURE 2.17 Cover of a special issue of *Política*: "Neoconservative Thinking" (1987, Volume 11)

too focused on the "infrastructure," and that while they may have been good at fighting Leninism, they did not notice the transformations within Marxist theory and practice that Gramsci had performed.

APS operated in an internationalized ideological framework that blended economic liberalism, a constrained form of political liberalism, and cultural

FIGURE 2.18   Picture of a talk by Julien Freund, the "Fundamental Questions of Contemporary Politics," in June 1982. Julien Freund was a philosopher from Strasburg University who was a student of Raymond Aron and a well-known scholar of Max Weber.

(Instituto de Ciencia Política, Universidad de Chile, 1982)

conservatism. Some of the recurring theoretical references in *Política* and *RCP* were Samuel Huntington (Cea Egaña, 1982b; Gajardo Lagomarsino, 1989a; Reichley, 1982), Friedrich Hayek (Hayek, 1982; Nishiyama, 1982), Carl Schmitt (Rojas Sánchez, 1980), and Joseph Schumpeter (Gajardo Lagomarsino, 1989a; Mertz, 1982; Nishiyama, 1982). Putting the authoritarian Schmitt aside, it is still the case that none of them are particularly progressive or radical in their approach to democracy. More significantly, however, APS incorporates liberalism in a way that is modulated and shaped by the obsession for order and stability.

The same logic of protected democracy's *international awareness* and *internal policing* was applied to culture and society. To be sure, the "enemies" of capitalism and Western civilization were discussed in both political and cultural terms. While Marx's presence within APS' analyses was constant, Nietzsche and Freud, along with some spiritual "deviations" such as liberation theology, were also identified as corrosive voices of the international (cultural) left that undermined the fundamentals of Western society *from the inside*. In this view, Marxism, psychoanalysis, relativism, and nihilism, among other threats, constituted a joint cultural offensive:

> The emancipatory scheme proposed by Marx, Nietzsche's instinctual vitalism and Freud's sexualism, have successfully merged in a common front to attack the traditional-Christian culture, without carrying the dead weight of Soviet-style bureaucratic collectivism and taking advantage of the political and economic structures of Western culture.
>
> *(Massini-Correas, 1988, p. 46)*

The ideological battle occurs at the intersection between the national and the global, which means that academic conversation cannot be narrowly local. Common sense depicts the Chilean dictatorship as a regime isolated from the international intellectual arena. However, APS was highly internationalized. I was able to trace the academic itinerary of most of the authors published in the main journals in this period. In *Política*, 46% of the contributors obtained their degrees in the US and Europe, while in *RCP* this was the case for 69% of the contributors. Even taking into account that I could not find information for 23% and 15% of *Política*'s and *RCP*'s authors respectively, 85 in 188 and 84 in 122 are still high numbers for the Latin American context (see Figures 2.19 and 2.20).

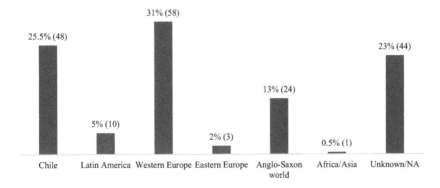

FIGURE 2.19 Country of academic training of contributors to *Política*, 1982–1989

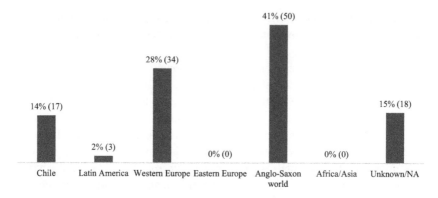

FIGURE 2.20   Country of academic training of contributors to *RCP*, 1979–1989

It should also be noted that *at least* 67 contributors to *Política* (1982–1989) and 39 to *RCP* (1979–1989) were foreigners. The presence of European scholars is remarkable in *Política* (34 from Western Europe and 8 from Eastern Europe) and the presence of Anglo-Saxon scholars (24) is prominent in *RCP*. Note that among the 103 confirmed Chilean authors in *Política*, 42 received foreign academic training, while the same holds for 39 of the 58 Chilean contributors to *RCP*. Furthermore, both journals, along with the *Memoria de Actividades* and many other historical records show extensive academic connections with Latin America, Europe, the United States, and South Africa.[25] In the case of *Política*, we have the curious presence of authors originally from Eastern Europe and associated with Soviet dissidence who in some cases were actually invited to Chile.[26] APS was not alone in the world: its protagonists and therefore its narratives and conversations were fairly international.

Around 30% of the articles in *RCP* and 20% of the articles in *Política* in this period correspond to research on IR and geopolitics. *RCP* and IPS-CU's external orientation is also expressed by their numerous international guest speakers (Dahl, 1985; Gershman, 1985; and Novak, 1983, to name just a few) and by the translation of articles published in prominent international journals such as *Government and Opposition*, *Hispanic Historical Review*, *Journal of Interamerican Studies and World Affairs*, *Philosophical Review*, *Political Science Quarterly*, *Revue Française de Science Politique*, *The American Political Science Review*, and *The Washington Quarterly*. *Política*, with a European orientation, only reproduced a couple of pieces from journals such as *Epoché* and *L'Altra Europa*.

However, IPS-CHU and *Política* also had intense connections with the United States. American conservative intellectual Paul Gottfried was one of its many international guests.[27] He participated in a 1986 seminar on "Neo-conservative Thinking" which also had speakers from England, Portugal, Italy, Spain, and France. In his talk, Gottfried argued that American culture and the arts had been captured by the left. He asked if it was possible to force a leftist, and sometimes nihilist, culture to support conservative writers, artists, and academics, thus breaking with the leftist rule over knowledge and the arts (Gottfried, 1987, p. 106). Interestingly, the piece refers to the need for conservative poetry and theater, talking about power broadly in a way that neo-Marxists and post-structuralists could agree with. As a discussant of Gottfried's intervention, Alejandro Silva Bascuñán was not a passive recipient of what the American intellectual forwarded. After making a joke about how misleading it was to call the United States by the single word "America" (given that Chile is also America), Silva Bascuñán talked about what he termed an inescapable paradox: on the one hand, the uniqueness of nations and peoples should be acknowledged, and therefore, whole cultural models should not be simply transplanted from one place to the other. On the other hand, we need to learn from international experiences (Silva Bascuñán, 1987).

Protected democracy is a local expression of the clash between two incompatible global projects. At a world scale, it is Western civilization itself that has to be defended. The East-West dichotomy is framed in Cold War, civilizational, and religious terms. The numbers in this regard are strikingly similar: 49% of *Política* articles and 47% of *RCP*'s defend or celebrate the West and/or Christianity (see Figures 2.21 and 2.22). Sometimes, the argument meshes anticommunist sentiment with civilizational arguments and Christian views.

Within this group of articles, I identified and analyzed those specifically focused on religion. They invariably do so by framing Christianity in anti-Marxist and frequently neoliberal terms. It is fascinating to see how APS assembled Catholic and pro-market discourses, given the emphasis in Catholicism on the spiritually purifying powers of poverty. Pope Juan Pablo II visited Chile in 1987, and the event was talked about by Domic (1987), Valdivieso Ariztía (1987), Hasbun (1987)—a priest himself—and Mac Hale (1987). These were all *Política* articles originally published in the press to confront what was perceived

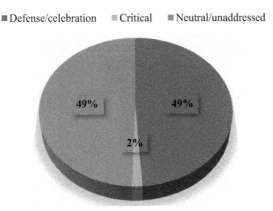

FIGURE 2.21 Attitude toward the West and Christianity in *Política*, 1982–1989

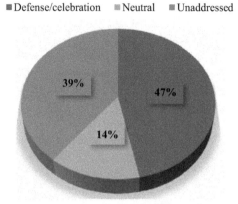

Defense/celebration   Neutral   Unaddressed

FIGURE 2.22   Attitude toward the West and Christianity in *RCP*, 1979–1989

as a communist campaign of misinformation against Chile that had human rights violations claims at its core. The issue closes with the transcription of a reflection by the pope. Fernando Moreno Valencia (1987) also refers to this visit in *RCP*, but in more theological and academic terms.

There were also highly conceptual theological interventions (Bentué, 1986; Cottier, 1985; Francou, 1986; Novak, 1983; Poradowski, 1984, 1986). Juan Antonio Widow (1979) offered a radical critique of modern democracy and modernity from a religious perspective in *RCP*, and articles by Joseph Ratzinger, who would later on become pope (2005–2013), appeared in both *RCP* (1984) and *Política* (1986, 1987).[28] Michael Novak, from the conservative American Enterprise Institute for Public Policy Research, was invited to a political theory seminar in 1983 hosted by the IPS-CU. His talk combined a Catholic framework with pro-capitalist advocacy: Adam Smith with the gospel.

In November of 1984, IPS-CU hosted a seminar titled "The Gospel, Ethics and Politics," which was published by *RCP* in 1985. The six interventions (Cumplido Cereceda, 1985; Flisfisch, 1985; Gaete, 1985; Ibáñez, 1985; Mifsud, 1985; Moreno Valencia, 1985) covered radically different views of the political role of the gospel and the working paper published by the Chilean Church at the time. On the right side of the ideological spectrum, Ibáñez (1985) challenged the "democratic dogma" that linked democracy to human rights and assumed that any other regime was immoral. That moderate alternative voices were also included in the conversation on spirituality reveals that APS allowed dissent to be expressed providing that—as with the transition to democracy—the pro-regime forces were dominant.

In the period 1979–1989, a significant number of *RCP* articles had religion as a main topic (22 in total, or 18%). One could assume that the institutional location of the journal within a Catholic university could be a factor explaining this remarkable presence of religion in a PS publication. I thus extended the analysis to all the articles published until 2012 (487 for *Política* and 544 for *RCP*): in

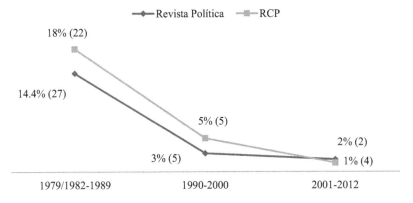

FIGURE 2.23   Religion as a main topic in *Política* and *RCP*

both journals, religion dramatically drops to the point that in the 2001–2012 period, it practically vanishes (see Figure 2.23). This might be the result of the professionalization of the discipline, but it seems that conservative spirituality and the Catholic religion were part of the regime's conceptual arsenal that were expressed through APS.

Academic Training, Law, Meaning(s), Terror

Contrary to the commonsensical idea that what happened during those years "was not really academic" (CHL4), as many colleagues argue today in different spaces, APS was, in the main, an academic space. Many of its protagonists were qualified scholars. Most of *Política*'s and *RCP*'s contributors had university-level education. *Política* had a more interdisciplinary orientation and was more open to non-academic contributors while *RCP* had a clear PS and strict academic orientation: around 60% of its contributors held PhDs (see Figures 2.24 and 2.25).[29]

It is well known that law and lawyers had an important role in incompletely consolidated PS academies in Latin America. The difference between the two journals in this respect is striking: at least 70 (37%) of *Política*'s contributors between 1982 and 1989 were lawyers, while this was the case for only 18 (15%) in *RCP* in the period from 1979 to 1989. The numbers fall dramatically in the following period, which speaks to the professionalization of PS, a process for which *RCP* and the department that hosts the journal are perceived as an emblematic example—"the guiding light," as one interviewee declared (CHL34; see also Figure 2.26).

Given the dominant, liberal assumptions linking lawyers and the law with democratic institutions and civic liberties, it may seem paradoxical that the law-oriented journal was the most aligned with the dictatorship of Augusto Pinochet.

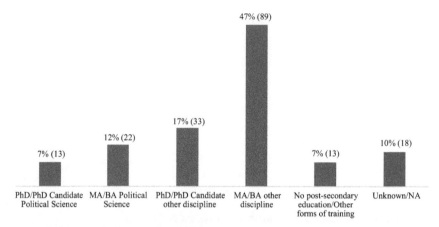

FIGURE 2.24 Academic training of contributors to *Política*, 1982–1989

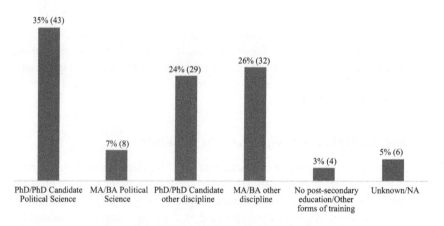

FIGURE 2.25 Academic training of contributors to *RCP*, 1979–1989

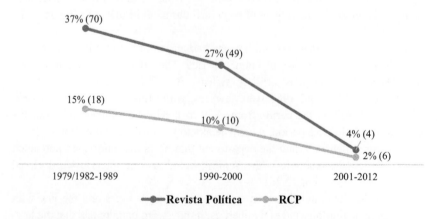

FIGURE 2.26 Lawyers in *Política* and *RCP*

However, let us not forget: dictatorships also have their laws and lawyers, after all. Many of *Política*'s articles were aimed at informing political debate, public policy decisions, and institutional reform processes; as such, lawyers' expertise was thus particularly relevant for this type of intervention.

A crucial point emerges through this search for meanings and discourses, which cannot be expressed by any numerical figure. *Política* and *RCP*, along with other key documents of the period under analysis, reveal a *mixture of discursive logics* within APS. On the one hand, there is what might be called a scientific will for the study of politics, expressed in the concern around methods and methodology, the defense of academic objectivity, as well as in profuse references to liberalism and its values (freedom in particular). On the other hand, this form of PS was functional to an authoritarian regime and was invested in the protection of Pinochet's legacy—i.e., in building a governable and stable democracy where capitalism flourishes and corporations' profits are secured.

Figure 2.27 analyzes Issues 1 through 28 of IPS-CU's *Cuadernos* [Notebooks] advertised by *RCP* in 1979. The titles corresponding to an authoritarian script were highlighted with orange, while those consistent with PS' standard language as we now know it were marked with blue. The same exercise was done with the 1988 curricula of IPS-CHU's MA program in political science (Figure 2.28). Both figures show the apparent contradiction mentioned above. In this period, a section of Chilean PS—APS—*talks and promotes* democracy and liberalism while being authoritarian. Thus, in APS' discourse, democracy and liberalism seem to peacefully coexist with authoritarianism, or, put differently, the latter operates as the limiting framework for democracy. These findings open up all sorts of empirical, theoretical, and *political* questions, some of which are addressed in the concluding chapter of this book.

Certainly, if PS could actually embody the knowledge of an authoritarian regime as it did, it seems imperative to reframe the notion that our discipline is an intrinsically democratic knowledge. Or perhaps, we, political scientists, *need to be more suspicious of those power relations that make of "liberal democracy" the ideological vocabulary that sanctifies PS*. It might be time to start thinking about PS' power relations *within* democracy.

The presence of the regime and the right-wing project that it incarnated, then, was performed *also* by PS, in its APS form. In different ways, the dictatorship *was in* academia, through both *RCP* and *Política*. The regime *killed and thought* at the same time—and, of course, it killed thought as well. From the point of view of critical theory, especially that of the power and knowledge literature (Foucault, 1991a; Gramsci, 2008), this double motion may help to explain the capacity of the regime to reshape Chilean politics, culture, and political economy.

Sometimes killing and thinking were done by the same people. Jaime García Covarrubias, a high-ranking military member and head of the National Intelligence Directorate (DINA), authored three contributions to *Política* (1987, 1988,

CUADERNOS DEL INSTITUTO
DE CIENCIA POLITICA

N° 1 ENRIQUE ORTUZAR ESCOBAR
"La nueva institucionalidad chilena".

N° 2 GERARDO CORTES RENCORET
"Introducción a la seguridad nacional".

N° 3 FREDERICK NUNN
"El profesionalismo militar chileno en el siglo XX: pensamiento y autopercepción de la clase de oficiales hasta 1973".

N° 4 ALVARO ALSOGARAY
"La democracia de masas y la crisis en países del mundo libre".

N° 5 GUSTAVO CUEVAS FARREN
"Cuando la rebelión es un derecho; el caso de Chile durante la U.P.".

N° 6 JOSE LUIS CEA EGAÑA
"Teoría de la libertad de opinión".

N° 7 CARLOS NAUDON DE LA SOTA
"La proliferación nuclear: ensayo sobre la diseminación de la muerte".

N° 8 RICARDO COX
"En torno al tema de la democracia".

N° 9 JOSE LUIS CEA EGAÑA
"La representación funcional en la historia constitucional de Chile".

N° 10 ALEJANDRO SILVA BASCUÑAN
"En torno al porvenir político de Chile".

N° 11 JULIO VON MUHLENBROCK
"La concepción de una nueva democracia para Chile".

N° 12 PABLO RODRIGUEZ GREZ
"Democracia liberal o democracia orgánica".

N° 13 FREDERICK NUNN
"Militares chilenos: desarrollo institucional; relaciones cívico-militares; consideraciones de política".

N° 14 TOMAS F. MAC HALE
"Poder político y comunicación en Chile: marzo a septiembre de 1973".

N° 15 FELIPE HERRERA
"Las políticas culturales y la seguridad latinoamericana".

N° 16 ATALIVA AMENGUAL B.
"El estudio científico de la política".

N° 17 OSCAR MERTZ
"El realismo político de Maquiavelo".

N° 18 IRIS VITTINI C.
"La unión Europea. El informe Tindemann".

N° 19 ALEJANDRO SILVA BASCURAN
"La experiencia chilena sobre Referendum y su valoración".

N° 20 EMILIO MENESES C.
"La organización del tratado del Atlántico Sur: una visión crítica".

N° 21 GISELA VON MUHLENBROCK
"La política laboral en Chile en 1977".

N° 22 CARLOS NAUDON DE LA SOTA
"El proceso de distención y América Latina".

N° 23 FELIPE HERRERA
"América Latina y el nuevo orden económico internacional".

N° 24 MERCEDES AUBA ASVISIO
"Los partidos políticos: un análisis descriptivo".

N° 25 GISELA VON MUHLENBROCK
"Participación política: algunas motivaciones y causas".

N° 26 CARLOS NAUDON DE LA SOTA
"El nuevo escenario latinoamericano: Un enfoque global".

N° 27 AUGUSTO MERINO MEDINA
"Reflexiones sobre la Cultura Política Chilena".

N° 28 FREDERICK M. NUNN
"El Chile antiguo y el nuevo: La Política de Transición 1973-1979".

Ventas y suscripciones: Avda. Vicuña Mackenna 4860, edificio N° 10, tercer piso, Santiago. Teléfono 519012, anexo 461.

REVISTA
DE CIENCIA
POLITICA

INSTITUTO DE CIENCIA POLITICA
PONTIFICIA UNIVERSIDAD
CATOLICA DE CHILE

Director: Gustavo Cuevas Farren
Santiago, 1979 - N° 2

Sumario:

GUSTAVO CUEVAS FARREN
3 Perspectiva del Proceso Institucional en Chile

MERCEDES AUBA ASVISIO
22 Ideología y partidos políticos

JOSE LUIS CEA EGAÑA
34 Fiscalización parlamentaria de los actos del Gobierno, 1925-1973

MARIA TERESA INFANTE
46 Orden jurídico y orden internacional: alcances teóricos actuales

DIRK KUNERT
56 Una contienda desigual: Estados Unidos y la Unión Soviética en Africa

94 Reseña de la actividad académica del Instituto de Ciencia Política durante 1979

Analysis of The Notebooks of Political Science (titles from 1 to 28). Pontificia Universidad Católica de Chile. Different logics: Orange = APS; Blue = 'Standard' PS.

FIGURE 2.27 List of political science notebooks published by the IPS-CU (left) printed in the second volume of *RCP* in 1979, with my own added annotations. In orange are notebooks I have identified as belonging to APS and blue those belonging to "standard" PS.

Asignatura: "CIENCIA POLITICA II".
N⁰ de Créditos: 10.
Nivel en que se imparte: 2 semestre.
Requisitos: "Ciencia Política I".
Profesor de la Asignatura: Augusto Merino Medina.
Descripción: El objetivo de este curso es hacer un estudio de la teoría de las élites y su importancia en el control del gobierno, abarcando tanto su formulación clásica como sus nuevas reediciones, y ofreciendo al alumno la oportunidad de apreciar sus pro y contras.

Asignatura: "GEOPOLITICA".
N⁰ de Créditos: 10.
Nivel en que se imparte: 2 semestre.
Requisitos: "Nociones sobre Historia Política Contemporánea" e "Historia de las Instituciones Políticas de Chile.
Profesor de la asignatura: Hernán Santis Arenas.
Descripción: El objetivo de este curso es estudiar el comportamiento especial de los Estados desde una perspectiva teórica y práctica, con énfasis en el caso chileno.

FIGURE 2.28   Curricula of the IPS-CHU's MA Program in Political Science

(Instituto de Ciencia Política, Universidad de Chile, 1988)

1989). To be sure, in the MA programs of both IPS-CHU and IPS-CU, but especially in the former, the presence of military members was significant in this period (see Figure 2.29; Ravecca, 2014); Covarrubias 1987, for example, is an article based on his MA thesis (he was a member of the 1985 cohort of the MA program at IPS-CHU and defended his thesis in 1987).

Professor Emilio Meneses published frequently in *RCP* (1979, 1981a, 1981b, 1982 [with Tagle & Guevara], 1992, 1995 [with Navarro Meza], 1998) and *Política* (1983). He was a professor at the War Academy of the Chilean Army where Pinochet had taught as well; his scholarly credentials linked him to a leading university, for he held a PhD from Oxford University.

In 1998, a well-known scholar, Felipe Agüero, published in *RCP* in the same issue as Professor Meneses (Agüero, Tironi, Valenzuela, & Sunkel, 1998). This would have been an unexceptional situation had Agüero not emailed some IPS-CU scholars two years later stating that Emilio Meneses, a faculty member of the institution, had participated in the interrogation team that tortured him at the National Stadium of Chile, which was used as a prison after the coup of 1973. Agüero also made this public in a widely read Chilean newspaper (*Diario La Segunda*, March 23, 2001). We have to read the silence(s), again: Meneses' voice is highly professional and academic. Even though some of his pieces are framed in Cold War terms, in only one of them does he refer to Marxism. And

FIGURE 2.29 Cover of the first MA thesis of IPS-CHU

even then, he does so in a rather neutral way. He explores very "scholarly" issues such as Chilean foreign policy in the first half of the 20th century (Meneses, Tagle, & Guevara, 1982).

That tortured and (alleged) torturer write in the same academic journal constitutes a crude manifestation of the interpenetration between academia and political context. As with the legacy of Pinochet, APS is still with us, circulating in the blood of Chilean institutions.[30] Current Chilean PS seems to be a blend of

APS and liberal political science; in other words, a mixture of authoritarianism and democracy. To put it more cautiously: a question for further research would be to what extent PPS in Chile today bears the imprint of the trajectories and forces from the so-called transition years.

Conclusion: The Banality of Institutionalization

The analysis offered in the preceding segments suffices to suggest that authoritarian political science formed a distinct version of PS, which was basically characterized by the academic promotion of the dictatorship's institutional and political legacies. Three pillars of APS were identified in the previous pages: the conceptual justification of a limited form of democracy (institutionalized transition, protected democracy); the defense of neoliberalism as the only economic approach that guarantees freedom; and the perceived duty of intellectuals to be custodians of the West and Christianity, both supposedly under threat in the Cold War context.

To be sure, the analyzed journals and APS were not the same. *RCP* in particular was both inside and outside of APS, inasmuch as it was significantly less aligned with the logics of the dictatorship. Both journals were, however, key sites where this set of discourses on democracy, the market economy, and the West/Christianity circulated. In other words, the two journals operated as suitable empirical locations for the task of grasping APS narratives and logics. Yet, APS was also a space of human interaction.

I refer to APS as a space because it operated as a *realm* of activities, dialogues, and encounters for scholars who supported Pinochet's regime that sometimes also included moderate opponents; dissidence was allowed as long as it was carefully policed. This realm was inhabited and crafted mainly by academics, but also by military members, businessmen, and religious authorities. What was circulated within the space of APS was both institutional and discursive. These two spatialities and registers were implicated in concrete power dynamics and mechanisms such as the 1980 Constitution, the crafting of the binominal electoral system, and a well-known set of neoliberal reforms. What I mean by this is that APS participated in the discussion of actual institutional design of post-transition Chile as well as in the ideological production that advanced such changes.

The authoritarian nature of APS was displayed in the kind of project it promoted: a limited form of pluralism that falls short of a fully polyarchic political system. Other features were significant and perhaps unexpected. For instance, APS was cosmopolitan: Chilean, European, North American, and even Russian dissidents were its protagonists, challenging common notions about academic life during that period as both irrelevant and isolated. The academic and political battle against communism and Marxism as well as the concomitant defense of the so-called market economy were both local and global enterprises, and so it was the neoconservative agenda that APS embraced at the socio-cultural level.

APS shares with many liberal thinkers and discourses the emphasis on order and stability, as well as the naturalization of capitalism. Such an emphasis did not go away after the transition and in fact it became an aspect of the common sense of the entire political system and academia in Chile and beyond. These shared concerns with liberals, however, were modulated by APS through its particular (authoritarian) framework. Thus, the feature that perhaps makes APS distinct is, in my view, an interesting phenomenon: it mobilized the language of democracy and liberalism within an authoritarian project that shaped Chile's future and forced the moderation of the left (Puryear, 2016, p. 155). This opens up questions about the ruptures and continuities between APS and "standard" PS. Granted, power does not disappear from knowledge when democracy arrives (I will be dealing with this issue by the end of this study in Chapter 5).

Finally, I want to conclude with a simple idea: APS was a space *of* the discipline. That is, *Chilean APS was political science:* it mobilized—in scholarly ways—typical categories and notions of the discipline such as political regime, democracy, electoral systems, competition, civic participation, transition, government, political stability, among numerous others. The implication is thus: our discipline can be authoritarian. Furthermore, APS exercised its own authoritarianism in the name of democracy. Democracy, as any other fragment of discourse, is polyvalent: what else can be done in the name of democracy? Or, more concretely: can we find authoritarian traces in the ways that mainstream polyarchic discourse captures, reduces, and disciplines democracy, or in the ways that some of my own colleagues laugh or get irritated when students question PS' dominant conception of democracy? Perhaps the authoritarianism of a discipline can be measured in the kinds of questions that it allows or does not allow to be asked from within; maybe we need to use the APS experience as an opportunity to exercise self-critique and test the force of the questions we are ready to ask. Dogmatism looks so clear from chronological distance: it is much harder to detect our own.

The exploration of the institutionalization of PS becomes purposeless or—even worse—*banal* without the analysis of the content and the socio-political role of the discipline. Knowledge is structurally implicated in power relations. Therefore, exploring academic discourses is just another way of studying politics. By expanding awareness of the impact that context has had on our science, this kind of epistemological exercise of self-clarification should help prevent our academic practice from becoming a mere echo of the dominant powers of our times, be they authoritarian or liberal democratic.

Notes

*   I am grateful to Mariana Mancebo for her assistance at all stages of the research that sustains this chapter. A preliminary draft of this chapter was presented at the Iberoamerican University in México City at the 50th Anniversary Celebration of the BA Program in Political Science and Public Administration ("Challenges for Political Science's Reflection in Mexico," October 27–29, 2014) and in Lima, Perú, at the

2015 annual conference of the Latin American Political Science Association; that previous version was published by *Revista de Ciencia Política*. The chapter has benefited from the comments of Pablo Bulcourf, Eduardo Canel, Elizabeth Dauphinee, Ruth Felder, Arturo Fernández, Juan Pablo Luna, David McNally, Viviana Patroni, María Francisca Quiroga, Diego Rossello, Antonio Torres-Ruiz, and Lilian Yap. María Francisca Quiroga and Mónica Tagle's help and guidance were crucial during the fieldwork in Santiago.

1. Heine (2006), for instance, addresses the flourishing of PS during the authoritarian period and in footnote 11 acknowledges the "ambiguous" relationship that the regime had with the discipline. However, his analysis of PS' takeoff does not fully consider the *active* role that the regime had in the process and its theoretical implications.

2. Marcuse (1991) is one of the very few books that address American PS from the perspective of critical theory (see Chapter 1).

3. The Pinochet regime's mobilization of neoclassical economics has already been abundantly explored (see Camou, 1997; Markoff & Montecinos, 1994; McNally, 2011).

4. While alternative voices continued to exist, they were produced in other settings. It is well known that universities in several other countries in Latin America (for instance, Costa Rica and Mexico) benefited enormously from the exodus of intellectuals from the Southern Cone.

5. These numbers do not include institutional memorandums published by the journals (seven pieces by *Política* and six by *RCP*), book reviews, and special issues without volume number. This material was analyzed but not included in the database used to process the information that follows. For these special issues, another database was created, and the results did not significantly change once they were included in the analysis.

6. The procedure was two-fold. Each article was read at least four times (twice by a research assistant, once by me, and a last time together). The pieces were assigned values using an SPSS database with 89 descriptive and conceptual variables that operationalized the dimensions of analysis already mentioned in this section. The articles were also analyzed in an interpretive fashion (Geertz, 1997) by reconstructing the main conceptual and political features of APS. I conducted 35 interviews with Chilean political scientists, and while they have not been systematically integrated into this chapter, the arguments proposed here were cross-checked and enriched with the evidence provided by them.

7. The Uruguayan dictatorship persecuted the social sciences and did not create its own institutional infrastructure of knowledge production in this realm (see Chapter 3).

8. In order to preserve the confidentiality of the interviewees, all interviews will be cited by interview code, with interviews from Chile beginning with CHL. Interviews were conducted in Spanish, and all translations from original transcripts are mine.

9. This becomes clear by contrasting his introduction to the first volume of *RCP* (Cuevas Farren, 1979b) or his first *RCP* article (Cuevas Farren, 1979a) with some of his later interventions (such as Cuevas Farren, 1990). His voice appears in both journals, mostly in *Política*, in different formats (articles, published seminar interventions, speeches, institutional reports, etc.). He published 21 pieces in *Política* and 1 in *RCP*. This difference is unsurprising given that he left the IPS-CU soon after *RCP* was founded. His last appearance was in 1993.

10. For instance, Mujal-León (1982) explores the Spanish transition and Gajardo Lagomarsino (1989b) studies what he calls the Mexican political transition.

11. All translations from Spanish to English are mine unless otherwise stated.

12. In August 1983, an international seminar on "Regional, Hemispheric and Global Tendencies of International Relations" took place at the IPS-CU. Theberge was a guest speaker along with David Singer, a Michigan University professor whose

complex and mathematically formalized contribution (1984) explores the possibility of identifying "cycles of war." *Anti-communism and complex science shared a stage.*

13. Howard J. Wiarda, a University of Massachusetts political science professor, was the director of the conservative American Enterprise Institute for Public Policy Research.

14. Raymond Aron (1984) also received attention (Durán, 1984; Godoy Arcaya, 1984; Lapouge, 1988).

15. See also Yrarrázaval (1982).

16. Rubio Apiolaza (2011) explores the legacy of Jaime Guzmán, a right-wing intellectual of the period who showcases the important political role performed by *part of* the Chilean academia during the dictatorship.

17. Child's (1981) work was also published by *RCP*.

18. Cheyre would become Commander-in-Chief of the Chilean Army from 2002 to 2006 and would distance the military from Pinochet's dictatorship. However, he was also involved in human rights controversies.

19. In fact, Robert Dahl gave a lecture titled "Controlling Nuclear Weapons: Democracy Versus Guardianship" in the launch of the 1985 academic year of the MA program of the IPS-CU. The title of his paper was translated in a way that affects the meaning: "Nuclear Weapons: Democracy and Protection. Why the Guardians Fail" (Dahl, 1985).

20. Lewis Tambs is a conspicuous member of the American right. His trajectory is analyzed in "Lewis Tambs, Latin American Geopolitics and the American New Right," by Prof. Leslie W. Hepple. The piece is available at www.bristol.ac.uk/media-library/sites/geography/migrated/documents/lewis.pdf

21. This exploration of the APS experience complements the more widely known story of the Chicago Boys who, at this point, even have a full-length documentary (Fuentes, Valdeavellano, & Mladinic, 2015) focused on them.

22. There are numerous references to Gramsci in *Política*. Volume 14, for example, alludes to an entire Metropolitan University seminar on the Italian thinker, with an intervention by *Política* editor Jaime Antúnez Aldunate (1987, p. 245).

23. Interestingly, Rojas Sánchez is also critical of the idealization of the ideological and political "center," and argues that there can be extremism there as well.

24. The reappearance of names, institutions and activities matter because they reveal that APS operated as a discursive and institutional (neoconservative) realm of experience where its protagonists met and interacted.

25. Kunert (1979) in *RCP* and Petrus Putter (1983) in *Política* develop discourses in support of South African apartheid within an anti-communist framework.

26. Interestingly, in 1988, the ICP-CHU hosted Nicolai Tolstoi, descendant of Leo Tolstoi, to give a talk on his book *Victims of Yalta* and on human rights in Eastern Europe.

27. APS' relationship with American and foreign institutions more broadly is interesting given that emphasis has typically been on the relatively strong development of Chilean academia before the coup (Beigel, 2014) and on academic activity during the dictatorship outside the country both through transnational networks and in private research centers associated with the political opposition against Pinochet's regime (Puryear, 1994).

28. Widow obtained his PhD in philosophy in Spain. As a committed far-right figure, he supported the dictatorship. In June 2010, Widow was harassed by human rights activists after he attended a documentary exhibition and tribute ceremony for Augusto Pinochet. Fascist websites described the attack as a manifestation of the "Demo-Marxist Hatred." In a lecture titled "Faith and Reason" in an academic course on Catholic culture at the Gabriela Mistral University in 2013, the professor concludes by saying that in our times, the main social and cultural discourses exclude the truth, which means to exclude God.

29. This information needs to be contextualized; these numbers are significant given that in Latin America (*a*) the PhD requirement for professors has been imposed only

recently; and, (*b*) the expectations around the BA degrees are still higher than in North America.

30. For more detailed information about this case see Verdugo (2004).

Works Cited

Agüero, F., Tironi, E., Valenzuela, E., & Sunkel, G. (1998). Votantes, partidos e información política: La frágil intermediación política en el Chile post-autoritario. *Revista de Ciencia Política, 19*(2), 159–193.

Alexander, J. M. (2005). *Pedagogies of crossing: Meditations on feminism, sexual politics, memory, and the sacred.* Durham, NC: Duke University Press.

Altman, D. (2005). La institucionalización de la ciencia política en Chile y América Latina: Una mirada desde el sur. *Revista de Ciencia Política, 25*(1), 3–15.

Altman, D. (2006). From Fukuoka to Santiago: Institutionalization of political science in Latin America. *PS: Political Science & Politics, 39*(1), 196–203.

Amadae, S. M. (2016). *Prisoners of reason: Game theory and neoliberal political economy.* New York: Cambridge University Press.

Amoureux, J. L., & Steele, B. J. (Eds.). (2016). *Reflexivity and international relations: Positionality, critique, and practice.* New York: Routledge.

Antúnez Aldunate, J. (1987). Estado, política y cultura. *Política, 11*, 55–63.

Auyero, J. (2002). Clientelismo político en Argentina: Doble vida y negación colectiva. *Perfiles Latinoamericanos: Revista de la Facultad Latinoamericana de Ciencias Sociales, Sede México, 10*(20), 33–52.

Aron, R. (1984). La alternancia de los gobiernos en los países industrializados. *Revista de Ciencia Política, 6*(1), 18–32.

Barrientos Del Monte, F. (2012). La institucionalización de la ciencia política en América Latina. In F. Reveles Vázquez (Ed.), *La ciencia política en México hoy: ¿Qué sabemos?* (pp. 21–48). Mexico City: Plaza y Valdés.

Beigel, F. (2014). Chile: Un centro periférico para la internacionalización de las ciencias sociales latinoamericanas y la construcción de un prestigio académico regional (1953–1973). *Revista de la Red Intercátedras de Historia de América Latina Contemporánea (Segunda Época), 1*(1), 101–105.

Benavente Urbina, A. (1985). La transición política: Aproximaciones a una clasificación teórica a partir del estudio de casos. *Política, 7*, 43–79.

Benavente Urbina, A. (1987). Movimiento de izquierda revolucionaria: Trayectoria y presente. *Política, 12*, 121–155.

Benavente Urbina, A. (1989). La estabilidad política en los procesos de transición. *Política, 20*, 57–84.

Bentué, A. (1986). Libertad y proceso de liberación. *Revista de Ciencia Política, 8*(1–2), 172–179.

Bravo Lira, B. (1987–1988). Crisis institucional en Chile: Precedentes y perspectivas. *Revista de Ciencia Política, 9–10*(2–1), 71–79.

Bruna Contreras, G. (1987). La libertad económica: Elemento de un nuevo orden político económico. *Política, 13*, 59–76.

Bruna Contreras, G., & Cumplido Cereceda, F. (1987). Intervenciones sobre comunicación social, totalitarismo y terrorismo. *Política, 13*, 135–160.

Butalia, U. (2000). *The other side of silence: Voices from the partition of India.* Durham, NC: Duke University Press.

Buquet, D. (2012). El desarrollo de la ciencia política en Uruguay. *Política, 50*(1), 5–29.

Camou, A. (1997). Los consejeros del príncipe: Saber técnico y política en los procesos de reforma económica en América Latina. *Nueva Sociedad, 152*, 54–67.

Carmona, J. D. (1983). Transición a la democracia: Problemas y perspectivas. *Política, 4*, 217–231.

Cea Egaña, J. L. (1982a). Representación política y social en la nueva constitución. *Revista de Ciencia Política, 4*(2), 5–49.

Cea Egaña, J. L. (1982b). Cinco paradigmas políticos. *Revista de Ciencia Política, 4*(1), 29–57.

Child, J. (1979). Geopolitical thinking in Latin America. *Latin American Research Review, 14*(2), 89–111.

Child, J. (1981). Pensamiento geopolítico y cuatro conflictos en Sudamérica. *Revista de Ciencia Política, 3*(1–2), 71–104.

Collados Núñez, M. (1987). El rol del estado en la economía. *Política, 13*, 77–85.

Cottier, G. (1985). El verdadero sentido del progreso. *Revista de Ciencia Política, 7*(2), 100–116.

Cox, R. (1987). *Production, power, and world order*. New York: Columbia University Press.

Cuevas Farren, G. (1979a). Perspectiva del proceso institucional en Chile. *Revista de Ciencia Política, 1*(2), 3–21.

Cuevas Farren, G. (1979b). Editorial. *Revista de Ciencia Política, 1*(1), 1.

Cuevas Farren, G. (1987). El principio de subsidiariedad en el régimen político chileno. *Política, 13*, 9–17.

Cuevas Farren, G. (1989a). Procesos de transición a la democracia: Una visión personal. *Política, 20*, 47–56.

Cuevas Farren, G. (1989b). Chile 1989: Las coyunturas de un proceso político. *Política, 21*, 11–27.

Cuevas Farren, G. (1990). Las fuerzas armadas y transición a la democracia en América Latina. *Política, 22–23*, 83–100.

Cuevas Farren, G. (1991). Discurso de Don Gustavo Cuevas Farren con ocasión del inicio de su nuevo periodo como director del Instituto de Ciencia Política de la Universidad de Chile (1990–1994). *Política, 26*, 113–119.

Cuevas Farren, G., Mac Hale, T., & Trucco, M. (1988). Homenaje a James Theberge. *Política, 17*, 139–152.

Cumplido Cereceda, F. (1985). Evangelio y organización político-jurídica. *Revista de Ciencia Política, 7*(1), 163–165.

Dahl, R. (1985). Las armas nucleares: Democracia y protección. Por qué fracasan los guardianes. *Revista de Ciencia Política, 7*(2), 83–99.

Dauphinee, E. (2013a). *The politics of exile*. New York: Routledge.

Dauphinee, E. (2013b). Writing as hope: Reflections on the politics of exile. *Security Dialogue, 44*(4), 347–361.

Dauphinee, E. (2016). Narrative engagement and the creative practices of international relations. In J. L. Amoureux & B. J. Steele (Eds.), *Reflexivity and international relations: Positionality, critique and practice* (pp. 44–60). New York: Routledge.

Díaz Gronow, R. (1987). Comentario a las intervenciones de Guillermo Bruna Contreras y Francisco Cumplido. *Política, 13*, 161–166.

Domic, J. (1987). Campaña comunista de desinformación internacional. *Política, 13*, 205–215.

Durán, R. (1980). La corriente funcionalista en la teoría de relaciones internacionales. *Revista de Ciencia Política, 2*(3), 20–32.

Durán, R. (1981). Apuntes para un proyecto de investigación en relaciones internacionales y geopolítica. *Revista de Ciencia Política, 3*(1–2), 17–25.

Durán, R. (1984). Las relaciones internacionales en la concepción de Raymond Aron. *Revista de Ciencia Política*, *6*(1), 12–17.

Enloe, C. (2004). *The curious feminist: Searching for women in a new age of empire*. Los Angeles: University of California Press.

Flisfisch, Á. (1985). Ética del evangelio y convivencia política. *Revista de Ciencia Política*, *7*(1), 130–146.

Fontaine, R. (1980). Perspectivas de las relaciones Estados Unidos-Latinoamérica: Problemas que confrontará la administración Reagan y sus proyecciones hacia el 2000. *Revista de Ciencia Política*, *2*(3), 86–100.

Fortou, J. A., Leyva Botero, S., Preciado, A. F., & Ramírez, M. F. (2013). Ciencia política en Colombia: Una revisión de la literatura sobre el estado e historia de la disciplina en el país. In S. Botero Leyva (Ed.), *La ciencia política en Colombia: ¿Una disciplina en institucionalización?* (pp. 27–56). Medellín: Colciencias, Asociación Colombiana de Ciencia Política, Centro de Análisis Político—Universidad Eafit.

Foucault, M. (1991a). *Historia de la sexualidad 1: La voluntad de saber*. Madrid: Siglo Veintiuno.

Foucault, M. (1991b). *Saber y verdad*. Madrid: Ediciones La Piqueta.

Francou, F. (1986). La segunda instrucción vaticana. *Revista de Ciencia Política*, *8*(1–2), 165–171.

Fuentes, C. (Producer & Director), Valdeavellano, R. (Producer & Director), & Mladinic, H. (Producer). (2015). *Chicago boys* [Motion picture]. Chile: La Ventana Producciones.

Gaete, A. (1985). Evangelio, ética y política: Algunas implicancias filosóficas y teológicas. *Revista de Ciencia Política*, *7*(1), 119–129.

Gajardo Lagomarsino, P. (1989a). La transición a la democracia en Chile: Desafíos y perspectivas a partir de un análisis teórico. *Política*, *21*, 53–62.

Gajardo Lagomarsino, P. (1989b). La transición política en México y la crisis del Partido Revolucionario Institucional. *Política*, *20*, 85–100.

García Covarrubias, J. (1987). El partido radical y su relación de intereses con la clase media en Chile en el período 1888–1938. *Política*, *12*, 49–119.

García Covarrubias, J. (1988). Una perspectiva del origen y presencia de la clase media en Chile (1810–1940). *Política*, *18*, 57–78.

García Covarrubias, J. (1989). Reflexiones en torno a la política y lo político. *Política*, *21*, 135–149.

García Rodríguez, R. (1987). El rol del estado en materia empresarial. *Política*, *13*, 19–27.

Geertz, C. (1997). *La interpretación de las culturas*. Barcelona: Gedisa.

Gershman, C. (1985). Nuevas perspectivas en las relaciones entre Estados Unidos y Latinoamérica. *Revista de Ciencia Política*, *7*(1), 199–204.

Godoy Arcaya, Ó. (1983). Tocqueville y la democracia de las libertades. *Revista de Ciencia Política*, *5*(1), 30–47.

Godoy Arcaya, Ó. (1984). Aron y la democracia pluralista. *Revista de Ciencia Política*, *6*(1), 6–11.

Godoy Arcaya, Ó. (1987–1988). Naturaleza y razón constructiva en Hobbes. *Revista de Ciencia Política*, *9–10*(2–1), 7–27.

Gottfried, P. (1987). Conservantismo y neo-conservantismo norteamericano. *Política*, *11*, 95–107.

Gramsci, A. (2008). *Selections from the prison notebooks* (Q. Hoare & G. Nowell, Trans. & Eds.). New York: International Publishers.

Gros Espiell, H. (1983). Control político de la constitución: El caso de Uruguay. *Política*, *2*, 9–50.

Hamilton, J., & Eluchans, E. (1987). Intervenciones sobre televisión y cultura política. *Política*, *13*, 97–122.

Hasbun, R. (1987). Dictadores y comunicadores. *Política, 13*, 223–225.

Hayek, F. A. (1982). Liberalismo. *Revista de Ciencia Política, 4*(2), 122–151.

Heine, J. (2006). Democracy, dictatorship and the making of modern political science: Huntington's thesis and Pinochet's Chile. *PS: Political Science & Politics, 39*(2), 273–280.

Huneeus, C. (2006). El lento y tardío desarrollo de la ciencia política en América Latina, 1966–2006. *Estudios Internacionales, 155*, 137–156.

Ibáñez, G. (1985). Evangelio, ética y política: Comentario a un documento episcopal de trabajo. *Revista de Ciencia Política, 7*(1), 150–162.

Infante, M. T. (1980). Nota sobre la conferencia de Naciones Unidas sobre el derecho del mar. *Revista de Ciencia Política, 2*(3), 55–66.

Instituto de Ciencia Política, Universidad de Chile. (1982). *Memoria de actividades.* Santiago de Chile: Instituto de Ciencia Política.

Instituto de Ciencia Política, Universidad de Chile. (1983). *Memoria de actividades.* Santiago de Chile: Instituto de Ciencia Política.

Instituto de Ciencia Política, Universidad de Chile. (1988). *Memoria de actividades.* Santiago de Chile: Instituto de Ciencia Política.

Jelin, E. (2011). Subjetividad y esfera pública: El género y los sentidos de familia en las memorias de la represión. *Política y Sociedad, 48*(3), 555–569.

Justo Lopez, M. (1963). *El mito de la constitución.* Buenos Aires: Abeledo-Perrot.

Kunert, D. (1979). Una contienda desigual: Estados Unidos y la Unión Soviética en África. *Revista de Ciencia Política, 1*(2), 56–93.

Labin, S. (1983). Intentos de descifrar una esfinge: François Mitterrand. *Política, 2*, 139–152.

Laclau, E., & Mouffe, C. (2004). *Hegemonía y estrategia socialista: Hacia una radicalización de la democracia.* Buenos Aires: Fondo de Cultura Económica.

Lapouge, G. (1988). Raymond Aron: Imperialismo, lo que queda del marxismo leninismo. *Política, 16*, 29–39.

Lechner, N. (1990). *Las condiciones políticas de la ciencia política en Chile* (FLACSO-Chile Working Paper No. 453). Santiago de Chile: FLACSO-Chile. Retrieved from http://flacsochile.org/biblioteca/pub/memoria/1990/000219.pdf

Leiva, F. I. (2008). *Latin American neostructuralism: The contradictions of post-neoliberal development.* Minneapolis: University of Minnesota Press.

Mac Hale, T. (1987). Desinformación de la visita papal. *Política, 13*, 225–228.

Marcuse, H. (1991). *One-dimensional man: Studies in the ideology of advanced industrial society.* Boston: Beacon Press.

Marín Vicuña, A. (1986). El sistema electoral binominal como una opción para el centro político. *Política, 9*, 139–145.

Markoff, J., & Montecinos, V. (1994). El irresistible ascenso de los economistas. *Desarrollo Económico, 133*(34), 3–29.

Massini-Correas, C. (1988). Socialdemocracia y liberación sexual. *Política, 15*, 35–47.

Mayol, A. (2012). *El derrumbe del modelo: La crisis de la economía de mercado en el Chile contemporáneo.* Santiago de Chile: LOM Ediciones.

McNally, D. (2011). *Global slump: The economics and politics of crisis and resistance.* Oakland: PM Press.

Mella, M. (2011a). *Extraños en la noche: Intelectuales y usos políticos del conocimiento durante la transición chilena.* Santiago de Chile: RIL Editores.

Meneses, E. (1979). El sistema internacional multipolar de equilibrio de poder: Una revisión histórica. *Revista de Ciencia Política, 1*(1), 67–79.

Meneses, E. (1981a). Política exterior, los fondos marinos y diversos intereses. *Revista de Ciencia Política, 3*(1–2), 7–16.

Meneses, E. (1981b). Estructura geopolítica. *Revista de Ciencia Política, 3*(1–2), 105–161.

Meneses, E. (1983). Futuras opciones nucleares de Francia. *Política, 2,* 51–72.

Meneses, E. (1992). La crisis fronteriza chilena: Primera parte, 1954–1973. *Revista de Ciencia Política, 14*(1–2), 129–147.

Meneses, E. (1998). La disuasión aérea chilena: Implicancias político-estratégicas. *Revista de Ciencia Política, 19*(2), 63–88.

Meneses, E., & Navarro Meza, M. (1995). Política de defensa: El caso de la adquisición de sistemas de arma. *Revista de Ciencia Política, 17*(1–2), 121–157.

Meneses, E., Tagle, J., & Guevara, T. (1982). La política exterior chilena del siglo XX a través de los mensajes presidenciales y las conferencias panamericanas hasta la segunda guerra mundial. *Revista de Ciencia Política, 4*(2), 50–61.

Mertz, Ó. (1982). La cultura adversaria en la sociedad contemporánea. *Revista de Ciencia Política, 4*(1), 7–27.

Mertz, Ó. (1984). Adam Smith: Los conceptos de naturaleza humana y gobierno en la teoría de los sentimientos morales. *Revista de Ciencia Política, 6*(1), 55–75.

Mifsud, A. (1985). El texto evangelio, ética y política y su status epistemológico. *Revista de Ciencia Política, 7*(1), 115–119.

Miranda, C. (1984). Hobbes y la anarquía internacional. *Revista de Ciencia Política, 6*(2), 71–84.

Miranda, C. (1986). Realismo e idealismo en el estudio de las relaciones internacionales: La influencia de Hobbes y de Kant. *Revista de Ciencia Política, 8*(1–2), 88–100.

Miranda, M. T. (1982). El sistema electoral y el multipartidismo en Chile 1949–1969. *Revista de Ciencia Política, 4*(1), 59–69.

Moreno Valencia, F. (1985). Reflexión a propósito de un documento episcopal chileno: Evangelio, ética y política. *Revista de Ciencia Política, 7*(1), 147–149.

Moreno Valencia, F. (1987). El mensaje de Juan Pablo II en Chile: Primera parte. *Revista de Ciencia Política, 9*(1), 17–26.

Moulián, T. (2002). *Chile actual: Anatomía de un mito.* Santiago de Chile: LOM editores.

Moulián, T. (2009). *Contradicciones del desarrollo político chileno 1920–1990.* Santiago de Chile: Editorial Arcis.

Mujal-León, E. (1982). En torno a la consolidación de la democracia en España. *Revista de Ciencia Política, 4*(2), 62–72.

Myers, J. (1989). Argentina: Una visión crítica de su historia política. *Revista de Ciencia Política, 11*(1), 20–29.

Neumann, I. B. (2016). Conclusion. In J. L. Amoureux & B. J. Steele (Eds.), *Reflexivity and international relations: Positionality, critique, and practice* (pp. 272–274). New York: Routledge.

Nishiyama, C. (1982). Capitalismo humano. *Revista de Ciencia Política, 4*(2), 152–181.

Novak, M. (1983). Democracia y desarrollo. *Revista de Ciencia Política, 5*(2), 83–94.

Núñez Tome, L. M. (1988). El plebiscito presidencial de 1988. *Política, 16,* 75–81.

Otero, R. (1987). Comentario a las intervenciones de Roberto Pulido y Abraham Santibáñez. *Política, 13,* 191–200.

Pazos, L. (1987). Relaciones entre pobreza y sobrepoblación. *Política, 12,* 183–193.

Petrus Putter, A. (1983). La política marítima de Sudáfrica. *Política, 3,* 159–168.

Pezoa Bissieres, Á. (1989). El nuevo autoritarismo en América Latina: Un análisis bibliográfico. *Política, 21,* 151–158.

Pinochet de la Barra, Ó. (1985). El tratado de paz y amistad entre Chile y Argentina. *Revista de Ciencia Política, 7*(1), 188–198.

Pittman, H. T. (1981). Algunas tendencias geopolíticas específicas en los países del ABC. Nuevas aplicaciones de la ley de las áreas valiosas. *Revista de Ciencia Política, 3*(1–2), 27–70.

Poradowski, M. (1984). La 'teología de la liberación' de Karl Marx. *Política, 5*, 69–107.

Poradowski, M. (1986). Teología de la liberación de Karl Marx (II). *Política, 9*, 147–171.

Pulido, R., & Santibáñez, A. (1987). Intervención sobre política, comunicación social y vida privada. *Política, 13*, 167–190.

Puryear, J. M. (1994). *Thinking politics: Intellectuals and democracy in Chile, 1973–1988*. Baltimore: Johns Hopkins University Press.

Puryear, J. M. (2016). *Pensando la política: Intelectuales y democracia en Chile, 1973–1988*. Santiago de Chile: CIEPLAN.

Ratzinger, J. (1984). Instrucción sobre algunos aspectos de la 'teología de la liberación.' *Revista de Ciencia Política, 6*(2), 138–162.

Ratzinger, J. (1986). Economía y responsabilidad moral. *Política, 10*, 243–249.

Ratzinger, J. (1987). Libertad y liberación. *Política, 12*, 159–182.

Ravecca, P. (2014). *La política de la ciencia política en Chile y Uruguay: Ciencia, poder, contexto. Primeros hallazgos de una agenda de investigación* (Working Paper No. 01/14). Montevideo: Instituto de Ciencia Política.

Reichley, J. A. (1982). Las raíces conservadoras en las administraciones de Nixon, Ford y Reagan. *Revista de Ciencia Política, 4*(1), 71–86.

Ribera Neumann, T. (1986). Más allá de una inconstitucionalidad. *Política, 10*, 29–70.

Riesco, R. (1985). Valoración geoestratégica del hemisferio austral. *Revista de Ciencia Política, 7*(1), 168–187.

Rodríguez Grez, P. (1986). Restauración de la democracia en Chile. *Política, 9*, 127–137.

Rojas Sánchez, G. (1980). Elementos de una concepción totalitaria. *Revista de Ciencia Política, 2*(3), 33–54.

Rojas Sánchez, G., Ribera Neumann, T., & Cumplido Cereceda, F. (1987). Defensa de la democracia [Special issue]. *Política, tomo I*, 97–153.

Rubio Apiolaza, P. (2011). Jaime Guzmán y la Unión Demócrata Independiente durante la transición: Una revisión de su aporte intelectual en los años ochenta. In M. Mella (Ed.), *Extraños en la noche: Intelectuales y usos políticos del conocimiento durante la transición chilena* (pp. 73–96). Santiago de Chile: RIL editores.

Said, E. (1979). *Orientalism*. New York: Vintage Books.

Sandoz, E. (1983). Reflexiones sobre naturaleza humana, política y democracia. *Revista de Ciencia Política, 5*(2), 95–116.

Sasse, G. (1980). La guerra subversiva como método en relaciones internacionales. *Revista de Ciencia Política, 2*(3), 67–77.

Shapiro, I. (2005). Problems, methods, and theories in the study of politics or what's wrong with political science and what to do about it. In K. R. Monroe (Ed.), *Perestroika! The raucous rebellion in political science* (pp. 66–86). New Haven, CT: Yale University Press.

Silva Bascuñán, A. (1987). Democracia: Nuevo conservantismo. *Política, 11*, 109–112.

Singer, D. (1984). Estabilidad e inestabilidad en el sistema internacional del futuro. *Revista de Ciencia Política, 6*(1), 33–54.

Spivak, G. C. (1988). Can the subaltern speak? In C. Nelson & L. Grossberg (Eds.), *Marxism and the interpretations of culture* (pp. 271–313). Basingstoke: Macmillan Education.

Tambs, L., & Aker, F. (1982). Cómo acabar con el síndrome de Vietnam en El Salvador. *Política, 1*, 117–131.

Theberge, J. D. (1979). Tendencias actuales en la política de América Latina y de Estados Unidos. *Revista de Ciencia Política, 1*(1), 52–66.

Theberge, J. D. (1983). La política de los Estados Unidos en América Central. *Revista de Ciencia Política, 5*(2), 75–82.

Theberge, J. D. (1984). El sistema político de los Estados Unidos de América. *Política, 6*, 189–201.

Theberge, J. D. (1988). Cuatro alocuciones. *Política, 17*, 129–138.

Tuteleers, S. (1982). Sobre la separación de los poderes del estado. *Revista de Ciencia Política, 4*(2), 73–97.

Urenda Zegers, C., & Eyzaguirre García de la Huerta, J. (1987). El derecho de la propiedad: Bases de la estabilidad democrática [Special issue]. *Política, tomo II*, 15–43.

Valdivieso Ariztía, R. (1987). Al servicio de la mentira. *Política, 13*, 217–221.

Verdugo, P. (Ed.). (2004). *De la tortura NO se habla: Agüero vs Meneses*. Santiago de Chile: Editorial Catalonia.

Viacava, J. (2012). La ciencia política en Chile: Una carrera en expansión y transformación. *Política, 50*(1), 93–110.

Wiarda, H. J. (1985). ¿Se puede exportar la democracia? La búsqueda de la democracia en la política norteamericana para América Latina. *Revista de Ciencia Política, 7*(1), 85–111.

Widow, J. A. (1979). Filosofía y lenguaje político. *Revista de Ciencia Política, 1*(1), 30–40.

Wilhelmy, M. (1982). Programas, ideologías y preferencias partidistas: El modelo de Anthony Downs. *Política, 1*, 89–114.

Yrarrázaval, J. (1979). Reflexiones sobre ideología, conflicto y consenso. *Revista de Ciencia Política, 1*(1), 4–10.

Yrarrázaval, J. (1982). La participación en la sociedad libre. *Revista de Ciencia Política, 4*(2), 98–121.

Zepeda Hernández, C. (1985). Límites al pluralismo: ¿Un caso de coincidencia inadvertido? *Política, 7*, 161–182.

Zipper, R. I. (1982). Reseña bibliográfica de Orientalismo de Edward Said. *Política, 1*, 147–151.

3

FROM REVOLUTION
TO TRANSITION

The Making of a Conformist Academia
in Uruguay and Beyond(?) (Warm)*

U10: Juan accompanied Rodney Arismendi to Moscow.[1]
    [Long silence]
PR: Impressive . . .
U10: *[Interrupting]* Héctor[2] was the representative of the Uruguayan Commu-
    nist Party in Cuba!
    [Very long silence]
PR: The ideological changes have been so profound . . .
U10: For the record, I am very interested in your research; it is really useful for
    me . . . for self-analysis.
PR: I know . . .
U10: To analyze myself . . .
PR: *[Interrupting]* For discernment, I see.
U10: *Self-discernment.* Because one lives, and the wave just takes you . . .

Is it worthwhile to tell a story about power and knowledge in the realm of political science (PS) in Uruguay—a small country mostly ignored by global academia?[3] And if so, what may we discover through such an exploration about
the society and the polis where the story takes place? This chapter explores the
following questions: What do the politics of political science (PPS) look like in
Uruguay? How do we write a *political* history of the discipline in this particular case? What are the similarities and differences with the Chilean experience,
and how can we account for them? What can be learned through a comparative
exercise of the ways their political regimes related to knowledge production, and
with what consequences? Finally, why does the case of Uruguay matter at all,
beyond its borders? What does it lend itself to showing?

    As shall be seen in the following pages, the social sciences developed late
in Uruguay and subsequently encountered a dictatorship that undermined their

institutions and persecuted their practitioners. The regime did not produce its own centers of knowledge production in these areas of study: in stark contrast to the case of Chile, in Uruguay there was no *authoritarian political science* (APS). Rather than focusing on a specific and rather peculiar phenomenon as was done for Chile with APS, I approach the Uruguayan case through a broader and longer exploration of the discipline through a problematizing re-description (Shapiro, 2005) of PS' history from the point of view of knowledge-power dynamics (Foucault, 1980, 1988, 1989, 1991a, 1991b, 1992, 1993, 2006; Gramsci, 2008; Marcuse, 1991). The exercise will highlight what the similarities and differences are compared to the Chilean case, how these similarities and differences may be accounted for, and why they matter for deepening our understanding of the role of knowledge production in power relations.

That PPS is posed in this study as a form of critique that transcends the divide between cultural and material analysis means that in exploring the dynamics of PS in Uruguay across time, I am interested in both the political economy *and* the discourse of the discipline. In order to keep the comparative eye widely open, I partially follow the previous chapter's structure and analytical strategy. I will proceed by exploring the conceptual and institutional components that, in my interpretation, constitute the Uruguayan PS discourse. As in the case of Chile, I will focus on problematizing the way democracy is approached by the discipline's mainstream. The discourse analysis will include contextual and structural factors, and the exploration will stop at the various intersections between power and knowledge that reveal significant similarities and differences with Chile. Unlike the previous chapter, however, this one will include the subjectivity of Uruguayan political scientists in the analysis, further expanding and complicating the meditation on power and knowledge.

Research for this chapter consisted of a systematic analysis of all of the articles published by the *Revista Uruguaya de Ciencia Política* [Uruguayan Journal of Political Science] (*RUCP*) from 1987 to 2012 and other relevant historical records. In addition, 22 in-depth interviews were conducted. These conversations do much more than simply provide information or empirical evidence. They constitute a step toward grasping the role of lived experience in intellectual and political transformations (Bevir, 2003; Bischoping & Gazso, 2016; Denzin & Lincoln, 2011, p. 54; Geertz, 2003; Guber, 2011, p. 84; Flick, 2007, p. 20; Merlino, 2009, p. 115), thus raising the epistemological temperature of PPS and deepening the disciplinary self-reflection that this book proposes.

The analysis shows that PS in Uruguay has mostly been acritical with respect to political parties and political elites. Concretely, PS has been mobilized into a set of practices that are, at the very least, functional to established mechanisms of power and its associated post-dictatorship narratives. These practices, which are both institutional and intellectual, turn democracy from an object of inquiry into *the* locus and idiom of the discipline; that is, into a thing from which the political scientist cannot have critical distance. How can we make sense of this academic *and* political process through which the political analyst becomes an activist of a political regime *in the name of* objectivity? This chapter addresses the question by exploring both the conditions and circumstances that account for the forging of a conformist PS as well as the discipline's main discursive features.

The chapter unfolds in nine sections. The first section locates the trajectory of PS within the history of social sciences in Uruguay. It specifically deals with the lateness of the discipline's development, a feature that is crucial to understanding the specificities of PPS in the country. The second section shows that in contrast with Pinochet's regime, the Uruguayan dictatorship (1973–1984) did not appropriate or mobilize the social sciences. On the contrary, the regime dismantled and displaced these disciplines from the system of public education. This reveals sharp differences in the way these two regimes exercised power, a finding that is relevant for discussions about authoritarian governments in South America and their different performances and trajectories. The absence of APS in Uruguay had implications for the democratic transition and PS' political role in the country. The third section explores the role of private research centers (PRCs) during the authoritarian 1970s. The traditional interpretation is that PRCs were sites of peaceful resistance that kept the social sciences alive. Here, I argue that they *also* embodied a temporary shift toward a neoliberal governmentality of academia and a *permanent* ideological mutation toward *radical asepsis* (de Sierra, 2005), which have had significant political and intellectual effects. Thus, thinking was "kept alive" in a particular way that had political implications. The final sections offer a deeper exploration of PS' democratic discourse.

Uruguayan PS has been imagined and narrated as entrenched within democracy. The fourth to eighth sections analyze the conceptual operations that shaped these claims about the discipline's identity, particularly: the rejection of Marxism and the embrace of liberalism; the uneasiness around sociology; the disciplinary appropriation of Carlos Real de Azúa, a well-known Uruguayan thinker; and the positive evaluation of the Uruguayan political system by PS. The eighth section approaches another point of entry to the relationship between PS and its context that sets Uruguay apart from Chile: Uruguayan PS has been liberal but never promoted neoliberal reforms, and unlike Chilean PS, it is also secular, reflecting the ethos of the country. The last section draws on my notion of complex relationality to grasp, in theoretical terms, the multidimensional conditions of PS' trajectory.

Framing the Uruguayan Case: Historical Overview or the Politics of Timing

In the social sciences, time means history. Timing, in this case, refers to the specific historical circumstances (within the longer context of Uruguay's history) in which the discipline was forged, and that bear crucial implications for its politics. Most fundamentally, Uruguayan PS was formed during the democratic transition and was liberal democratic *at birth*. The following pages begin the exploration of PPS in Uruguay by locating its itinerary within the broader landscape of the social sciences in the country.

In the last decade, there has been increased interest in discussing the state of PS in Uruguay (some recent examples are Bentancur & Mancebo, 2017; Garcé & Rocha Carpiuc, 2015; Moraes, 2015; Ravecca, 2014; Rocha Carpiuc, 2017).[4] The late arrival of the discipline *vis-à-vis* the rest of the Southern Cone is widely acknowledged as one of its main features (Altman, 2005; Filgueira, 1974, 1986; Garcé, 2005; Pérez Antón, 1986, 1992).[5] Social sciences were, in general, late-comers in Uruguay. The Social Sciences Institute at the Universidad de la República [University of the Republic] (UdelaR) was formally created in 1956 (Filgueira, 1974, 1986; Solari, 1959), while the Instituto de Ciencia Política [Institute of Political Science] (ICP) was not founded until 1985—that is, after 13 years of (brutal) right-wing authoritarian rule.

PS is among the last of the social sciences to be institutionalized in the country.[6] For years (at least since 1957), political science was taught at the School of Law as well as at the School of Economics only in specific courses (called *cátedras*). It lacked an institutional base that could signal its boundaries—that is, it lacked disciplinary autonomy, and, it should be noted, was not yet differentiated from sociology. Both the aforementioned institutes were originally located in the law school of UdelaR.[7] Indeed, social sciences did not have their own institutional home until the founding of the School of Social Sciences in 1989. The first sociologist trained in the country graduated in 1973 (Filgueira, 1974), while the first political scientist defended his BA thesis in 1994.[8]

There is a small body of literature on the trajectory of the social sciences in Uruguay.[9] It consistently refers to this lateness and inquires into its possible causes in a country that is otherwise well known for its relatively high standard of living, relatively developed welfare state, and strong university structures in traditional areas such as medicine, law, and architecture (de Sierra, 2005; Filgueira, 1974, 1986; Rama, 1977). Gerónimo de Sierra (2005, p. 476), for instance, argues that local elites' self-perception of Uruguay as a successful country prevented them from developing "official" social sciences. The high national self-esteem, sustained by favorable international conditions and a sequence of social-democratic governments, observers argue, might explain why no population census was done between 1908 and 1963 (Buquet, 2012; de Sierra, 2005; Filgueira, 1974, 1986; Pérez Antón, 1986, 1992; Prates, 1987). Carlos Filgueira (1986, p. 174) claims that the need for systematic knowledge was precluded by a "false optimism" and a parochial attitude.[10]

Carlos Filgueira is considered one of the founders of modern sociology in Uruguay. In a text written after the coup, Filgueira (1974) develops a detailed, and at moments bitter, analysis of the situation of the discipline in the country.[11] He makes a number of points that are also relevant for us here, given that they refer to the conditions that precede the emergence of PS. First, in the early 1970s, the "subsystem" of social sciences was particularly underdeveloped in the context of an underdeveloped institutional and cultural framework for science; up until 1950, there were only seven institutions, including departments and research units (Prates, 1987, p. 13). Second, the institutionalization of the social sciences was a late process in comparison to other disciplines and to other Latin American countries. Third—and this is an important feature to remember—this development was happening almost exclusively in the public system (which made the social sciences very vulnerable to policy changes; see Figure 3.1).[12] Finally, Filgueira (1974) notes that economics was the social science garnering most of the resources and research centers; sociology came second, and the other disciplines were practically nonexistent (p. 8).

A main issue for Filgueira (1974) was sociology's persistent lack of intellectual and institutional autonomy *vis-à-vis* law and lawyers in particular. During the 1950s, a group of "sociologist-lawyers," "sociologist-architects," and "sociologist-historians" emerged whose activity was located in the sociology courses of their respective schools (i.e. law, architecture, etc.)

1. El proceso de creación de centros dedicados a las ciencias sociales en el Uruguay indica un considerable crecimiento que se dio recién en la última década (1961-1971). Es en este período que se constituyen las dos terceras partes de los centros existentes (64 %), como resultado de un cre cimiento exponencial muy nítido. (véase el Cuadro No. 1) (4)

CUADRO No. 3

Centros dedicados a las Ciencias Sociales

según dependencia administrativa (en %)

Administración Central	25
Entes Autónomos	18
Universidad	32
Municipio	–
Para-estatal	9
Sector privado	16

100 (37)

FUENTE: Conicyt, Uruguay.

FIGURE 3.1 Social science research centers: Lateness and concentration in the public sector

(Extracted from Filgueira (1974, p. 25))

(Filgueira, 1974, p. 10). This amateurism, Filgueira argues, was an obstacle for both the individual training of scholars and the institutionalization of a realm where sociologists could interact with each other and forge a common identity.[13]

However, in the pre-coup period of the 1960s and early 1970s, social sciences went through a process of consolidation. The author divides these years into two moments. In the early 1960s, the crisis of the development model based on import substitution industrialization was clear. Amid Cold War tensions and in the aftermath of the Cuban Revolution, the Alliance for Progress was launched. In this context, the Uruguayan government created the Comisión de Inversiones y Desarrollo Económico [Commission for Investment and Economic Development] (CIDE), an inter-institutional organism that was tasked with formulating a development plan for the country.[14] This attempt to rationally plan the future favored the social sciences. According to Filgueira, in this phase, UdelaR did not operate as a dynamic pole but was driven by external forces toward an expansion of the social sciences. He adds that in this period, the influence of Marxism was scarce and in fact US academia was already the dominant model. He also notes the fading of the French influence (1974, p. 23). This challenges the overarching description of the social sciences of the decade as dominated by Marxism and radical politics (Garcé, 2005).

During the second half of the 1960s, what Filgueira calls "the expansion of the university" takes place amidst rising political polarization and state repression. The militarization of state conflict with guerrilla groups precipitated— and increased—the political involvement of the military, which culminated in the 1973 *coup d'état*. These were agitated times for the university. Significant changes were introduced in the *planes de studio* [the BA curricula] of different schools. Sociology was incorporated into the mandatory introductory courses in several programs (Filgueira, 1974; U13; U21). This meant an enormous *quantitative* growth (i.e., expansion). One of my interviewees describes this dual dynamic of growth and politicization thus:

> In the School of Law and to some extent in the School of Economics, the syllabi were reformed. I did the 1971 *plan* as a student representative.[15] We moved social sciences to the introductory courses. Now the number of students in the first year was not 10, like in the PS course of the 6th year. They were 600, 700, 800! This change occurred in 1971 and many high school teachers became university professors. Some of them came from the School of Humanities but others came directly from high school institutions. In some cases, they had a political motivation: the communists, the philo-tupamaros, the socialists, everyone perceived those law students as a bastion for political recruitment, and in fact they were. These people measured success not in the number of lawyers but in how many new activists would go to protest in the streets or would join the *Tupamaros* or the parties.[16]

(U13)

Multiple and sometimes contradictory registers and aspects mesh in the complex story that I am trying to tell: contrary to what the mainstream narrative would argue later, this same move toward politicization meant an expansion of the social sciences as an *autonomous* field. Thus, another interviewee remembers: "The great move of the 71 *plan* was to say, 'social sciences are not an ornament for lawyers.' The law diploma used to say 'Doctor in Law and Social Sciences.' The certificate of my dad reads that: Doctor in Law and Social Sciences!" (U21). We will see later that PS' separation from sociology will happen in a radically different political atmosphere. Note, however, that in contrast with other countries in the region, in Uruguay, social sciences were still part of the curricula of other academic degrees.

This ideologically charged academic environment was not formed in a historical vacuum. Academia was one among many realms where the Cold War and political polarization manifested. Carlos Filgueira, who was at the time perceived as a conservative scholar by the student unions, argued that rising state repression stemmed from a class-based process whereby the role of professional politicians was taken over by members of the economic elite "who began to exercise power in a more direct way" (1974, p. 26). That Filgueira uses a language so close to Marxism's class struggle is remarkable, especially given that the class dimension of this political polarization has been erased by official accounts adopted by the Uruguayan political system and academia.

Filgueira (1974) was also highly critical of the left and aspired to a kind of objective social science which, I will argue, was achieved a decade later with the emergence of PS. One of his main concerns was local academia's cultural isolationism. In 1969, the Institute of Social Science presented a report that condemned "any policies of funding or subsidies in any form coming from foreign or domestic capital" because of its corrupting powers (cited in Filgueira, 1974, p. 27). Susana Prates (1987) argued that institutional, professional, and ideological obstacles limited the development of social sciences before 1973. Political radicalization, in particular, prevented "systematic empirical research" (Prates, 1987, p. 17). In the view of Filgueira, some of these problems persisted even after the dictatorship when the public university came to life again. Indeed, more than a decade later, he (1986, p. 166) claimed that the problems of sociology were still the old issues of organization, institutionalization, and consolidation. This is connected with the alleged distortions introduced by the "bureaucratic" and "politicized" public university into the organization of science. The threat of ideologically driven isolationism was persistent. For these authors, clearly, an activist social science is perceived as an undesirable moment of academic destruction. This is important because PS practitioners today—including those colleagues who have written on the history of the discipline—see Filgueira as a modernizer of the social sciences in Uruguay, whose narrative and legacy they now ardently inherit.

Filgueira's and Prates' reflections are representative of a two-dimensional narrative of collective self-blaming that will consolidate after the dictatorship.

First, at the epistemological and academic levels, radicalization is argued to have meant the impossibility of serious—that is, objective—science. Second, the social sciences are seen as part of the process of radicalization that contributed to the loss of democracy; thus, academics were partially responsible for the worst tragedy the country has gone through in the 20th century: the 1973 *coup d'etat*. This double accusation, both academic and political, has been adopted by the mainstream PS narrative, and its final implication is that we social scientists must be, from now on, neatly objective *and* unrelentingly liberal. PS has been a main protagonist of this shift within the discourse of the social sciences in Uruguay. To analytically grasp the apparent move from "politicized" to "objective" social sciences, regardless of the historical or conceptual accuracy of this characterization, it is necessary to examine what happened with the social sciences during the years of the dictatorship. I turn to this issue in the following section.

Dictatorship, Transition, and Trauma

The Uruguayan dictatorship (1973–1984) persecuted political dissent, and was particularly brutal with those organizations it deemed to incarnate the so-called communist threat, such as trade unions and leftist political parties (Caetano & Rilla, 1987). The repression and surveillance included a wide range of practices from classifying citizens into categories (A, B, or C), to imprisonment, torture, and forced disappearances (Gil & Viñar, 1998; Giorgi, 1995; Marchesi, 2017; Marchesi, Markarián, Rico, & Yaffé, 2003; McSherry, 2005; Perelli & Rial, 1986; Rico, 2007; Serpaj, 1989; Sempol, 2010). In such a context, intellectuals and the social sciences were per se suspicious: in Uruguay, "social sciences meant left-wing" (U15).

The dictatorship removed the introductory courses recently created by UdelaR and, with them, most of the social science courses offered by the institution. Sociology was wiped out from the upper-year curricula of the BA programs. The Institute of Social Sciences was shut down and many of its members were fired. At the same physical venue, a new Institute of Social Studies was created whose academic activity was scarce and that did not produce any relevant research during its whole existence (Filgueira, 1986). From the point of view of the professionalization of sociology, the creation of this institute was, according to Filgueira, a regression in the development path, a sort of process of de-institutionalization. Vania Markarián (2015) notes that an estimated 45% of the faculty at the University of the Republic was fired for political reasons.

The consensus among interviewees and authors is overwhelming: the dictatorship was devastating for the social sciences (U4; U5; U13; U15; U18; U21). Filgueira (1974, pp. 31–32) explains that the regime's intervention within the university ("la intervención de la Universidad," as the experience was named) unleashed a period of *destruction* of these disciplines. Public offices that housed some social science activity also saw the disintegration of their technical teams

(Filgueira, 1974). Given that most social science research and teaching was located in UdelaR and other public organizations (see Figure 3.1), this meant an appalling situation. The terms employed by other authors to describe the period are consistently negative. Gerónimo de Sierra (2005) mobilizes the same notion of destruction and adds *dismantling*, while Romeo Pérez Antón (1992, p. 49) argues that anything perceived as critical or disruptive was *amputated*. For Adolfo Garcé (2005) and David Altman (2005), the social sciences were *interrupted*. Finally, Susana Prates (1987) refers to a *freezing* process of the university in general.

Most social sciences academic activity during the dictatorship moved to private research centers and was under permanent threat. This also had its consequences during the transition, as the efforts of institutional reconstruction and meeting the very practical needs of a "devastated" UdelaR (U12) drastically diminished the room for conceptual debate. According to Stephen Gregory (2009, p. 78), it is difficult to find major work in the Uruguayan social sciences published in the mid-to-late1980s that had no support from privately funded research institutes. It seems revealing that in his study on intellectuals and the left in Uruguay, the chapter on the dictatorship is called "Interlude." Gregory suggests that the military was its own organic intellectual, pointing out that the situation was such "that they produced a gargantuan two-volume account of their motives and actions in the unremittingly dense, monochromatic prose of a battlefield report, modeled on the doctrine of national security promoted in United States military centres and widely practiced throughout the Southern Cone" (p. 75).

From a comparative perspective, even though Uruguay's and Chile's dictatorships had a lot in common—an authoritarian right-wing ideology and a robust record of human rights violations, for a start—they dealt with knowledge in radically different ways. As shown in Chapter 2, Pinochet's regime deployed neoconservative forms of knowledge to dispute the terrain of hegemony of the cultural left, and this battle included academia and PS. This created an enormous capacity to create "positive" legacies (multiple durabilities claimed as successes by a significant part of the population even today). APS did not exist in Uruguay. The Uruguayan dictatorship did not create any "good memories" among social scientists. Nobody in the academic world has publicly vindicated the regime in any way. This overly destructive nature of the dictatorship is revealing of how the regime exercised power and helps to explain how PS would relate to liberal democracy after the transition. As I discuss later, the linkage between liberal democracy and PS appears accurate for the Uruguayan case (Buquet, 2012; de Sierra, 2005; Garcé, 2005; Pérez Antón, 1986).

Granted, the Uruguayan dictatorship did produce a legacy, and it did change Uruguayan society (Caetano & Rilla, 1987; Cosse & Markarián, 1996; Menéndez-Carrión, 2015; Yaffé, 2010). Furthermore, *any* power entails the mobilization of knowledge. Thus, I am not arguing for the stereotypical notion of the dictatorship as a "long night" or a "blackout," nor for the idea that the military was somehow primitive. I do argue, however, that the lack of interest in academic intellectual production, particularly in the realm of the social sciences, as well as the undermining of the university seem to contrast with the Chilean case, which is analytically significant when reading these regimes and their trajectories both historically and in peoples' memories.

Markarián (2015) goes beyond the widespread analytical emphasis on the repressive aspects of the dictatorship by exploring its public policies on education, particularly those directed toward the public university. According to her findings, it seems that at the beginning, there was not a global and systematic project of modernization for the institutions of higher education. However, she qualifies this assessment with a thought-provoking observation: the dictatorship privileged the technical dimensions of education as well as problem-solving and market-oriented types of knowledge. This, again, contrasts with the Chilean case, at least with the experience of APS and its philosophical density. The Uruguayan dictatorship seemed to focus on changing the relationship between academic knowledge and society toward the depoliticization of academia. An important piece of this historical puzzle is that one of the very last decisions made by the dictatorship was to allow the creation of private universities in the country.

In two interviews with ICP founders (U13; U18), a member of a generation of scholars prior to their own was mentioned. At the time of the interviews, I was already active in the local PS community and I had been working on disciplinary introspection for some time. Nevertheless, this was a new name for me. Since he had been one of the very few who taught political science during the dictatorship, interviewing him seemed warranted.

The most interesting part of the conversation with this political scientist—totally forgotten by PS academics today—was not recorded upon the interviewee's request: according to him, during the dictatorship there was an unexpected academic freedom because of the inefficiency of the censors. They represented themselves as warriors of democracy and where there was no need for military interventions, they did not interfere. Because of his relationship with a leftist professor, U8 was almost assigned the citizenship category of C, which meant that the person was considered a threat to the nation, and consequently, would not be allowed to serve as a civil servant. Luckily, it was proved that U8 did not engage in subversive activity. This is an important point:

> They persecuted communists and guerrilla members, but they felt that they were defending democracy, so where there was no danger in their eyes, they pretended not to notice anything [*hacían la vista gorda*]. . . . They wanted a protected democracy, which would not be a rare thing in the international realm.

(U8)

In other words, in U8's narration, the military persecuted *people* involved in radical politics rather than ideas, theories, or disciplines. He surprised me by showing me a syllabus and a textbook from the 1970s that included Marxism. Nonetheless, either because of the military's anti-intellectualism or because Uruguayan social scientists were overwhelmingly involved in radical politics, the global result remains the same: *social sciences were under siege during the dictatorship in Uruguay.* Even economics, a friendly knowledge for this type of regime, did not flourish in the same way as in Chile (Markoff & Montecinos, 1994).

In short, the Uruguayan military operated through negation and censorship. They may have tolerated social sciences in some exceptional cases as U8 suggests, but they did not cultivate these knowledges. Their brutality and lack of cultural sophistication (the jokes about this in popular culture are abundant; see Chapter 4) remained in the memory of Uruguayans of all political views to the extent that it is rare to find anyone, not only scholars but also politicians, journalists, activists, or cultural workers of all stripes, who would say *anything* positive about the period. This sheds analytical light onto the relationship between academia and the regime. Even though authoritarianism's effects on the intelligentsia require further exploration for the purposes of this study, for the moment I would like to preliminarily explore the interplay between the dictatorship, subjectivity, and political and intellectual transformations.

The images with which interviewees describe their relationship with the authoritarian regime are very powerful and revealing. The dictatorship was a "monster" unto which one dreams of extirpating an eye or an arm (U3). It was also "a long road with a dense fog that paralyzes you" (U5) or simply a terrifying, oppressive regime that controlled your movements, conversations and thoughts:

> We were all terrified. We only had spaces in the interstices because control over society was brutal. . . . You walked on 18 de Julio Avenue and it was full of cops. They passed by all the time. I was socialized with cops beside me. I still carry my ID everywhere. *It is a mark that I carry.*
>
> *(U15, emphasis mine)*

For U4, it was an entire period of life that Uruguayans were dispossessed of: "The dictatorship took away so many things from us. It took so many things away from me. I was 15 in 1973. Imagine everything they took from me from when I was 15 to 24 years old!"[17]

The dictatorship produced deep changes in how academia relates to politics, democracy—and socialism. Through negative example, it "taught" scholars about the importance of the rule of law (U1; U3; U6; U7; U10; U12; U13; U14; U17; U18; U22). One interviewee asserted, for instance, that "the dictatorship made me categorically embrace democracy" (U18). Scholars were not "loyal" to democracy before: "Democracy was just a form, democracy was of others. Democracy was not yours" (U12). Given that this democratic learning process (González, 1993) included persecution and exile, it was deeply traumatic. The emotionally charged narratives of distress, suffering, loss, struggle, and damage embody the historical interweaving between subjectivity and political transformations (Fleming, 2005; Freud, 1986; Horowitz, 2003, 1977; Marcuse, 1974). In a way, the trauma *is* the ideological transformation: if scholars cared about socialism and dismissed democracy, and if their quest for utopian equality contributed to the political polarization responsible for the coup, then they were guilty for their own collective pain and, even worse, for the horrific consequences of the dictatorship for the country as a whole.[18] The traumatic betrayal (Edkins, 2003) here operates on two levels articulated in a discourse that goes something like this: the state, instead of protecting me, attacked me; but I deserved to be attacked. I am betrayed because I betrayed first. There is guilt and there is punishment for academia and for the left in general. It is understandable how in this context, Marxism and socialism became "despicable" (U17), "shameful" (U5), or "ridiculous" (U20).

Trauma may or may not produce personal and collective growth (Tedeschi & Calhoun, 2004). In this case, it did not leave space for critical reflection and the expansion of imagination (Ravecca, 2010). The conceptual shift toward liberalism was mechanical and thus it produced a particular form of intellectual narrowness and rigidity.[19] If the dictatorship is the enemy, then democracy becomes a political aim more than an object of critical inquiry. In some cases, the fall of the Berlin Wall finished the traumatizing task of emphasizing the liberal aspect of liberal democracy (U5; U2) as well as of expelling socialism from acceptable vocabulary. Thus, the global US-led enterprise of defeating alternative projects to neoliberal capitalism and its National Security Doctrine were successful. The body of thinking also received "electrical shocks" and suffered "disappearances."

The democratic transition consolidated the project of US-backed dictatorships: to enforce the unthinkability of socialism and the naturalization of liberalism. This has been a continental and, for the most part, efficacious enterprise. The radical ideological mutations of academia during the authoritarian period described above were instrumental for such a process: they were directly linked to the dismantling of *infrastructures of dissent* (Sears, 2012). The consolidation of social disciplines *as* objective idioms happened and participated in a moment of liberal victory. Ideological asepsis, if Marxism is understood to be the bacteria, naturalized dominant views: in this context, liberalism and capitalism (Alexander, 2005; Gramsci, 2008; Horkheimer, 1978; Marcuse, 1991). Socialism became unthinkable by the imposition of liberalism *as* unthinking, as nature—it was a transition *against* revolution (U6). This was buttressed by the narratives adopted by both the political establishment and the media that blamed radicalism for the institutional collapse of 1973.

It was in these ideological circumstances that Uruguayan PS, which was institutionalized *after* the transition, was forged *as* the knowledge *of* democracy. The ideological move can be characterized as a synecdoche because a universal— i.e., democracy—was reduced to a very specific (liberal) kind involving elections, stability, order and, very importantly, private property, and represented as if it were the whole. The discipline participated in and embodied these theoretical transformations. Paradoxically, that democracy would soon break the sacred liberal rule of law to protect human rights violators.

Rethinking Epic Narrative(s): Private Research Centers During the Dictatorship—Resistance . . . Through Neoliberalization?

As a reaction to the dictatorship's sweeping institutional dismantling of the social sciences (de Sierra, 2005, p. 499) and the firing of many researchers from the public sector, between 1973 and 1979, several private research centers were established, including four that would have the opportunity to network and take part in regional conferences thanks to their membership in the Consejo Latinoamericano de Ciencias Sociales [Latin American Council of Social Sciences] (CLACSO) established in 1967 (Prates, 1987).[20] An epic tone predominates in the narration of this experience (de Sierra, 2005; Filgueira, 1974, 1986; Prates, 1987; U3; U4; U9; U12; U13; U14; U15; U18). For Prates (1987), for instance, they kept critical consciousness alive. The PRCs are perceived to have advanced the institutionalization of the social sciences and are understood to have constituted important sites of peaceful resistance against the authoritarian regime. In this view, the PRCs were bastions of both science and democracy.

While acknowledging its valuable contribution to making sense of the period, I depart from this narrative and furthermore conceptualize the PRCs as part and parcel of the power-knowledge dynamics to be scrutinized. In my view, the emphasis on the PRCs' contribution to the professionalization of research and the defense of democracy conceals the fact that the dictatorship pushed scholars toward a neoliberal model of management, which has had ideological implications. Furthermore, the embrace of objectivity and of liberalism can be conceptualized as epistemological and political shifts in the direction of producing a conformist academic community that perceives itself as non-ideological (Marcuse, 1991; Alexander, 2005; Horkheimer, 1978). This modernized structure for the practice of science (as embodied in the PRCs) was, in my view, the organizational setting for the rise of a new way of practicing social science that assembled objectivism and democracy.[21]

In the brief exploration of the PRCs' experience that follows, I draw on secondary literature and 22 interviews with political scientists conducted between 2012 and 2013. It should be noted, as a methodological caveat, that I do not contest the empirical data of the authors cited below. Rather, I propose a problematizing reinterpretation[22] of the PRCs that situates their experience under a different analytical light.

Prates (1987) offers a detailed analysis of the PRCs. The author views their emergence and consolidation as part of a rich range of forms of peaceful resistance to the dictatorship (p. 10). Furthermore, in her assessment, the PRCs took social sciences to a more advanced stage, achieving goals that the pre-coup UdelaR did not because of its heavy bureaucratic structure and its over-politicized dynamics. In terms of academic internationalization, she observes that these centers made great progress: they engaged with regional social science networks such as CLACSO before the research units at UdelaR did.

Meanwhile, for Filgueira (1974), the establishment of PRCs meant the possibility of leaving behind what he deemed "the provincialism" and "isolationism" of the country's social sciences (p. 24). At the same time, he notes that this meant confronting an enormous challenge in terms of management, administration, and fundraising. Prates (1987) makes a similar point about the learning process undergone by scholars during this period:

> If we take into account the ideological perspective and the political practices that guided social sciences within the university in the pre-coup period, it becomes easy to understand that, especially for those teams that came from that institution, building managerial capacity implied a huge learning effort.
>
> *(p. 23)*

For present purposes, it is analytically relevant to identify how the authors' politics shape their descriptions. Given that the perspective that they represent has become hegemonic—and thus naturalized—in the post-transition academia, it is not easy to uncover its ideological dimensions in a Marxist move or to show its power effects in a Foucauldian fashion. But the promise of analytical returns is worthy of the effort. I suggest here three points: first, the need to search for funding is a powerful intellectual disciplining force. Second, if the new material conditions had transformed the way of *being* an academic in the country, that transformative process included epistemology *and* ideology. Consequently, what Prates called a "learning effort" and Filgueira "an enormous challenge" can be read as a shift in the terrain of power (Menéndez-Carrión, 2015) and of the governmentality of academia (Foucault, 2006).

Prates (1987, p. 52) makes another observation that furthers my argument on neoliberalization: at the risk of making "dubious transpositions," she evokes the notion of the informal sector in describing the process of establishment and organization of the PRCs. That is, like the informal sector, it was constituted by a highly competitive academic market structured by organizations with small-scale operations and scarce resources that achieved high productivity through labor-intensive strategies. In other words, the researchers became amateur entrepreneurs, funding seekers, and precarious workers experiencing firsthand what happens when the state withdraws from an economic activity—it was neoliberalism applied to academia. For Prates, this form of organizing academic activity allowed the social sciences to consolidate.[23]

The situation described *and* the celebratory tone in which it is narrated have a clear neoliberal logic. Given that this point is controversial, let me extensively quote Filgueira (1986) here:

> There are differences in the organizational forms that these private centers adopted. However, in my opinion, the most important point is that they achieved efficient decision-making structures thanks to their way of funding, the relatively reduced membership, their efficient way of relating to Latin American institutions and the rest of the world and, fundamentally, because of their *flexibility* and rapid adaptative capacity to *the demands to which they were subjected*. This contrasts with *the heavy and complex bureaucratic mechanisms of the preceding institutions (i.e. the public university)*. To this we should add *an intense competition* in which the centers had to engage in order to survive in a context where *research by contract* or defined by grants/projects with their pre-established schedules and terms, proved to be more adequate for the new discipline that was taking shape.
>
> *(p. 183, emphasis mine)*

Filgueira reinforces the point in subsequent paragraphs of his study in no uncertain terms: the PRCs were undeniably successful in doing research and teaching, demonstrated that sociology could be developed in unwelcoming conditions, and found efficient ways of "organizing science." Hence, their flexibility and speed in the orientation and reorientation of research and teaching *is an example to emulate in the future*, especially given the "tremendous difficulties" that the public university normally represented as a host for science, the implication being that UdelaR's parliamentary structure and fragmented power prevented efficient decision-making (Filgueira, 1986, p. 184). In his view, the PRCs' experience should be projected into the future way of organizing social sciences in the country, especially in terms of the institutions upon which disciplinary development will be based.

Note that Filgueira is writing in the mid-1980s, when Uruguayan democracy had just been recuperated, which meant a window of opportunity for policy innovation in higher education. His proposal goes in the direction of minimizing the role of the public university in knowledge production. Filgueira is well aware of the destructive role of the dictatorship, which is a point of departure of his analysis and a feature of his own lived experience. It is significant that instead of arguing for a full recovery of UdelaR, the author places the blame for the previous backwardness of the social sciences on the public university and embraces, for all intents and purposes, an organizational model imposed, intentionally or not, by the dictatorship.

To be sure, from the 1960s to the 1980s, the mutation of the academic landscape would be quite remarkable: it moved from a general stance of firm rejection of external funds for ideological reasons to a situation in which 50% of the PRCs' funding was provided by international institutions (Prates, 1987, p. 50). The lack of any critical or more balanced reflection about the problematic aspects of this transformation in the literature seems rather striking, and, I would add, runs parallel to (or, better yet, is intertwined with) the lack of critical thinking concerning the *visceral rejection* of Marxism that would subsequently take hold within the social sciences, and in PS particularly.

The aforementioned shift within the governmentality of academia had significant intellectual consequences. During the dictatorship, these centers were always under suspicion and therefore self-censorship was common (U4; U15). This "training" in self-disciplining can be, for interpretive purposes, projected into the future. Conversely, if Carlos Filgueira—as stated to me in the course of the interviews—"saved two generations of scholars" and social sciences in general (U15), it is because he was not prevented from doing so by the far-right dictatorship. The reason why is clear: the kind of social science that he practiced and promoted was not perceived as a threat, and perhaps even fit in with a disciplined society devoid of "ideologisms."[24]

As mentioned earlier, Markarián (2015) argues that the dictatorship seemed to have aimed for a more technical or practical form of knowledge within the university. Paradoxically, this was achieved by the PRCs. In practice, social sciences would become what Carlos Filgueira thought they were and *should* be: "la penosa descripción de lo obvio" [the pathetic description of the obvious] (U15), a merely *useful* empirical type of knowledge. Probably the dictatorship could approve of such an atheorical and acritical type of social science.

If depoliticization was functional to the dictatorship, why would it disapprove of a "useful" type of knowledge production? After all, the forging of a non-ideological social science represented a shift in the direction of both the professionalization *and* the disciplining of intellectuals. To be sure, in the hearts and minds of many practitioners, what they were doing at the PRCs during the dictatorship was resisting. Be that as it may, a highly empiricist and anti-critical theory version of the social sciences became dominant in Uruguay in this period.[25]

According to de Sierra (2005), during the dictatorship, "the issues analyzed did change, as did the discursive contexts, predominant ideologies and explicit political referents but the conceptual core of the situation remained basically as it had been before the coup" (p. 493). But if the issues, discourses, ideologies, and political referents changed, it is hardly likely that the conceptual core of "the situation" could remain unchanged. Note, however, that the author himself qualifies that intriguing phrase when proposing, in the same article, that an epistemology of radical "asepsis" became dominant in those years. That kind of epistemology is best understood as part and parcel of the process "of detoxification from Marxism" (U5), which would be completed during the transition,

when, in the words of one of my interviewees, political scientists would defini-
tively escape "the Marxist Church" (U7).

Some firm steps in the direction of the hegemony of objectivity and liberalism—
or toward the representation of liberalism as the objective idiom—were taken
in this period. While persecution, torture, and exile taught scholars about the
importance of the so-called rule of law, those who could work at PRCs learned
about the imperatives of objective science. Indeed, the kind of reactivation of
social science that the PRCs performed goes well with the language of liberalism and the celebration of liberal democracy—this was the "great discovery" of
the transition. The renewed (i.e., non-ideological) social sciences were ready to
contribute to the restoration of liberal citizenship and governmentality in post-
authoritarian Uruguay, a role that PS would extend and improve. Prates (1987,
p. 33), for instance, details the PRCs' active participation in CONAPRO (the
Programmatic National Commission), a multi-sectorial space to discuss the
transition to democracy, while Pérez Antón (1992, p. 56) emphasizes the collaboration between social scientists and political parties in this period.

While the institutional horizon of basing social science on the PRCs' structure
and political economy disappeared after the intervened university recovered its
formal autonomy,[26] the major ideological and epistemological shifts unleashed
during—and through—the dictatorship years seem to have consolidated in the
past three decades. The type of social science that emerged may be read as a victory for the US-led project of dismantling socialist politics and delegitimizing
the radical left as an acceptable epistemological base for thinking politics in the
process.

What happened after the dictatorship in Uruguay as far as "thinking politics" as an academic endeavor is concerned? As one interviewee put it, it meant
"exiting Marxism, going back to reality" (U5). I was struck by the unexpected
similarity between that statement from a Uruguayan political scientist who self-
defined as a liberal democrat and Yrarrázaval (1979), who, from an extreme
neoconservative view, describes Marxism as a simulation of reality. Years
before interviewing U5, as an undergraduate student in the early 2000s, I had
been intrigued and shocked by the radical and all-encompassing rejection of
Marxism by most of my professors in Uruguay.

In the section that follows, I intend to show how these transformations played
out. I will do so by examining the forging of PS identity in Uruguay, paying
special attention to its ideological dimensions.

The Limits of Pluralism: Identity Building, Epistemological Policing, and the Shadows of Marx

The academic experience during the transition was framed by a public university
devastated by the dictatorship (U12; U13; U15; U18; U21; among others). Many
of the stories that I collected situated the university and academia as a lived

experience in this particular historical context. Several interviewees referred to the years of democratic transition as marked by severe material scarcity and as a veritable "institutional mess." The latter explains why it seemed that almost everything needed to be done "from scratch" in quite literal terms (U12; U13; U21). I find the following testimony revelatory and in its own way moving:

> [Name of person omitted] and U21. . . those guys were there for whatever the ICP needed. If you had to steal a table from the law school because we did not have any, we were ready . . . [Names omitted], U21 and myself. There is a famous episode from the early days of the ICP that someday we should recreate: when we stole a desk for the [Institute's] Director. We stole my desk from the law school and we carried it along Frugoni Street. At some point the Dean saw us from his car and screamed at us while we were running with the damn desk!
>
> *(U13)*

Another interviewee—one of the participants in the episode (U12)—also remembered how angry the Dean was. But in his memory, what was stolen were a couple of doors *to make* a desk. In both versions, the anecdote is both slightly ridiculous and heroic: it shows, in a funny way, the effort of the pioneers in building the discipline. The fact that PS did not even have a desk for the director of the nascent Institute of Political Science speaks to the state of disarray in which the dictatorship had left the public university. But perhaps most importantly, it also speaks to the lack of academic legitimacy of PS *vis-à-vis* the law profession at the time. After all, the directors of the School of Law did have a desk—and some to spare . . . otherwise, the desk in the anecdote could not have been stolen in the first place. It is interesting to note in this regard that one of the earliest BA students of political science at UdelaR refers to the days when the program, originally hosted by the university's law school, did not even have permanent classrooms to hold classes (Altamiranda, 2009).

In the words of the founding Director of the ICP, one of the protagonists of the desk hunting anecdote, the birth of the ICP "was done like a nest with sticks stolen from everywhere. It was amazing!" (U13). Clearly, there was no stealing in the literal sense. And, to be sure, the story does not imply a real robbery. Rather, it portrays an ad hoc and unauthorized re-allocation of a very basic resource from an office with a surplus to another with none.

There are a couple of points to highlight here: first, U13 refers to "the Director's desk" and immediately afterwards, to "my desk." Besides the intention behind this gesture, U13 has a clear institutional orientation and a long-term vision. As an institution-builder, he can see the process in detached terms. Second, the very unlikely idea of "recreating" this episode in an amateur play of some sort, speaks to the perceived need to narrate local PS history to the younger generations as a way of reassuring the identity of the discipline. I will come back to the issue of the protection and narration of identity later, about which U13 also has an interesting and distanced perception, even though he was a key protagonist in the militant rejection of "sociologism" and even sociology as such within PS. An additional point should be added: the anecdote does not solely portray a kind of desperate attempt to equip the director's office with something as elementary as a desk. More importantly, the desk incident was emblematic of a pioneer's resolve to build an institution—as well as an institutional identity— out of whatever resources could be made available.

The resources "from everywhere" were material as well as intellectual. To be sure, the pioneers had different disciplinary backgrounds (U19). The phrase "a political science almost without political scientists" (U1) says it all. The question is, how was it possible to forge PS under these conditions? I find this issue particularly interesting: how could an interior be built from "the outside"? That is, how could any semblance of a defined identity be built on the basis of scarce resources and with people who came from outside the discipline? How were the needs of incorporation and the urge for exclusion woven? It seems that the *lack* that marked the initial situation of PS was compensated for with an assertive identity discourse that strived for the discipline's growth—and, paradoxically, policed its boundaries. Narratives and memories are key in this regard: while they reconstruct the past, they also do work in securing PS, and in so doing, exercise the politics of political science.

The institutional precariousness shown in the preceding paragraphs coupled with the transition to democracy are the two markers of the birth of PS in Uruguay (Buquet, 2012; de Sierra, 2005; Garcé, 2005; Pérez Antón, 1986). Both markers are closely intertwined. The urge for institutional and disciplinary assertiveness was also fueled by ideology. The PS narrative radicalized the ideological mutations that we noted with the PRCs. As the discipline's identity was being forged, objectivity as science and liberalism as politics became signs of the new times.

Embracing the New Times—and "Reality"

I am interested in the analytical power of details and gestures, and their implications for social research (Dauphinee, 2013a, 2013b; Geertz, 1997). Aggregated data and nomothetic attempts risk erasing *the experience of meaning*. Let me mobilize this theoretical statement through a concrete example. It may be recalled from the previous section that Filgueira (1974) had described pre-coup Uruguayan academia as both "parochial" and "ideologically narrow," to the point of rejecting any collaboration with international institutions. Accused of being "an agent of imperialism" due to his ties with the Ford Foundation (U7; U13), Filgueira had experienced this "narrowness" first hand; there were others who could make the same claim (U10). Before the coup, some of the future founders of the ICP participated in a sort of popular trial against him that involved a public statement of condemnation. Upon his return to Uruguay, one of the first things U13 did as an ICP director was to apologize to Filgueira. In his words:

U13: There were also acts of mea culpa. One of the first things I did when I returned to Uruguay was to apologize to Carlitos Filgueira. He ranked first in a contest at the Institute of Sociology in 1970. We [the student body] publicly shamed him, because he had ties with the Ford Foundation. Of course, during and after the dictatorship *everybody worked for the Ford, Rockefeller, and other foundations* that kept the little candle's flame alive. This episode [of repentance] took place in a context of vindication of democracy, pluralism, and political parties . . . the traditional political parties and the party system.[27]

PR: So it was a sort of critique of the critique of the system.

U13: Exactly! Exactly!

This act of "mea culpa" stands as a powerful and complex fragment of experience. It shows how two academic biographies, inextricable from the political life of the country, intersect at two different points that delineate a collective trajectory. This micro-experience reveals much more than just a strong sense of *guilt* around Filgueira's treatment. The narration embodies the prevailing discourse around the wrongs of the left. To be sure, both during the transition and after, leftist "illiberal" and "anti-democratic" views and practices were seen by the media and the political establishment as at least partially responsible for the political polarization that destroyed Uruguayan democracy in 1973. This accusation included the social sciences and social scientists, massively identified with the left (U1; U3; U6; U7; U10; U12; U13; U14; U17; U18; U22).

PS tries to undo the path that connects social science and leftist ideology. Given that the discipline was born as a pro-systemic creature that embraces stability, order, and the rule of law from the very beginning, it is only natural for Marxism to be seen as narrow-minded, dated, and even dangerous, as needing to be expelled from the realm of acceptability. Furthermore, taking distance from Marxism and radical politics was also a way of legitimizing PS *vis-à-vis* the traditional political parties, which in a party-centric society (Caetano, Pérez Antón, & Rilla, 1987) have a powerful capacity to regulate public conversation.

The Autonomy of Politics and the Limits of Academic Pluralism

It has been argued that the ICP was a plural space from its inception (Rocha Carpiuc, 2012a, 2012b; Garcé, 2005). Garcé's exultant description of the intellectual forging of the institute is illustrative. In his words: "A very important achievement of his [the director's] administration has been to assemble [haber amalgamado] different political, ideological, and theoretical tendencies, stimulating the formation of a plural environment [that was] highly beneficial for academic debate and learning" (Garcé, 2005, p. 237).[28]

This plurality was a tangible reality at different levels. The institute's pioneers came from different disciplinary backgrounds (history and sociology, in the main), studied and worked in different countries, and had diverse professional trajectories (U12; U13; U18). Furthermore, no single theory or set of theories were imposed on research and in the classroom. Multiple testimonies and analyses concur about the absence of any overt intellectual policing of any kind (Garcé, 2005)—and, I may add, my own experience as an undergraduate student at ICP bears witness to this kind of intellectual openness. Nevertheless, the institute's academic comfort zone has been built on the basis of some conspicuous exclusions, casting a shadow on the depth and scope of its purported pluralism.

Figure 3.2 provides elements with which to grasp the dominant conception of the political realm in *Revista Uruguaya de Ciencia Política*, the ICP's journal: topics covered by the journal are, first and foremost, political parties and party politics, to which was added public policy in the 2000s (Buquet, 2012; Garcé & Rocha Carpiuc, 2015; Bentancur & Mancebo, 2013). The insignificant presence of non-mainstream authors and alternative views is striking. Taking this as a guideline, the reader would be led to believe that partisan politics, elections, and public policy are the sole protagonists of politics. This is consistent with Table 3.1, which presents the most cited authors. On the whole, then, the *RUCP* tends to publish articles that have a narrow and elitist perspective of politics to the exclusion of articles on other aspects of the political (grassroots movements in particular). Figure 3.3 confirms that a narrow conception of politics (basically, government and political parties) prevails (for an explanation of the construction of this variable, see Appendix A). I will expand on this later.

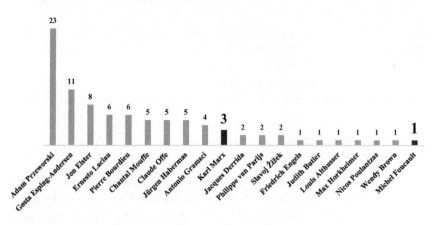

FIGURE 3.2 "Critical" authors cited in *RUCP*, 1987–2012

TABLE 3.1 "Popular" authors in *RUCP*, 1987–2012

Most cited authors	Number of citations
Lanzaro	47
Sartori	46
Mainwaring	45
Buquet	39
Caetano	38
Lijphart	35
O'Donnell	35

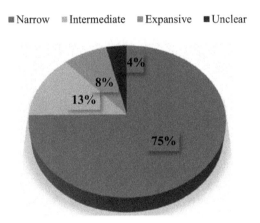

■ Narrow　▨ Intermediate　■ Expansive　■ Unclear

4%
8%
13%
75%

FIGURE 3.3　Conception of the political in "spatial" terms in *RUCP*, 1987–2012

Meanwhile, Uruguayan PS has ignored, almost completely, Marxism, neo-Marxism, and critical theory of *any* kind throughout its trajectory—a reality that was crystal clear at the time of completion of my fieldwork (Ravecca, 2014). This remains the case even though the topics covered by the journal has expanded in the last few years with the publishing of a special issue on feminism (in 2014, though entirely focused on government and its institutions), another one on ideas, discourse, and politics (in 2015), and one article on disability studies (Castro, 2018); in 2017, most of the 15 articles published belong to conventional PS.

Marx has been ignored, even from the point of view of the history of ideas. The consensus around such an indifference is overwhelming (U1; U2; U3; U4; U5; U6; U7; U9; U10; U11; U12; U13; U14; U15; U16; U17; U18; U19; U20; U21; U22).[29] In contrast with the cases of Alexis de Tocqueville and John Locke, for instance, there is not a single *RUCP* article that addresses Marxist theory as its main theme (see Figure 3.4). Furthermore, contemporary critical

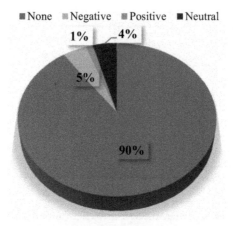

FIGURE 3.4 View of Marxism in *RUCP*, 1987–2012

thought has not been included either, as we can see in Figure 3.2. Marx has been quoted three times in the entire history of the journal; Michel Foucault once. In terms of theory, the *RUCP* seems to have been more welcoming for the tradition of analytical philosophy. More generally, Figure 3.2 shows the marginality of critical political theory in Uruguayan PS.

Given the overwhelming consensus around the strong connection between the social sciences and the left in the 1960s and early 1970s (U1; U15), the almost absolute absence of Marxism (including neo- and post-Marxism) in the *RUCP* is striking. Communism as a historical reality has not been addressed either, even though the *RUCP*'s first issues were contemporary with the agonizing years of the Soviet Union (see Figures 3.5 and 3.6).

In what constitutes a sharply dissimilar power-knowledge formation and ideological timing from the one shown for APS in the preceding chapter, such an indifference needs to be situated within an academia that looks inwards *and* a liberal discourse that despises communism without embracing anti-communist narratives. The point is worth elaborating. Uruguayan PS is a creature of the transition to democracy that was forged by scholars (leftists, moderates, as well as the democratic right) who unanimously opposed the dictatorship (U1; U2; U3; U4; U5; U6; U7; U8; U9; U10; U11; U12; U13; U14; U15; U16; U17; U18; U19; U20; U21; U22). Protected democracy is consequently absent in the *RUCP*: Uruguayan PS is fully polyarchic (see Figure 3.7). And, in the words of one of the interviewees, "Marxism, from the perspective of the polyarchy, is idiotic" (U17).

The Cold War framed PS in both Chile and Uruguay, but in different ways. In Chile, PS was *cultivated* (not denied) by the dictatorship, so the enemies of the regime had to be addressed. Uruguayan PS was born within and for liberal

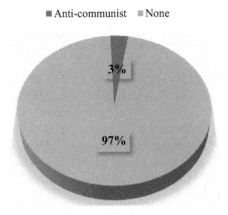

FIGURE 3.5 View of communism in *RUCP*, 1987–2012

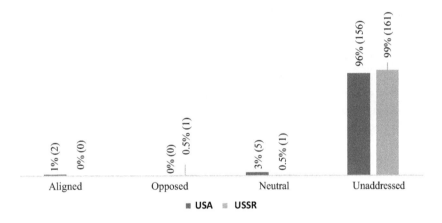

FIGURE 3.6 Position toward the US and the USSR in *RUCP*, 1987–2012

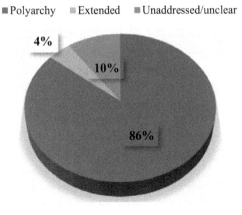

FIGURE 3.7 Type of democracy promoted in *RUCP*, 1987–2012

democracy in the context of the intellectual and political collapse of socialism. There was no need to talk about communism, a topic that actually—and perhaps inconveniently—reminded some political scientists of their self-perceived anti-democratic beliefs of not too long ago.

In hindsight, the resulting architecture of the field had a serious drawback. If explanations for political processes should be sought in the political system in Sartori's sense (1984), in terms of what the political system does or does not do, then the rudimentary conception of the autonomy of politics implicated in this narrative maneuver also narrowed the pluralism celebrated by Garcé (2005). For all intents and purposes, the boundaries of this logic (that is, that the study of politics is the study of the political system) have operated as a principle of regulation of PS' pluralism. Everyone is welcome as long as he or she adjusts to this norm, which is what permits the separation of political science from sociology, with the latter being equated to Marxism and radical politics.

If during my years as an undergraduate student I was disturbed by the dogmatic and uninformed disdain for Marxism that many of my professors transmitted in the classrooms, I was also intrigued by the conceptual easiness displayed by academics in conferences and other academic spaces when they declared, without any sense of complexity, that the development of PS was possible *because* socio-centric theories, such as Marxism, had been abandoned. What was most striking to me was not the existence of such narratives, but that nobody seemed to be bothered by them, with the exception of a few students who sensed that mainstream PS was concealing important questions about power and political life.

If, as posed at the outset of this study, epistemological, theoretical, and political changes are part and parcel of human experience, and ideological transformations have an experiential and biographical dimension, it follows that the transitions from Marxism to liberalism and from sociology to political science in Uruguay from the 1960s to the 1990s have been interwoven with the fabric of scholars' lives. Hence, it is useful to go back to and expand on the point about the interconnection between subjectivity, epistemology, politics, and the global political arena (Agathangelou, 2004; Brigg & Bleiker, 2010; Dauphinee, 2013a, 2013b; Löwenheim, 2010). I will thus now turn to discourse (Foucault, 1991a; Said, 2003) and language (Laclau & Mouffe, 2004), always conceptualized in terms of their role on truth formation, identity building, and power, but in the register of the subjective, personal, and testimonial (Butalia, 2000). First, let me elaborate more on the connection between trauma, language, and the identity of the discipline.

From the beginning of this book, I understood the social sciences *as* human activity in the very basic sense of Marx. PS is a space of human action and interaction. That is, the discipline has its own social life, and is at the same time part of broader social life. Therefore, the theories and ideologies of scholars and intellectuals are *also* historical and biographical entities. We also know that time, memory, and subjectivity are milieus where domination and resistance are manifested (Alexander, 2005; Edkins, 2003; Fleming, 2005; Marcuse, 1974). If we put these insights to work together, the result is that: (*a*) social sciences are not exterior to power relations, and (*b*) the memories and subjectivities of scholars have a role in their scholarship and its changes, especially in the case of social sciences, where we study dynamics in which we are heavily involved. Scholarship is made by the *subjects* of social reality: scholarship, as a human activity, is affected by its *object* (which is also human activity). This is not only an epistemological insight but also a political perspective with significant implications for understanding the politics of academic knowledge and PS in particular. What does this mean for the case under study?

The *coup d'état* in general and the persecution of intellectuals in particular constituted traumatic experiences for scholars—and for scholarship as well. At the time of the dictatorship, academic life revolved heavily around the University of the Republic. And, as a major component of the infrastructures of dissent, the university was directly targeted by a dictatorship bent on dismantling them. The story has two key elements of trauma (Edkins, 2003; Giorgi, 1995; Kellermann, 2001; LaCapra, 2009; Sneh & Cosaka, 2000): there is (*a*) a moment of unprecedented and unexpected violence, a brutal exercise of force that hurt students, scholars, and intellectuals. Some of them were already adults and heavily involved in left-wing politics, while others were youngsters who went through the dictatorship as young adults. Both groups suffered the dictatorship at different levels and in diverse ways; (*b*) a mainstream and hegemonic narrative—promoted by influential politicians—both during and after the dictatorship that blamed radical politics, which included students, scholars, and intellectuals, for the fall of democracy. The issue of language here is key: within the dominant narrative, both the left wing and the military appear as equally responsible for the coup. In short, the university community, so the narrative goes, was responsible for its own sorrows.

A self-directed guilt located Marxism and its theoretical surroundings as politically and conceptually *wrong* and therefore they had to be expelled as far as possible. This trauma was instrumental for the separation from sociology. The emotional intensity of the representations of Marxism through images laced with derogatory adjectives speak of something more than just an intellectual shift—perhaps because intellectual changes are never *just* that. They seem to reveal the tremendous impact of historical experience on scholars' views: "swindler," "untrustworthy," "shameful," "ridiculous," "dogmatic," "Church," "mocked," "expiated guilt," "crude," "repented," "obsolete," "precarious," "anti-science," "toxic," "erased," "despicable," "stupid," "idiotic," "a path that I interrupted forever," "I threw it in the garbage," "shit," "crisis," "mea culpa" (U1; U5; U7; U10; U13; U15; U16; U17; U18; U20; U21; U22).

It would be difficult to measure the relative weight of the collapse of the Soviet Union and the effect of the dictatorship in this process of ideological shift; both appear prominently in the interviews. Besides, I am not particularly interested in such a positivist procedure. My aim is to craft a vocabulary to navigate the complexity of this story. I find it more fruitful to situate the dictatorship and the fall of the Soviet Union as components in a series of interlocked factors, both internal and external—a complex relationality—that affected scholars' subjectivities and views. Academic transformations are a nodal point in the larger, multidimensional transformation that the country and the region experienced.

This process had concrete effects on the lived experience of scholarship. Indeed, colleagues with a Marxist and neo-Marxist background had to negotiate their professional space within a new—and considerably more difficult—environment. In the words of one interviewee: "Some of us were forced to unlearn much of what we knew" (U1). As a new scholar at the time of the transition, U1 had to change his research topic because his theoretical views were perceived as unacceptable within the field of political parties and government, which was the mainstream area of research of the discipline in the 1990s (Buquet, 2012; Rocha Carpiuc, 2012a). U17, the only scholar singled out in many interviews as a neo-Marxist, experienced a feeling of inadequacy both in research and in teaching at the MA level in particular. He characterized some of his colleagues as "aggressive liberals" and recalled some "violent" exchanges with students (scholars identified as Uruguayan "big names" today) in which they asked him not to teach those "dated" theories anymore. "I threw all of that in the garbage," he concludes. At the time of the interview, he described his situation as "extremely depressing" and thus detrimental to his academic productivity. This rejection or embarrassed "escaping" (U7) denotes trauma at the ideological level. And it exceeds the experience of single individuals, shaping power relations within the field of Uruguayan PS.

In the course of the interviews, these kinds of transits were not described or experienced as gradual and meditated changes, but as violent rupture: as an *act* perpetrated with words through which the *other*, in this case the beliefs of the past, are completely dismissed. I am not suggesting that these scholars are individually traumatized. I am not a psychologist. The point lies elsewhere: for interpretive purposes, the category of trauma lends itself to productively frame the impact of the dictatorship on the narratives that shaped the birth and development of PS in Uruguay in subsequent decades. The traumatic dimension of the dictatorship had intellectual manifestations and consequences for the way in which PS was born and developed during the transition and beyond. This constitutive component of the discipline cannot be captured by solely focusing on the institutional history of PS. Scholars' subjectivity is a crucial component of PS' complex relationality.

This note on subjectivity, complex relationality and the abandonment of Marxism should not end without raising the question: How strong was Marxism actually in the late sixties? And what does strong mean in that specific context and point in time? Clearly, Marxist politics were salient in academia.

However, the intellectual referents of the left at the time seem to have belonged to the political parties. Indeed, Marxist scholarship does not seem to have been abundant. According to a testimonial account, academic Marxism in Uruguay was "weak." That is, they (i.e., the Marxists) did not create a school of thought or a tradition (U19). The "weakness of Marxism's scholarly and institutional implantation" explains why it was relatively easily displaced (U19). For U12, the political discussion was regulated by Marxist categories, and scholars were simply immersed in that environment. This is corroborated by U8, the academic who taught PS during the dictatorship: the regime, in his view, persecuted leftists, not theories.

Interestingly enough, it seems that the party-centric theory about Uruguay works well once again (Caetano et al., 1987). This partisan form of Marxism only needed to be inverted to become dogmatic liberalism (U12). The academic weakness of Marxism problematizes the narrative that identifies this school of thought as the main obstacle to the emergence of PS. It was Uruguayan society and its socio-political dynamics that, during the 1960s, politicized knowledge in the plainest sense of the term. The source of the "problem" was beyond academia. It is not surprising, given their power and legitimacy for framing collective thinking, that the traditional political parties would ultimately manage to impose their interpretation(s) of reality (including that the left was guilty for the coup). The lack of academic density of Uruguayan Marxism made it vulnerable to partisan debacles: and that is what happened.

In the end, the dictatorship successfully obliterated socialism as a political horizon and pushed scholars to bury radical politics and Marxism. Interestingly, they literally did so, sometimes, as a way of keeping them alive.

U15: We did read Marxism during the dictatorship, but we had to dig the books up because they were buried . . . so we read from very wet and deteriorated books!

PR: Dig them up?

U15: Yes, we somehow got a bunch of books such as *Capital, The Economic and Philosophical Manuscripts*, and *The Eighteenth Brumaire* through a senior researcher, but they were buried in the backyard of his house. So, we had to go there and dig them up. We read them . . . it was a very thin paper with silk texture. They were really wet!

Another scholar mentioned that he mostly reads and sees the world from a critical theory perspective, but that he does not engage with it in any way in his writing today. I could see his discomfort during, and because of, the interview. He was angry at something. It seems that it is hard to write—to think—when you bury authors.

In the following section, I explore how, and with what consequences, a remarkable Uruguayan intellectual, Carlos Real de Azúa, has been enthroned as *the* pioneer of contemporary Uruguayan PS. Through this worshiping, the complexity of his *oeuvre* has been avoided, even erased, and a particular version of the discipline has been promoted. The mainstreaming and appropriation of Real de Azúa is thus an operation of interest to understand PPS and the knowledge-power dynamics of the forging of the discipline in Uruguay.

Appropriating Carlos Real de Azúa: Teleology and Destiny

In a move that mimics the narratives that singularize Machiavelli as the founder of modern PS in the so-called Western world, Carlos Real de Azúa (1916–1977) is praised for fully acknowledging the specificity of politics (Aguiar, 1984) in the context of Uruguayan academia. Since Real de Azúa, one of the most acclaimed Uruguayan intellectuals of the 20th century (Mallo, 2011),[30] has been widely regarded as the predecessor, or even the founder, of PS in the country (Aguiar, 1984; Buquet, 2012; Garcé, 2005; González, 2007; Pérez Antón, 1986, 1992; Ravecca, 2014), it seems warranted to examine how he has been read and appropriated by the narratives of disciplinary identity-building.

Since the mid-1980s to this day, the practitioners of Uruguayan PS have unfailingly kept Carlos Real de Azúa's presence alive. The following are just some examples. An early text on the development of political science in Uruguay devotes an entire section to "The Foundational *Oeuvre* of Real de Azúa" (Pérez Antón, 1986, p. 228). The title of an academic event celebrating the intellectual's legacy held in 2001 was a reminder in itself: "Carlos Real de Azúa: A Pioneer of Political Science in Uruguay."[31] In 2007, the Centro Latinoamericano de Economía Humana [Latin American Centre for Human Economy] (CLAEH) organized a colloquium on Real de Azúa's life and work featuring the participation of a prominent Argentine historian, Tulio Halperin Donghi (1926–2014), where I contributed as a discussant.[32] On March 15, 2016, a roundtable celebrated the "First 100th Anniversary" of Real de Azúa, and on December 15, 2017, historian José Rilla presented a paper exploring his engagement with Spain and its political ventures.

An article published in 1984 shows that the central place attributed to Real de Azúa was framed early on. But how was it framed? César Aguiar's "Notes on Real de Azúa and Political Science in Uruguay" (1984) links the birth of PS to the work of Real de Azúa as follows: "There has not been an inventory made of PS in the country (in fact, there is not much to make an inventory of). But with justice and certainty we can assert that PS in Uruguay could not exist without Real de Azúa" (p. 5). The emphasis is put on Real de Azúa's alleged rejection of Marxism's anti-political reductionisms. One of the main merits of Real de Azúa, so the argument goes, was to acknowledge that the political system has its own logic and rules. Politics cannot be reduced to the social: "Something similar to what Althusser and Poulantzas, who would probably be dismissed by Real de Azúa's intellectual style and greatness, failed to explain when they talk about 'relative autonomy'" (p. 3).[33] Once again, this time invoking Real de Azúa's "intellectual style and greatness" as source of legitimation, PS' identity is placed—or made to reside—on a version of the notion of the autonomy of politics that expels Marxism (and in this case also neo-Marxism) as a sensible academic perspective.

The framing of Real de Azúa's place in/for PS resorts to other operations as well. Some identify "PS moments" within Real de Azúa's trajectory, in a curious effort to separate them from other moments of his work, which (sadly, one could add with irony) were mostly grounded in sociology and the humanities. The narrative is subtle, but, when fully unfolded, it becomes clear that Real de Azúa went through a teleological journey toward PS: "In his intellectual history, Real de Azúa went through a focus on literature to a focus on political science" (Aguiar, 1984, p. 4). Others refer to his transition from historical sociology to political science (Pérez Antón, 1992, p. 46; Pérez Antón, 1986, pp. 228–229). The idea is constant: that Real de Azúa has overcome something else (literature, sociology), to reach a new (and better) intellectual stage—i.e., our discipline— and that such a journey is parallel to the transition that Uruguayan academia went through from *ensayismo* [roughly, essayism] to science (more on this below).

While I do not intend to evaluate the accuracy of these kinds of accounts, in closing this subsection, I will add a couple of complicating notes. First, in contrast with PS narrative, Uruguay's internationally celebrated literary critic and scholar Angel Rama (1926–1983) held the view that Real de Azúa was "first, a literary critic and literature professor that, as time went by, *became a critic of culture, of thought, and* that which Mexicans name with the ugly word *politólogo* [political scientist]" (Rama, 1977, p. 3; emphasis mine). In other words, PS was never alone in Real de Azúa's repertoire. Second, an essay written just before Real de Azúa's death in 1977 and posthumously published in 1983 is quite far from offering a PS perspective, at least *not* in the mainstream sense: indeed, a reflection entitled "The World Euro-Center-Periphery Cleavage and the Excepted Areas, 1500–1900," where the object of study is different development paths from an interdisciplinary perspective, hardly could.

What matters here is how Real de Azúa, who defined himself as "a specialist on generalities," is appropriated and mobilized to manufacture PS identity.[34] The narrative operation sets aside and dismisses his complex form of writing to overemphasize his rejection of Marxism and underemphasize his later commitment with the left—as well as his interdisciplinary vocation. In the name of politics and its autonomy, this form of discursive identity regulation produces, to some extent, a fictional Real de Azúa. This reminds me of how families and nation-states administer selfhood through essentializing tales and linear time sequences that erase contingency and the accidental dimension of collective history (Butler & Spivak, 2010; Edkins, 2003; Buck-Morss, 2009).

In a beautiful and nuanced text about Latin American political theory, Real de Azúa problematizes "the urge for the immediate and 'drastic' use of the social sciences" and the notion of science itself "as a missile to be hurled at some enemy" (Real de Azúa, 1973, para. 21; Mallo, 2011, p. 182). Real de Azúa was critical of activist versions of the intellectual endeavor and thus also of the instrumentalization of thought for immediate political purposes. In his view, and this formulation is in my opinion superb, the social sciences are a weapon for the "liberation of Man" *and* also for "*the liberation of/from the partial libera-tions*" (Real de Azúa, 1973, para. 24, emphasis mine). To be sure, though with a much smaller readership and fame, Real de Azúa argued before Judith Butler that theoretical interrogation should not be stopped in the name of action, secu-rity, or justice. "Partial liberations" should also be critiqued in order to prevent them from becoming *total* oppressions, especially given that, as Butler notes, oppression names itself as its other (Butler, Laclau, & Zizek, 2003).

The reification and simplification of alternative perspectives, Marxism included, is foreign to Carlos Real de Azúa's impressive intellectual openness. His version of the political realm attests to that openness. In the text cited above, he argued that Latin Americans were in a privileged position for combining dif-ferent intellectual traditions—including Marxism (Real de Azúa, 1973). In this regard, and keeping in mind my reading of the dictatorship developed in previ-ous sections, I cannot avoid quoting extensively the following fragment written in the early days of the dictatorship. In these lines, Real de Azúa's perspective on the Uruguayan plight at the time leaves no doubt as to how he views the contribution of Marxism *vis-à-vis* other approaches to understanding politics:

> If you allow me a *confidence* even more confessional than what I have said until now, I will say that I am a citizen of a nation that in less than four years went from a system of coalitions and equilibrium at various social levels; from government action that respected legality and all individual rights; from the hegemony of a middle class political personnel trained in the everyday exercise of different forms of compromise . . . we went from a nation with all these features to an opposite system of a practically auto-cratic imposition, illegality and limitless repression executed by a bunch of government agents—military members, big bankers, land owners—who one day stormed the roles and functions they—as a collective—had been foreign to until then. If we take a look at this picture—unsophisticated but, I believe, essentially accurate—*we can suspect that the Marxist insights about social domination, the relationship between economic and political power, class antagonisms, the effect of money over politics, and democ-racy as a mere appearance that vanishes because of social pressures are useful. They have been more useful than the behaviorist and functionalist typologies and models in order to understand what has happened in my and everyone's surroundings.*
>
> *(1973, para. 44; emphasis mine)*

The quote brings to mind Filgueira (1974), a scholar far from being identified with the left, and his observation regarding the role of the economic elites and the benefits they attained during the dictatorship (a topic which has by now acquired a body of published research but is not said enough in Uruguayan PS classrooms and texts). These are intellectual and political moments erased by the mainstream narrative because within Uruguayan PS ignoring *social* classes became a mandate—a constitutive moment of who "we" are supposed to be. There are other things that get erased too.

At the book launch of Susana Mallo's *Carlos Real de Azúa: Un Intelectual Inasible* [Carlos Real de Azúa: An Inapprehensible Intellectual] (2011), one of the panelists, Uruguayan cultural critic Hugo Achugar, challenged the sharp distinction that mainstream academia today draws between *ensayismo* and science. This distinction is worth commenting upon for present purposes, albeit briefly.

If *ensayo* [an essay] refers to a piece that proposes a reflection about an issue, then *ensayismo* refers to a style of writing that has been very present among intellectuals in Latin America. However, in the past few decades, and among practitioners of the social sciences throughout the region including Uruguay, *ensayo* has become a derogatory term to name an unscientific form of knowledge that is not based on research. Throughout the interviews, the notion of *ensayo* operated as a volatile category, or floating signifier (Laclau & Mouffe, 2004), to disqualify the intellectual production of others. The notion was mobilized in extremely different ways and with different targets; interestingly, the "accuser" often turned out to be "the accused" on different occasions.

It is revealing that the only colleagues who were not named as *ensayistas* (i.e., those who write *ensayos*) by anyone were the specialists on political parties who base their research on quantitative methods and rational choice institutionalism—that is, the most mainstream group. In contrast, this group considers everyone else (i.e., the colleagues who work on public policy, history, and political theory) as *ensayistas*. The research on public policy was described by one interviewee as descriptive "*ensayismo*," later on adding that "when they explain anything they have a sociological hypothesis. . . . There is no academia here; you can caption this interview this way: this [i.e., the ICP] is not academia" (U13). The problem of disqualifying narratives is widespread. Indeed, the need for an evil or inferior otherness has been a very consistent finding throughout my research. All of my interviewees are sophisticated people, and yet, it seems that the building of the academic self needs to be done in antagonistic ways (Ravecca & Dauphinee, 2018). The other is permanently thought of as a threat: in academia, policing and securitization are prominent (Marcuse, 1991). In the impoverishing and divisive dialectics of *ensayismo*, a very conservative notion of science wins. It is really the voice of the master that speaks and rejoices in the self-hatred and the false consciousness of the subaltern—the non-mainstream scholar.

Ensayismo is seen as an underdeveloped form of knowledge. This narrative opposes Latin America (and to some extent continental Europe) to the allegedly more advanced US, where academics do not write *ensayos*. Global politics, writing, and epistemology meet again. It is particularly interesting the role that the unilateral representation of US academia plays in the use of the accusatory term *ensayismo*, as tool to locate oneself in the hierarchy of knowledge. This is remarkable in a generation that followed the pioneers. Scientism would become aggressive in the academic community, especially in PS (see, for instance, Buquet, Chasquetti, & Moraes, 1998). The generational ruptures that are part and parcel of the social sciences were, in this case, mostly methodological. The generational crusade never presented itself as ideological. It did not have to. The most salient members of the second generation of mainstream PS scholars, who achieved prominence in the late 1990s and early 2000s, did not challenge the older generation (i.e., the pioneers) at the ideological level—liberalism still reigns today—but they radicalized the notion of the autonomy of politics, worshiped methodology, and even concrete methods (statistics in particular).

Real de Azúa has been symbolically consumed by narratives that, while enthroning him as the first political scientist in Uruguay, deny his embrace of complexity and interdisciplinarity. For him to become the father of PS, it was necessary to "unwrite" his *ensayismo*, his political involvement, and, in the words of Hugo Achugar, his "baroque" style of thinking (Asuntos Públicos, 2011).

Real de Azúa has been unwritten in another way. He was gay, and I think that matters. *The father of Uruguayan PS was queer.* What kinds of meanings can be found in *that*? I wonder how his internal struggles between, for instance, his Catholic background, the hostile environment toward "homosexuals," and his sexuality played out in his intellectual ruminations. This is also a story of writing masculine epistemologies on a queer-erased body (of life and of writing). The way he wrote and the way he was read were shaped by homophobia. Until recently, in events and in texts on Real de Azúa, the issue was elusively referred to. While reducing someone's writing to his sexuality would be reductive, to assume a radical separation between how we think and write and our life experiences erases, once again, the fact that thinking is part of life. Separation as an epistemological principle conceals power and disintegrates the integrity of the socially concrete (Bannerji, 2005). I will come back to the theme of sexuality, PS, and Real de Azúa in Chapter 4, and I resume the critique of separation as an epistemological principle in Chapter 5.[35]

The ultimate erasure. . . . . During the dictatorship, and by then exiled in Venezuela, Angel Rama writes about Real de Azúa's legacy. He refers to the destruction of the education system in the hands of the dictatorship. As he recounts the losses, Real de Azúa himself comes up as a major one: "it is not excessive to compute [Real de Azúa's] death among the sorrows that we owe to the unwieldy militarism that has taken over Uruguay" (Rama, 1977, p. 40).[36] Death is, in this case, an important moment in the shifting of political theory: the moment of *exiling* critical thinking even when the body of the thinker remained at (a no longer recognizable) home.

Narrative Power(s): Storytelling and the Delineation of the Disciplinary Self

The ways in which the history of the discipline has been narrated symptomatize liberalism's naturalization as the uniquely acceptable theoretical idiom. This has implications for the inside and the outside of PS.

Garcé (2005) discusses the lateness of PS' development and considers three hypotheses. The first is taken from Pérez Antón (1992), according to whom the high-quality reflections of Uruguay's politicians about their own practice made PS unnecessary or redundant.[37] The second and third hypotheses seem more plausible. The second suggests that the centrality of political parties may have inhibited, instead of stimulated, political reflection. In other words, the extensive and intensive politicization of the country may have prevented analytical approaches to political issues from flourishing. Incidentally, this resembles the argument of U19, a scholar highly critical of mainstream PS who argues that during the 1950s and 1960s, Marxism in Uruguay was academically weak because it was not located in the university but in political parties and groups. This *subjection* to its object of analysis (i.e., political practice) made Marxist thinking vulnerable to changes in social circumstances. In other words, there was not "theory," only thinking circumscribed to concrete situations. When the situations that sustained Marxism disappeared, this school of analysis vanished with them. This incestuous relationship with the object that inhibits theoretical reflection, I argue, is also practiced by PS today, but in the name of objectivity.

The third hypothesis offered by Garcé, however, is the one that matters for the critical analysis of the accounts of PS' development: that the most likely obstacle for the development of PS in the 1950s and 1960s may have been the predominance of Marxism and other socio-centric theories among Uruguayan intellectuals and academia. Let us unpack the implications of this perspective.

The very notion that these supposedly anti-political theories could prevent the birth of the discipline is in itself a symptom of the ideological climate of academia in Uruguay in the early 2000s, which was rather hostile to radical politics both in theory and practice—a feature that was strongly emphasized during the interviews (U1; U7; U10; U13; U17; U18; U19; U20; U21; U22). Garcé links the very birth of PS to the crisis of Marxism. The latter and its derivatives are located not only as exterior to the discipline, but also as its enemies. A complex discursive formation (Foucault, 1984) such as Marxism became essentialized as mechanistic and dogmatic, being conceptually reduced to its poorest version. This operation is entrenched in Uruguayan PS, and it is also a component of the (meta-)discourse around PS' development.

This was so not only in Uruguay. To illustrate how entrenched that narrative has become within the discipline, suffice it to note that it came up once again as a consensus at a 2012 roundtable with the presidents of the national political science associations of the region.[38] Some of the interventions of the presidents referred to "dated paradigms" that subsumed politics to society that prevented PS from flourishing in the past. The resistance against a "fictional American academic dominance" was singled out as a current problem, particularly in Argentina. The current challenges mentioned included the ("ridiculous") notion of academic imperialism, the anti-empirical mentality, the absence of institutionalized standards (i.e., peer review and indexation), and the persistence of *ensayismo*. The authoritarian experience was also listed among the negative factors in the trajectory of PS because, "as Huntington says, where democracy is weak, political science is weak." The consensus view did not have to state it upfront to reveal it: Marxism and authoritarianism collude against pristine democratic liberalism and PS, the discipline that upholds liberal democracy.

When the floor was open for a conversation about the state of the discipline in the region, I asked the panelists for their thoughts on the Perestroika movement (see Monroe, 2005) and its implications—if any—for Latin America. The answer was that the only perestroika they knew was the Russian one. . . . Clearly, up until 2012, this narrative framework was prevalent among the PS national associations of the region. Otherwise, the shocking response would not have had an expert congress in which to be uttered with such great confidence, as if it were the question—rather than the reply—that was out of place. The US that mainstream Latin American scholars "consume" is fictional; it is partial, and tailored to fit into a hegemonic project. The symbolic consumption of the US, imagined as a homogeneous space where "there are rules and standards" (as it is said once and again), is mobilized by mainstream scholars in the South to reinforce their position of power—as administrators of the discipline's canon.[39]

Historians of Latin American PS (i.e., political scientists who publish articles on the history of the discipline) tend to reproduce PS' biases. Their accounts lack criticality and operate as activist narratives that forge and reproduce an official representation of PS (its past, present, and hence its desirable future). Going back to Uruguay, a piece published in 2012 reproduces the equation between PS and liberalism: in its view, there was no space for PS in the 1960s because of the predominance of "structuralist" views (Buquet, 2012, p. 6). If we push the logic to its extreme, the ultimate result is, once again, clear: there is a trade-off between PS and Marxism. Interestingly enough, some of the authors arguing this used to belong to the Communist Party (U2; U5; U7).

Many colleagues seem not to be aware of how violent this form of academic identity regulation is. The expulsion of Marxism is also the expulsion of *people* from the space of acceptability, from journals (such as *RUCP*), and other academic sites. Not surprisingly, U17, a scholar whose work was informed by neo-Marxism, felt that there was no space for him in the ICP, which had a detrimental impact on both his academic productivity and emotional well-being. Recently, U17 was challenged for using the notion of a neoliberal state in one of his articles, even though such a notion was conceptually based on international literature—peer reviewers are not only gatekeepers but also function as ideological police sometimes, as the Perestroika movement and many others have denounced (Monroe, 2005; Holt, 2003; Ravecca, 2016).

This is about politics, again: the meta-narratives about PS' trajectory are also a point of entry into broader political transformations. Politics are immanent to the production and reproduction of meta-narratives regarding PS' trajectory, or any other discipline, for that matter, in Uruguay and elsewhere. In previous sections, I examined how Uruguayan social scientists were subjectively affected by the dictatorship, the defeat of Marxism, and the collapse of the Soviet Union, analyzing how PS was forged under these political conditions. In the course of this section I have advanced the proposition that not only knowledge but also the reflection *about* knowledge in Uruguay has been shaped by PS' object of study (i.e., politics).

The Uruguayan experience can neither be reduced to nor be read in isolation from global tendencies and international debates—which are mostly US-led (Bulcourf, Gutiérrez Márquez, & Cardozo, 2015; Torres-Ruiz & Ravecca, 2014). Mainstream PS does not tend to have epistemological density—it does not "need" to, given that neopositivism (Marcuse, 1991; Jackson, 2011; Monroe, 2005), which offers new and reinvigorated forms of objectivism (Isaac, 2015; Fujii, 2016; Trent, 2012), and even strategic and neoliberal rationality (Amadae, 2016; Brown, 2015), have been on the rise both in society and within the social sciences in recent years. However, in a sort of cruel anti-positivist joke, knowledge without critical self-reflection becomes highly ideological. Objectivity has become the Trojan horse of conservatives, neoliberals, and simply status quo minded scholars and intellectuals alike. The next section explores how, in the case of Uruguayan PS, objectivity, liberalism, and praise of the political establishment mingled in troubling ways.

Objectivity and Romance: Uruguayan Political Science and Liberal Democracy

> In the School of Law, I had a lot of advantage because PS was built against sociology. We were the nice, neat and good, and they were the fat, dirty and leftist.
>
> —U13

Time and place—that is, the specific historical juncture of the transition—situated PS in a political and intellectual environment that wedded it to liberalism, an ideological feature that did not change over time (whereas scientism would make its appearance later). Political scientists' very identity has been ideologically set *against* "economic reductionism" (i.e., Marxism) and "socio-centric views" (i.e., sociology). For such a disciplinary design to work, three things needed to happen. First, the sources to describe and explain "politics" had to come from "within." Second, the scope and boundaries of the discipline had to be conceived of in ways that excluded "the economy" and "society." And, third, broader conceptions of what political scientists "do" had to be wary of interdisciplinary approaches and political economy—for that might bring along the contamination of Marxist economic reductionism and socio-centric views that the narrative sets itself to stay clear from in the first place. This is what happened in Uruguay. Though the timing, as well as the specific contextual features, vary, the forging of PS identity in this country offers glimpses into broader stories about ideological change and about the mainstream of the discipline in both the North and the South.

In what follows, I show that PS' departure from the leftist legacy of the 1960s and early 1970s, its acritical embrace of liberalism, and its fixation with the autonomy of politics have their own type of hubris. I highlight also PS' complacency and submission *vis-à-vis* Uruguay's political system and political establishment. This love story with Uruguayan democracy, and with the traditional political parties in particular, has been written with the epistemological alphabet of scientific objectivity—a paradox that requires some investigation.

The Changing Shapes of Constant Love: PS and Uruguayan "Partyocracy"

Filgueira (1986) presciently complained in the late 1980s about the politics-centered type of sociology practiced in the country as well as about the general dismissive indifference toward psycho-cultural phenomena. PS radicalized these two features as it reduced the political into "politics," successfully displacing political sociology as the authoritative academic voice on the study of political issues (de Sierra, 2005).

The transition to democracy, political parties and government were the interests that presided over the formative period of PS. Most of the academic conversation revolved around the political system and later included public policy, an area of study that would exponentially grow by the 2000s (Bentancur & Mancebo, 2013; Buquet, 2012; Rocha Carpiuc, 2014). Such a change, however, did not function as a stepping-stone to expand the narrow conception of politics that was dominant at the time, at least not until 2012 (see Figure 3.3).[40] Uruguayan PS continued approaching the country on the basis of an overriding assumption: Uruguay is a *partyocracy* (Caetano et al., 1987). It is the task of PS to follow the comings and goings of its defining polyarchy. Social movements and what others understand as 'the political' have not been considered relevant to politics, if not overtly dismissed through the frequently uttered phrase "too sociological."

If Carlos Real de Azúa is considered a pioneer of Uruguayan PS, the father-hood that Jorge Lanzaro represents is more tangible in terms of its institutional legacy. He led the creation of the ICP, the leading PS department in Uruguay even today, an institution with enormous achievements in terms of teaching, research, and consolidating the discipline. In the words of an interviewee with a very long history in Uruguayan PS (in fact, one of its founders):

> We have a very important figure: Jorge Lanzaro. . . . He not only led the ICP for ten years but also conceived and created the institution. To under-stand the first period of PS' institutionalization I would refer to the fig-ure of Jorge Lanzaro and to a process which was the convergence of the PS that had been elaborated in the country and the academic training of those who had studied abroad because of exile or choice. That conver-gence was peaceful, loyal and very fecund. Both coincided indeed: the figure and the process. Jorge Lanzaro was decisive.
>
> *(U18)*

Widely acknowledged for his leadership in forging PS, Lanzaro speaks very openly about the "crusade" to separate from sociology and law, which he argues was necessary to build a PS community and identity. However, Lanzaro's account is sophisticated enough to show a reflective and *ironic* distance from the process.[41] Lanzaro's social sciences background and general culture allows him to steer clear from making naive distinctions among disciplines and sub-scribing to radical notions of autonomy.[42] As for later generations, that kind of self-ironic awareness seems to have been lost. On many occasions, the name of Jorge Lanzaro is symbolically mobilized and consumed to reify PS identity (Ravecca, 2014), which is characterized as openly "anti-sociological" and, thus, only focused on the political system.

The attachment to political parties and democracy has not been merely ana-lytical, but political as well. There is, indeed, a general acknowledgment from all former directors of the ICP that PS has not been critical enough *vis-à-vis* Uruguayan democracy and the political parties. This celebratory perception of political elites radically challenged the traditionally critical view that (leftist) intellectuals held of the political system before (Lanzaro, 2000). Thus:

> Uruguayan PS takes distance from historiographic perspectives that were quite drastic in their censorship of the traditional political parties. . . . [The political parties] were accused of empiricism, an internal heterogeneity that was paralyzing, and submissiveness to the upper classes. Besides internal disagreements, PS authors *acquitted* political parties on the basis of a more refined reconstruction of the problems that they faced along with the concrete alternatives that they had available.
>
> *(Pérez Antón, 1992, pp. 57–58, emphasis mine)*

This positive assessment of the traditional political parties' role in the life of the country was amplified by the following generation educated by the ICP's founders. These are the main components of the dominant PS narrative about Uruguayan democracy:

- Uruguay's exemplary democracy was built by the traditional political parties. In more elegant words, "the centrality of the political parties as dominant political actors is a line of *long durée* of our history and a key feature of our politics" (Caetano et al., 1987, p. 4). This feature (the centrality of political parties) has led political scientists to conceive of the Uruguayan political system as a *partidocracia* [partyocracy], a polyarchy presided over by a party system that accounts for the exemplary character of its (political) democracy. Note the reference to history to make sense of the present. The three proponents of the partyocracy hypothesis are historians that vindicate the autonomy of politics. They represent the first generation of PS scholars.
- Uruguay's political system has functioned and continues to function satisfactorily. From this, a sense of pride is derived: "Uruguay is admired because of the balanced and democratic ways of processing reforms in politics, the State and the market" (Buquet et al., 1998, p. 83). The quote above is extracted from a foundational text of the generation that followed the founders, including the first ICP BA graduate.[43]
- Uruguayan democracy has been and remains a gradualist political system that has been temperate in introducing pro-market reforms. Note that in contrast with APS, moderation—instead of neoliberal standards of efficiency—is valued and celebrated by this narrative. Balanced and negotiated arrangements (Real de Azúa, 1984) as well as the centrality of the state (Rama, 1987; Filgueira, Garcé, Ramos, & Yaffé, 2003) have been seen as a core feature of Uruguayan politics. To see gradualism, particularly in the terrain of pro-market reforms, as a self-evident merit is an example of the interpenetration between PS and its political context.[44]

The predominant optimism about the political establishment and Uruguayan democracy as well as the explicit embrace of liberalism are well represented by the next quote from the first ICP Director: "The revisionism—of anti-critical critique—that this book cultivates, and which is the product of careful and to some extent provocative explorations . . . refers to the quality of the government and to the parties' dynamics" (Lanzaro, 2000, p. 13). The "anti-critique" of Uruguayan democracy implied a critique of the critical view held by the left in the past. Jorge Lanzaro candidly analyzes PS' normative narrative during the 1990s:

> I mean, given that we *had to be* so laudatory of Uruguayan political history, of the political system, of democracy, which is linked to the autonomy of politics . . . we were not critical enough. On the contrary, we were

the defenders of our politicians even more than they were defenders of themselves; we were more invested than them, especially in the traditional political parties. We lost a little bit of . . . *we needed to do* a lot of work in one direction and we abandoned the other direction, the direction of critique. There were a lot of things to be critical about.

(Personal communication, March 14, 2013, emphasis mine)

It is interesting that this form of optimism, which seems to be more of a political than a scientific or analytical disposition, is conceptualized as a necessity for both Uruguayan democracy (harshly criticized by intellectuals before) and PS (whose fate is perceived as attached to that of the political system). Such an attachment to its object has had consequences for both research and education—as we have seen, the topics and the approaches of PS were shaped by the transition.

The 1990s were a period of ideological shift "toward the right," as Lanzaro recognized. In the Uruguayan context, this meant that some leading political scientists moved from the radical left during the 1960s, 1970s, and even the early 1980s, to an ideological area ranging from moderate left (perceived as "reasonable") to the center-right. Even though these labels seem imprecise, the collective self-perception of ideological mutation, via the critique of the left's dismissive attitude toward democracy, is clear (U1; U2; U3; U4; U5; U6; U7; U9; U10; U11; U12; U13; U14; U15; U17; U18; U19; U20; U21; U22). According to a leading political theorist, "scholars moved from the paradigm of revolution to the paradigm of liberal democracy" (U6), a mutation that expelled the radical left from the academic map.

Its alignment with mainstream politics has shaped the political role of PS. There were challenging aspects of Uruguayan democracy that were ignored by PS scholarship and by the interventions of political scientists in the media, particularly during the 1990s.[45] Álvaro Rico (2005) critically explores some of them. The unacknowledged effects of the dictatorship and the infamous Ley de Caducidad de la Pretensión Punitiva del Estado [Law on the Expiration of the Punitive Claims of the State, hereafter Expiry Law] is a case in point, and I explore it in the section that follows.

The Dark Side of the Partidocracia Uruguaya: When Politics Trumped the Rule of Law and Established Criminal Impunity in the Name of Order, Stability and . . . Democracy

The Expiry Law (15.848) was approved in 1986. The law stated that the state's intention of legally persecuting the crimes committed by the police and members of the military during the dictatorship up until March 1, 1985, had expired. Such a limitation on the reach of the justice system was the result, according to the text of the law, of the "logic of the facts" originated by the "agreement between political parties and the army in August 1984." The Expiry Law gave the Executive—in the hands of Julio María Sanguinetti, its leading proponent—the prerogative to decide whether an alleged illegal act was or was not comprehended by this norm.[46] In practical terms, the Expiry Law has effectively served to shield the military from the legal repercussions of the human rights violations perpetrated during the dictatorship. The reason proclaimed for this amnesty—granted (mostly) to men who tortured, killed, and "disappeared" political opponents—was to secure a peaceful transition toward constitutional order.

A coalition of the victims of the repression and their relatives, the leftist political party Frente Amplio [Broad Front], some dissenting figures of the traditional parties, students and workers unions, as well as other civil society organizations gained the necessary popular support in order to force the government to hold a referendum on the law, which took place in 1989 under abnormal circumstances of fear and unequal campaign conditions. The threat of authoritarian backlash if the law was revoked was expressed by the Commander-in-Chief of the Uruguayan army, Lt. Gen. Hugo Medina, warning that the judicial citations to military members were locked in his strongbox. The message was clear: the military was not going to allow its members to be incarcerated, regardless of the crime they might have had committed. Furthermore, the unequal access to the media was notorious: most of the press and all of the television channels were against the referendum. The government of Julio María Sanguinetti and its social and political allies won the ballot: 58% of the electorate supported the Expiry Law.

It goes without saying that the result was traumatic for the families of the victims, human rights activists, and, more generally, for those who promoted the *voto verde* [green vote] against the law. Once upheld by an absolute majority of the electorate, the Expiry Law interrupted the rule of law. By condoning the notion that powerful criminals cannot be punished, Uruguay's "admired democracy" normalized state repression.

More research needs to be done around the psycho-sociological and cultural effects of a legal disposition that, in the name of the "logic of the facts" (as it reads in its text), bypasses basic notions of justice (Rico, 2005). That such a law was democratically sanctioned does not take away the problem: it actually makes the situation even more traumatizing. Professional lawmakers asked the people they represented to undermine the mechanisms that we, collectively, had to achieve justice, and they got a positive answer; this is somehow the very definition of trauma! From a liberal perspective (a view that, as we already saw, became dominant in Uruguayan PS), this law distorts the roles given to different state powers in favor of the executive: in other words, the separation of powers, a basic feature of constitutional rule, was undermined. Liberalism, embraced by political parties and academia, was the victim of its own hegemony.

There was and is a lot to reflect, analyze, and critique regarding this law.[47] If narratives are about "accounting for," they are also about silences and sometimes about silencing (Butalia, 2000; Buriano & Dutrénit, 2017; Dauphinee, 2013a; Ravecca & Dauphinee, 2018; Spivak, 1988). An article published in UdelaR's

Revista de la Facultad de Derecho [Journal of the Faculty of Law] notes the silence surrounding the law between 1987 and 1989, when Uruguayan social scientists' research interests are taken into account (Arias, 2012). Regardless of the intention of the researchers, their silence has reproduced the narrative of Uruguay's traditional political parties and elites regarding how the transition should be understood and even justifies the Expiry Law's disquieting implications. Meanwhile, Rico (2005) as well as other leading historians such as U22 argue that PS ignores the dictatorship altogether. What happens once we tie these two silences together?

Only 4 articles (out of 163) in the *RUCP* address human rights issues and *none* focuses on the law in question, which, needless to say, was a salient political issue of Uruguay's very recent past that shaped the country's present. In Aria's view (2012), between 1985 and 1989, academia jumped onto the bandwagon of erasing the past, and thus proceeded to "omit" the topic of the Expiry Law, "promoting the option of forgetting" in the process (p. 32). As for my interviewees, in an admirable collective gesture of raw honesty, today bitterly agree with such an assessment, particularly in the case of PS (U4; U6; U10; U13; U18; U20; U22). In the view of some, to the extent that the discipline has been thought of as "the science of democracy," it simply ignored the dictatorship and, at least to some extent, its dark legacies:

> What happened? I think that reality was like *a stone that covered a veil*[48] that created a social environment that strongly conditioned [public debate]. After the ratification of the Law through the referendum of 1989, at the social and political level the topic was not spoken of anymore, and I believe that in academia we followed that path. This generated an absolute disregard for addressing the problem. *I don't have a more specific explanation than that.* 'Well, this issue was solved by our society,' so nobody felt that it was necessary to problematize it.
>
> *(U22, emphasis mine)*

If PS (*a*) is thought of as "the science of democracy"; (*b*) the definition of democracy limits itself to the political party system, elections, the assessment of political variables (narrowly understood in terms of classifying a whole host of actors in a matrix through public opinion surveys), and the assessment of how parties behave in the exercise of executive and parliamentary functions; and (*c*) political economy and socio-cultural dimensions are dismissed as out of the discipline's scope and boundaries, then there is no reason for the dominant PS narrative to contemplate the implications of the Expiry Law in ways other than those enabled by the narrow view. These features of PS worked to conceal the complexity of the circumstances of Uruguayan democracy after the transition.

This logic can be represented in a rather crude formula: what matters is that the people voted, period.[49] In fact, as the narrative goes, that the Uruguayan polyarchy as such (i.e., in institutional terms) worked well is what counts.

The commentary of one of Uruguay's leading political analysts and electoral experts on the Expiry Law serves to illustrate this logic. Óscar Bottinelli (2011) dismisses the argument that fear played a role in the victory of the yellow vote that upheld the law. By showing the consistency between electoral support for the yellow and green options on April 16, 1989, with support for political groups who promoted each option in the national elections on November 26 of that same year, he concludes that people simply followed their partisan preferences in both instances. Within that logic, the result had nothing to do with fear.

In the name of science—and discarding as empirical evidence anything that cannot be quantified—Bottinelli, who had participated in the foundation of the leftist Broad Front now in power and who was a close collaborator of its founder, Líber Seregni, reinforced the legitimacy of the law. Such a perspective, and the general logic it represents, actually reduces Dahl's (1991) vision of the democratic process into its Schumpeterian components (Schumpeter, 1985): bearing Dahl's vision in mind, it seems unlikely that citizens' "enlightened comprehension" could have been possible within a political context where the country's President and the TV channels resorted to censorship. This was the case for a TV spot that broadcasters in the country had refused to air that featured Sara Méndez—a former political prisoner and mother of a disappeared child—pleading for truth and justice.[50] Furthermore, Bottinelli does not ask how and why the elite had opted for "the transitional politics of oblivion" (Fried Amilivia, 2016) in the first place: must it only be the people who are fearful and not the elites? Does focusing on electoral numbers allow us to unpack the complex politics of fear, trauma, and power? In any case, this reduction of the Expiry Law issue is a clear example of the political implications of the narrow way Uruguayan PS approaches the political realm. The following exchange with a scholar of ICP is revealing in this regard:

PR: I've never heard a conversation around, just to put an example, "the deficits of Uruguayan democracy."

U18: That's right.

PR: It could have happened; something could have been said about that.

U18: You are right; you are right.

PR: We have been "optimistic" to say the least.

U18: Look, as a citizen and as an academic, I was always critical of the Expiry Law. I was always critical. I voted green, etcetera.

PR: The topic of the law was never incorporated into a reflection about the quality of our democracy . . .

U18: That is why I agree in that that was a mistake and I agree that, for instance, a book so . . .

PR: *[Interrupting]* Why do you think that happened?

U18: Why?

PR: Yes, why . . . isn't the issue an obviously relevant one?

U18: Yes, absolutely.

PR: It did merit a reflection on the quality of our democracy.

U18: I think you are right. I think you are right.

PR: Why do you think there is not such a reflection, then?

U18: Because there is no critique. . . . Yes, yes, this reflection was lacking when the traditional parties were in office, so we cannot say "there was a sort of political solidarity." [The interviewee is basing his analysis on the fact that scholars in Uruguay broadly self-identified with the left.]

PR: Exactly. That is not the register; that is not the issue.

U18: That is not the issue or the cause, I agree. I don't have an answer for that question. It's a great question!

The sharp contrast between this critical assessment and some of the celebratory texts that this same scholar has written about the traditional political parties in Uruguay leaves me perplexed without eroding my empathy: after all, it would be rather scandalous for a "critical" scholar to look at PS narratives in Uruguay from the conceptual window offered by trauma while, at the same time, turning one's back to them in a unilateral and arrogant gesture of condemnation. The *lack of language* and *lack of knowledge*—and here I am just re-stating the words of my interviewees (U8; U22)—around *why* PS has not had an interest in human rights is consistent with other testimonies. This, in a community whose expertise is to talk about, and indeed explain, political issues is revealing (especially given that the last two testimonies are from political scientists with a strong training in history). These perplexities—these holes in the narrative—fuel my drive to think about these complex issues of academia, biographies, and power.

A More Open Mainstream? New Closures?

The analysis of *RUCP* articles and the interviews reveal that Uruguayan PS is characterized by the embrace of liberalism and the absence of critical theory; its focus on politics and policies; the avoidance of alternative conceptualizations of the political realm (what some authors call "the political"); a relatively positive assessment of Uruguayan democracy; and a lack of criticality *vis-à-vis* the political establishment. Parallel to these developments, there are two more: the tendency to abandon *ensayismo* (portrayed by some as a problematic and, by many, as a desirable development) and the increasing quantification of the discipline (Rocha Carpiuc, 2017), the still enormous distance from the highly formalized and mathematized American PS (Sartori, 2004; Monroe, 2005; Isaac, 2015) notwithstanding.[51] Furthermore, analysis of the three curricula structures that the BA program in political science has had until today (1988, 1992, and 2009) shows that the main tendency has been the expansion of the study of the state and public policy. Epistemological reflections have, again, been absent (Rocha Carpiuc, 2017).

However, it seems that room for critical reflection has been at least partially expanded. The financial crisis of 2002, which revealed some failures of the Uruguayan political system, for instance, in terms of the lack of oversight of financial institutions, free-riding, and political irresponsibility (Garcé, 2012), was pointed out as a moment of critical awakening by some political scientists (U7; U4; U22). I have the impression—and this is just an informed impression—that there have been some political and thematic openings within the PS community as well.

The course curricula are slowly changing. For example, in the fourth year of the BA, a set of optional courses are offered that cover a more diverse set of topics than before. According to an ICP 2016 official report, in 2017, courses on emotions and politics, critical theory, and political ecology, among others, were added. Courses on international relations and the military, and gender and sexual diversity were included even before then (ICP, 2016). Granted, these are small steps for an institution whose officially sponsored books never stepped outside the realm of mainstream PS: government, elections, and public policy.

Thus, in closing this section, a couple of notes should be added. First, the database of *RUCP* articles that I created for this research ends in 2012. Interestingly, the last article of the series explores the economic and legal implications of the financial support provided by lenders to the Uruguayan dictatorship (Bohoslavsky, 2012). The issue raised in the article complicates the relationship and clear-cut distinction between democracies and dictatorships, given that powerful democracies, either through public or private agents, can sustain authoritarian regimes overseas and, therefore, function as a factor preventing democracy from developing globally (Torres-Ruiz & Ravecca, 2014). I mention this article because it is located outside the realm of mainstream PS and because it unpacks the dictatorship under renewed—and very critical—lenses.

Second, my research has not covered the relationship of PS with the progressive governments of the Broad Front from 2004 to the present. Be that as it may, there are indications that the lack of critical distance *vis-à-vis* political elites and the government persists, though in new forms, particularly through the economic bonds generated by consulting projects financed by the Broad Front administration (Garcé & Rocha Carpiuc, 2015; Ravecca, 2014; U5). One of the interviewees who mentioned how hard it was to be a sympathizer of the leftist Broad Front in the ICP of the 1990s recently told me that after 2004—when this party won the elections—"everyone became a Broad Front supporter" (U10). It is important to note, however, that the Broad Front has moved to the center of the political spectrum (Yaffé, 2005), so closeness to the government may indicate the persistence of the lack of critical engagement with the political establishment rather than a leftist comeback.

Besides its multiple definitions, it seems clear that neoliberalism has become globally hegemonic (Amadae, 2016; Brown, 2015, 2010; Harvey, 2005; Saad-Filho & Johnston, 2005; Menéndez-Carrión, 2015). Uruguay is not an exception.

Carlos Moreira (2001) challenges the common sense prevalent among academics, technocrats, and politicians that depicts the introduction of neoliberal reforms in this country as "gradual" and "heterodox." Amparo Menéndez-Carrión (2015) takes it a step further and, in line with other interesting scholarly theoretical developments in the area (Amadae, 2016; Brown, 2015), locates neoliberalism far beyond (though including), the realm of policy. This major three-volume research on the Uruguayan polis conceptualizes neoliberalism as a discursive logic that undermines public space and all things public, which was a distinct feature of Uruguay up until roughly the mid-1950s.

In relative terms, however, and regardless of how it is defined, neoliberal discourse and policymaking has not been as prominent in Uruguay as it has been in Chile. In the following pages, I show how this has manifested itself in Uruguayan PS.

The Limits of Conformism? State-Centrism and the Containment of Market Utopias (With a Note on Secularism)

It is impossible for me to remember how many times I have heard and read that Uruguay is resistant to neoliberal discourses and policies. In relative terms, and in contrast with the Chilean trajectory in particular, the introduction of structural adjustment in this country has been moderate (Alegre, 2008; Gonzalez Candia & Zapata Schaffel, 2015; Hernández, 2000; Forteza et al., 2007).[52] Direct democracy (in the form of plebiscites and referenda in the years 1989, 1992, 2003, and 2004) undermined the neoliberal agenda on a few occasions. This feature of Uruguayan society is reflected in the academic production of PS in particular. In sharp contrast with APS, contributors to the *RUCP* have been, since its inception, very reluctant to endorse neoliberalism. In fact, some of the most field-shaping texts praised the Uruguayan political system for its supposedly gradualist and moderate approach (Buquet et al., 1998, p. 83; Lanzaro, 2000).

Uruguayan PS does not usually address neoliberalism or economic philosophies as a main area of research. Having said that, it is interesting that while similar percentages of *RUCP* articles do not address the issue compared to the Chilean journals (between 76% and 82%), the percentage of articles critical of neoliberal reforms in the *RUCP* (16%) is similar to the percentage that support neoliberalism in the two Chilean journals (18% and 22%) (see Figure 3.8). Once again, science is not immune to its politico-temporal context: Uruguayan PS is Uruguayan, and it follows the social-democratic pattern of its host country; this pattern has been widely documented by academic research, and is most notably illustrated by the expression of Wilson Ferreira Aldunate, a historic leader of the National Party: "In Uruguay, there are three million *batllistas* [a supporter of José Batlle y Ordóñez]," implying, among other things, that the entire

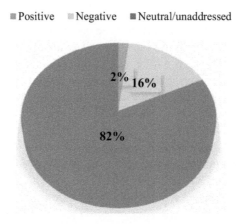

■ Positive   ▨ Negative   ■ Neutral/unaddressed

2% 16%

82%

FIGURE 3.8   View of neoliberal reforms in *RUCP*, 1987–2012

population of the country supports government intervention in the economy.[53] It seems that academics are also *batllistas*. The *RUCP* simply is not a host of neoliberal discourse: only 2% of the articles promote liberalizing reforms.

As I have argued before, the Chilean dictatorship had a clear sense of direction and it achieved not only political and economic reforms, but also cultural change, something celebrated by its organic intellectuals (Bruna Contreras, 1987; Gajardo Lagomarsino, 1989). In the case of Uruguay, neoliberal values and reforms have not been incorporated into large arenas of social activity— *at least not with the same intensity*, even though the Uruguayan dictatorship did have a neoliberal orientation in several policy areas and neoliberalism has had tremendous implications for the country (Finch, 1992; Menéndez-Carrión, 2015; Vacs, 1998).

According to Tomás Moulián (2002, p. 11), in Chile corporations "have been the stronghold of the capitalist revolution through the mediation performed by the dictatorship." In his view, there has been an economization of political rationality that narrows the realm of what is democratically debatable. In 1990, Norberto Lechner forwarded a similar argument:

> With the reigning neoliberal discourse since 1975, political categories (popular sovereignty, state, representation) are substituted by economic categories (comparative advantages, market, transaction). While the official doctrine of the regime (National Security Doctrine) keeps a low profile, a factual hegemony of the market is imposed.
>
> *(p. 16)*

These reflections echo Marcuse's (1991) notion of technological rationality discussed in Chapter 1. Marcuse's concern was how contemporary capitalist power dynamics affected freedom through narrowing the realm of thinking, even in the context of liberal democracy. His analyses of social science, and American PS in particular, unpack its militantly anti-reflexive ways of writing as well as its reification of capitalism and consumer society.[54] At a simpler register, the point is that Chilean corporations and entrepreneurs are powerful political agents that have an important section of the intelligentsia as their organic intellectuals; "order and stability over democracy" (Álvarez Vallejos, 2011, p. 125) is a summary of their vision. This corporate empowerment had an academic expression in APS.

The connection between Chile and the United States is, in this regard, interpretively powerful,[55] and allows us to theorize the relationship between social and epistemological transformations at the international level. Neoliberalism is also an international intellectual and academic project. However, the local has its own density and historicity (Menéndez-Carrión, 2015): Uruguayan political scientists' thinking reproduces a radically different environment than the Chilean. Not even the most liberal academics in Uruguay would declare: "less fiscal pressure and less public spending; competition creates inequality and that is good" (Fernández de la Mora, 1987, p. 20).[56] In contrast, constant references to "statism" (the ideology of big government)—the nightmare of neoliberals—crowd Uruguayan scholarship and the press. The columnists of conservative newspaper *El País* complain about it daily.

Neoliberalism entails a form of regulation—and production—of the subject (Read, 2009; Brown, 2015). Much of the scholarship on neoliberal subjectivity has focused on the case of Chile.[57] It seems that in this terrain, again, besides the tremendous impact that neoliberal logic has had on Uruguay (Menéndez-Carrión, 2015), the contrast between the two cases is sharp, an issue that requires further comparative research, particularly as it pertains to the implications of neoliberalism on scholarship. Relatedly, recent intellectual transformations involving, for instance, the regulation of academic writing is another interesting issue.

In mainstream American PS, at least since the 1960s, and in Latin America at least since the 1980s, intellectuals and scholars are frequently counterposed. The mainstream notion of the scholar comes hand in hand with a departure from the allegedly baroque style of writing of *ensayistas*, who position themselves as universal thinkers (that is, *pensadores* [thinkers/intellectuals] with a capacity to say anything they feel like saying with little or no scientific basis), and with the embrace of systematicity and rigor. The problem arises when linearity becomes a rule that undermines thinking—and learning! One of my interviewees referred to the policing of BA students' writing in a revealing way. The colleague insisted that one of his/her students had to "straighten" his language because it was "too philosophical"—even though, and the clarification is important here, "he was a good writer." This version of the mandate for clarity and transparency in academic language reminds me (again) of Marcuse's observation of the imposition of a sanitized form of writing. In this style of thought, the given universe of facts is the final context of validation (thus, "philosophy" has no room in it). The distance between actuality and potentiality collapses. The writer cannot doubt, cannot have emotions, and should hide in a bunker while strangling her imagination (Ravecca & Dauphinee, 2018).

It seems that leading PS institutions in Chile went further in the process of embracing mainstream American political science as a model, adopting neo-classical economics as the epistemological idiom, and consequently abandoning *ensayismo* (defined in way that sometimes includes rigorous non-positivist forms of research). Most of my interviewees did perceive this process, regardless of their evaluation of it (CHL1; CHL4; CHL5; CHL6; CHL7; CHL9; CHL10; CHL11; CHL12; CHL13; CHL14; CHL15; CHL16; CHL17; CHL18; CHL19; CHL21; CHL22; CHL23; CHL24; CHL25; CHL26; CHL27; CHL29; CHL30; CHL31; CHL32; CHL34).

The interpenetration between context and science is revealed sharply in another area: religion. Uruguay has been characterized as a relatively secular country; at least this has been the cultural reality for broad sectors of society, particularly the intelligentsia (Da Costa, 2009). Thus, some aspects of Chilean academia were surprising to me. The analysis of *Política* and *RCP* required changes to the conceptual structure of the original database. In fact, an important variable was added: The West and Christianity. In both journals in Chile during the period 1979–1989, around half of the articles defended the West as a political-cultural identity threatened by the East, understood in both Cold War and religious terms (communism and Islam respectively). Chile is perceived as being monolithically Western and Catholic—erasing the Mapuche community and other groups from the map. In the whole history of the *RUCP*, there are no traces of this type of discourse (see Figure 3.9). This example illustrates the power of context in shaping the text of science.[58]

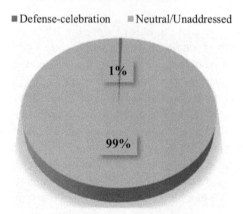

■ Defense-celebration   ■ Neutral/Unaddressed

1%

99%

FIGURE 3.9 Attitude toward the West and Christianity in *RUCP*, 1987–2012

Concluding Remarks: Complex Relationality and Liberal Unthinking

In the preceding pages, I examined the politics of Uruguayan political science from two standpoints: the circumstances and conditions of the discipline's emergence, as well as its main conceptual features. The analytical emphasis was put on the latter—on PS' narratives—and the underlying theme was how the relationship between knowledge and power played out in the way democracy was constructed and studied. With this purpose in mind, I explored some of Uruguayan PS' major features: the rejection of Marxism and embrace of liberalism; the uneasiness around sociology; the disciplinary appropriation of Carlos Real de Azúa; and the positive evaluation of the political system. If the question I sought to address by examining these dimensions was whether PS took part in broader ideological transformations that located liberalism as unquestionable, the conclusion is clear: on the whole, Uruguayan PS can be conceptualized as an acritical form of knowledge *vis-à-vis* liberal democracy and—even more—the local political establishment.

During the 1990s and early 2000s, the discipline was able to establish an identity and produce a mainstream that upholds this identity, ensuring the stability of its scope and boundaries through discursive and institutional operations. For all intents and purposes, upholding that identity has required that Marxism and other socio-centric views be kept out. Even though these conceptual fences do not hold—the social and the political are stubbornly intertwined—the rhetoric around boundaries matters, and it does have performative effects. The act of keeping out the other demands a whole host of knowledge operations through which vigilance can deploy its power to ensure the reproduction of the stability thus conquered and the expansion of its—very political—might: establishing what may be said and what ought to be excluded from the practice of the discipline. To be sure, this kind of reactionary (academic) formation (Ravecca, 2016) has internal and external political implications. Among the former is the establishment of a hierarchy between colleagues. The closer to the mainstream a research program is, the higher it sits in the curious scale of PS. In terms of the latter, taking the institutional(ist) road has limited PS' criticality.

What has been shown in this chapter needs to be conceptualized and analytically gathered with the assistance of theory. In what follows, while keeping in the mind the broad Marxist orientation of this project, I mainly mobilize post-structuralist insights (especially that of queer theory) around discourse, identity, and power.

Foucault's (1991a) hypothesis on power rejected the notion that its fundamental function was to repress and deny people's sexuality. In fact, one of the main insights of Foucault's investigations is that subjects, such as "the homosexual," were produced through discourse. Furthermore, according to his rule of immanence, power and knowing are inseparable: the knowledge of sexuality is part and parcel of the power dynamics involving the constitution of sexualized subjects. Queer studies (Butler, 1990) have built on these insights and are mostly known for radically politicizing and de-naturalizing gender (feminine-masculine) and even sexual (female-male) identities. At first sight, queer theorizing may understandably be regarded as an awkward companion for a book on the politics of knowledge. However, dislocating a theory from its natural realm (a paradoxical formula for a post-structuralist approach) and re-locating it in a new milieu to observe its operations may be a productive move. In other words, the insights of queer theory may help us (re-)read the politics of disciplinary identity configuration.

We can expand the scope of the insight about the discursive constitution of gender to show that the cultural production of a naturalized self is also at play within knowledge and academia. Foucault (1980) already challenged the claims that psychoanalysis and Marxism were "sciences" by asking what kind of power dynamics are deployed through such struggles for scientificity and what kinds of knowledges they disqualify. From a comparable logic, the following question arises: What is happening politically through the narratives of PS' identity? And what kinds of knowledges do they disqualify?

The formation and reproduction of PS identity has involved internal power dynamics linked to the stabilization—and securing—of its features. They have also implied the naturalization of specific ways of defining and framing politics. The adoption of a conventional conception of politics has political consequences, but it is purposely depoliticized (i.e., presented as neutral and inevitable) by the dominant PS narrative. This depoliticization is a fundamental political act. In other words, the reification of political science projects the reification of politics. These two processes of reification travel through an epistemological tissue made of positivist objectivity. PS is objective, and its notion of politics is therefore objective as well. This is an operation that conceals the ideological dimension of interpretation and analysis. It also protects political scientists in a fortress form of writing that allows them to hide their subjectivity (Ravecca & Dauphinee, 2018).

This illusory separation between academia and ideology has meant that the international academic dominance of the US, and the intellectual shifts this dominance has implied, has been perceived as politically neutral, and the slight suggestion to the contrary awakens almost hysterical accusations of being *sesentista* [of the sixties], synonymous with being ideological. Through these lenses, academic imperialism becomes unthinkable. More importantly, liberal capitalism has disappeared as a scholarly issue for the students of politics. It is a thought-provoking paradox that a postmodern theory—queer theory—and not Marxism, is so instrumental in identifying this *political economic* consequence of the way PS' identity has been forged. *The gender of Uruguayan PS is liberal and capitalist*. Let me elaborate on this.

As was shown above, while for Chilean APS they were an obsession, Marxism, and communism never appeared in Uruguayan PS. The contrast is sharp. The predominant Uruguayan way of dealing with Marxism has been indifferent silence in writing, supplemented by mocking in classrooms and hallway conversations. One could guess that leftists converted into liberals who somehow remain progressive do not become anti-communists; in this regard, they can be classified as *converts* in Keucheyan's (2013) sense. I want to highlight the following point: that *PS itself* has been thought of and narrated as incompatible with Marxism reveals the *porosity* (Buck-Morss, 2009) between internal and external power relations. The ideological shift from the radical 1960s to the moderate 1990s at the very core of the PS identity-building process was crafted by domestic and international conditions. I want to suggest that the encounter between discourse analysis and international political economy allows for a better understanding of the *complex* and *relational* layers of power.

The reification of the self requires a careful delineation of exteriorities and alterities, of those who are not *us*. In this case, the not-us are the sociologists. The move away from ideology and toward objectivity was linked to PS' suspicion of sociology, both in terms of competing paradigms and resource-seeking. Through the notion of discarding socio-centric theories—the cornerstone of PS—a project of independence, and perhaps of supremacy, was deployed. While the expansion of sociology happened in the 1960s in a context of political polarization (Filgueira, 1974), PS was forged during the democratic transition and after (in the 1980s and 1990s). In this context of the return of democracy, PS would find in the rejection of sociology and Marxism a window of opportunity for identity building. This double rejection is a contingent event that has been essentialized by the mainstream narrative.

The overcoming of radicalism and socio-centric approaches was assembled, on an explicitly political level, as a (self-) critical reading of the traditional leftist critique of the mainstream political parties and liberal democracy—i.e., *the critique of the critique* (Lanzaro, 2000; U10; U13). This operation was internalized into PS identity. As if socio-centrism, along with Marxism and/or the "Marxist overtones" sometimes attributed to socio-centrism, needed to be literally reversed in order for the critique of the critique to be put to good use, Uruguayan PS became blatantly liberal and party-centric. The very *fact* of the (narrow) definition of the political embraced by the discipline is a foundational political act with significant consequences (as we saw in the case of the Expiry Law).

"The Uruguayan Partyocracy" (Caetano, Pérez Antón, & Rilla, 1987) and *The Second Transition* (Lanzaro, 2000) are academic *and* political interventions. Their exclusive focus on the political system and their praise for the traditional political parties are linked to a mode of thinking about the transition, democracy, the dictatorship, and the desirable future of the country that put an emphasis on moderation, order, and stability. The dictatorship traumatized the intellectual left who, in her attempt to rescue the main protagonists of liberal democracy, the political parties (and thus rescuing herself in the process), committed hubris.

The theoretical density of time (Buck-Morss, 2010) is of interest in this analysis. Time and timing were indeed crucial: all that has been described and conceptualized here was situated in, and interlocked with, the context of the fall of the Berlin Wall and the consolidation of US hegemony in the region, both politically and academically. These international and historical circumstances are also theoretical: they framed the positive reevaluation of democracy linked to the transition in entirely liberal terms. Marxism and the radical left were perceived as something *of the past* and associated with an underdeveloped version of science, while liberalism *and* objectivity were thought, in a sort of postmodern pastiche, as the language of the future. The politics of temporality are also attached to ideology. The syllogism of the present was: democracy is liberal; PS is democratic. Therefore, PS is, and should be, liberal. In other words, one ideology was perceived as non-ideological, as the way things are. Objectivity naturalized liberalism and representative government as the unique idiom and form of democracy—it was Schumpeter on steroids.

At the most abstract level, the consequence of the equation between PS' very identity and this sort of objectivist liberalism is the naturalization of capitalism as the uncontested (back)ground for democracy. In other words, capitalism is trafficked under the cover of democracy. This implication (as any good ideological move) remains invisible, but it is really crucial, as it reveals how capitalism succeeds in naturalizing itself through academic knowledge. This goes back to the fascinating reflections of Karl Marx in *Capital* about how certain knowledges (classical political economy, in his case) sanction capitalism at the level of knowledge production and re-create false consciousness.[59] This, as we saw, does not necessarily mean support for neoliberal policies. In this regard, the Chilean and the Uruguayan cases have significant differences. And these variances really matter, politically and analytically, as they speak of the density of the local and the importance of keeping a situated analysis.[60]

Uruguayan PS was born during the democratic transition *as* a liberal democratic discourse. The very notion of transition was more of a political project than a carefully crafted scientific category (Lesgart, 2003, p. 242). Such a political condition transcends text and involves the materiality of social life. In all of his studies, Foucault made the point very clear: discourse is always linked to institutional and material power dynamics. His notion of governmentality shows how multiple sets of components and levels are linked in a configuration of knowledge and power (Foucault, 2006). In my argument, PS was part of how power was exercised in the post-transition period, a power that was classed (capitalism was protected) and elitist (the party system was idealized).

The constitution of the contemporary political subject in Uruguay is the product of a dictatorship sponsored by the US, which had powerful disciplining effects on action and thinking. The socialist project, democratic or not, was erased from the cognitive and political map; such an operation is clearly evident today, as when the progressive Broad Front gained power, it migrated to the center of the ideological spectrum (Garcé & Yaffé, 2005). Rather than critically analyzing this process and Uruguayan democracy, PS *embodies* them.[61] This *disciplined* social science in both senses of the term, an endeavor celebrated from Filgueira (1974) to Buquet (2012), naturalized the status quo, and from the point of view of critical theory, embodied the rationality of domination (Horkheimer, 1978; Marcuse, 1991).

To sum up, the complex relationality that shaped PS involved different, intertwined registers: political economy (the definitive defeat of any alternative to capitalism), the international (the collapse of the Soviet Union and US hegemony in the region), theory, ideology and epistemology (the hegemony of liberalism and neopositivism, the abandonment of Marxism, and the separation from sociology), the institutional enterprise (the creation of the ICP) and, last but not least, subjectivity (trauma, guilt). This multilayered dynamic regulated what can be considered PS and what was expelled beyond the walls of the discipline's identity. The consequences have been multiple, going from micro-practices of intellectual policing of undergraduate students ("your research about social movements is not political science"), to the lack of critical distance with its object of study, the mainstream political parties in particular.

As shown in the previous sections, the process of formation of PS involved different moments: the social substance of time—that is, history and its multilayeredness—shaped PS.[62] If knowledge is historical (Buck-Morss, 2009), then to understand history we need to (re)examine knowledge *and* the politics immanent to its production (Jackson, 2011). Indeed, the study of knowledge production may reveal significant aspects of the society that is being known. From this particular perspective, epistemology is about society—and ethics (Marcuse, 1991).

On Tuesday, October 30, 2006, President Tabaré Vázquez spoke at the central roundtable of the First Uruguayan Conference of Political Science. He shared the stage with two other presidents: the President of the Uruguayan Association of Political Science (AUCiP), Daniel Buquet, and the President of the International Political Science Association (IPSA), Lourdes Solá, who also gave speeches. Buquet solemnly declared that PS is not neutral when it comes to political regimes:

> There is only one principle to defend to death; and that is democracy. . . .
> In this case Political Science is not neutral because it supports democracy
> and makes a contribution to keep and improve it.[63]

If democracy should not be taken for granted, if it is more than an object of inquiry and should be thought of as a system that ought to be upheld (bearing in mind that this system is currently the status quo), then a series of questions comes to mind. What does the statement that political science supports democracy mean and do, and to whom is it directed? Should I be "democratic" to be a political scientist? And if so, what does that mean, exactly? What kind of democracy is being talked about? Must the political scientist become a pro-systemic creature, a guardian of the status quo? Is someone being silenced through this apparently reasonable statement? What kind of violence is being deployed here? Can we find traces of the logic of Marxism-Leninism or any other dogma? If political science *is* democratic, what happens—or should happen—to those political scientists or discourses that challenge liberal democracy as the uniquely acceptable political option... Should they be "disappeared"? If something should be defended "to death," where is the room for free thinking and critical reflection? Is the role of the scientist to die in the name of her object of study? Is that really "science"? It seems that, here, we have reached the limits of PS' episteme.

This attachment to what currently *exists* (for instance, the democracy currently in place) may also become a consistent celebration of the successful politician (U18). "Give me something with power, and I will like it," joked a colleague in an academic meeting a few years ago. Uruguay is a politics-centered society, and PS follows its path: political analysis lacks critical reflection about, and distance from, its object of study. In the words of one of my interviewees, "scientific embodiment of political parties allows very little space for reflection and theory" (U6).

Pérez Antón (1992, p. 56) celebrates that, during the transition, the PRCs and UdelaR organized inter-partisan forums to discuss the political future of the country; PS was a builder of Uruguayan democracy. This proactive civic engagement had its troubling side. U1 remembers how uncomfortable ICP's academic seminars during the 1990s were for him, because some of the politicians invited ("from center-left to right, but *right* right") used to arrogantly lecture the scholars. The scene suggests the collapse of the necessary (analytical) distance to cultivate knowledge, but not in the critical way of assaulting reified definitions of science. In this case, science becomes ideology by naturalizing certain political discourses *while* allegedly embracing objectivity.

The acknowledgment of PS' political nature and of the historical condition of our knowledge may furnish PPS with more distance, criticality, and independence. For now, the indications are only partially promising: not so long ago, in 2015, I received an invitation for the ICP's 30th anniversary celebration. Former presidents Julio María Sanguinetti and Luis Alberto Lacalle, as well as then Vice-President Raúl Sendic, were invited to speak about the "Present and Future of Democracy in Uruguay." It seems that our second story on power and trauma persists in compulsive repetition.

This exercise of disciplinary introspection has unfolded a political analysis of Uruguay that can offer potential insights into the experience of other Latin American countries. This story has shown something that happened almost everywhere: the rise of liberal capitalism and US hegemony (Gramsci, 2008), which also had manifested within academia. This universality (Butler et al., 2003), however, does not imply that the local lacks density. In simple language, the outputs were consistent, but the paths were different. Yet that dissimilarity also has implications for the outputs (for instance, in the rejection or acceptance of neoliberalism). The Chilean and Uruguayan cases display complex academic and ideological paths of convergence and divergence.

Notes

* This chapter benefited from exchanges with historians Juan Andrés Bresciano, Diego Sempol, and María Eugenia Jung. I am grateful for my exposure to their deep knowledge of Uruguayan history. Alan Sears helped me to refine my engagement with liberalism as a political philosophy and ideology. Amidst the crafting of my reflections on trauma, Barbara Soren rightly suggested exploring the US Holocaust Memorial Museum website as well as studying some of the vast scholarly literature on the Holocaust. Amparo Menéndez-Carrión and her insightful, theoretically dense reading of the Uruguayan polis (Menéndez-Carrión, 2015) is always inspiring for my own analyses and this is, once again, the case. A preliminary version of this chapter was presented at the 8th Latin American Political Science Conference of the Latin American Political Science Association (ALACIP) in Lima, Perú. The multiple conversations sponsored by the Research Group on the History of Political Science in Latin America were encouraging and fruitful. From the outset of this chapter, I would like to acknowledge the work of Álvaro Rico (2005), one of the rare attempts to understand the political transformations in Uruguay from a critical perspective that looks at the role of academic knowledge, including that of political science. Belén Villegas and Camila Zeballos assisted me with the pre-classification of the *RUCP* articles for the database and Mariana Mancebo collaborated with me on the second pre-classification and data analysis, among other tasks.

1. Rodney Arismendi (1913–1989) was a historical leader of the Communist Party in Uruguay. He was also a leading communist ideologue in the South American context.

2. This is a pseudonym, and the only time I employ fake names. To preserve the confidentiality of the interviewees, they are named using codes: *CHL* corresponds to Chileans and *U* to Uruguayans. Translations for all interviews and other quoted material originally in Spanish are mine.

3. The causes of this relative indifference go beyond the small scale of the country. For one thing, Uruguay is not "dangerous" or strategically relevant from the point of view of mainstream or conservative academia. For another, it may not seem exotic or "revolutionary" enough to catch the attention of progressive or critical eyes and may be deemed "unsexy" because it shows boring sameness: "white" people not-in-war, relatively impoverished but not to the point to make the experience interesting or moving for the critical graduate student *à la* Indiana Jones. That is, Uruguay is hard to romanticize or to *use* to satisfy desires of transcendence of any kind. Amparo Menéndez-Carrión (2015) counters such an environment of indifference: focusing on the question of citizenship and its different collective moments, the book argues for the significance of the Uruguayan experience for political theory.

4. Interventions have been published by *RUCP* and other Latin American journals, and have been presented in national and international events, including the Latin American Political Science Association's (ALACIP) annual conference.

5. The delay is clear if we take into account that in Chile, the Institute of Sociology and its BA program were created in 1954. The comparison with Brazil and Argentina (Filgueira, 1986; Bulcourf, 2012; Cardoso Keinert & Pinheiro Silva, 2010; Pessanha, 2017) confirms this paradox of a secular and modern society that puts a strong emphasis on education but did not develop an efficient system for science and technology (Filgueira, 1974, p. 173).

6. Pérez Antón (1986, p. 225) goes as far as to say that PS is chronologically the last social science to appear in the country.
7. UdelaR was the only university in the country until the dictatorship, and it remains the most important institution for higher education today.
8. The 1990s have been described by many as the neoliberal peak in the region, when communism was indeed a specter, but in a radically different way as the one imagined by Marx.
9. Among others: Altman (2005), Bentancur (2003), Buquet (2012), Busquets, Sarlo, and Delbono (2015), Chasquetti (2013), de Sierra (2005), Filgueira (1974, 1986), Garcé (2005), Garcé and Rocha Carpiuc (2015), Pérez Antón (1992), Prates (1987), Ravecca (2010a, 2014), Rocha Carpiuc (2012a, 2012b, 2014), and Solari (1959).
10. Pérez Antón is a good representative of the optimistic perspective that de Sierra and Filgueira criticize. For Pérez Antón, during the 20th century, social sciences were not necessary given that the political parties' reflections about the national reality were of high quality. This author was one of the founders of the ICP and a proponent of the party-centric hypothesis about the Uruguayan polis, as we will see.
11. Filgueira understood the consolidation of the social sciences as a process of institutionalization—a process encompassing the creation of courses, programs, research centers, training for researchers, and academic production. But in his view, the process also entailed the creation of a legitimated space in society, the demand for sociological expert knowledge as well as an academic community with shared values, common dialogue and evaluation criteria of quality standards. Thus, Filgueira's notion of institutionalization goes beyond the mere production of institutions, centers or activities (Filgueira, 1986, pp. 166–167).
12. Taking into account all of the periods studied by Prates (1987), 82% of social science research units belong to the public sector. This feature is more salient for the period 1961–1971, which is the most dynamic in terms of the creation of institutions: only 15% of the new institutions were founded by the private sector.
13. Disciplinary independence and identity would be the exact same motives for future PS. Sociology will change roles from being oppressed (*vis-à-vis* law) to being the oppressor that should be defeated.
14. If the Alliance for Progress was a soft version of American imperialism, then "development" was the strategy to confront the influence of the Cuban revolution and the communist threat in general.
15. UdelaR is autonomous from the government and has a tripartite structure of governance: faculty, students, and alumni.
16. The MLN-Tupamaros is a leftist movement that operated as an urban guerrilla during the 1960s and the beginning of the 1970s.
17. These types of manifestations of the dictatorship at the micro-level have been abundantly registered in theater plays, literature, and academic research. Menéndez-Carrión (2015, Chapter 7), for instance, analyzes strikingly similar testimonies.
18. In this narrative, scholars are self-perceived as leftists. What is interesting is that even scholars who were never part of the left would perceive Uruguayan academia *as such* as left-wing. These colleagues locate themselves as exceptions without contesting the general characterization.
19. Something close to "positive thinking" in Marcusian terms: "a syntax in which the structure of the sentence is abridged and condensed in such way that, no tension, no 'space' is left between the parts of the sentences" (Marcuse, 1991, p. 86). In this case, such a reifying language reproduces democracy and liberalism as unthinkable, naturalized realms.
20. CIESU (Centro de Informaciones y Estudios del Uruguay [Center of Information and Studies of Uruguay]) and CINVE (Centro de Investigaciones Económicas [Center of Economic Research]) were created in 1975; CIEDUR (Centro Interdisciplinario de

Estudios sobre el Desarrollo [Interdisciplinary Center for Studies on Development]) in 1977; and GRECMU (Grupo de Estudios sobre la Condición de la Mujer en Uruguay [Study Group on the Condition of Women in Uruguay]) in 1979. CLAEH (Centro Latinoamericano de Economía Humana [The Latin American Center of Human Economy]), founded in the late 1950s, also played an important role during the dictatorship in sheltering research and hosting social sciences training. See http://claeh. edu.uy/v2/index.php?option=com_content&view=article&id=2&Itemid=118.

21. Menéndez-Carrión (2015) conceptualizes the experience of (at least some of) the PRCs in an entirely different fashion. She highlights the role played by some NGOs (as well as private homes) within the politics of *insilio* [a state of being "in exile," while remaining in the country] in keeping the possibility of talking-and-thinking and of being political (that is, of "being of the *polis*" in/at/through being there, at those places) throughout the dictatorship. The argument is convincing. Both logics (*insilio* and neo-liberalization) might have been at play during the period, probably with differentiated and specific intensities in the different PRCs.

22. I am combining the conceptual vocabularies of Geertz (1997) and Shapiro (2005) here.

23. The hesitation of Prates in applying the notion of informal sector to academia is interesting. The risk of "dubious transposition" means in this context that academia should not be analyzed with the same categories employed for our objects of study. One can see in such a position the resistance to accepting that academic institutions and discourse are part of the social realm in which they are embedded.

24. Quite tellingly, economics survived, institutionally speaking, the authoritarian assault on the social sciences.

25. In the sense of Marcuse (1991) and Horkheimer (1978): a merely useful knowledge that collapses the difference between actuality and potentiality.

26. The dictatorship intervened in the political economy of the sector through strangling sources of funding and the creation of private universities. However, UdelaR has remained the leading institution for teaching and research in the system of higher education up until today.

27. The Partido Colorado [Colorado Party] and the Partido Nacional [National Party] are among the oldest political parties in the world. The former was in office for most of the 20th century, going through different ideological mutations. Both parties have been on the right side of the ideological spectrum after the dictatorship.

28. The original in Spanish reads: "Un acierto muy importante en su gestión fue el de haber amalgamado distintas corrientes teóricas, ideológicas y políticas, estimulando la conformación de un ambiente pluralista, altamente beneficioso para el debate y el aprendizaje académico" (Garcé, 2005, p. 237).

29. In this regard, the testimony of U11, a British scholar living and working in Uruguay, is interesting, given that it sheds comparative light onto the case: "In British academia and intellectual life [Marxism] was present . . . here not at all!"

30. Mallo (2011) is based on the author's PhD dissertation on Carlos Real de Azúa's life and writing. A vast literature about him can be found at: www.autoresdeluruguay.uy/ biblioteca/Carlos_Real_De_Azua/doku.php?id=sobre.

31. Awkwardly, but meaningfully, this activity was sponsored by *and physically located in* parliament. One of the participants, Luis Eduardo González, questioned the location of the seminar, saying that Real de Azúa was particularly jealous of his independence from the political system.

32. "Carlos *Real de Azúa:* 1916–1977. Evocación y *Coloquio* con Tulio Halperin Donghi." I recall Susana Mallo asking some interesting questions about the political radicalization of Real de Azúa and his support to the political left. She was preparing Mallo (2011) at the time. The portrayal of Real de Azúa as a radical did not please one of the organizers.

33. The translation is mine and is not literal. The original reads: "Algo así como lo que Althusser y Poulantzas, que probablemente producirían escalofríos al estilo y la envergadura intelectual de Real de Azúa, intentan explicar y no lo hacen al hablar de 'autonomía relativa'."
34. See, for instance: www.autoresdeluruguay.uy/biblioteca/Carlos_Real_De_Azua/doku.php?id=entrevistas.
35. Given that it is the first time that sexuality makes an appearance in the book—at least in its analytical body—I feel compelled to make the following theoretical point: to assert that the personal is political might imply an essentialist move. The political is not out there prior to its definition in discourse. Therefore, the personal is politicizable. Assuming that the personal cannot be politicized is another essentialist move. Clearly, analytical separations (private—public, civil society–the state, society—the economy), when reified, become an ideological move that erases the relationships that constitute what we call reality. This reality, therefore, becomes ungraspable and power relations cannot be understood. This is the theoretical context in which I situate my reading of Real de Azúa's queerness.
36. The original reads: "No es exceso poner esta muerte en la cuenta de las penas que debemos al militarismo torpe que se ha apoderado del Uruguay" (Rama, 1977, p. 40).
37. In my view, Pérez Antón's hypothesis may be regarded as an example of what Filgueira (1974) and de Sierra (2005) identify as an excessive optimism about the country's reality, with conservative consequences.
38. Roundtable titled "Political Science in the Region," held during the 2012 Uruguayan Conference of Political Science.
39. In this regard, some of the comments made by Kathryn Sikkink in this roundtable are interesting (see Asuntos Públicos, 2014).
40. It was not until very recently—the last five years or so—that Uruguayan PS' research agenda started comprising subjects decidedly outside the mainstream such as critical theory (still extremely marginal), political economy, and social movements, among others.
41. Bear in mind that Uruguayan PS started with a call by Lanzaro to a diverse set of scholars without political science degrees; hence, its birth was interdisciplinary. Perhaps that is why launching a crusade for its identity was perceived as needed.
42. As I said before, the rupture between generations operated in the realm of methodology and methods, not in the realm of ideology:

> There was a very strong vindication of political parties by the scholars from CLAEH, which we also embraced. Jorge Lanzaro and Luis Eduardo González were more moderate, but we (their students) got extremely passionate . . . until the *coup d'état*, intellectuals and academia were critical of the parties; we all used to think that they were just trash but after the end of the dictatorship the parties were celebrated.
>
> *(U5)*

Another interviewee from the same generation confesses:

> We sang praises, praises to the Uruguayan political system! That is what *The Imaginary Invalid* is all about [this is a reference to an important book in Uruguayan PS]. Among all the contributions to *The Second Transition* [another important book of Uruguayan PS], the worst text, the most acritical, is the one I wrote; I am sure; that was the spirit of the age.
>
> *(U7)*

43. In the case of these authors, they obtained their BAs in Political Science from ICP between 1994 and 1997. Adolfo Garcé defended his in 1996 and Jaime Yaffé in 1999.

This generation of scholars that was educated during the 1990s became extremely academically active soon after the completion of their degrees. Their research agenda focused, in different ways, on government, political parties and politics.

44. In Volume 1, Chapter 5, Menéndez-Carrión (2015) offers a detailed examination of what she terms "deceitful gradualism" and, in the process, challenges the gradualism narrative as it has been applied to Uruguay (pp. 343–358).

45. The, at times, acritical engagement with the political system suffered shifts over the years. For some interviewees, (U4; U7) the financial crisis of 2002 made some PS practitioners reconsider their overwhelmingly positive views of the political establishment. Leading PS practitioners also made public declarations about this (see Garcé, 2012).

46. Sivolobova (2010) offers a succinct legal discussion of the law.

47. For a succinct and recent reflection on the law and its implications, see Buriano and Dutrénit (2017). The article refers to some of the authors who have researched and reflected on this law such as Eugenia Allier, Gianella Bardazano, Ana Buriano, Gerardo Caetano, Carlos Demasi, Silvia Dutrénit, Gonzalo Varela, Gabriela Fried, Álvaro De Giorgi, Ana Laura De Giorgi, Francesca Lessa, Aldo Marchesi, Álvaro Rico, and Diego Sempol. A relatively recent article in English is Fried Amilivia (2016).

48. Even though the notion of a stone covering a veil is awkward and the phrase is highly unstructured—the product of the messiness of oral language—I decided to go for accuracy rather than grammar and aesthetic perfection when I translated the testimony. My aim was to keep its expressive power.

49. This was the response of a colleague, who distances himself ideologically and theoretically from the mainstream, to my critique of PS for not problematizing Uruguayan democracy in light of the Expiry Law, during a personal conversation in the 8th Latin American Conference of Political Science (July 2015).

50. An extensive interview with Sara Mendez is available at Raquel Daruech TV (2013).

51. In a critical tone, former Editor-in-Chief of *Perspectives on Politics*, Jeffrey C. Isaac, has argued that "in the highest reaches of rigorous American political science, empiricism increasingly means elaborate statistical, mathematical, and experimental research that is far removed from the empirical world as lived and experienced" (2015, p. 21).

52. On the contrasts between Chile and Uruguay in terms of the model of capitalism adopted, see Bogliaccini (2012). Chile is widely identified as an early and prominent neoliberal experiment (Brown, 2015; Saad-Filho & Johnston, 2005; Harvey, 2005; Moulián, 2009).

53. Batllismo is a faction of the Colorado Party that takes its name from José Batlle y Ordóñez (1856–1929), a Uruguayan president (1903–1907; 1911–1915) who had a key role in the building of the Uruguayan welfare state and the advancement of several progressive social and economic reforms. Traditionally, the label has thus been linked to a political program that could roughly be called social democratic.

54. Moulián (2002) argues that, in Chile, the contemporary mechanization of politics "where a decision around the final aims in society that differs from the currently accepted ones becomes irrational, is contradictory with the essence of democracy" (p. 13). The political elites *and academia* narrow the realm of the thinkable and debatable. The result: "once the 'unrealistic' excess of meaning is abolished, the investigation is locked within the vast confine in which the established society validates and invalidates prepositions. By virtue of its methodology, this empiricism is ideological" (Marcuse, 1991, p. 114). This is just power at work. Marcuse is one of few critical theorists who unraveled the profound relationship between liberal PS and neoliberalism.

55. I do not refer to "imperialism" here, given the multiple contributions that, as Ananya Mukherjee-Reed once reminded me, "the South" and Southern scholars have made in the forging of neoliberalism. However, the United States clearly functioned as a "toxic democracy." The toxicity of a regime, government or society "has to do with . . . the little space left for the expression of other socio-political possibilities, and the actual actions taken by state representatives and political/economic elites to block and derail autochthonous and/or alternative democratic experiences and models at home—think McCarthyism—and abroad (e.g. Chile in 1973, Guatemala in 1954, Mexico in 1913, etc.)" (Torres-Ruiz & Ravecca, 2014, p. 130).
56. As one leading Uruguayan political scientist who works and lives in Chile said as a compliment: "Competition is not a bad word in Chile" (CHL1).
57. For instance, Pozo Cisternas (2016), Román Brugnoli and Energici Sprovera (2010), and Véjar (2012).
58. It goes without saying: the absence of a strong Catholic influence over the social sciences does not imply the absence of racism and rampant inequalities. Uruguayan society has traditionally been proud of being supposedly white and there is no reason to assume that academia is different.
59. In the *Economic and Philosophical Manuscripts of 1844*, there are also profound epistemological reflections about how knowledge is a manifestation of its own object.
60. These contrasts reveal different levels of capitalist naturalization, as well as the crucial importance of discourse and the superstructure.
61. I have not fully engaged with postcolonial thinking in this book but, clearly, PS has also had its (post)colonial moments and dynamics that should be explored (see Chapter 1).
62. This interpretation operationalizes my conception of power relations as a complex relationality between knowledge production and dissemination, identity, subjectivity, political economy, conventional politics, and the transnational dimension of the political. I have shown that all these aspects dynamically affect (or mutually constitute) each other. However, I am not a structuralist, and that is why "mutual constitution" is, in my view, full of accidents that can only be apprehended through looking at concrete h*istories*, which is what I have attempted to do in this chapter.
63. The original: "En este ámbito hay un único principio para defender a muerte que es la democracia . . . ahí sí la Ciencia Política toma partido y no es neutral porque está a favor de la democracia y hace su aporte en la medida de lo posible para que la misma dure y mejore."

Works Cited

Agathangelou, A. (2004). *The global political economy of sex: Desire, violence, and insecurity in Mediterranean nation states*. New York: Palgrave Macmillan.
Aguiar, C. (1984, July 13). Notas sobre Real de Azúa y la ciencia política en el Uruguay. *Jaque*, p. 6–7. Retrieved from www.autoresdeluruguay.uy/biblioteca/Carlos_Real_De_Azua/lib/exe/fetch.php?media=cesaraguiar.pdf
Alegre, P. (2008). Democracia y reformas en el Uruguay: Un caso de gradualismo perverso. *Revista Uruguaya de Ciencia Política, 17*(1), 137–158.
Alexander, J. M. (2005). *Pedagogies of crossing: Meditations on feminism, sexual politics, memory, and the sacred*. Durham, NC: Duke University Press.
Altamiranda, J. J. (2009). *Veinte años de la creación de la Licenciatura de Ciencia Política (1989–2009)*. Asociación Uruguaya de Ciencia Política, Montevideo. Retrieved from www.aucip.org.uy/index.php/institucional/publicaciones/14-veinte-anos-de-la-creacion-de-la-licenciatura-de-ciencia-politica-1989–2009.html

Altman, D. (2005). La institucionalización de la ciencia política en Chile y América Latina: Una mirada desde el sur. *Revista de Ciencia Política, 25*(1), 3–15.

Álvarez Vallejos, R. (2011). Gran empresariado, poderes fácticos e imaginarios políticos: El caso de la transición democrática chilena (1990–2000). In M. Mella (Ed.), *Extraños en la noche: Intelectuales y usos políticos del conocimiento durante la transición chilena* (pp. 97–149). Santiago de Chile: RIL editores.

Amadae, S. M. (2016). *Prisoners of reason: Game theory and neoliberal political economy.* New York: Cambridge University Press.

Arias, C. (2012). Los conceptos de transición y democracia en el pensamiento de las ciencias sociales: Uruguay 1985–1989. *Revista de la Facultad de Derecho, 32*, 23–38.

Asuntos Públicos [Asuntos Públicos]. (2011, December 3). *Carlos Real de Azúa. Un intelectual inasible.* [Video file]. Retrieved from www.youtube.com/watch?v=uLx WQu-Mwi8

Asuntos Públicos [Asuntos Públicos]. (2014, November 7). *¿Qué ciencia política para qué democracia? Parte 4: ¿Clima de perestroika?* [Video file]. Retrieved from www.youtube.com/watch?v=CrHCvveeN98

Bannerji, H. (2005). *Building from Marx: Reflections on "race," gender and class.* Retrieved from http://davidmcnally.org/wp-content/uploads/2011/01/bannerji.buildingfrommarx.pdf

Bentancur, N. (2003). *La ciencia política en Uruguay: Creación e institucionalización de un campo disciplinario.* Unpublished paper.

Bentancur, N., & Mancebo, M. E. (2013). Pensando "lo público": Los desarrollos de la ciencia política sobre estado y políticas públicas en Uruguay (1987–2012). *Revista Debates, 7*(3), 9–30.

Betancur, N., & Mancebo, M. E. (2017). ¿Cómo se forma a los científicos políticos en Iberoamérica? Análisis de la oferta de titulaciones de grado en ciencia política en doce países. *Revista Española de Ciencia Política, 43*, 161–185. doi: 10.21308/recp.43.07.

Bevir, M. (2003). Interpretivism: Family resemblances and quarrels. *Qualitative Methods Newsletter of the American Political Science Association, 1*(2), 18–20. doi: 10.5281/zenodo.998729.

Bischoping, K., & Gazso, A. (Eds.). (2016). *Analyzing talk in the social sciences.* Thousand Oaks, CA: Sage Publications.

Bogliaccini, J. A. (2012). *Small latecomers into the global market: Power conflict and institutional change in Chile and Uruguay* (Doctoral dissertation). Retrieved from https://cdr.lib.unc.edu/indexablecontent/uuid:617a0663-6b00-4469-b798-410f5794141a

Bohoslavsky, J. P. (2012). El eslabón financiero en la justicia transicional uruguaya. *Revista Uruguaya de Ciencia Política, 21*(1), 153–179.

Bottinelli, O. A. (2011, April 3). ¿Voto amarillo = voto por miedo? *Factum Digital: Revista de Análisis Político, Opinión Pública, y Estudios Sociales.* Retrieved from www.factum.uy/analisis/2011/ana110403.php

Brigg, M., & Bleiker, R. (2010). Autoethnographic international relations: Exploring the self as a source of knowledge. *Review of International Studies, 36*, 779–798.

Brown, W. (2010). *Walled states, waning sovereignty.* Brooklyn: Zone Books.

Brown, W. (2015). *Undoing the demos: Neoliberalism's stealth revolution.* New York: Zone Books.

Bruna Contreras, G. (1987). La libertad económica: Elemento de un nuevo orden político económico. *Política, 13*, 59–76.

Buck-Morss, S. (2009). *Hegel, Haiti and universal history.* Pittsburgh: University of Pittsburgh Press.

Buck-Morss, S. (2010). The second time as farce . . . historical pragmatics and the untimely present. In C. Douzinas & S. Žižek (Eds.), *The idea of communism* (pp. 67–80). New York: Verso.

Bulcourf, P. (2012). El desarrollo de la ciencia política en Argentina. *Política, 50*(1), 59–92.

Bulcourf, P., Gutiérrez Márquez, E., & Cardozo, N. (2015). Historia y desarollo de la ciencia política en América Latina: Reflexiones sobre la constitución del campo de estudios. *Revista de Ciencia Política, 35*(1), 179–199.

Buriano, A., & Dutrénit, S. (2017). A 30 años de la ley de caducidad uruguaya. ¿Qué y cómo debemos conmemorar? *Antíteses, 10*(19), 351–375.

Buquet, D. (2012). El desarrollo de la ciencia política en Uruguay. *Política, 50*(1), 5–29.

Buquet, D., Chasquetti D., & Moraes, J. A. (1998). *Fragmentación política y gobierno en Uruguay: ¿Un enfermo imaginario?* Montevideo: Taller de impresiones de la Facultad de Ciencias Sociales, Universidad de la República.

Busquets, J. M., Sarlo, O., & Delbono, A. (2015). La recepción de Maquiavelo y los neo-maquiavelistas en la ciencia política, con especial referencia al caso uruguayo (1957–1985). *Revista de la Facultad de Derecho (2° época)*, (38), 49–85.

Butalia, U. (2000). *The other side of silence: Voices from the partition of India*. Durham, NC: Duke University Press.

Butler, J. (1990). *Gender trouble: Feminism and the subversion of identity*. New York: Routledge.

Butler, J., Laclau, E., & Zizek, S. (2003). *Contingencia, hegemonía, universalidad: Diálogos contemporáneos en la izquierda*. Buenos Aires: Fondo de Cultura Económica.

Butler, J., & Spivak, G. C. (2010). *Who sings the nation-state?: Language, politics, belonging*. New York: Seagull Books.

Caetano, G., Pérez Antón, R., & Rilla, J. (1987). La partidocracia uruguaya. *Cuadernos del CLAEH, 12*(44), 37–61.

Caetano, G., & Rilla, J. (1987). *Breve historia de la dictadura*. Montevideo: CLAEH/ Banda Oriental.

Castro, M. M. (2018). El accionar colectivo en torno a la discapacidad en Uruguay. *Revista Uruguaya de Ciencia Política, 25*(2), 79–98.

Chasquetti, D. (2013). Construyendo instituciones: Examen de las asociaciones de ciencia política en el Cono Sur. In S. Leyva Botero (Ed.), *La ciencia política en Colombia: ¿Una disciplina en institucionalización?* (pp. 287–308). Medellín: Universidad Eafit-Biblioteca Luis Echavarría Villegas.

Cosse, I., & Markarián, V. (1996). *1975: Año de la orientalidad. Identidad, memoria e historia en una dictadura*. Montevideo: Trilce.

Da Costa, N. (2009). La laicidad uruguaya. *Archives de Sciences Sociales des Religions, 146*, 137–155.

Dahl, R. (1991). *La democracia y sus críticos*. Buenos Aires: Paidos.

Dauphinee, E. (2013a). *The politics of exile*. New York: Routledge.

Dauphinee, E. (2013b). Writing as hope: Reflections on the politics of exile. *Security Dialogue, 44*(4), 347–361.

De Sierra, G. (2005). Social sciences in Uruguay. *Social Science Information, 44*(2–3), 473–520.

Denzin, N. K., & Lincoln Y. S. (2011). *Manual de investigación cualitativa*. Barcelona: Gedisa.

Edkins, J. (2003). *Trauma and the memory of politics*. New York: Cambridge University Press.

Fernández de la Mora, G. (1987). El método y el ideario conservadores. *Política, 11*, 13–21.

Filgueira, C. H. (1974). *25 años de sociología uruguaya*. Montevideo: Centro de Investigaciones y Estudios Sociales del Uruguay (CIESU).

Filgueira, C. H. (1986). Sociología. In *Ciencia y tecnología en el Uruguay* (pp. 163–191). Montevideo: Centro de Investigaciones Económicas (CINVE).

Filgueira, F., Garcé, A., Ramos, C., & Yaffé, J. (2003). Los dos ciclos del estado uruguayo en el siglo XX. In B. Nahum (Ed.), *El Uruguay del siglo X:. La política* (pp. 173–204). Montevideo: Banda Oriental.

Finch, H. (1992). Uruguay since 1930. In L. Bethell (Ed.), *The Cambridge history of Latin America, volume 8: Latin America since 1930: Spanish South America* (pp. 195–232). Cambridge: Cambridge University Press.

Fleming, P. (2005, July). *Marcuse, memory and the psychoanalysis of workplace resistance*. Paper presented at the meeting of Critical Management Studies, Cambridge, UK. Retrieved from www.mngt.waikato.ac.nz/ejrot/cmsconference/2005/proceedings/psychoanalytic/Fleming.pdf

Flick, U. (2007). *Introducción a la investigación cualitativa*. Madrid: Ediciones Morata y Fundación Paideia.

Forteza, Á., Buquet, D., Ibarburu, M., Lanzaro, J., Pereyra, Á., Siandra, E., & Vaillant, M. (2007). Pro-market reform in Uruguay: Gradual reform and political pluralism. In J. M. Fanelli (Ed.), *Understanding market reforms in Latin America: Similar reforms, diverse experiences, varied results* (pp. 227–265). New York: Palgrave Macmillan.

Foucault, M. (1980). Two lectures. In C. Gordon (Ed.), *Power/knowledge: Selected interviews and other writings 1972–1977* (pp. 78–109). New York: Pantheon.

Foucault, M. (1984). What is an author. In P. Rabinow (Ed.), *The Foucault reader* (pp. 101–120). New York: Vintage Books.

Foucault, M. (1988). L'anti-oedipe: Une introduction a la vie non fasciste. *Magazine Littéraire, 257*(September).

Foucault, M. (1989). *Vigilar y castigar*. Mexico City: Siglo Veintiuno Editores.

Foucault, M. (1991a). *Historia de la sexualidad 1: La voluntad de saber*. Madrid: Siglo Veintiuno de España Editores.

Foucault, M. (1991b). *Saber y verdad*. Madrid: Ediciones La Piqueta.

Foucault, M. (1992). *Microfísica del poder*. Madrid: Ediciones La Piqueta.

Foucault, M. (1993). *Genealogía del racismo*. Montevideo: Nordam.

Foucault, M. (2006). *Seguridad, territorio, población: Curso en el Collège de France (1977–1978)*. Buenos Aires: Fondo de Cultura Económica.

Freud, S. (1986). El malestar en la cultura. In J. Stratchey (Ed.) & J. L. Etcheverry (Trans.), *Obras completas, Volumen XXI (1927–1931)* (pp. 57–140). Buenos Aires: Amorrortu Editores.

Fried Amilivia, G. (2016). Sealing and unsealing Uruguay's transitional politics of oblivion: Waves of memory and the road to justice, 1985–2015. *Latin American Perspectives, 43*(6), 103–123.

Fujii, L. A. (2016). The dark side of DA-RT. *Comparative Politics Newsletter, 26*(1), 25–27.

Gajardo Lagomarsino, P. (1989). La transición a la democracia en Chile: Desafíos y perspectivas a partir de un análisis teórico. *Política, 21*, 53–62.

Garcé, A. (2005). La ciencia política en Uruguay: Un desarrollo tardío, intenso y asimétrico. *Revista de Ciencia Política, 25*(1), 232–244.

Garcé, A. (2012, July 18). Crisis de 2002: La otra cara. *El Observador.* Retrieved from www.elobservador.com.uy/crisis-2002-la-otra-cara-n228388

Garcé, A., & Rocha Carpiuc, C. (2015). La ciencia política en Uruguay: Entre la profesionalización, la partidización y el fantasma del "movimiento perestroika." *Revista Ciencia Política, 35*(1), 121–144.

Garcé, A., & Yaffé, J. (2005). *La era progresista.* Montevideo: Fin de Siglo.

Geertz, C. (1997). *La interpretación de las culturas.* Barcelona: Gedisa.

Geertz, C. (2003). Interview with Clifford Geertz (J. Gerring, Interviewer). *Qualitative Methods Newsletter of the American Political Science Association, 1*(2), 24–28. doi: 10.5281/zenodo.998745.

Gil, D., & Viñar, M. (1998). La dictadura militar: Una intrusión en la intimidad. In J. P. Barrán, G. Caetano, & T. Porzecansky (Eds.), *Historias de la vida privada en el Uruguay 3: Individuo y soledades 1920–1990* (pp. 301–326). Montevideo: Taurus.

Giorgi, V. (1995). Represión y olvido: El terrorismo de estado dos décadas después. In V. Giorgi (Ed.), *Represión y olvido: Efectos psicológicos y sociales de la violencia política dos décadas después* (pp. 53–66). Montevideo: Roca Viva Editorial.

González, L. E. (1993). *Estructuras políticas y democracia en el Uruguay.* Montevideo: ICP-FCU.

González, L. E. (2007). *Carlos Real de Azúa.* Asociación Uruguaya de Ciencia Política, Montevideo. Retrieved from www.aucip.org.uy/index.php/institucional/publicaciones.html

Gonzalez Candia, J. C., & Zapata Schaffeld, F. (2015). Reformas estructurales y su impacto en las bases de poder del sindicalismo chileno y uruguayo. *Trabajo y Sociedad, 24,* 5–32.

Gramsci, A. (2008). *Selections from the prison notebooks* (Q. Hoare & G. Nowell, Trans. & Eds.). New York: International Publishers.

Gregory, S. (2009). *Intellectuals and left politics in Uruguay, 1958–2006.* Brighton: Sussex Academic Press.

Guber, R. (2011). *La etnografía: Método, campo y reflexividad.* Buenos Aires: Siglo Ventiuno.

Harvey, D. (2005). *A brief history of neoliberalism.* Oxford: Oxford University Press.

Hernández, D. (2000). *Acerca del aprendizaje democrático: Seguridad social en el Uruguay, una perspectiva comparada.* Informe final del concurso: Democracia, derechos sociales y equidad; y Estado, política y conflictos sociales. [Final Report of the Competition: Democracy, Social Rights, and Equality; State, Politics, and Social Conflicts.] Programa Regional de Becas CLACSO [Regional Scholarship Program of CLACSO], Buenos Aires, Argentina. Retrieved from http://bibliotecavirtual.clacso.org.ar/ar/libros/becas/1999/aragon.pdf

Holt, N. L. (2003). Representation, legitimation, and autoethnography: An autoethnographic writing story. *International Journal of Qualitative Methods, 2*(1), 18–58.

Horkheimer, M. (1978). *Théorie critique.* Paris: Payot.

Horowitz, G. (1977). *Basic and surplus repression in psychoanalytic theory: Freud, Reich and Marcuse.* Toronto: University of Toronto Press.

Horowitz, G. (2003, October 29). On intellectual life, politics and psychoanalysis: A conversation with Gad Horowitz (C. Campbell, Interviewer). *CTHEORY,* Article a135. Retrieved from www.ctheory.net/articles.aspx?id=397

Instituto de Ciencia Política. (2016). *Informe de la dirección del departamento de ciencia política a la sala docente período julio 2013- julio 2016.* Montevideo: ICP.

Isaac, J. C. (2015). The parochialism of the universal, or beware of American political scientists bearing gifts. *The Romanian Journal of Society and Politics*, *10*(2), 7–25.

Jackson, P. T. (2011). *The conduct of inquiry in international relations: Philosophy of science and its implications for the study of world politics*. New York: Routledge.

Keinert, F. C., & Silva, D. P. (2010). A gênese da ciência política brasileira. *Tempo social*, *22*(1), 79–98.

Kellermann, N. P. F. (2001). *Transmission of holocaust trauma*. Jereusalem: Yad Vashem, The World Holocaust Rememberance Center. Retrieved from www.yad vashem.org/yv/en/education/languages/dutch/pdf/kellermann.pdf

Keucheyan, R. (2013). *The left hemisphere: Mapping critical theory today*. New York: Verso.

LaCapra, D. (2009). *Historia y memoria después de Auschwitz*. Buenos Aires: Prometeo.

Laclau, E., & Mouffe, C. (2004). *Hegemonía y estrategia socialista: Hacia una radicalización de la democracia*. Buenos Aires: Fondo de Cultura Económica.

Lanzaro, J. (2000). *La "segunda" transición en el Uruguay*. Montevideo: Fundación de Cultura Universitaria/ICP.

Lechner, N. (1990). *Las condiciones políticas de la ciencia política en Chile* (FLACSO-Chile Working Paper No. 453). Santiago de Chile: FLACSO-Chile. Retrieved from http://flacsochile.org/biblioteca/pub/memoria/1990/000219.pdf

Lesgart, C. (2003). *Usos de la transición a la democracia: Ensayo, ciencia y política en la década del '80*. Rosario: HomoSapiens.

Löwenheim, O. (2010). The "I" in IR: An autoethnographic account. *Review of International Studies*, *36*(4), 1023–1045.

Mallo, S. (2011). *Carlos Real de Azúa: Un intelectual inasible. El papel de los intelectuales, la política y los vaivenes del Uruguay y la región en la segunda mitad del Siglo XX*. Montevideo: Banda Oriental.

Marchesi, A. (2017). *Latin America's radical left: Rebellion and cold war in the global 1960s*. New York: Cambridge University Press.

Marchesi, A., Markarián, V., Rico, A., & Yaffé, J. (2003). *El presente de la dictadura: Estudios y reflexiones a 30 años del golpe de estado en Uruguay*. Montevideo: Ediciones Trilce.

Marcuse, H. (1974). *Eros and civilization: A philosophical inquiry into Freud*. Boston: Beacon Press.

Marcuse, H. (1991). *One-dimensional man: Studies in the ideology of advanced industrial society*. Boston: Beacon Press.

Markarián, V. (2015). La universidad intervenida: Cambios y permanencias de la educación superior uruguaya durante la última dictadura (1973–1984). *Cuadernos Chilenos de Historia de la Educación*, *3*(4), 121–153.

Markoff, J., & Montecinos, V. (1994). El irresistible ascenso de los economistas. *Desarrollo Económico*, *133*(34), 3–29.

McSherry, P. (2005). *Predatory states: Operation condor and covert war in Latin America*. New York: Rowman and Littlefield.

Menéndez-Carrión, A. (2015). *Memorias de ciudadanía: Los avatares de una polis golpeada. La experiencia uruguaya*. Montevideo: Fin de Siglo.

Merlino, A. (2009). *Investigación cualitativa en ciencias sociales: Temas, problemas y aplicaciones*. Buenos Aires: Cengage Learning.

Monroe, K. R. (Ed.). (2005). *Perestroika! The raucous rebellion in political science*. New Haven, CT: Yale University Press.

Moraes, J. A. (2015). Del pluralismo incómodo a la comodidad del pluralismo: Una respuesta a Adolfo Garcé y Cecilia Rocha sobre el estado de la ciencia política en Uruguay. *Revista de ciencia política*, *35*(3), 629–636.

Moreira, C. (2001). La reforma del estado en Uruguay: Cuestionando el gradualismo y la heterodoxia. In P. Calame & A. Talmant (Eds.), *Con el estado en el corazón: El andamiaje de la gobernancia* (pp. 167–202). Montevideo: Ed. Trilce.

Moulián, T. (2002). *Chile actual: Anatomía de un mito*. Santiago de Chile: LOM editores.

Moulián, T. (2009). *Contradicciones del desarrollo político chileno 1920–1990*. Santiago de Chile: Editorial Arcis.

Perelli, C., & Rial, J. (1986). *De mitos y memorias políticas: La represión, el miedo y después* . . . Montevideo: Banda Oriental.

Pérez Antón, R. (1986). Ciencia política. In *Ciencia y tecnología en el Uruguay* (pp. 223–233). Montevideo: Centro de Investigaciones Económicas (CINVE).

Pérez Antón, R. (1992). Ciencia política. In G. Caetano, P. Mieres, R. Pérez, & J. Rilla (Eds.), *Partidos y electores: Centralidad y cambios* (pp. 41–62). Montevideo: Centro Latinoamericano de Economía Humana (CLAEH).

Pessanha, C. (2017). 50 Anos de "DADOS—Revista de Ciências Sociais": Uma Introdução à Coleção. *DADOS—Revista de Ciências Sociais*, *60*(3), 605–622.

Pozo Cisternas, C. (2016). El psicoanálisis y la actualidad de la subjetividad neoliberal en Chile. *LIMINALES: Escritos sobre psicología y sociedad*, *1*(10), 71–84.

Prates, S. (1987). *Los centros autónomos en ciencias sociales en el Uruguay: Trayectoria y perspectivas*. Montevideo: Centro de Investigaciones y Estudios Sociales del Uruguay (CIESU).

Rama, A. (1977). Carlos Real de Azúa (1916–1977). *Escritura: Teoría y Crítica Literaria*, *2*(3), 35–40. Retrieved from www.autoresdeluruguay.uy/biblioteca/Carlos_Real_De_Azua/lib/exe/fetch.php?media=ar_-_cra.pdf

Rama, G. (1987). *La democracia en Uruguay*. Montevideo: Editorial Arca.

Raquel Daruech TV [Raquel Daruech TV]. (2013, October 24). *Sara Méndez uno x uno bloque 1*. [Video file]. Retrieved from www.youtube.com/watch?v=7Dd5L2zAGsY

Ravecca, P. (2010). La política de la ciencia política: Ensayo de introspección disciplinar desde América Latina hoy. *América Latina*, *9*, 173–210.

Ravecca, P. (2014). *La política de la ciencia política en Chile y Uruguay: Ciencia, poder, contexto. Primeros hallazgos de una agenda de investigación* (Working Paper No. 01/14). Montevideo: Instituto de Ciencia Política.

Ravecca, P. (2016). The intimate architecture of academia. In E. Dauphinee & N. Inayatullah (Eds.), *Narrative global politics* (pp. 51–63). London: Routledge.

Ravecca, P., & Dauphinee, E. (2018). Narrative and the possibilities for scholarship. *International Political Sociology*, *12*(2), 125–138.

Read, J. (2009). A genealogy of homo-economicus: Neoliberalism and the production of subjectivity. *Foucault Studies*, *6*, 25–36.

Real de Azúa, C. (1973). *La teoría política latinoamericana: Una actividad cuestionada*. Retrieved from www.autoresdeluruguay.uy/biblioteca/Carlos_Real_De_Azua/lib/exe/fetch.php?media=teoriayetica.pdf

Real de Azúa, C. (1983). *El clivaje mundial eurocentro—periferia y las áreas exceptuadas 1500–1900*. Montevideo: CIESU/Acali Editorial.

Real de Azúa, C. (1984). *Uruguay, ¿una sociedad amortiguadora?* Montevideo: Banda Oriental/CIESU.

Rico, Á. (2005). *Cómo nos domina la clase gobernante: Orden político y obediencia social en la democracia posdictadura, 1985–2005*. Montevideo: Ediciones Trilce.

Rico, Á. (Ed.). (2007). *Investigación histórica sobre detenidos desaparecidos*. Montevideo: IMPO.

Rocha Carpiuc, C. (2012a). La ciencia política en Uruguay (1989–2009): Temas, teorías y metodologías. *Revista Uruguaya de Ciencia Política, 21*(2), 97–127.

Rocha Carpiuc, C. (2012b). *El desarrollo de la ciencia política en Uruguay (1987–2009): Temas, teorías y metodologías*. Unpublished BA dissertation, ICP, Faculty of Social Sciences, University of the Republic, Uruguay.

Rocha Carpiuc, C. (2014). ¿Hacia una hegemonía del "modelo mainstream norteamericano"? Enfoques de la ciencia política en América Latina (2000–2012). *Revista Latinoamericana de Investigación Crítica (I+C), 1*(1), 131–166.

Rocha Carpiuc, C. (2017). La ciencia política en Uruguay: Profesión, enseñanza e investigación. In F. Freindenberg (Ed.), *La ciencia política en América Latina* (pp. 247–274). Santo Domingo: Fundación Global Democracia y Desarrollo.

Román Brugnoli, J. A., & Energici Sprovera, M. A. (2010). La solidaridad de mercado y sus sujetos en el capitalismo de consumo: Un análisis del discurso neoliberal sobre piezas de publicidad en Chile. *Psicologia & Sociedade, 22*(2), 247–258.

Saad-Filho, A., & Johnston, D. (Eds.) (2005). *Neoliberalism: A critical reader*. London: Pluto Press.

Said, E. (2003). *Orientalismo*. Barcelona: Debolsillo.

Sartori, G. (1984). *La política: Lógica y método en las ciencias sociales*. Mexico City: Fondo de Cultura Económica.

Sartori, G. (2004). Where is political science going? *PS: Political Science & Politics, 37*(4), 785–787.

Schumpeter, J. (1985). *Capitalismo, socialismo y democracia*. Barcelona: Folio.

Sears, A. (2012). *The next new left: A history of the future*. Halifax: Fernwood Publishing.

Sempol, D. (2010). Homosexualidad y cárceles políticas uruguayas: La homofobia como política de resistencia. *Revista Latinoamericana Sexualidad, Salud y Sociedad, 4*, 53–79. Retrieved from www.sexualidadsaludysociedad.org

SERPAJ (Servicio Paz y Justicia) Uruguay. (1989). *Uruguay, nunca más*. Montevideo: SERPAJ.

Shapiro, I. (2005). Problems, methods, and theories in the study of politics or what's wrong with political science and what to do about it. In K. R. Monroe (Ed.), *Perestroika! The raucous rebellion in political science* (pp. 66–86). New Haven, CT: Yale University Press.

Sivolobova, E. (2010, June 10). URUGUAY: Approaches to the expiry law. *JURIST Student Commentary*. Retrieved from www.jurist.org/dateline/2010/06/uruguay-approaches-to-the-expiry-law.php

Sneh, P., & Cosaka, J. C. (2000). *La shoah en el siglo: Del lenguaje del exterminio al exterminio del discurso*. Buenos Aires: Xavier Bóveda.

Solari, A. E. (1959). *Las ciencias sociales en el Uruguay*. Río de Janeiro: Centro Latinoamericano de investigaciones en Ciencias Sociales.

Spivak, G. (1988). Can the subaltern speak? In C. Nelson & L. Grossberg (Eds.), *Marxism and the interpretations of culture* (pp. 271–313). Basingstoke: Macmillan Education.

Tedeschi, R. G., & Calhoun, L. G. (2004). Posttraumatic growth: Conceptual foundations and empirical evidence. *Psychological Inquiry, 15*(1), 1–18.

Torres-Ruiz, A., & Ravecca, P. (2014). The politics of political science and toxic democracies: A hemispheric perspective. *Crítica Contemporánea. Revista de Teoría Política, 4*, 107–136.

Trent, J. (2012). Issues and trends in political science at the beginning of the 21st century: Perspectives from the World of Political Science book series. In J. Trent & M. Stein (Eds.), *The world of political science: A critical overview of the development of political studies around the globe: 1990–2012* (pp. 91–153). Toronto: Barbara Budrich Publishers.

Vacs, A. (1998). Between restructuring and impasse: Liberal democracy, exclusionary policymaking, and neoliberal programs in Argentina and Uruguay. In K. von Mettenheim & J. Malloy (Eds.), *Deepening democracy in Latin America* (pp. 137–172). Pittsburgh: University of Pittsburgh Press.

Vejar, D. J. (2012). Dispositivos de disciplinamiento en el trabajo: Relaciones laborales y subjetividad(es) en Chile. *Si Somos Americanos, 12*(2), 109–131.

Yaffé, J. (2005). *Al centro y adentro: La renovación de la izquierda y el triunfo del Frente Amplio en Uruguay.* Montevideo: Linardi y Risso.

Yaffé, J. (2010). Economía y dictadura en Uruguay: Una visión panorámica de su evolución y de sus relaciones con la economía internacional (1973–1984). *Revista de Historia, 61–62*, 13–35.

Yrarrázaval, J. (1979). Reflexiones sobre ideología, conflicto y consenso. *Revista de Ciencia Política, 1*(1), 4–10.

4

DOING RESEARCH, FROM FORTRESS TO INTIMACY (HOT)*

> Placing [the] internal-external entwinement at the centre of research . . . is not to abandon the idea of science: quite the contrary, closely engaging the network of relations in which the author produces knowledge promises to deliver more nuanced, comprehensive, and perhaps even more scientific forms of insight than approaches that strive for authorial self-sufficiency and detachment.
>
> —Morgan Brigg and Roland Bleiker (2010, p. 794)

> The starting point of critical elaboration is the consciousness of what one really is, and is 'knowing thyself' as a product of the historical process to date which has deposited in you an infinity of traces, without leaving an inventory.
>
> —Antonio Gramsci (2008, p. 324)

The theoretical underpinnings of this study on the politics of political science (PPS) are based on the following premises: (*a*) the discipline is, following Marx, a form of human activity; (*b*) therefore, it is necessarily intertwined with the context of social relations in which it finds itself, including those relationships that are its object of analysis. From this, it logically follows that as practitioners of the discipline, or more specifically, as we go through the motions of practicing the discipline, *we, the political scientists*, are political; (*c*) additionally, and complementarily, if on the one hand participating in PS politicizes our experience (i.e. we are political *because* we are part of a political space called political science), on the other hand we are also bringing our human condition to the discipline, and our human activity constitutes the political motions of the discipline (i.e., PS is political because we, human beings, practice it). These premises are the fundamentals of the exercise that follows. There are other points of departure that are not less important: for instance, that (*d*) the narratives of reality and the knowledge that we produce as PS practitioners are, in Foucauldian terms, part of the discursive dynamics that regulate our social existence and have power effects over ourselves and others; but that (*e*) nonetheless, PS has its own density and gravitas. That our discipline has an ideological dimension that is linked to power dynamics does not mean that its practices of knowledge production can be *reduced* to ideology, power, or politics.

This chapter explores the *inter*play—perhaps, the inextricability—between knowledge production, power relationships, and the lived experience of being part of the discipline (or the discipline *as* personal experience) through an "I" narrative.[1] To be sure, the intimate architecture of any academic story is always personal. This does not make the idea of sharing that existential substratum with others necessarily interesting; and yet, at times, there may be a purpose it can serve beyond that of disclosure (Brigg & Bleiker, 2010; Naumes, 2015; Ravecca & Dauphinee, 2016, 2018). Here, personal self-reflection is meant to function as an analytical resource as well as an opportunity to theorize the politics of knowledge, and as such, politics—period. Granted, my own story is implicated in the theoretical relevance I attach to situating the discipline itself as a political question. However, I do not want to offer a positivist search for the "ultimate causes" of this research project. I am not displaying personal material in order to explain *why* I have embarked on the endeavor called PPS, a usual practice in the epilogues of academic books where the subjectivity of the scholar is finally (if at all) allowed to appear (King, Keohane, & Verba, 2000, p. 25). Quite the contrary, this chapter is part of the core of the analysis. Following the premises stated above, my aim is to take stock of the personal story *inside* the history that my research explores: situating disciplinary introspection through personal introspection may open fruitful paths to interrogate and unravel knots of experience made of knowledge, power, and politics.

The risk, of course, is always there. Revealing the personal may be dismissed by some as analytically irrelevant, and by others still as obscene, even. I fear more the former than the latter. I do not care that much about being perceived as obscene. But I do care about producing some form of significant knowledge (even "useful" knowledge). I care about the relationship between knowledge and power because I have experienced that encounter in ways that both destroyed and saved me, and it still does. I am not alone in this. Many of us have been made and unmade by knowledges and powers. I do not want to say "all of us," because that would hide oppression: we are not all equally made and unmade *vis-à-vis* knowledges and powers. In any case, and this is what matters the most here, that process is always social and political. It is from this standpoint that I turn to self-reflection or reflexivity (Amoureux & Steele, 2016) as an analytical strategy and, even more, as my way to cope with—to *do* something about—the troubles this research studies. In this way, disclosing the personal becomes a risk worth undertaking.[2]

The following pages engage with my experience (though experience that is hardly only mine) from the point of view of the theoretical insights presented above. They explore, and also embody, significant linkages between personal trajectory, family structure, the nation-state, the political system, world politics, and the discipline of political science. By looking at meaningful encounters between realms of experience that we are trained to keep separate, and by paying attention to how power travels faster, and in more complicated ways, than the categories with which we try to apprehend it, we will reach, I hope, a deeper knowledge of the politics of the discipline and, also, of the political in general.

Looking for a Perspective

In 2012, an immigration officer decided to give me zero points on "adaptability to the country," which at the time meant the denial of my permanent residency application. The immigration process into Canada became uncertain and frightening. This unexceptional experience transcends the personal: by showing the power that states (and the corporations that they structurally tend to represent) exercise over average people, it incarnates a tiny moment of international politics, political economy, and power relations. The distance is short from the international political economy to our bodies (Agathangelou, 2004, 2006; Alexander, 2005; Ciriza, 2010; Enloe, 1989; Persaud, 2016; Segato, 2016). The state names you, and as we all know, this naming has material implications, such as the power of rejection and expulsion (Butler & Spivak, 2010).[3]

For me, this event also evoked older moments of rejection and painful othering. The scrutiny over my persona resembled the rejection and insults hurled at me by other kids for being an undesirable subject called a "fag" in both elementary and high school.[4] These experiences are different. Temporal, geographical, and even institutional settings set them apart. Yet, notwithstanding these contrasts, both involve power relations and are part and parcel of the social. "Inequality between countries and their citizens" and "discrimination and bullying" are the distant and sanitized labels used by mainstream social science, which somehow washes out the pain from the analysis. And pain, as Elaine Scarry (1987) reminds us, is of theoretical and political interest.[5]

The editor of an academic journal recently rejected one of my articles. His language resembles that of the letter from the immigration officer. Cold, disengaged, impersonal. Besides the debatable unfairness in both judgments, what I find quite intriguing and sad at the same time is the capacity of language to devastate.[6] Realizing that I need to get used to rejections in my academic activity, I think that this may have been a powerful moment of learning. I fear my defensiveness and my potential incapacity to accept tough critique. But I also wonder to what extent we, students and scholars, are allowed to actually *create* in these anti-intellectual and managerial times (Gaulejac, 2012; Marcuse, 1991), when many claim that graduate school is merely a means to get a job

(Kelsky, 2012) and, as Nicholas Kristof (2014) pointed out in the *The New York Times*, "rebels are too often crushed or driven away." Academia has its security borders, gatekeepers, and bullies, in mainstream and critical orthodoxies alike. Herbert Marcuse (1991) noted that "defense and security are still large items in the intellectual as well as the national budget" (p. 211). In the current climate of relentless careerism, exacerbated competition, obsession with productivism, and funding-disciplined practices in which we live our (mostly, for most of us anyway) unhappy academic lives—*how far can reflexivity go*?[7] And what can it do for us? What are we here for? Are there limits that we simply cannot trespass? Where and what are those?

In the three cases referred to above—immigration policies, anti-queer bullying, and academic policing—language hurts, creating a situation that prevents dialogue of any kind. The nation-state, sexuality, and academia are all carefully policed (Alexander, 2005; Butalia, 2000; Marcuse, 1991; Smith, 1999). I wonder if this violent policing is a necessary moment of (all) identity building. . . . What are, if they exist, the alternatives beyond a reactionary (academic) "we" formation (Brown, 2010, 2013)?[8] In any case, the wounds left by these forms of policing, which give shape to personal and social circumstances, need to be dealt with, analytically *and* politically.

Whose Dictatorship(s)?

I was born in Montevideo, Uruguay, at the end of a dictatorship that had horrendous consequences for the people around me. I was five years old when the transition to democracy took place in 1985. Soon thereafter, Uruguay disappeared from the international news for years. Horror always leaves traces, however, and pain never goes away completely (Agathangelou & Killian, 2009; Edkins, 2003; Kellermann, 2001; LaCapra, 2009; Scarry, 1987).[9]

The dictatorship radically affected most of the scholars I interviewed in my research (see Chapter 3). It also shaped the texture of my home life. My mother was a communist activist whose family was endangered and disrupted. Her brother and her then-husband were imprisoned and tortured. My brother Daniel was kidnapped and savagely beaten. He was found unconscious in random parks a couple of times. My mother would sometimes receive anonymous death threats and telephone calls telling her that her daughter (who was at that moment playing in the garden of the house) could suddenly disappear. Families are vehicles for political experiences and the emotions involved (Greco & Stenner, 2013; Kellermann, 2001; Fried, 2016). Even though I did not directly experience any of these events, I absorbed a profound repulsion for the military and authoritarianism. This was something that traveled with me to Toronto (and back to Montevideo) that led me to read militaristic nationalism and police brutality as ugly redundancies, which often seemed offensive to liberals of the Global North.

Politics was everything in my family. It was more important than money and love. Money was despised, while love and personal life were subordinated to the search for "justice." Yet I absorbed the unconditional love of my mother, and that was, in itself, a great training for life and politics. Knowledge was also part of the repertoire of important things. I now see the violent dimension of this enlightened posture that subordinates the personal and the emotional (and, sometimes, the body). Nevertheless, I appreciated the belief that oppression could be overcome with *reflexive* knowledge. Despite Nietzsche and Foucault, or perhaps enriched by them, that belief lingers in me still.

Today I realize that, for me, the dictatorship was (and still is) a bunch of stories told by others. In fact, I experienced liberal freedom all my conscious life. But those narratives were a crucial part of my reality;[10] they produced many powerful emotions and thoughts. The materiality of those memories and the pain they carry are hard to apprehend with words (Edkins, 2003; Hite & Huguet, 2016; LaCapra, 2009; Scarry, 1987; Sneh & Cosaka, 2000). I grew up listening to stories of the dictatorship, receiving traumas and treasures (traumatic treasures?): women being savagely beaten by soldiers and fighting back with their high heels; my grandfather (a doctor, a poet, and a politician highly idealized by my family) protecting leftist activists from right-wing mobs; the ignorance of the *milicos* [a derogatory term for soldiers] who solemnly declared that "our society should be protected against the testicles of communism" (they meant tentacles), that "Uruguay is one step behind the abyss and we should take a step forward," and that "meetings of more than one person are forbidden!" It seems that bitter and ironic storytelling about the military's "primitivism" became a form of resistance and of cultivating collective memory about the dictatorship.[11] Such a memory was not without problems.

The *milicos*, I was taught, were ignorant and stupid. Interestingly, in that narrative, sometimes they (as a collective) were also *pardos* [brown] . . . a word that mixed class and race. I wonder now about the weird politics at play in mocking them. Somehow, when the middle-class leftist activist was tortured by a *milico*, there was a paradoxical form of inverted class struggle—so different from Chile, where the military officers were much more prestigious (and probably richer). These two were similar and yet very different dictatorships, as I would find out a couple of decades later through my research. In any case, that bizarre form of racism of left-wing politics was paradoxical and confusing for me—later I would realize that confusing paradox may be a good starting point for theory.

I was not "there" during the dictatorship, but I have many memories of it. As a child, I used to have spectacular images in my mind: tanks on the streets, soldiers everywhere hunting my mother and her *compañeros* [comrades]. It was hard to understand that the mundane was still going on during the dictatorship, and that was in fact the unique reality for a vast part of the population. I would later meet some people who did not even notice the regime change! Years later, talking to Dora, an older university classmate who was a member of the guerrillas in the sixties,[12] I also realized that during that period my mother and her *compañeros* were actually *young*. Until that point, I would imagine my mother, Dora and the others as they looked at that present moment, which somehow made me feel more connected with their pain and perhaps more outraged. Mine was a dislocated temporality, with all of the inaccuracies of life and politics.

My family's situation and stories forged my relationship to the official world of politics and its institutions. We were "the communists" (an insult for many people at that time), at best suspicious subjects located at the margins of mainstream society. I also learned about the role of knowledge in power relations: years before reading Gramsci, I was told many times that, during the dictatorship, schools at all levels became caves of indoctrination and symbolic violence. (So many stories, again. One day, one of those "teachers" appointed by the dictatorship, a military member without any credentials, terrified my brother Daniel and his classmates when he put his gun on the desk—a not so subtle way to show who was in charge in the classroom.) After the transition to democracy, the mainstream media framed public debate in terms used by the right-wing and the TV channels became another antagonist for me. The suspicious attitude and the experience of isolation did not go away.

When I was a child, my mother used to recite poems to me. I have a remote memory of how awkward I used to find Gustavo Adolfo Becquer's mannered texts. Books were a solace in a situation of relative economic deprivation and the rejection of bourgeois life. They were also political allies. Knowledge was deeply appreciated at home. Even though the menu was sometimes biased (Soviet propaganda was welcomed, and I read all those dubious booklets from the communist *Editorial Progreso*), the idea that thinking and critique were part of a meaningful life was very much present, and I treasured it. Books were never forbidden, and thinking was never repressed, as my extensive and obsessive reading of Marquis de Sade and Nietzsche as well as my own book of dark poetry written in my troubled early 20s would prove. They were gestures *against* my family's narrative, but located in a register that was perceived as legitimate. *That* Marxism could be turned against itself and become something different. (There is not one but multiple Marxisms, and all of them are lived experiences of oppression, liberation, or both, as the long and humbling conversations with my friends from Eastern Europe and other places frequently remind me.)

After the tragic period of the dictatorship, scholars massively turned to liberalism, and (liberal) democracy became the new fetish; I turned to something else that I am still discovering. There are two issues that I feel compelled to explore: what did these experiences—the dictatorship and what came after—do to me, and what have they meant for the discipline that I am studying (what did they do to PS)? I want to know more about the encounter between these two registers, and that is why I am telling this story.

I just called my mother to confirm some facts that show up in the paragraph below. I could not do so. She was heading to the Feria Tristán Narvaja, one of the main Sunday street markets in Montevideo, to get some fresh fruits and vegetables. The background noise made the conversation difficult. Amidst the noise, I could at least get one phrase clearly. She said: "in the early 1980s I was *militando* [doing political work] a lot, and I used to take you everywhere."

On December 29, 1983, I turned 3 years old. That same day, Germán Araújo finished his famous hunger strike against political censorship.[13] So my birthday party ended (too) early, and my mother took my sister and me to the huge demonstration organized for his support. Quite unexpectedly, the peaceful protest was brutally repressed with horses and *chanchitas* [colloquial term for an armored vehicle].[14] Someone in the crowd screamed that they were shooting and panic spread. We ran; we ran so much. We ended up in front of the closed doors of a *parrillada* [barbecue restaurant] called Taití. A tall guy took me in his arms to protect me. The soldiers were coming. My mother was holding hands with my scared sister. *I guess* I was scared too. We did not know what was going to happen. Everyone was pushing the door and screaming to the owner: "please open the door, open the fucking door!" Finally, the door was opened and that particular crowd, us included, escaped the beating batons.

After writing the paragraph above, I could finally have a conversation with my mother without the annoying background of Tristán Narvaja's unpleasant noises. And it seems that my story makes several mistakes! I am conflating two different situations. In one of them I was present; in the other one I had not even been born yet. According to my mother, everything is "true," but the sequence and characters of the events are mixed. Should I go back to correct the story? Is that really the point? I wonder if narrative, with its positivist tendency toward factual reconstruction and its well-organized way of saying (even when it tries to portray discontinuity and rupture), can be reflexive enough (Edkins, 2003; Hamati-Ataya, 2014).[15] In this chapter, I choose a different direction: the direction of unfolding questions and exploring meanings. And of mixing narrative, theory, and science.

It seems to me that others remember things about us that we forgot or never knew. I am thinking not only about information but also about representation. The other carries pieces of us. The other's unique reading of us contributes to our uniqueness in the world. We are singular only because we are among others, as I learned from Hannah Arendt's books during those endless hours of class preparation in the tiny garage that served as reading space in the house of the old Institute of Political Science (ICP), itself indicative of the poverty of the Uruguayan public university at the time.[16] When someone who knows you dies, a version of yourself dies with her. And because you could never know that version of yourself completely, now you cannot be certain about which part of you just died: our own death does not belong to us, and it goes unnoticed.[17] Happily, my mother is alive, and her version of the past expands and complicates my own and vice versa.

In any case, the ways in which I remember have effects on the affects and thoughts that shape my politics—subjectivity and social relations encounter in our desires, memories, and nightmares. The story I just told above did happen *to me*. It is about my family, Uruguay, the discipline, myself, and I remember it. I will not correct it. Not here; not now.

I also remember seeing my mother crying in front of our black-and-white TV. *El voto verde* [the green vote] lost the referendum against the Expiry Law, and this meant that the Uruguayan population decided not to judge human rights violations committed by the dictatorship (see Chapter 3). It was 1989, and I was eight years old. We hugged, and I could feel her pain in my chest. State terrorism, democratically sanctioned: how to make sense of that? What kinds of feelings and questions were opened that day? Abuse and powerlessness were markers of the dictatorship, and the transition to liberal democracy extended that profound trauma and sense of betrayal. Social justice, kicked on the head countless times by military boots, was now abandoned in agony by the establishment of liberal democracy.

My professors did not problematize the quality of the democracy that left my mother crying and trembling. They were also traumatized: the pain that the dictatorship imprinted on bodies and souls transformed political scientists' relationship to socialism and liberal democracy. The former was despised; the latter was worshiped. They blamed radicalism, in academia and beyond, for contributing to political polarization and the collapse of our democracy. They blamed the left for its obsession with equality and for not caring enough about the rule of law. In other words, my professors, many of them with a leftist past, felt ideologically and politically guilty. They became liberal and elitist. They celebrated the same political parties that, in the name of protecting democracy, prevented judges from doing their job.

Liberalism is always raping itself—for it consistently violates its own principles to favor the powerful. At its core, it is still the ideology of proprietors and modern slavery (Losurdo, 2011), even when it becomes democratized.[18] In post-transition Uruguay, private property rights and the military were protected, and order and stability imposed. This sacred "rule of law" celebrated by my professors was the rule of injustice. And it was this (self-inflicted) violence that eventually made me obsess over the politics of political science.

PS' Positivist Masculinity and Straightness

> *¿Qué cosa fuera la maza sin cantera?* [What would a sledgehammer be without a quarry?]
>
> —Silvio Rodríguez (1982)

Urvashi Butalia (2000) says that we need to have "the language to describe our own experience, to make sense of it" (p. 200). But for me there were no words for many years. In a personal world so full of books and eloquent phrases, there was not a single (permissible) word to name my experience. When I was 16 years old, in one of our first sessions, Cristina, my psychoanalyst, uttered a frightening one: "homosexuality." I covered my mouth with my hands and shouted: "Oh no!" The vocabularies for healing would be slowly, slowly crafted. In my early 20s I wrote a piece for *Brecha*, a respected weekly in Uruguay, in which I could finally put words to my experience and circumstances.

The publication of that text was a special moment for me (years later, for the same weekly, I wrote an article on "The Politics of Political Science," another self-reflexive exercise). Cristina still sometimes refers to that piece in our sessions. *"Au commencement, il y a l'injure* [In the beginning, there is the injury/insult]," insisted Didier Eribon (2001, p. 29). His book spoke to me, about me. And a simple book review became a manifesto, a text coming from deep inside, crafted for others.[19]

In the first place, there is the polymorphous attack, states Eribon, and there is the injury. *In the first place, there is the injury.*[20] Humiliation creates a very disturbing kind of pain. The residues of shame and guilt for not being strong enough to defend yourself accumulate somewhere and poison you—you cannot defend yourself from homophobia because you are guilty, because they are saying the truth: you are the insult. The location of the forces that attack you is so unclear . . . outside or inside? Both? This experience leaves you in a deep and inexplicable loneliness: you are alone *vis-à-vis* yourself because your self is not yours. I keep wondering how to communicate this to people who have not experienced it. The critique of political correctness so fashionable today even amongst self-identified progressives—with its blind celebration of free speech and proud lack of empathy—has an awful outcome: the trivialization (again) of the pain that comes from discrimination. The banalization of others' pain can never be progressive, critical, or leftist (Ravecca, 2017a, 2017b).

The political is personal because politics affect lives: Marxism, for me, has been homophobic and queer at the same time.[21] I *made it* queer. (In its turn, subjectivity affects politics.) Something similar can be said about Uruguayan secularism and rationalist culture: my family's discourse on justice and assertive atheism helped me to make sense of myself and my circumstances; it was also definitely helpful in a more strategic fashion when I came out to them. I could mobilize their vocabulary to challenge them, making their own beliefs work in my favor. If they were defenders of the marginalized, the poor, and the oppressed, if they were against dogmatism and on the side of science, how could they oppress me?

I remember sharing with my mother the letter Freud wrote to another mother of a "homosexual," saying that homosexuality was not an illness. This was in contrast to Gramsci, who would soon become so fundamentally helpful in challenging my professors' very conception of politics, yet was a foe of "sodomites." I would later write "Fuck you" many times on the margins of the pages of the *Prison Notebooks*. Yet, my love *and* compassion for Gramsci persisted, which in itself is a sign of the complexity of politics and affects. In the end, the violent modern rationalism of Uruguayan communism, mediated by Freud, proved to be queer-able.[22] I did not choose my material and discursive circumstances, but I did my part in shaping them—Marxism and queer politics make "history" and "story" intersect. My family changed along with the country's transformation, becoming more and more accepting. At the beginning, it was difficult. Full acceptance took time, and I guess it is always on its way.[23] I always felt the love of some, and that is perhaps what matters the most.

Meanwhile, mainstream PS in Latin America, following its American role model, became obsessed with democratic institutions and political tolerance, yet like the "antidemocratic" left that it (self-)critiqued so harshly in Chile and Uruguay, it has also been quite homophobic: sexuality has not been deemed material for democracy in either theory or practice—at least not until very recently. Homophobia within PS has been, for me, a lived experience rather than an abstract entity. It is quite remarkable how illiberal liberals can sometimes be. . . .

It was the first time that I was attending the ICP's *fiesta de despedida del año* [end of year party]. I had just started working there 10 hours a week and my (symbolic) salary was around US$100 a month. I was 24 or 25 years old. It was a big deal: I was becoming part of the PS community and being there was a sign of this significant achievement. I was also uncomfortable and nervous: male political scientists in the early 2000s tended to be unapologetically aggressive and assertive. I can handle that very well today. I perhaps became one of them in some way. But in those years, I was vulnerable.[24]

At some point, a senior colleague said loudly that he did not understand why faggots in the university did not *confess*. His words hit my stomach with paralyzing anxiety. The scene resembles the declaration of "Democratic Faith" that the dictatorship pushed on the people, and the classification of subjects performed through the categories A, B, and C. Being assigned a C meant that you were a threat to the nation and an undesirable subject. Now we were in democratic times, but for this progressive and liberal academic, I was a C. I had to *confess* that I was queer. I remained in silence: a silenced silence. At our table there was an older man that I thought to be gay. I did not know if the "joke" was directed to me, to him, to both of us, or if it was just another random bullying comment. The older man and I did not build any solidarity. We just could not do anything. The horrific feeling of transparency assaulted me once more: the childhood fear and anxiety of entering the classroom. Of going to my high school. To school. To the Institute of Political Science. I broke again.

The space of PS has warning signs and one-way roads, and it is not just about dominant ideology and liberalism. Our discipline's sexuality is an extension of the aggressive masculinity of politics.[25] Homophobia, inside and outside, affected my way of being a political scientist in those years. It dictated with whom I would engage intellectually in the department and with whom I would speak for any purpose. They were not free choices. Marginalities frequently magnify each other: my theoretical preferences (let's say, Michel Foucault over Anthony Downs) and my lack of enthusiasm for liberal democracy were somehow an additional form of academic queerness. That the PS I was taught by my professors would never reflect on the regulation of identities and bodies that affected my life so much—and even worse, that they openly and proudly exercised forms of power that subordinated women and queer people, a power that did not have room or a name in their conception of politics—made me suspicious of it. Was PS a place of depoliticization? Was PS a space and discourse for the naturalization of the status quo (political and sexual)? Mainstream PS needs a political and sexual critique, and memories of the oppressions within the discipline need to be written in Uruguay, in Latin America, and elsewhere . . . even if they are disruptive. Even if they sound "out of place." Because it is the being out of place that is inflicting harm—not this writing.

I remember a different party where another senior scholar told a "funny" story about a world-famous soccer player. Apparently, his team was involved in the raping of a "faggot" (the professor's word) and he had been asked in an interview if he had taken part in it or not. The player originally suggested that he did. The professor thought that the situation of a soccer player raping a queer was hilarious. Another time, I saw a drunk colleague simulating that he had dropped something from his chair to only grab the neck of his male interlocutor and playfully simulate to force him into oral sex. Another day, at the school I heard a discriminatory comment made by one of my professors while he ran away, perhaps to go back to a classroom. Another professor, more amused than annoyed, loudly called him "homophobe!" in a tone that made it clear that he was not making fun of homophobes but of homosexuals. In an elegant lunch, a senior colleague—polite, formal, conservative—voiced his outrage about the rumors that one of the leaders of the (conservative) National Party was involved in gender violence against his wife. In his view, that issue was a private affair. The phenomenalist mindset (Jackson, 2011), concerned with empirical evidence sustaining claims, would have its criteria fulfilled if proving the existence of sexism and homophobia in Uruguayan and Latin American political science was the goal.

> *I want to leave.*
> *I will leave. I have to.*
> *I did.*

Years later, I would occasionally collaborate with the protagonist of the first story. Our conversation has changed; Uruguay has changed. I think he changed. But overall, I did. Today, we have a gender and sexual diversity section in the ICP. I teach queer theory in one of my courses, and I critique gay marriage (approved by the Uruguayan parliament in April 2013) and its neoliberal co-optation. True: mainstream PS does not critically reflect on liberal democracy and liberalism in Uruguay, but the intolerance against critical views has weakened. In October 2016, I was invited to a roundtable at the 10th Anniversary of the Uruguayan Political Science Association. Nobody contested my claim that we, as an academic community, need to make room for critical theory in the discipline. Perhaps because power mechanisms are shifting toward how academic careers are conceived and regulated in the direction of a sort of academic *homo economicus* (Shepherd, 2016; Brown, 2015)—the neoliberalized university allows you to produce critical theory as just one more regular commodity (Keucheyan, 2013, 2016). Indeed, that was the focus of the intervention of David Altman that day: the professors of the ICP have to "work harder" (publishing in venues with high impact factors, teaching more courses, etc.). Furthermore, the jock attitude that looks at you as if you were talking nonsense if you are not a hardcore, hypothesis-testing positivist did not go away.

We still inhabit the positivist trap, which is, by definition, gendered. In what we call an internal seminar, I was recently advised that scholarship might elude ideology by purging "normative" terms such as "neoliberalism"—as if wording, and not theory, was the fuel for science. That exiling words appears as an antidote against subjectivity reveals that epistemological poverty has not been overcome. The cosmetic solution at the level of language in its plainest sense performs a pantomime of neutrality that naturalizes dominant biases as "objectivity" and ignores entire research programs on neoliberalism (Amadae, 2016; Brown, 2015, 2017; Harvey, 2005; Saad-Filho & Johnston, 2005; Menéndez-Carrión, 2015).[26] In my view, it is the awareness of how our theoretical lenses frame social reality that can protect us from arbitrariness: objectivity is the ultimate hiding place of passions, trauma, and power.

Un-changing changes? Variations of the same? Only to an extent. We are not stacked. Personal and social changes *did* reshape power relations, inside and outside. For me, self-exploration, psychoanalysis, and critical theory made the words appear, and stay. Silence and the body—the very infrastructure of our human existence—also started to mean something different. One day I want to write about critical theory *and* yoga (one of the many gifts that Toronto gave me).

I learned the register of love and care from my mother. Politically speaking, I think that register is also one of compassion *vis-à-vis* a cold ethicality. Until very recently, many of us were denied the possibility of love and having a home that transcends one's mother, one's friends, one's cat. The impossibility of love is highly political: it is socially produced, also by closeting forms of PS and those theories that naturalize this specific form of oppression (homophobic Marxism included). Homophobia is like a war that destroys one's infrastructures of love. Those infrastructures need to be built; the construction process is a political and personal gain in itself, and needs to be celebrated. The terrain of emotions and affections has been conquered by many of us. Space has been expanded, inside and outside. In recent years, the Toronto-Montevideo (and, more recently, NYC) dialectics of my existence has expanded and nuanced my range of movement and experience. All of this is political not only because "the personal is political" but because the political is always *already* personal: it is people's lives that are at stake and that are affected by public decisions and conversations.

I remember my deep smile when I learned that Carlos Real de Azúa, the great intellectual and *father* of Uruguayan PS was a "homosexual" (in his time, "gay" was not part of the available vocabulary in Uruguay).[27] It was in 2007, in an informal conversation after a seminar at CLAEH[28] where I was speaking about him. "I knew it," I thought. "The tortured sinuosity of his writing was always saying something else." Tulio Halperin Donghi, the main speaker of the event, did not feel comfortable when I shared this thought with him: he stated that his homosexuality had no connection with Real de Azúa's personality as a writer.[29] Afterward, I walked up along Zelmar Michelini Street (another man killed by the dictatorship) to join the annual (sexual) Diversity March in the center of the city.

I have never been happy in my department: I said that as a guest speaker in a panel that launched a 2015 special issue of the Chilean *Revista de Ciencia Política* focused on the state and the development of the discipline in Latin America. I talked about homophobia in PS in front of many Uruguayan and Latin American colleagues: I could barely walk afterwards. I was sad and exhausted. In times of tensions between feminist gains and aggressive reactionary politics (Dragiewicz, 2008; van Wormer, 2008; Faludi, 1991),[30] leftists complaining against the "totalitarianism" of "political correctness,"[31] and of demonstrations against sexual education,[32] it seems that in the view of many, we (queer people and other minorities) should feel okay because people do not openly verbally attack or mock us anymore. A dear queer scholar told me that there is no discrimination in our school and that the anti-racist and queer positive references in the syllabus of my course on critical theory could be read as exaggerated and somehow artificial. The question, then, remains: when do discrimination and oppression cease? Varied events and experiences reveal that they have not yet ceased: I still see them every day in full operation—inside and outside. Granted, they have been resituated, displaced. The conditions of power have shifted in Uruguay and beyond, but the moving and complex structures of racism and homophobia are still in place. Uruguay is gender progressive as much as Charlottesville, Virginia, has overcome racism while hosting a rally that included KKK and Nazi sympathizers.[33] I still have to think twice before openly referring to my partner in my professional and everyday life. And that is unfair. If that is my reality . . . it is hard to grasp how tough the experience is for vulnerable populations, particularly transgender people who, according to official reports in Uruguay, are expelled by the educational system and have a lower life expectancy than the rest of the population (MIDES, 2017).

Love for PS and Its Complicated Temporalities and Geographies

> Empathy with the victor invariably benefits the rulers.
>
> —Walter Benjamin (1969, p. 256)

In the United States, some canonic PS authors such as Gabriel Almond and Sidney Verba (1963) praised American democracy for being the most civic and humane in the world while ignoring the horrors of racial segregation at home and imperialism abroad. Verba would later be, paradoxically (or perhaps not paradoxically at all), the coauthor of a widely read handbook on methodology that advises researchers to not allow their subjectivity and politics to contaminate their analysis of reality (King et al., 2000, p. 25). At the other end of the Americas, Uruguayan PS was institutionalized later, after the democratic transition of 1985. None of my professors had any sympathy for the military government that, with the support of the US, oppressed Uruguayans from 1973 to 1984. Many of them had, in fact, a history of engagement with left-wing organizations and were traumatized by the dictatorship and the collapse of the Soviet Union. They tried to undo their dogmatic past with another dogma, radically embracing liberalism and (American) pluralism.[34] I still get upset when I think about the absurdity of the enterprise. Someone told me that they escaped the "Marxist Church" that contributed to political polarization. "And then you quickly jumped into another temple, which contributed to neoliberalism and injustice," I thought.[35]

During the 1990s, along with the consolidation of US hegemony in the region, a narrow discourse of moderation and reasonability appeared. In Uruguay, neo-positivist and liberal PS gained its place in—and contributed to producing—the privileged space of *the center*, getting both political credit as democratic and epistemological credit as objective science, a seemingly strange but powerful combination of attributes. Marxism and socialism were rejected and ridiculed not just by the media but in the classroom as well. Liberalism can become Stalinist in its own way, and it indeed did so (Guilhot, 2001; Ravecca, 2017a). Dogmatic liberalism proved to be as intellectually oppressive (and boring) as simplistic forms of Marxism (Rico, 2005). This outcome of history and politics did not help to expand thinking and political imagination in Uruguay.

I have loved PS since the day I set foot in the School of Social Sciences at the University of the Republic. Knowledge was, and still is, precious for me. But I also started thinking, early on, that PS could, at times, be quite oppressive. My professors celebrated the quality of our democracy, even when their beloved political system did not judge the crimes of the powerful. As one of my interviewees said, in a self-critical tone, after the transition they "sang praises to the Uruguayan political system" (U8). This was painful for me. Those same crimes that they ignored could have killed my mother, as they indeed killed other mothers. I still remember her devastated expression when the electorate decided not to prosecute the dictatorship's human rights violations, a decision promoted by Julio María Sanguinetti, our president, in the name of the ethics of responsibility: our democracy was menaced by the potential return of the military into power, so the responsible thing to do was to acquiesce to the situation and renounce justice. Thus, within the dominant narrative, one of the most widely read PS founders, Max Weber, who coined the notion of the ethics of responsibility used by Sanguinetti, became a weapon in the same fashion as Nietzsche or Marx did several times in different ways in the 20th century.

My professors did not have the language to problematize this discourse, which in the name of building the conditions of possibility for the rule of law, dismissed those very fundamentals. They lacked the words; the only words available were those of the powerful. The fear of authoritarian backlash undermined liberal democracy: a blind liberalism, problematically fearless (Shklar, 1998) about the devastating effects of its own fears and its pathetic concessions, dictated that Uruguayan society had to forget the crimes of the dictatorship. The political use of fear and this oblivion toward crime were traumatic. And trauma undermines language and speech (Edkins, 2003; Sneh & Cosaka, 2000); it *is* paralysis and repetition, a mistaken path forward.

Scholars' bodies and subjectivities were involved in theoretical and epistemological transformations. The trafficking of dogmatic liberalism (again, a liberalism ready to betray its own tenets if stability and order were, presumably, at stake) in the guise of objective science was a symptom of guilt and trauma that fed the machinery that re-traumatized people, including myself. The killing and torturing done by the dictatorship affected both scholars (and therefore scholarship) and my family.[36] At the same time, PS participated in a public discourse that affected my family, while my family affected my way of being in PS. They all inhabit the same history, and here they cross paths in the same story.

In conceptual (but somehow very material) terms, the very definition of politics that mainstream PS holds and that has been acritically imported by Uruguayan academia is violent, exclusive, and invisibilizes the painful experiences of many. A more expansive conception of politics makes it possible to interrogate and question those forms of oppression that remain undetected by only looking at electoral systems, elections, and public policy. My experience exemplifies this: queer theorizing came *from outside my own discipline* and not only helped me to politicize my own (queer) experience of oppression but also to reclaim the classroom and academic meetings as a space that I could legitimately, and genuinely, inhabit. If PS is conceptualized as human activity (Marx, 1978a) done by people and as a space with formal and informal institutions (North, 1990), then the homophobic and sexist conditions in which the activity of political scientists is performed (not only or mainly in Latin America) do matter: PS is still white, male, and straight (Ahmed, 2012; Brettschneider, 2011;

Breuning & Sanders, 2007; Fujii, 2016; Htun, 2016; Rocha, 2016; Smith, 2011; Trent, 2009, 2012).[37]

Words are helpless in organizing the multiple times, spaces, and contradictory experiences that sustain a perspective. My interest in the political power of self-reflection and in the politics of political science lie on a fluid theoretical and geographical place, an always-in-between that I am not able to fully capture.

Contemporary paradox accumulation: without Uruguay and its wonderful, public, *and free* university, Toronto and York University would not have been the same for me. I am also immensely grateful to the amazingly dense cultural fabric of Montevideo—from the Cinemathèque, where I have watched movies from all over the world since I was a teenager, to its epic theater companies, to its small and friendly bookstores, to my readings of Uruguayan and international poets and philosophers, where another, richer, and more intriguing version of the political was always available to me.[38] My days as a graduate student in Toronto did not rescue me from homophobia at home, as most people usually assume when I tell them that I am from Montevideo. Discrimination and acceptance are evenly distributed between these two cities and, in fact, my social circle "here" is more open-minded than many people "there." What neoliberal Toronto offered me, along with its fascinating cosmopolitan fabric, was . . . Marxism and other critical theories. While Uruguayan academic Marxism had been decimated, York University, where critical theory was alive and another type of PS was possible, became an epistemological and theoretical refuge.

Ironically, the cultural and political left in Uruguay is much more powerful and *developed* (labels are never innocent or harmless) than the Canadian. The streets of Montevideo have traces of Marxism and class politics everywhere. Toronto doesn't . . . or at least it doesn't in the same way. Bizarre and primitive conservative Rob Ford would have been unthinkable as Montevideo's mayor because people here are, at least in relative terms, politically cultivated. Be that as it may, at my York refuge, submerging into different vocabularies—from Marxism to queer theory, to post/anticolonial thought—helped me to put words to the fact that academia is never outside power (Alexander, 2005; Butler, 1990; Foucault, 1991a; Horowitz, 1977; Jackson, 2011; Marcuse, 1991; Said, 2003; Smith, 1999; the list is endless). These theories sometimes treat each other with violence. I have seen them doing great things, as well as regrettable ones, if emancipation and perhaps the (unambitious) aim of minimizing cruelty is used as a criteria of assessment.

Privilege is a moving constellation, and heroes do not exist (Ravecca & Dauphinee, 2018). Every subject ("workers," "gays," "women," "people of color") can be the locus of oppression. All of these theories and constructs, however, helped me to challenge dominant PS and its narrowly liberal, elitist and, at the end, pro-capitalist narratives.

Our disciplinary science belongs to history and to politics; thus, through the critical analysis of PS, we can better understand the politics of the time.

Knowledge is involved in power from the personal to the social. Knowledge has a material history, or as Naeem Inayatullah suggested to me, knowledges *are* material history. Knowledges may, sometimes, be grounded in the body; at other times, they may move in more abstract registers; but they are always linked to power and its materiality. PS is also (part of) our material history. Knowing the ways of knowing is a way of (re)knowing the object known. By this meta-navigation through the mediations performed by official knowledge, by dismantling their positivities and unpacking their silences, one can better understand power itself.

But if knowledges are always linked to power dynamics and their materiality, does that mean that our disciplines are not lovable? Let me go back to a story to tackle this question. My grandfather was a center-right-wing politician and powerful figure in his province. His daughter, my mother, moved to the capital when she was 16 and became a communist. They accepted and loved each other, and my mother still has an inflated, sometimes even annoying, admiration for him. In her eyes, my grandfather was a wise man. And yet, she could still radically disagree with him to the point that in the local elections she supported the leftist opposition. Once, my mother cried while staring at her father's name and "big and beautiful picture" on the ballot paper. . . . She did not vote for her beloved father. After that, she transferred her formal residence to her actual address in Montevideo and thus to another electoral district, where the ideological adversaries were outside the family. Luckily, she did not have to face that dilemma again. I felt respect for her when she told me this story. She cried, yes, but she did what she thought she had to do and that was, for me, a precious lesson on politics, difference, acceptance, and love. It could as well be read as a lesson about knowledge: The critique of knowledge comes from love for knowing.[39] Cannot we feel empathy for PS and critique it at the same time? Are narrow corporatism and blind defense, or rejection and resentment, the only choices available?[40]

PS for PS

> There is no such thing as an expert on human relationships.
> —Woodrow Wilson (1911, p. 9)

The opening anecdotes of this chapter are a reminder that power travels through nation-states, sexualities, and academic disciplines without caring about the conceptual boundaries that we erect between them. Narrative as a form of writing is political and epistemological because it can pull back together what analysis separates. By restoring the integrity of the socially concrete (Marx, again, through Himani Bannerji), writing and reading stories may perhaps become a powerful way of reclaiming free movement *vis-à-vis*, as well as within, theories, classrooms, airports, and further beyond. Introspection is a desperate need for both people and sciences. And self-reflexive, theoretically informed narrative may become an antidote against a reactionary (academic) "we" formation.

Autobiography and auto-ethnography may: (*a*) involve theoretical awareness and density; (*b*) show not only the power effects of knowledges, but also how subjects confront, navigate, and mobilize knowledges in transformative ways (agency within knowledge-power relations); and (*c*) deploy a multilayered self-consciousness that problematizes the reification of the self that autobiography/ethnography risks implying. "I" narrative writing, in short, offers possibilities for scholarship (Ravecca & Dauphinee, 2018).[41] In committing to those possibilities, I decided to take my own excavation as far as I am able to. The next section does not constitute a mere addition to the previous ones. In fact, the opposite can be said: up to this point, I have written an addendum and now I feel that *I can at least try* to express the core of my experience of the politics of knowledge.

So far, the exploration of the personal experiences that are intertwined with the scholarly and intellectual journey of which this book is a product is rather incomplete. My way of reading knowledge/power dynamics and my conception of the politics of political analysis come also, fundamentally, from *somewhere else*. Certainly, my aim with the next section is not to unfold a reifying narrative about origins (an operation despised by Nietzsche), that would (re)insert linearity into "trauma time" (Edkins, 2003), concealing the contingency of this intellectual enterprise. However, there is a point in my experience that changed everything for me; maybe because of its intrinsic significance, perhaps because of its social implications. Either way, I think and feel that it is relevant, for present purposes (i.e., exploring how life, knowledge, and power are related), to engage with that event here. It was the extensive reading of different literatures on trauma that persuaded me to connect the questions around the politics of academic knowledge to this specific event of my personal trajectory. Thus, if in the previous sections I have delineated a sort of intimate architecture of my research project, what follows opens the possibilities of digging deeper into the very foundations of the PPS house: the subsequent pages rewrite the preceding ones.

Horror in the Body of Thought: Undoing Harm

> *Wo Es war, soll Ich werden.* [Where It was, shall I be.]
> —Sigmund Freud (1933, p. 80)

> To be radical is to grasp the root of the matter. But for man, the root is man himself.
> —Karl Marx (1843, para. 30)

> *En Montevideo hay biromes. . ./desangradas en renglones . . .* [In Montevideo there are pens. . ./bleeding in lines. . .]
> —Leo Masliah (1984)

In 1993, I came back from spending eight months with my eldest half-brother in Europe. He, as thousands of Uruguayans, had been in "economic exile" since I was 9. The trip had failed to rebuild our relationship. Our family was dealing with the tensions produced by the issues we had during my visit.

I was 13 years old at the time. I do not remember why I decided to visit my siblings' father (I think that I am blocking out that piece of my memory, afraid of what I might find there). He and my mother had been separated for many years, and they never had a good relationship. But he was still somehow part of my family. Maybe, on some level, he was a phantom of the male parental figure that I always lacked. I visited him at his place in my old neighborhood. That day, *what happened with my siblings' father*, as I would call that event for many years, happened. I remember running out from the dark apartment and going straight to my sister's place. I do not know how I managed to tell her, but I did. I still do not know how to make sense of that night (or was it an afternoon?).

When my mother arrived home, she was looking elegant and smelling wonderful, as usual. When she tried to hold me, I shouted, "Please don't touch me, I'm dirty!" How cliché, I now think smiling, but I was definitely not smiling then. Yet I was, somehow, performing. I felt that what had happened was my fault, and given that I was guilty of the family tragedy about to come, I needed to exaggerate. But what was being exaggerated, exactly? I actually did not know what I was feeling or what I was supposed to feel. I only knew, rationally, that what had just happened was wrong, and that I was hurting my mother and destroying my family. I was certain that they would choose and protect *me* and somehow expel and punish *him*: I felt confusedly guilty for that. I felt as if I were lying about everything: my language was a lie. Where was the dirt? Did I not voluntarily go to his place? Had I fulfilled an obscure desire to take their father away, too?

Harm in its purity—that was what I discovered that day. I still do not have the words to name this. I cannot organize such a conflation of times, spaces, and emotions. What I do know is that since *what happened with my siblings' father* happened, I have always had a sort of estrangement with my own feelings and desires. The desire to oppress is never totally exterior . . . or is it the experience of being oppressed that makes us attached to oppression and get dangerously close to transitioning into the oppressor? Where is the way out after power, violence, and desire become entangled? Mainstream forms of morality seem pathetically weak *vis-à-vis* the motions of life. What they do achieve, though, is to bury and poison urgencies and impulses that would be less destructive if they were aired out. Abuse thus projects itself over the multiple registers of time as an endless trap, somehow sustained in strange ways by the attempts to suppress it from memory and discourse. Reflexivity, to put a name to this voyage inwards and outwards, is the opposite of suppression: it is the *courage* of looking at how abuse became part of our flesh. Reflexivity is a struggle for freedom, which, even more in this case, *has to be* endless (Davis, 2016). I am still looking for mine.

My mother and my sister supported me in a radical, visceral way. My brothers chose silence and distance. They only said that I did not have any responsibility for what had happened and, after some months, decided to resume their relationship with their father, something that my mother and my sister could not understand.[42] I did not know what to think, and *how to think*, about that. I am still figuring it out, but around the whole situation there is a blind spot that seems to be unthinkable. I know that I will always be trying to grasp an unnamed area where (my) thinking cannot be. Nobody ever blamed me but myself (so everyone did). From my family to my therapy, the mobilized script sentenced "abuse," and I came to terms with such a notion. But for a long, long time it was very hard for me to understand that I was not guilty. I think that I will never fully understand it.

There are knowledges that cannot be known. How could this *communist hero*, imprisoned by the dictatorship for many years, do what he did? My brothers found a consoling explanation: alcoholism. My mother and my sister rejected the hypothesis, and articulated the situation in a radically alternative manner: pedophilia. Sometimes I think that he tried to destroy my mother. The politics of naming and narrative, again. In this case, this aphorism, though extreme, applies: "In the animal kingdom, the rule is, eat or be eaten; in the human kingdom, define or be defined" (Szasz, 1973, p. 200). I cannot go into his mind and body—especially now, given that he died a number of years ago. I do not feel the need to make sense of him anymore. I can only try to make sense of this for myself.

The very possibility of thinking (and, therefore, of being) would become a question for me: the very experience of trauma. I still have to conquer thinking every day. My extreme forms of marking up texts as I go through them enact my struggle to be able to think in spite of the wounds (see Figure 4.1). And yet, that traumatic experience opened up countless possibilities *for* thinking and creation, thanks to psychoanalysis, critical theory, and love. Abuse, trauma, and beauty meet in forms that we are obliged to hide: Nietzsche saw how cruelty, oppression, creativity, and knowledge amalgamate—what to do about that? Moralizing and hiding those connections just does not work.

Today I read this event as an opportunity to learn about power, theory, and knowledge. *What happened with the father of my siblings* has become a sharp lesson on power relations and the volatile nature of names and structures of moral intelligibility; it also engrained me in the role of knowledge, thinking, and language in conflict and struggle (note how I still name this event, even today, after years of working on it). That day confronted me with a difficult aspect of the human condition: the point where the good-evil divide becomes blurry (Dauphinee, 2013a, 2013b). Again, and again: a communist hero imprisoned by the evil military abused me. What is the deeper meaning and the full implications of *that*? My family, where so much love was available for me, could not protect me. And later, PS (at least the one that I first encountered)

FIGURE 4.1   "The language of the conquerors soon came to supplant the other languages" (Ghosh, 1992, p. 101)

would declare that this (the private sphere) is not political (therefore, it does not matter), and so we do not need to talk about it. (Particularly, according to many, I should not include this "anecdote" in a book on comparative politics or the politics of knowledge.)

I obviously disagree, given that the following remains, I think, a main lesson for life and politics: those who represent "the good" can hurt you. They can kill you; or they may push you to kill yourself. "*Los representantes de la luz construyen patíbulos* [The representatives of the light build gallows]," I would write many times as an adolescent. You can be hurt by socialists, sometimes in the name of socialism (also by democrats, sometimes in the name of democracy). My siblings' father inoculated me with torture. And innocence died for me that day. Desire was obscured. Marquis de Sade (1977, 1986, 1987, 1996, 1999a, 1999b, 1999c) and Nietzsche (1989, 1992, 1999a, 1999b, 1999c) provided me with the vocabulary and imageries that portrayed the contradictions that hurt me. I am grateful to horror and darkness because they were such powerful sites for thinking and creation for me during an important period of my life. That meant a great deal for my politics and my future ways of theorizing. Oppression is not the monopoly of the other. Neither is abuse. I think that once we get this, (self-) critique can become more than just a rubric.

I rediscovered Carlos Real de Azúa, the great Uruguayan intellectual, during the writing of this book. As in critical theory, for him, thinking is a tool for human liberation, yes, but it is also a tool for liberation of/from *partial liberations* (Real de Azúa, 1973; also, see Chapter 3).[43] For me, that insight has the power of revelation. The partial liberations change in history, of course. They may be called democracy, the market, communism, feminism, anti-racism, social justice, etc., etc. *Every* position and perspective has its own economy of violence: theories are emancipatory and oppressive at the same time, and thus critique is *always* needed. I learned this years ago in an experiential fashion from the father of my siblings, and I am somehow grateful to him. Real de Azúa provides me with a vocabulary to theoretically translate this experience.

The experience of trauma—*un*scripted and *re*narrated through psychoanalytic tools, blended with others attempts of translation—showed to me *how* it is that knowledges are intrinsically part of power, abuse, and resistance. Inside the individual, within the family structure, and in larger communities, including academic disciplines and the nation-state, there are always knowledges and narratives battling. Power relations connect the dots from child abuse to the nation-state to the market (let us not forget the market as a site of, and excuse for, abuse and cruelty), and not only because all these forms of domination are sexualized and complicate desire, but also because they show how political knowledge and narration are. From the justifications of domestic violence to the technical excuses for austerity measures, whatever the site is, when power happens, there is a war between views—sometimes, a narrative hosts a war within.

Introspection is key if we do not want our knowledge practices to be part of abuse. In other words, I conceptualize self-reflection as a way *out* of the position of the abuser and, therefore—and this is vital—as a way to re-appropriate and transform desire. This insight *becomes* political if we think of it *as* political.

Today, the American Psychological Association is discussing its role in torture in the context of the war on terror. In 2016, I attended the Latin American Political Science Association annual conference and in 2017, the Latin American Studies Association annual meeting, both in Lima, Perú. During my visits to some of the historical sites, I learned about the role of prestigious American universities in stealing Incan treasures. My own abuser tried to convince my family that I "provoked" the situation (I was lucky: many *many* families accept this kind of framework, support the adult, and silence the child). And Donald Trump, from the center of the global stage, equates anti-racist activists with the white supremacists who killed Heather Heyer in Charlottesville.[44] Black Lives Matter activists are named terrorists (Khan-Cullors & Bandele, 2018).[45] In all these cases, an alternative form of knowledge needs to be created in order to open up the space for thinking and confronting the powerful knowledge that justifies oppression (sometimes in the name of its opposite).

Oppression comes from unexpected places from the private to the public, and that is important for theory. In Uruguay, the highly admired trade-union federation (PIT-CNT) has protected civil servants involved in the torture of minors (as children and youth in conflict with the law are called in the country) (Corti, 2015). The same trade unions that suffered torture by the state during the dictatorship and are well known for their heroic resistance had a vice-president who sanctioned human rights violations. The abused children invariably come from the poorest and most vulnerable sectors of society, which makes it even more significant that a Marxist-inspired organization is the one that sentences them to death—the collective death of innocence. It is a part of the "turn to the left" in Latin America that should not be romanticized by any means. As I write this, the government of Nicolás Maduro's bloody repression and crude dogmatism distresses anyone who, while finding them unacceptable, also fears the return of neoliberalism. In any case, partial liberations should be kept partial if we do not want failed projects to ruin the very capacity *to project* a more livable society.

I might not have enough "theory" to articulate the next thought, but I do want to make the point. The narrative of monstrous exceptions does not undo the practices it tries to denounce, and even less so their conditions of possibility. Quite the contrary. The problematic exteriorizing of the criminal from the social body has been critically analyzed for the case of the Holocaust (LaCapra, 2009). The issue was explored by Hannah Arendt (1999) around Eichmann's story. The contemporary figure of the pedophile is particularly clear to me: the notion of an evil radical-other erases the crucial question of the gendered social norms that sustain and indeed normalize abuse of power. Colonialism, narratives of superiority, and dynamics of prestige and power allowed universities to engage in crimes in the Global South and African Americans to be killed by the police today. In Uruguay, widespread punitive desires close to what has been called "social fascism" (Escobar, 2004) sanctions the torture of minors. Paradoxically, the logic that locates the civil servants involved in these horrific practices as criminals completely foreign to "us" seems similar to the narrative that erases the systemic marginality in which the kids in conflict with the law have to survive and that partially explain their disruptive behavior. What the narrative of the monstrosity of the pedophile shares with that of the blaming of children is that, through both of them, "society" (i.e., the rest of us) becomes innocent. Wrapping the social majority in a mantle of innocence has the regrettable outcome that abuse becomes a purely exterior accident and, therefore, unexplainable. Such an operation is the opposite of reflexivity, because though abuse is inhumane, it is radically human.

Ethical arrogance is dangerous. Excessive confidence hides the precarity of the terrain on which the representation of the self has been built. In order to be vigilant of our potential crimes, the productivity of the crisis/critique of the ethical self-image needs to be acknowledged. Critique, in order to unfold its transformative powers, needs to go where it is difficult, and hurts. Refining our grasp of the structures of oppression implies shaking the (fictional) pure exteriority between us and their crimes. In significant ways, we (including academics) are also the criminals. How can we navigate such an insight? In *The Politics of Exile*, Elizabeth Dauphinee (2013a) undoes the ontological divide between victims and perpetrators; and together we have argued that the subaltern is not inherently better than the oppressor (Ravecca & Dauphinee, 2018).[46] Following this view, the theorization of emancipatory politics gets complicated by the mobility and nuance of oppression, which is expressed in the motion of changing constellations of power and privilege. Resistance against oppression can be oppressive; oppression is not only of the other. An example of this nuance is Angela Davis' (2016) critique of "carceral feminism."[47]

For Davis, "simply by focusing on the individual," without acknowledging the structural forces at play, "as if the individual [and, I would add, his/her act] were an aberration, we inadvertently engage in the process of reproducing the very violence that we assume we are contesting" (2016, pp. 138–139). I want to take this insight further. The demonizing and singularizing of the criminal by both left and right remove collective responsibility and are part of the same mechanism that erases the voice and the writing of the victims *of the present moment*. The victims of the Holocaust were silenced at the beginning (LaCapra, 2009) and today they are mobilized to silence the Palestinians. The exceptionalization of abuse favors the powerful *of the present moment*. In other words, the persecution of the criminal, whoever he or she might be (the pedophile, the capitalist, the racist, the terrorist, the minor, the abuser man) is also a dangerous partial liberation that needs to be critically addressed. Sadly, it seems that power can be analytically dismantled only after it "happens." While a power dynamic or a form of domination is unfolding, academia and society at large seem to work to repress attempts to expose the widespread complicity that makes it possible, thus concealing, and contributing to, the complicity. Confronting dominant current biases is regarded as biased, as "ideological." Being on the side of the victims *of the present moment* is frequently seen as even obscene and distasteful. Critical self-reflection seems to arrive too late. This text also arrives too late and embodies such a tragedy.[48]

If, as Walter Benjamin argued, the victors write history, then counter-reading, reevaluation, or redescription comes from an ethical commitment. Yet the previous paragraph posed a more troubling question. If what we consider treasures today were built on the backs of the oppressed, if "they owe their existence not only to the efforts of the great minds and talents who have created them, but also to the anonymous toil of their contemporaries" and, thus, "there is no document of civilization which is not at the same time a document of barbarism" (Benjamin, 1969, p. 256), then, who is writing the present—and how? Where are our treasures, perhaps the "traumatic treasures" I have referred to, being crafted, by whom, and at what cost? Can we critically confront the new (Buck-Morss, 2010)? Do we have to wait for the future in order to unveil the crimes and horror we embody today? What kind of political commitment is required to keep us awake?

In the way I understand such a political commitment, it entails the refusal to conceal complexity. Not even in the name of justice. The imperative of *sapere aude* remains valid, as well as Kant's (2008) warning that putting an end to an autocratic government is easier than achieving "a true reform in the ways of thinking" (p. 55).[49] The following thought of Judith Shklar (1989) has had an impact on my own thinking: "the idea of joining a movement and submitting to a collective belief system strikes me as a betrayal of intellectual values" (p. 13). To be sure, both claims—particularly Shklar's—if read literally, have conservative implications. However, I read them as provocations for a creative response from the perspective of radical theorizing, which, in my view, demands the acceptance that thinking has its own dignity and its own (precious) space. Critical academia needs to resist attempts to discipline and narrow imagination's scope: not only those done in the name of the market, but also those in the name of socialism, feminism, or any other social justice idiom. Judith Butler distances herself from the notion of academic excellence:[50] I wonder if, instead, what is needed is to contest the neoliberal translation of excellence while exploring likelihoods of beauty *and excellence*, which, by creating something transformative and nurturing for the world, makes of it a better place to inhabit collectively.

Thinking, in order to survive, needs to be aware of its intrinsic partiality. Being critical is, from this perspective, cultivating an awareness of the historical nature of how we ask, feel, and think—being aware, in other words, of the contingency of who we *are*. If this ethical commitment is truly historical, it needs to be self-reflexive in order to detect and maintain its own conditions of possibility (Real de Azúa, 1973; Butler, Laclau, & Zizek, 2003, p. 263).[51] De-essentializing operations do not imply a crude relativism that denies any form of universality (Buck-Morss, 2009; McNally, 2002). It is precisely the need to challenge abuse that sustains the "suspicion." It is an attempt to remain ethically awake. It is the urge to effectively confront the capitalist totalization constantly engulfing us, and that requires the immanent critique of any attempt to escape the dictatorship of the fragments (Floyd, 2009).

PS may benefit from engaging with its own partiality and contingency.[52] If the discipline needs more critical epistemological reflection at the international level, this is even more so in Latin America (Ravecca, 2010b; Baquero, Ortiz, & Noguera, 2015; Bulcourf, Gutiérrez Márquez, & Cardozo, 2015). This book can be read as an attempt to convince my fellow political scientists that critical self-reflection is both a constitutive part of good political analysis as well as a refusal to reproduce dominant powers through our academic practices.

How is political analysis related to the powers under study? If we situate this question in Latin America, then it becomes more specific: what is being trafficked through contemporary commitments to liberalism? As long as liberal democracy remains uncritiqueable, it will be a locus and a discourse where abuse happens. Democracy, as any other partial liberation, needs to be de-totalized and be treated as a dangerous "fragment." This exploration transcends the Latin American milieu: a more self-critical examination of the failures of political and economic liberalism might be needed if a serious reflection about how Donald Trump could be elected as President of the United States is going to happen. The de-fetishization of the liberal order is coming from the right, and that is a not a very promising scenario.

In this book, the critical analysis of PS' embrace of liberal democracy has been an unexpected and productive occasion to explore the relationship between knowledge and power. The closure of discursive and political imagination can be (and has been) done through "democracy." Furthermore, crimes were erased in its name. The query expands and translates an older and more intimate question: how could a political hero hurt me and make me hurt myself? Such a point of departure, where the expected terms of reference are inverted, allow us to perform the needed epistemological rupture in order to situate democracy within the discourse of PS as part of the power relations this discipline embodies through its analyses—which implies a sort of meta-epistemological rupture.

Names and stories (i.e., knowledge) do things to us and we do things through them (Nagar, 2016). The location of that doing is always multiple and messy in time and space. Something is clear though: interrupting reification to expand thinking, in *any* context, challenges domination. And academia is no exception.

The location and the making of an authorial voice are consubstantial to what is authorized and, therefore, to what is and can be known. I wanted to (de)locate myself within my research, and in searching for the tools to do so, neither a rationalist methodological individualism nor a radical anti-identitarian constructivism seemed convincing. "The author is a shifting node in a larger and constantly moving network of experience," say Morgan Brigg and Roland Bleiker (2010, p. 794), and yet, they also suggest, we somehow know that *we are we*; we are not someone else. Judith Butler (1999) argued that post-structuralism does not entail

> the death of autobiographical writing but it does draw attention to the difficulty of the "I" to express itself through the language that is available to it. . . . I am not outside the language that structures me but neither am I determined by the language that makes this possible.
>
> *(pp. xxv–xxvi)*

In my view, that we are structured through language and that we can think of the self as a journey of narration (Bischoping & Gazso, 2016)—thus, neither a fixed essence nor a pure dispersion of events—is what makes the "I writing" exciting and important. It is precisely the *relative* indeterminacy—allow me to call it *freedom* for present purposes—of the subject that is reintroduced by the autobiographical critique that mobilizes theory in order to dismantle a reified identity, opening possibilities for politics, new subjectivities, and futures.

The author has a voice and is not only an arbitrary social construction; the subject is not just an accident. Foucault-inspired anti-essentialism needs to be contextualized, and even dismantled, because taking it too literally seems unproductive. I am not "fully" post-structuralist because the *experience of* psychoanalysis (and, in a different way, Marxism) was also critical in the incomplete reflexive journey of becoming myself. My intuitions on the self and on politics (to retheorize, the *and* is needed) lie on a never-fixed point of tension or friction between different critical theories and experiences, including the poetic. Marcuse's (1991) reflections on the political role of the poetical seems to be very important today. Furthermore, science, as an institution and as a mode of studying the world, may gain a lot from engaging its others—feelings, intuitions, spirituality, disavowed knowledges, fragmented voices, broken memories, nude doubts, ontological crises, madness, and more. Such a search for its other might make science and the scientist less dogmatic, less oppressive, and better at what they are fundamentally trying to do: to understand the world.[53] Today I am grateful to any intellectual vocabulary that helps me to heal—and healing is, or can be, a collective endeavor.[54] In this regard, I wonder about the possibilities for the politicization of self-care, which goes back to my vision of an encounter between Marxism and yoga.

This narrative on trauma, healing, politics, life, and theory, along with all of its unresolved queries, is a way—my current way—of continuing to question a reactionary (academic) "we" formation based on privilege and power. It is also an attempt to engage *our* contingencies and partialities in order to interrupt cruelty within PS and beyond. Even though the rescuing powers of (self-)reflection are limited, it seems to me that we become subjects, that we are constituted as academics or citizens, through the questions we ask (Kovach, 2010, p. 111), particularly through the questions we are ready to ask ourselves.

Notes

* Art Babayants, Elizabeth Dauphinee, Ana Laura De Giorgi, Naeem Inayatullah, Shelley Liebembuk, Robert Kohls, David McNally, Viviana Patroni and Cecilia Rocha read and provided feedback on the numerous versions that this chapter has gone through. Elizabeth Dauphinee, Cristina Barcia, Marta Fonseca and Andrew Soren together *and* in different spaces, times, and registers make the *ongoing* journey of this piece of writing possible: my gratitude to them expands every day. I also want to thank my students in my course on Critical Theory at the Universidad de la República for their respectful and enthusiastic engagement with a previous version of this text.
1. Roughly since 2010, there has been an expansion of scholarship that is either narrative in form (including what is varyingly termed autobiography or auto-ethnography) or that engages in debate around the scholarly pertinence of narrative approaches.

See, for example, the forum on auto-ethnography in the *Review of International Studies* (Volume 36, Issue 3, July 2010), Inayatullah (2011), Löwenheim (2014), Dauphinee (2013a, 2013b), Muppidi (2013, 2016), Naumes (2015), a special issue on *The Politics of Exile* in *Security Dialogue* in 2013 (Volume 44, Issue 3), and Bleiker (2009). A recent piece on the issue is Ravecca and Dauphinee (2018). Other notable pieces in the feminist tradition that either utilize or endorse narrative approaches include Sylvester (2013), Zalewski (2013), and Wibben (2011). The following are examples of critiques of narrative approaches: Hamati-Ataya (2014) and Knafo (2016).

2. Jack L. Amoureux and Brent J. Steele (2016) differentiate between three meanings of reflexivity: as positionality, as critique, and as practice. With Elizabeth Dauphinee, I understand this endeavor here as a critique, as a process, *and* as positionality, as "an ethos through which I strive to keep my own thinking mobile and fluid" (Dauphinee, 2016, p. 51). As Richardson (1994) argued, "evocative representations are a striking way of seeing through and beyond sociological naturalism. . . . Through it we can experience the self-reflexive and transformational process of self creation" (p. 521).

3. At the time of the revision of this text, a few years after I finally got the permanent resident status, I might lose it for not staying in the country for enough time. The story repeats but it is not the same story. . . . The condensation of temporalities makes narrative an impossible endeavor: reality has changed already once we start writing about it.

4. Even though from the point of view of current queer theorizing it may be regarded as mainstream, I consider the work of Didier Eribon (2001), and particularly his reflections on the role of harmful insults in the production of gay subjectivities, a significant contribution to understanding this type of othering.

5. Trump effectively assembles bullying and foreign policy. Examples of this assemblage are the deportation of undocumented immigrants and immigration activists as well as the attempts to ban members of entire groups and nationalities from entering the US.

6. I have explored the conceptual underpinnings of this notion in Chapter 1. The theoretical perspectives that propose language and knowledge as playing a significant role in power relations are multiple. Nietzsche (1989), Marx (1978a, 1978b, 1990), Freud (Castoriadis, 1990; Fleming, 2005; Floyd, 2009; Freud, 1986a, 1986b), Horowitz (1977), Marcuse (1974, 1991) and Foucault (1980, 1984, 1988, 1989, 1991a, 1991b, 1992, 1993, 2006) linked language to power in different ways. They opened up paths that were further explored by others. Postcolonial studies, queer theory, and poststructuralist trends in political theory have also politicized language and knowledge, arguing that the ways in which objects of study such as sex/gender and the Global South are approached are actually part of the problem to be addressed. Judith Butler (1990), Ernesto Laclau (Laclau & Mouffe, 2004), and Edward Said (2003) were particularly helpful during my BA years to explore politics from a cultural perspective. The conversation between Butler, Laclau, and Zizek (2003) was in this regard especially significant. Politicizing language means to politicize academic discourse. In order to understand politics in depth, we need to explore the role that our languages and knowledges have in them. I acknowledge that my intellectual itinerary was shaped by Eurocentrism. Decolonizing and indigenous methodologies (Kovach, 2010; Smith, 1999) share with critical scholarship the perspective that subjectivity, self-location, and storytelling have a central role in knowledge production. That domination is also an epistemological process is a premise of indigenous scholarship, which is not surprising given the marginalization that the knowledge of indigenous peoples has been subjected to.

7. In defending his decision to bike everyday back and forth from home to the university as an intellectually productive "experiential and explorative decommuting,"

Löwenheim (2014) states: "I don't want to open a Pandora's box here, but against this criticism of my supposed waste of time, I must ask, in our day, how much time do we actually have to think in academia? Not much, I fear." And he convincingly adds: "A great deal of the current structure of incentives and constraints in academia reproduces and enhances an anti-intellectual climate in universities" (pp. 30, 35).

8. I borrow some words from Wendy Brown's intervention here (Resist Network, 2009). Brown (2010) theorizes this reactionary I/we defensiveness through psychoanalytic lenses thus:

> What does the ego, the conscious "moi," become consequent to these battles? "The defended ego," Anna Freud says, "takes the form of bodily attitudes such as stiffness and rigidity, a fixed smile, contempt, irony, and/(or) arrogance." Defense paradoxically produces a fragility and brittleness, what, borrowing from Wilhelm Reich, Anna Freud identifies as the "armor plating of character," which, again, more than merely attaching to the ego, transforms it. Hegel's shadow is discernible here as defenses come to reduce the resilience, adeptness, and flexibility—the powers—of the entity they are built to secure. (Consider this paradoxical effect in the state of Israel today.) Moreover, the ego thus constructed will inevitably block not only untoward impulses or experiences, but analysis itself; where analysis stands not simply for formal psychoanalytic work, but for all forms of self-reflexivity. The ego comes to be defined by these defenses, and not merely protected by them. Consequently, it fiercely resists submitting them to critical undoing.
>
> *(pp. 128–129)*

In this perspective, analysis becomes a political process of opening possibilities for the self by challenging the symbolic and subjective bunker that was supposed to protect her, but that ended up severely limiting her movements. Elizabeth Dauphinee and I have theorized the interplay between anxiety and what we call academic fortress writing (Ravecca & Dauphinee, 2018). The rules of academia also become rigid, resist analysis, and limit movement (in this case, of thinking). Narrative approaches, in our view, are an attempt to un-wall academic writing.

9. During the Uruguayan dictatorship between 1973 and 1985, private space and the cultural realm were disrupted (Cosse & Markarián, 1996; Gil & Viñar, 1998; Giorgi, 1995; Paternain, Ravecca, & Somma, 2005). The horrendous abuses have been abundantly proved by, among many others, the courageous report titled *Nunca Más* [Never Again], which was published by a human rights advocacy group (Serpaj, 1989). I do not remember how old I was when I read it, but I do recall the physical experience of horror that the reading produced on me. I want to highlight an important project called "*Memoria para armar*" [Memory to assemble] that collects the testimonies of women who experienced the dire effects of the dictatorship. Some of these texts were performed in a series of shows by the Teatro Circular of Montevideo. All of these are efforts to "do something" with the experience of trauma, which, in Edkins' (2003) words, "takes place when the very powers that we are convinced will protect us and give us security [in this case the security forces, precisely] become our tormentors" (p. 4).

10. We can call it discourse, or language, or whatever other category we may choose. Even though they have different implications, in this context, they have something relevant in common: the insight that the way reality is talked about is itself constitutive of reality.

11. On the inter-generational transmission of trauma from a psychological perspective, see Kellermann (2001), among others.

12. While the Communist Party opted for a peaceful path toward revolution, other groups, such as the MLN (the National Liberation Movement), chose armed struggle.

13. Germán Araújo (1938–1993) was a Uruguayan journalist and politician. He was the director of CX 30 The Radio, from whence he systematically opposed the right-wing military regime (1973–1985). His speeches on the radio became a symbol of the resistance against the dictatorship. In 1984, amid the transition to democracy, Araújo was elected senator by a coalition of leftist groups identified with the number 1001, itself a member of an even larger progressive coalition called the Broad Front, which eventually won the national elections 20 years later. He was a ferocious critic of the Ley de Caducidad (i.e., the Expiry Law) that prevented judges from prosecuting human right violations perpetrated by the military. He was a constant presence in the conversations of my family during my childhood.

14. *Chanchitas* [small female pigs] was the popular name given to the armored vehicles used by the military for repressive purposes and sometimes kidnapping.

15. Here, following Löwenheim (2014), I hope that by "identifying the *limits* of my reflexivity in this subjective account, one could learn more about the reality I describe. Things that remain hidden from my eyes or underappreciated by me might be very visible and important to other readers" (p. 22, emphasis in original).

16. In Uruguay at that point, it was not unusual to start working as a university instructor early on, right after completing the BA degree. Even so, I was precocious there: I was 25 years old when I started TAing Contemporary Political Theory, a challenging course that closes the BA in Political Science; some of my students were older than me.

17. Without others, we simply cannot exist. We know all these things already (and smart people have taught us about them, from Aristotle to Arendt), but in this text that I am writing now, I want to experience and *feel* theory; because experiencing and feeling theory is theoretically and politically relevant.

18. I assume the "reductionism" into which I am falling in this analysis. For a nuanced exploration of the itinerary of transatlantic liberalism, see Adcock (2014). However, as it is argued in that book, liberalism became "democratized," which means that was not initially democratic. It was also the language of patriarchy, racism, and colonialism, which engulfs PS' political history as well. As Adcock (2014) observes:

> Talk of "universal suffrage" and "democracy" at this time did not, as we do today, look upon racial and gender exclusions from political rights as inimical to these concepts. Exclusionary assumptions regarding what was *not* at stake when American politics was characterized in terms of a rising tide of "universal suffrage" and "democracy" would, in turn, be extended by American political science as it developed in subsequent decades. In later chapters, when I treat political scientists engaging "democracy," racial and gender exclusion will be a constant background fact. At no point was such exclusion recognized by the political scientists that I study as a challenge to their view of post-1820s America as a "democracy."
>
> *(p. 33)*

But should not these features be theoretically explored, instead of just leaving them to an additive logic through which, later on, gender and race would be incorporated into the democratic language?

19. About the operations of homophobia in Uruguay see Ravecca (2010a, 2013); Ravecca and Sempol (2013); Sempol (2008, 2010), and especially Sempol (2013). On the operations of discourses on tolerance see Gioscia and Carneiro (2013).

20. What matters here is the experiential appropriation of Eribon's work, not the assessment of how "queer" or "radical" his book is. Books are *bio*graphical creatures.

21. Needless to say, this does not refer only to a personal experience but to the complicated historical relationship between socialist politics, including Marxist theorizing, and the struggles for gender equality and sexual freedom. Eley's (2002) work shows that, in Europe, left-wing forces have traditionally been indifferent and sometimes even hostile toward feminist and anticolonial struggles. The Southern American experience was not different, and the Uruguayan left was not exceptional. In fact,

discrimination against "homosexuals" was a common practice in moderate and radical left-wing groups, even after the transition to democracy in the mid-1980s (Sempol, 2008, 2010). My family was active in the (sometimes subtly, sometimes not so subtly) homophobic Communist Party, and as a child I heard stories about "homosexual" comrades being almost expelled by their fellows. I remember my mother saying that she and others protested against that because "it was unfair." I remember another comment about a gay activist who, against all expectations, did not betray the party when he was caught and tortured by the military. He resisted the torture without "talking" and everyone was surprised. The framework of this story is problematic from every angle, and it is very revealing of the type of othering to which queers were subjected by "progressive" families and political groups. In terms of theory, while in 1935, Sigmund Freud told a mother that the homosexuality of her son was not an illness (1951, pp. 786–787), around the same time, Antonio Gramsci's conservative reflections on the "sexual question" described homosexuality as "bestiality" (2008, p. 295). Marxism is, of course, a complex body of practice and theory; if it has marginalized some subjects and struggles, it has also bred resistance to this marginalization from its own margins. Anderson (2010), McNally (2002), Roediger (2017), the tradition of Marxist feminist thinking and political economy (Hennessy, 2000), and the recent call for more collaboration between queer and Marxist perspectives (Floyd, 2009; Sears, 2005), among countless others, are signs of this complexity. Because of all of this, Marxism may be viewed as homophobic and queer at the same time.

22. A seemingly strange strategic ally if we think of the critique that feminist and queer theory have later made of psychoanalysis. Theories and names lack essence but have history.
23. The incomplete condition of acceptance, I think, might be read in isolation from the "gay issue" for it to reach its complete theoretical and political potential.
24. Connected to this issue of maleness in PS and its performative power, something has always caught my attention: how many women perform *within* PS a sort of masculine assertive academic identity. I know that my observation is hugely problematic (why should I assume that women are feminine, and what does that mean anyway?), and yet, both in academic approaches and personal interaction, I have observed this so many times. Niki Johnson, a feminist scholar who lives and works in Uruguay, with fine irony mentioned to me in a conversation, "you have to be tough and good on charts and numbers to become respectable!" Within mainstream PS, the macho rational choice boy is a centripetal force that has the power to craft his surroundings.
25. The gendered cultural politics of the discipline needs to be explored in-depth, a task that is beyond the scope of this book. Particularly, manly anti-intellectualism and the scorn of the unconventional is a tendency that I have observed across borders in different departments and international conferences. Judith Shklar (1989) has some fascinating comments linking American politics in the era of McCarthyism and the shifts within PS' environment:

> The effects of McCarthyism were less crude and immediate than subtle and latent. . . . What it did was to enhance a whole range of attitudes that were there all along. Young scholars boasted of not being intellectuals. Among many no conversation was tolerated except sports and snobbish gossip. A kind of unappetizing dirty socks and locker room humor and false and ostentatious masculinity were vaunted. . . . More damaging was that so many people who should have known better, scorned the poor, the bookish, the unconventional, the brainy, the people who did not resemble the crass and outlandish model of a real American upper-crust he-man whom they had conjured up in their imagination. For any woman of any degree of refinement or intellectuality, this was unappealing company.

(p. 7)

26. Amadae (2016) is an in-depth exploration of the role of game theory in the internal mutations and ruptures within liberalism. She notes that game theory reinterpreted the notion of rationality to divorce it from its original attachment to the no-harm principle, such that for neoliberal political economy, "[t]he no-harm principle at the root of classical liberalism no longer, neither in theory nor in practice, animates the action of rational actors who instead seek gain despite others" (p. xvi).

27. Carlos Real de Azúa (1916–1977) is one of the most relevant Uruguayan thinkers. In classrooms and academic forums, he is acknowledged as the father of PS in the country for his sharp historical and political analyses. His books constitute an essential component of how Uruguayan society has represented itself. See, for instance, Real de Azúa (1984). For a more in-depth exploration of the author, see Chapter 3 of this book.

28. The Centro Latinoamericano de Economía Humana [Latin American Center of Human Economy] (CLAEH) is a non-profit academic center for higher education and research in Uruguay, inspired by Christian and progressive ideals. During the dictatorship, public institutions for education were under the scrutiny of the military. CLAEH was an important refuge for social research and academic life. It is still a very active institution. For more information see Chapter 3.

29. Halperin Donghi (1987) seems to elliptically allude to Real de Azúa's homosexuality, perceived, in his time, as his most radical extravagance. Rilla (2017) and Espinosa (2016) also refer to this and the latter mentions the fact that Real de Azúa's sexuality was part of the anecdotes of Montevideo's cultural milieu. He adds that this condition did not leave visible signs that are traceable in his writing—I am not sure about that (see Espinosa, 2016).

30. Given its limitations and ambiguous politics, I avoid the term "anti-feminist backlash." On this issue, see Braithwaite (2004).

31. Snapshots of a new political and cultural terrain: While the election of Donald Trump poses an obvious challenge to advocates of race and gender equality, the wide online public support received by University of Toronto professor Jordan Peterson's fierce critique of gender studies and political correctness reveals that Canada is also home to a conservative discourse on the rise. South America is not an exception: in Brazil, in 2017, Judith Butler was assaulted in an airport, and her talks were widely protested; in Argentina, an aggressive conservative discourse has come back after the election of Mauricio Macri. And in Uruguay, the weekly *Voces* has become a leading voice of protest against political correctness. These attacks on social justice are truly an ideological mélange that needs to be seriously engaged with: when they show up in the camp of the left it is by reactivating the centrality of class in order to diminish the relevance of other forms of oppression. Sometimes this perspective links feminism to a global neoliberal agenda imposed by NGOs and other foreign powers. In contrast, Peterson sees the proliferation of gender pronouns as part of a global and radical leftist project of domination. In the case of the US, the constellation of discourses around Trump's campaign actively delinked the working class from racial and gender minorities, representing the former as white, and conceptually situating those subjects at odds with each other. These are all examples of a challenging environment that requires ideological innovation and to rethink the relationship between the cultural and the economic, particularly in leftist politics. Furthermore, the support that Peterson has received by trans-activists such as Theryn Meyer is also a call for theoretical and political innovation (see TVO, 2016). How can we deal with the fact that a transgender activist asserts the binary sexual order that has been problematized by queer and gender studies?

32. See Martínez (2017).

33. As is well known, the discussion around race and racism is, in the US, extremely intense right now.

34. There is consensus regarding this, and it is shown by the set of interviews analyzed in the previous chapter.
35. Texts *cannot* be dogmatic; readings of texts and of authors can: the intellectual working of a text/author is activated through the agency of reading (Ravecca & Dauphinee, 2018). The possibility of resignifying what an author (such as Marx) wrote is where creativity's potential lies. Some of my professors who needed to abandon Marxism fell into the trap of dogmatism, believing, like the teenager who yells and shuts the door hysterically, in the illusion that such a gesture inaugurates independence and free thinking. As Iver B. Neumann (2016) argues, "a scholar who leaves no room for answering, is by definition part of the discourse police" (p. 274)
36. In Ravecca (2014), I refer to torture as a material act with powerful "theoretical" effects. As Foucault and Marx showed in different ways, the body is a site of theory. While torture was applied to individual bodies, the effects were collective and extensive. The tortured/disappeared/exiled body of the socialist activist performed the theoretical act of eradicating socialism as a thinkable political aim. Put torture in this way, and the boundaries between theory, experience, and the body collapses: there is porosity between these realities. The interpretations (from center-left to right) of the collapse of the democratic system reproduce *the act of torture* (of people and of socialism) at the level of discourse. The victim is guilty. Torture and pain were the result of embracing socialism.
37. In her 1989 lecture titled "A Life of Learning," Judith Shklar has some thought-provoking passages on the situation of women in the discipline at the time:

    The atmosphere for women is, however, far from ideal. There is certainly far less open discrimination in admissions, hiring, and promotions, and that is a very genuine improvement. However, there is a lot of cynical feminism about that is very damaging, especially to young women scholars. The chairman who calls for hiring more women, any women, for, after all, any skirt will do to make his numbers look good, and to reinforce his own liberal credentials. The self-styled male feminist who wildly overpraises every newly appointed young woman as 'just brilliant and superb,' when she is in fact no better or worse than her male contemporaries, is not doing her a favor, just expressing his own inability to accept the fact that a reasonably capable woman is not a miracle. The male colleague who cannot argue with a female colleague without losing his temper like an adolescent boy screaming at his mother, and the many men who cannot really carry on a serious professional conversation with a woman, are just as tiresome as those who bad-mouth us overtly. And they are more likely to be around for a long, long time proclaiming their good intentions without changing what really has to change most of all: they themselves.

    (1989, p. 12)

    These subtle observations remain revealing of power relations that are still in operation today in different locations—and versions—as is shown by Berdahl (2017) and her opportune critique of the crazy/bitch narrative about senior academic women, regardless of the troubling elitist comments about "lesser institutions" made by the author (para. 5); and by my own interviews in Argentina, Chile and Uruguay (A1; CHL19; CHL31; U11). Ahmed's (2012) critique of the whiteness of institutions of higher education include white critical theorists: "When criticality becomes an ego ideal, it can participate in not seeing complicity" (p. 179). Indeed, the parallelism between the "self-styled male feminist" of Shklar and the critical male scholar of Ahmed is interesting. In the countries I studied in this book, whiteness within PS and in academic departments is not even an issue of conversation.
38. I have always had a broad conception of politics. As an adolescent I used to read poetry, for instance, thinking that its work of meaning-making was deeply political.

After a systematic training in political science, I still persist in this view. In 2004, I started working as a research assistant for Amparo Menéndez-Carrión, who challenges mainstream PS by conceptualizing places such as theater companies, cooperatives of different kinds, and the streets of the city as political sites. On the political function of these kinds of places for "the space of the *polis,*" see Menéndez-Carrión (2015), especially the theorization she offers in Chapter 3 (Volume I). On the "Rise and Fall of the Uruguayan *Polis*" and the deleterious impact of authoritarianism and the penetration of neoliberalism, see especially Chapters 7 and 8 (Volume II), as well as Chapters 10, 12–14 (Volume III).

39. This is a highly philosophical exercise; philosophy may be understood as the critique of thinking and, therefore, of truth (Foucault, 1998, p. 12). Such a critique is *the practice* of the love for knowledge and truth. And introspection, I would argue, is part of the philosophical way of relating to the world, including of course the internal one. The critique of our families, disciplines, and ourselves. The critique of our critique.

40. A practical way to answer this question is to clarify that I have been heavily involved with the *Uruguayan Journal of Political Science* (*RUCP*) as an assistant editor for some time now; it is the same journal I critically engaged with in Chapter 3.

41. Shepherd (2016, pp. 13–14) expresses the need to narrate herself "in relation to [her] multiple others in order to understand the quality and texture of those connections, and to understand how they will continue to nourish [her]." Neoliberal academia is blind to those connections. Narrative might function as an alternative way to think of knowledge production as a collective endeavor, even when it is only one person who executes the physical act of typing.

42. Now, as I wonder about how they lived this experience, an awareness of otherness and a feeling of compassion expands.

43. The sentence can be interpreted in two ways: (*a*) that critique may protect us *from* the partial liberations or (*b*) that critique may liberate partial liberations from themselves. Even though both go in the same direction of the crucial role of critical thinking within politics, I opted for the latter, because it does not stress negative freedom (i.e., the individual *versus* projects of liberation). In my interpretation, self-critique makes radical politics more emancipatory, but not "less radical." The original in Spanish reads: "*la teoría política latinoamericana tiene que preocuparse por servir, en tanto el destino de toda ciencia y toda cultura es ser función de las necesidades del hombre, arma para la liberación del hombre y aún liberadora de sus parciales liberaciones*" (Real de Azúa, 1973, p. 10). This piece was written in 1973, the same year as the *coup d'état.* Such an encounter of theory and history is very powerful: Real de Azúa reflects about the different forces, from left to right, that obliterate the possibility of thinking, and, therefore, of freedom. He would die in isolation in 1977 in a context of state repression.

44. A detailed report of the incident was broadcasted by *Democracy Now* (2017).

45. *Democracy Now* (2018) has an excellent interview with Patrisse Khan-Cullors, co-founder of Black Lives Matter, and journalist Asha Bandele. Their book is an example of the ability of narrative writing to assemble aspects and dimensions of experience that mainstream forms of analysis keep apart, from everyday love and violence to the politics of mental illness and structural oppressions.

46. In this regard, the notion of porosity between identities and locations (Buck-Morss, 2009) needs to be applied to trauma and guilt as a way to shake off the condition of victimhood and overcome trauma.

47. Davis also uses "punitivism," to refer to those "feminisms that call for the criminalization and the incarceration of those who engage in gender violence." For Davis, they "do the work of the state as surely as they focus on state violence and repression as the solution to heteropatriarchy and as the solution, more specifically, to sexual assault" (2016, p. 138).

48. Opening the space for critique is the opposite of fascism's logic, whose core operation is the obliteration of thinking. The destruction of the possibility of engaging in reflection about ourselves has taken varied historical forms, all of them connected to some kind of oppression or/and repression: neurosis and surplus-repression (Horowitz, 1977; Marcuse, 1974), fascism (Gramsci, 2008), positivism and *reified* formal reason (Bourdieu, 1973; Marcuse, 1974, 1991), subjugating knowledge dynamics (Foucault, 1993), and neoliberalism, which has recently been theorized as opposed to individuality, should be added to the list. For a sociological theorization of individuality, see Corcuff (2008).

49. Later on, Kant (2008) insists that "the possession of power inevitably corrupts the free judgment of reason. . . . [T]he class of philosophers is by nature incapable of forming seditious factions and clubs" (p. 115).

50. See her answer in this Q&A (Peter Wall Institute for Advanced Studies, 2012).

51. The conception of our thinking as historical implies that the categories through which we apprehend reality are consubstantial to the events that they name. For Susan Buck-Morss (2009), we need "to recognize not only the contingency of historical events, but also the indeterminacy of the historical categories by which we grasp them" (p. 11). If categories "happen" within history and belong to it, then the Foucaldian approach to philosophy as the critique of truth is in itself an interrogation of history. Self-reflection (the interrogation of the ways in which *we are thinking*) is the only possible way to grapple with the new.

52. Besides the cliché that teaching is political, there is something about knowledge and abuse that I want to say, and I can only say it fully in Spanish: *Sabemos que el que no sabe puede saber cuándo el que sabe se equivoca y que es importante en la práctica docente saber eso. Hay que reconocer el derecho del que no sabe a resistir y contestar no lo que sabe el que sabe sino la posición de privilegio del saber.* [We know that s/he who does not know may know when s/he who does know is wrong. It is very important to acknowledge this in our teaching practice. We need to recognize the right of those who do not know to resist and contest, not the knowledge of the person who knows, but the privileged position of knowledge itself.] The classroom is sacred.

53. "When did social science stop being literature?" Roxanne Doty (2015) asks, and continues: "When did the political and the poetic become separated? When did we become so certain of the border between fact and fiction? When did the academic writer become prisoner to the comforting area of ordered space?" (p. 23). Narrative approaches offer possibilities to momentarily exit the ordered space (Ravecca & Dauphinee, 2018).

54. I borrow this notion from Angela Davis (SSEX BBOX, 2017).

Works Cited

Adcock, R. (2014). *Liberalism and the emergence of American political science: A transatlantic tale*. Oxford: Oxford University Press.

Agathangelou, A. (2004). *The global political economy of sex: Desire, violence, and insecurity in Mediterranean nation states*. New York: Palgrave Macmillan.

Agathangelou, A. (2006). Colonising desires: Bodies for sale, exploitation and (in) security in desire industries. *The Cyprus Review, 18*(2), 37–73.

Agathangelou, A., & Killian, K. (2009). The discourse of refugee trauma: Epistemologies of the displaced, the state, and mental health practitioners. *The Cyprus Review, 21*(1), 19–58.

Ahmed, S. (2012). *On being included: Racism and diversity in institutional life*. Durham, NC: Duke University Press.

Alexander, J. M. (2005). *Pedagogies of crossing: Meditations on feminism, sexual politics, memory, and the sacred.* Durham, NC: Duke University Press.

Almond, G., & Verba, S. (1963). *The civic culture: Political attitudes and democracy in five nations.* Princeton, NJ: Princeton University Press.

Amadae, S. M. (2016). *Prisoners of reason: Game theory and neoliberal political economy.* New York: Cambridge University Press.

Amoureux, J. L., & Steele, B. J. (Eds.). (2016). *Reflexivity and international relations: Positionality, critique, and practice.* New York: Routledge.

Anderson, K. (2010). *Marx at the margins: On nationalism, ethnicity, and non-western societies.* Chicago: University of Chicago Press.

Arendt, H. (1999). *Eichmann en Jerusalén: Un estudio sobre la banalidad del mal.* Barcelona: Lumen.

Baquero, S. A., Ortiz, J. A. C., & Noguera, J. C. R. (2015). Colonialidad del saber y ciencias sociales: Una metodología para aprehender los imaginarios colonizados. *Análisis Político, 28*(85), 76–92.

Benjamin, W. (1969). *Illuminations.* New York: Schocken Books.

Berdahl, J. (2017, July 15). Jennifer Berdahl: The 'crazy/bitch' narrative about senior academic women. *The Georgia Straight.* Retrieved from www.straight.com/news/937181/jennifer-berdahl-crazybitch-narrative-about-senior-academic-women

Bischoping, K., & Gazso, A. (Eds.). (2016). *Analyzing talk in the social sciences.* Thousand Oaks, CA: Sage Publications.

Bleiker, R. (2009). *Aesthetics and world politics.* New York: Palgrave.

Bourdieu, P. (1973). *El oficio del sociólogo.* Buenos Aires: Siglo Ventiuno.

Braithwaite, A. (2004). Politics of/and backlash. *Journal of International Women's Studies, 5*(5), 18–33.

Brettschneider, M. (2011). Heterosexual political science. *PS: Political Science & Politics, 44*(1), 23–26.

Breuning, M., & Sanders, K. (2007). Gender and journal authorship in eight prestigious political science journals. *PS: Political Science & Politics, 40*(2), 347–351.

Brigg, M., & Bleiker, R. (2010). Autoethnographic international relations: Exploring the self as a source of knowledge. *Review of International Studies, 36*, 779–798.

Brown, W. (2010). *Walled states, waning sovereignty.* Brooklyn: Zone Books.

Brown, W. (2013, January 30). Reclaiming democracy: An interview with Wendy Brown on occupy, sovereignty, and secularism (R. Celikates, & Y. Jansen, Interviewers). *Critical Legal Thinking: The Law and the Political.* Retrieved from http://criticallegalthinking.com/2013/01/30/reclaiming-democracy-an-interview-with-wendy-brown-on-occupy-sovereignty-and-secularism/

Brown, W. (2015). *Undoing the demos: Neoliberalism's stealth revolution.* New York: Zone Books.

Brown, W. (2017, April 25). Interview—Wendy Brown (A. Hoffmann, Interviewer). *E-International Relations.* Retrieved from www.e-ir.info/2017/04/25/interview/

Buck-Morss, S. (2009). *Hegel, Haiti and universal history.* Pittsburgh: University of Pittsburgh Press.

Buck-Morss, S. (2010). The second time as farce . . . historical pragmatics and the untimely present. In C. Douzinas & S. Žižek (Eds.), *The idea of communism* (pp. 67–80). New York: Verso.

Bulcourf, P., Gutiérrez Márquez, E., & Cardozo, N. (2015). Historia y desarollo de la ciencia política en América Latina: Reflexiones sobre la constitución del campo de estudios. *Revista de Ciencia Política, 35*(1), 179–199.

Butalia, U. (2000). *The other side of silence: Voices from the partition of India*. Durham, NC: Duke University Press.

Butler, J. (1990). *Gender trouble: Feminism and the subversion of identity*. New York: Routledge.

Butler, J. (1999). *Gender trouble: Feminism and the subversion of identity* (2nd ed.). New York: Routledge.

Butler, J., Laclau, E., & Zizek, S. (2003). *Contingencia, hegemonía, universalidad: Diálogos contemporáneos en la izquierda*. Buenos Aires: Fondo de Cultura Económica.

Butler, J., & Spivak, G. (2010). *Who sings the nation-state?: Language, politics, belonging*. New York: Seagull books.

Castoriadis, C. (1990). *El mundo fragmentado*. Montevideo: Editorial Nordam-Comunidad.

Ciriza, A. (2010, October 17). A propósito de una controversia feminista: Sobre ambivalencias conceptuales y asuntos de disputa. Las relaciones entre cuerpo y política. *Herramienta: Debate y Crítica Marxista, 45*. Retrieved from www.herramienta.com.ar/revista-herramienta-n-45/proposito-de-una-controversia-feminista-sobre-ambivalencias-conceptuales-y-

Corcuff, P. (2008). Figuras de la individualidad: De Marx a las sociologías contemporáneas: Entre clarificaciones científicas y antropologías filosóficas. *Cultura y Representaciones Sociales, 2*(4), 9–41.

Corti, A. (2015, June 25). ¿Compañero de quién? *Brecha*. Retrieved from https://brecha.com.uy/companero-de-quien/

Cosse, I., & Markarián, V. (1996). *1975: Año de la orientalidad: Identidad, memoria e historia en una dictadura*. Montevideo: Trilce.

Dauphinee, E. (2013a). *The politics of exile*. New York: Routledge.

Dauphinee, E. (2013b). Writing as hope: Reflections on the politics of exile. *Security Dialogue, 44*(4), 347–361.

Dauphinee, E. (2016). Narrative engagement and the creative practices of international relations. In J. L. Amoureux & B. J. Steele (Eds.), *Reflexivity and international relations: Positionality, critique and practice* (pp. 44–60). New York: Routledge.

Davis, A. (2016). *Freedom is a constant struggle: Ferguson, Palestine, and the foundations of a movement*. Chicago: Haymarket Books.

Democracy Now. (2017, August 14). *Daily show: Mon. August 14, 2017*. [Video file]. Retrieved from www.democracynow.org/shows/2017/8/14?autostart=115.0

Democracy Now. (2018, January 16). *'When they call you a terrorist': The life of black lives matter co-founder Patrisse Khan-Cullors*. [Video file]. Retrieved from www.democracynow.org/2018/1/16/when_they_call_you_a_terrorist

De Sade, M. (1977). *Juliette 2*. Madrid: Espiral.

De Sade, M. (1986). *Juliette 3*. Madrid: Espiral.

De Sade, M. (1987). *Juliette 1*. Madrid: Espiral.

De Sade, M. (1996). *Las 120 jornadas de Sodoma*. Madrid: Espiral.

De Sade, M. (1999a). *Cuentos, historietas y fábulas*. Madrid: Edimat Libros.

De Sade, M. (1999b). *La filosofía del tocador*. Barcelona: Edicomunicación.

De Sade, M. (1999c). *Los infortunios de la virtud*. Barcelona: Edicomunicación.

Doty, R. L. (2015). A mostly true day in Eloy, Arizona. *Journal of Narrative Politics, 2*(1), 22–24.

Dragiewicz, M. (2008). Patriarchy reasserted: Fathers' rights and anti-VAWA activism. *Feminist Criminology, 3*(2), 121–144.

Edkins, J. (2003). *Trauma and the memory of politics*. London: Cambridge University Press.

Eley, G. (2002). *Forging democracy: The history of the left in Europe, 1850–2000*. New York: Oxford University Press.

Enloe, C. (1989). *Bananas, beaches and bases: Making feminist sense of international politics*. London: Pandora Press.

Eribon, D. (2001). *Reflexiones sobre la cuestión gay*. Barcelona: Anagrama.

Escobar, A. (2004). Beyond the third world: Imperial globality, global coloniality and anti-globalisation social movements. *Third World Quarterly, 25*(1), 207–230.

Espinosa, G. (2016, March 15). Fundador de panoramas: Se cumplen 100 años del nacimiento de Carlos Real de Azúa. *La Diaria*. Retrieved from https://ladiaria.com. uy/articulo/2016/3/fundador-de-panoramas/

Faludi, S. (1991). *Backlash: The undeclared war against women*. New York: Three Rivers Press.

Fleming, P. (2005, July). *Marcuse, memory and the psychoanalysis of workplace resistance*. Paper presented at the meeting of Critical Management Studies, Cambridge, UK. Retrieved from www.mngt.waikato.ac.nz/ejrot/cmsconference/2005/proceed ings/psychoanalytic/Fleming.pdf

Floyd, K. (2009). *The reification of desire: Toward a queer marxism*. Minneapolis: University of Minnesota Press.

Foucault, M. (1980). Two lectures. In C. Gordon (Ed.), *Power/knowledge: Selected interviews and other writings 1972–1977* (pp. 78–109). New York: Pantheon.

Foucault, M. (1984). What is an author. In P. Rabinow (Ed.), *The Foucault reader* (pp. 101–120). New York: Vintage Books.

Foucault, M. (1988). L'anti-oedipe: Une introduction a la vie non fasciste. *Magazine Littéraire, 257*(September).

Foucault, M. (1989). *Vigilar y castigar*. Mexico City: Siglo Veintiuno Editores.

Foucault, M. (1991a). *Historia de la sexualidad 1: La voluntad de saber*. Madrid: Siglo Veintiuno de España Editores.

Foucault, M. (1991b). *Saber y verdad*. Madrid: Ediciones La Piqueta.

Foucault, M. (1992). *Microfísica del poder*. Madrid: Ediciones La Piqueta.

Foucault, M. (1993). *Genealogía del racismo*. Montevideo: Nordam.

Foucault, M. (1998). *Historia de la sexualidad 2: El uso de los placeres*. Madrid: Siglo Veintiuno de España Editores.

Foucault, M. (2006). *Seguridad, territorio, población: Curso en el Collège de France (1977–1978)*. Buenos Aires: Fondo de Cultura Económica.

Freud, S. (1933). New introductory lectures on psycho-analysis. In J. Stratchey (Ed. & Trans.), *The standard edition of the complete psychological works of Sigmund Freud, Volume XXII (1932–1936)* (pp. 1–182). London: Hogarth.

Freud, S. (1951). Letter to an American mother. *American Journal of Psychiatry, 107*, 786–787.

Freud, S. (1986a). El malestar en la cultura. In J. Stratchey (Ed.) & J. L. Etcheverry (Trans.), *Obras completas, volumen XXI (1927–1931)* (pp. 57–140). Buenos Aires: Amorrortu Editores.

Freud, S. (1986b). El porvenir de una ilusión. In J. Stratchey (Ed.) & J. L. Etcheverry (Trans.), *Obras completas, volumen XXI (1927–1931)* (pp. 1–56). Buenos Aires: Amorrortu Editores.

Fried Amilivia, G. (2016). Sealing and unsealing Uruguay's transitional politics of oblivion: Waves of memory and the road to justice, 1985–2015. *Latin American Perspectives, 43*(6), 103–123.

Fujii, L. A. (2016). The dark side of DA-RT. *Comparative Politics Newsletter, 26*(1), 25–27.

Gajardo Lagomarsino, P. (1989). La transición a la democracia en Chile: Desafíos y perspectivas a partir de un análisis teórico. *Política, 21*, 53–62.

Gaulejac, V. (2012). *La recherche malade du management.* Versailles: Quae.

Ghosh, A. (1992). *In an antique land.* New York: Vintage Books.

Gil, D., & Viñar, M. (1998). La dictadura militar: Una intrusión en la intimidad. In J. P. Barrán, G. Caetano, & T. Porzecansky (Eds.), *Historias de la vida privada en el Uruguay 3: Individuo y soledades 1920–1990* (pp. 301–326). Montevideo: Taurus.

Giorgi, V. (1995). Represión y olvido: El terrorismo de estado dos décadas después. In V. Giorgi (Ed.), *Represión y olvido: Efectos psicológicos y sociales de la violencia política dos décadas después* (pp. 53–66). Montevideo: Roca Viva Editorial.

Gioscia, L., & Carneiro, F. (2013). Tolerancia y discursos de poder en el Uruguay progresista. *Revista Estudos Hum(e)anos, 6*, 3–20.

Gramsci, A. (2008). *Selections from the prison notebooks* (Q. Hoare & G. Nowell, Trans. & Eds.). New York: International Publishers.

Greco, M., & Stenner, P. (2013). *Emotions and social theory: A social science reader.* New York: Routledge.

Guilhot, N. (2001). Les professionnels de la démocratie: Logiques militantes et logiques savants. *Actes de la recherche en sciences sociales, 139*, 53–65.

Halperin Donghi, T. (1987). Prólogo. In T. Halperin Donghi (Ed.), *Escritos de Carlos Real de Azúa* (pp. 5–47). Montevideo: Arca.

Hamati-Ataya, I. (2014). Transcending objectivism, subjectivism, and the knowledge in-between: The subject in/of 'strong reflexivity.' *Review of International Studies, 40*(1), 153–175.

Harvey, D. (2005). *A brief history of neoliberalism.* Oxford: Oxford University Press.

Hennessy, R. (2000). *Profit and pleasure: Sexual identities in late capitalism.* London: Routledge.

Hite, K., & Huguet, J. (2016). Luz guía. *Crítica Contemporánea: Revista de Teoría Política, 6*, 43–52.

Horowitz, G. (1977). *Basic and surplus repression in psychoanalytic theory: Freud, Reich and Marcuse.* Toronto: University of Toronto Press.

Htun, M. (2016). DA-RT and the social conditions of knowledge production in political science. *Comparative Politics Newsletter, 26*(1), 32–36.

Inayatullah, N. (ed.) (2011). *Autobiographical international relations: I, IR.* New York: Routledge.

Inayatullah, N. (2013). Pulling threads: Intimate systematicity in the politics of exile. *Security Dialogue, 44*(4), 331–345.

Jackson, P. T. (2011). *The conduct of inquiry in international relations: Philosophy of science and its implications for the study of world politics.* London: Routledge.

Kant, I. (2008). An answer to the question: 'What is the enlightenment?' In H. S. Reiss (Ed.) & H. B. Nisbet (Trans.), *Kant: Political writings* (pp. 54–60). Cambridge: Cambridge University Press.

Kellermann, N. P. F. (2001). *Transmission of holocaust trauma.* Jereusalem: Yad Vashem, The World Holocaust Rememberance Center. Retrieved from www.yad vashem.org/yv/en/education/languages/dutch/pdf/kellermann.pdf

Kelsky, K. (2012, March 27). Graduate school is a means to a job. *The Chronicle of Higher Education.* Retrieved from http://chronicle.com/article/Graduate-School-Is-a-Means-to/131316/

Keucheyan, R. (2013). *The left hemisphere: Mapping critical theory today*. New York: Verso.

Keucheyan, R. (2016). Las mutaciones de la teoría crítica: Un mapa del pensamiento radical hoy. *Nueva Sociedad, 261*(enero-febrero), 36–53.

Khan-Cullors, P., & Bandele, A. (2018). *When they call you a terrorist: A black lives matter memoir*. New York: St. Martin's Press.

King, G., Keohane, R. O., & Verba, S. (2000). *El diseño de la investigación social: La inferencia científica en los estudios cualitativos*. Madrid: Alianza.

Knafo, S. (2016). Bourdieu and the dead end of reflexivity: On the impossible task of locating the subject. *Review of International Studies, 42*(1), 25–47.

Kovach, M. (2010). *Indigenous methodologies: Characteristics, conversations, and contexts*. Toronto: University of Toronto Press.

Kristof, N. (2014, February 15). Professors, we need you! *The New York Times*. Retrieved from www.nytimes.com/2014/02/16/opinion/sunday/kristof-professors-we-need-you.html?nytmobile=0

LaCapra, D. (2009). *Historia y memoria después de Auschwitz*. Buenos Aires: Prometeo.

Laclau, E., & Mouffe, C. (2004). *Hegemonía y estrategia socialista: Hacia una radicalización de la democracia*. Buenos Aires: Fondo de Cultura Económica.

Losurdo, D. (2011). *Liberalism: A counter-history*. New York: Verso Books.

Löwenheim, O. (2014). *The politics of the trail*. Ann Arbor, MI: University of Michigan Press.

Marcuse, H. (1974). *Eros and civilization: A philosophical inquiry into Freud*. Boston: Beacon Press.

Marcuse, H. (1991). *One-dimensional man: Studies in the ideology of advanced industrial society*. Boston: Beacon Press.

Martínez, I. (2017, August 12). Manifestación en ciudad vieja contra la guía de educación sexual de primaria. *La Diaria*. Retrieved from https://ladiaria.com.uy/articulo/2017/8/manifestacion-en-ciudad-vieja-contra-la-guia-de-educacion-sexual-de-primaria/

Marx, K. (1843). *A contribution to the critique of Hegel's philosophy of right: Introduction*. Retrieved from www.marxists.org/archive/marx/works/1843/critique-hpr/intro.htm

Marx, K. (1978a). Economic and philosophic manuscripts of 1844. In R. C. Tucker (Ed.), *The Marx-Engels reader* (pp. 66–125). New York: W.W. Norton & Company.

Marx, K. (1978b). Theses on Feuerbach. In R. C. Tucker (Ed.), *The Marx-Engels reader* (pp. 143–145). New York: W.W. Norton & Company.

Marx, K. (1990). *Capital* (Vol. I). London: Penguin Books.

Maslíah, L. (1984). *Biromes y servilletas. On Canciones y negocios de otra índole* [Audio cassette]. Montevideo: La Batuta.

McNally, D. (2002). *Bodies of meaning: Studies on language, labor, and liberation*. New York: State University of New York Press.

Menéndez-Carrión, A. (2015). *Memorias de ciudadanía: Los avatares de una polis golpeada. La experiencia uruguaya*. Montevideo: Fin de Siglo.

Ministerio de Desarrollo Social. (2017). *Claves para la discusión del proyecto de ley integral para personas trans*. Montevideo: MIDES.

Muppidi, H. (2013). *The colonial signs of international relations*. London: Routledge.

Muppidi, H. (2016). *Politics in emotion: The song of telangana*. Oxford: Oxford University Press.

Nagar, R. (2016). Editor's interview with Richa Nagar (E. Dauphinee, Interviewer). *Journal of Narrative Politics, 2*(2), 73–80.

Naumes, S. (2015). Is all 'I' IR? *Millennium: Journal of International Studies, 43*(3), 820–832.

Neumann, I. B. (2016). Conclusion. In J. L. Amoureux & B. J. Steele (Eds.), *Reflexivity and international relations: Positionality, critique, and practice* (pp. 272–274). New York: Routledge.

Nietzsche, F. (1989). *Genealogy of morals*. New York: Vintage Books.

Nietzsche, F. (1992). *Así habló Zarathustra*. Barcelona: Planeta-Agostini.

Nietzsche, F. (1999a). *Ecce homo*. Madrid: Edimat Libros.

Nietzsche, F. (1999b). *El caminante y su sombra*. Madrid: Edimat Libros.

Nietzsche, F. (1999c). *El ocaso de los ídolos*. Madrid: Edimat Libros.

North, D. C. (1990). *Institutions, institutional change and economic performance*. New York: Cambridge University Press.

Paternain, R., Ravecca, P., & Somma, N. (2005). *El golpe de estado en Uruguay: Tres miradas desde la teoría social* (Department of Sociology Working Paper No. 74). Montevideo: Facultad de Ciencias Sociales, Universidad de la República.

Persaud, R. B. (2016). The reluctant immigrant and modernity. In E. Dauphinee & N. Inayatullah (Eds.), *Narrative global politics* (pp. 5–24). London: Routledge.

Peter Wall Institute for Advanced Studies [Peter Wall Institute for Advanced Studies]. (2012, December 20). *Judith Butler: Q & A with UBC faculty*. [Video file]. Retrieved from www.youtube.com/watch?v=4ECjyoU6kGA

Ravecca, P. (2010a). *'Progressive' government (2005–2009) and the lgttbq agenda: On the (recent) queering of Uruguay and its limits* (Working Paper No. 01/10). Montevideo: Instituto de Ciencia Política. Retrieved from http://cienciassociales.edu.uy/wp-content/uploads/sites/4/2015/04/DOL_10_01_Ravecca.pdf

Ravecca, P. (2010b). La política de la ciencia política: Ensayo de introspección disciplinar desde América Latina hoy. *América Latina, 9*, 173–210.

Ravecca, P. (2013). Sobre la aprobación del matrimonio gay en Uruguay. *Periferias, 21*, 185–193. Retrieved from https://fisyp.org.ar/media/uploads/p.21-ravecca.pdf

Ravecca, P. (2014). *La política de la ciencia política en Chile y Uruguay: Ciencia, poder, contexto. Primeros hallazgos de una agenda de investigación* (Working Paper No. 01/14). Montevideo: Instituto de Ciencia Política.

Ravecca, P. (2017a, June 17). Paulo Ravecca, politólogo: El liberalismo también puede ser estalinista (J. Lauro, & A. García, Interviewers). *Voces del Frente*. Retrieved from http://semanariovoces.com/paulo-ravecca-politologo-el-liberalismo-tambien-puede-ser-estalinista/

Ravecca, P. (2017b). Sobre capitalistas llorones y machos en pena: Teorías críticas y producción ideológica hoy. *Revista Bravas, 3*. Retrieved from http://revistabravas.org/article/168/ensayo-sobre-capitalistas-llorones-y-machos-en-pena-teorías-críticas-y-producción

Ravecca, P., & Dauphinee, E. (2016). Narrativa (y) política: Ideas que solo se pueden contar. *Crítica Contemporánea. Rev. de Teoría Política, 6*, 1–4.

Ravecca, P., & Dauphinee, E. (2018). Narrative and the possibilities for scholarship. *International Political Sociology, 12*(2), 125–138.

Ravecca, P., & Sempol, D. (2013). Triángulos rosas y negros en Uruguay: Un memorial del 'genocidio gay' ante la tolerancia integracionista uruguaya. In J. A. Bresciano (Ed.), *La memoria histórica y sus configuraciones temáticas: Una aproximación interdisciplinaria* (pp. 385–407). Montevideo: Ediciones Cruz del Sur.

Real de Azúa, C. (1973). *La teoría política latinoamericana: Una actividad cuestionada*. Retrieved from www.autoresdeluruguay.uy/biblioteca/Carlos_Real_De_Azua/lib/exe/fetch.php?media=teoriayetica.pdf

Real de Azúa, C. (1984). *Uruguay, ¿una sociedad amortiguadora?* Montevideo: Banda Oriental/CIESU.

Resist Network. [resistnetwork]. (2009, November 27). *The psychological need to create "us" and "them."* [Video file]. Retrieved from www.youtube.com/watch?v=rrbnbmA3n 5o&feature=related

Richardson, L. (1994). Writing: A method of inquiry. In N. K. Denzin & Y. S. Lincoln (Eds.), *Handbook of qualitative research* (pp. 516–529). Thousand Oaks, CA: Sage Publications.

Rico, A. (2005). *Cómo nos domina la clase gobernante. Orden político y obediencia social en la democracia posdictadura, 1985–2005.* Montevideo: Ediciones Trilce.

Rilla, J. (2017). *Carlos Real de Azúa viaja a España: Ratificación/rectificación.* Montevideo, manuscript in preparation.

Rocha Carpiuc, C. (2016). Women and diversity in Latin American political science. *European Political Science, 15*(4), 457–475.

Rodriguez, S. (1982). *La maza. On Unicornio* [LP]. Havana: Egrem.

Roediger, D. (2017). *Class, race and marxism.* New York: Verso Books.

Saad-Filho, A., & Johnston, D. (2005). *Neoliberalism: A critical reader.* London: Pluto Press.

Said, E. (2003). *Orientalismo.* Barcelona: Debolsillo.

Scarry, E. (1987). *The body in pain: The making and unmaking of the world.* New York: Oxford University Press.

Sears, A. (2005). Queer anti-capitalism: What's left of lesbian and gay liberation. *Science & Society, 69*(1), 92–112.

Segato, R. (2016). *La guerra contra las mujeres.* Madrid: Editorial Traficantes de Sueños.

Sempol, D. (2008). *Informe Uruguay: La historia de la sexualidad.* Buenos Aires: Red Académica LGTB MERCOSUR.

Sempol, D. (2010). Homosexualidad y cárceles políticas uruguayas: La homofobia como política de resistencia. *Revista Latinoamericana de Sexualidad, Salud y Sociedad, 4,* 53–79.

Sempol, D. (2013). *De los baños a la calle: Historia del movimiento lésbico, gay, trans uruguayo (1984–2013).* Montevideo: Random House Mondadori.

SERPAJ (Servicio Paz y Justicia) Uruguay. (1989). *Uruguay, nunca más.* Montevideo: SERPAJ.

Shepherd, L. J. (2016). Research as gendered intervention: Feminist research ethics and the self in the research encounter. *Crítica Contemporánea: Revista de Teoría Política, 6,* 1–15.

Shklar, J. N. (1989, April 6). *A life of learning* (Charles Homer Haskins Lecture, American Council of Learned Societies (ACLS) Occasional Paper 9). Washington, DC: ACLS. Retrieved from www.acls.org/uploadedFiles/Publications/OP/Haskins/1989_Judith NShklar.pdf

Shklar, J. N. (1998). The liberalism of fear. In S. Hoffmann (Ed.), *Political thought and political thinkers* (pp. 3–20). Chicago: University of Chicago Press.

Smith, C. A. (2011). Gay, straight, or questioning? Sexuality and political science. *PS: Political Science & Politics, 44*(1), 35–38.

Smith, T. (1999). *Decolonizing methodologies: Research and indigenous peoples.* London: Zed Books.

Sneh, P., & Cosaka, J. C. (2000). *La shoah en el siglo: Del lenguaje del exterminio al exterminio del discurso.* Buenos Aires: Xavier Bóveda Ediciones.

SSEX BBOX. [SSEXBBOX]. (2017, May 22). *On inequality: Angela Davis and Judith Butler in conversation.* [Video file]. Retrieved from www.youtube.com/watch?v=-MzmifPGk94

Sylvester, C. (2013). *War as experience: Contributions from international relations and feminist analysis*. London: Routledge.

Szasz, T. (1973). *The second sin*. Garden City, NY: Anchor Press.

Trent, J. E. (2009, July). *Political science 2010: Out of step with the world? Empirical evidence and commentary*. Paper presented at the 21st International Political Science World Congress, Santiago, Chile. Retrieved from www.johntrent.ca/published-writings/IPSAIsPolSci-0709.html

Trent, J. (2012). Issues and trends in political science at the beginning of the 21st century: Perspectives from the World of Political Science book series. In J. Trent & M. Stein (Eds.), *The world of political science: A critical overview of the development of political studies around the globe: 1990–2012* (pp. 91–153). Toronto: Barbara Budrich Publishers.

TVO. (2016, October 26). Gender, rights and freedom of speech. [Video file]. *The Agenda with Steve Paikin*. Retrieved from https://tvo.org/video/programs/the-agenda-with-steve-paikin/genders-rights-and-freedom-of-speech

Van Wormer, K. (2008). Anti-feminist backlash and violence against women worldwide. *Social Work & Society, 6*(2), 324–337.

Wibben, A. T. R. (2011). *Feminist security studies: A narrative approach*. London: Routledge.

Wilson, W. (1911). The law and the facts: Presidential address, seventh annual meeting of the American Political Science Association. *American Political Science Review, 5*(1), 1–11.

Zalewski, M. (2013). *Feminist international relations: Exquisite corpse*. London: Routledge.

5

THE TEMPERATURES OF THINKING AND POLITICS

An Assemblage of Critical Theories and a Problematizing Re-Inscription of Political Science

> Man cannot be, never was, without property, without mine and thine.
> —Francis Lieber[1] (1890/2003, p. 112)

> Prisons are a quintessential democratic institution.
> —Angela Davis (SSEX BOXX, 2017)

This book is a meditation on power and knowledge. Though located within political science, this reflection does not belong to the discipline's mainstream (Bulcourf, Krzywicka, & Ravecca, 2017).[2] Informed by critical theory, it has appealed to diverse epistemologies and methodologies, practicing an "unhomed interdisciplinarity" (Puar, 2007, p. xvi). Such a variety of points of departure and perspectives was given cohesiveness by a consistent problem of inquiry, and a recurring set of theoretical questions.[3] The problem explored has constantly been the intermingling of science—political science in particular—and power. The study asked how this relationship operated in the cases under examination, showing how Chilean and Uruguayan PS have had a more complex relationship with their political context than the narratives of objectivity and detachment are ready to recognize. Indeed, it was shown how political regimes and international political economy affect the discipline, while at the same time the latter partici-pates in public discourse, for instance, by reinforcing the common sense that liberal democracy is the only possibly desirable way of organizing society. The implication of this is that by attending to the power dynamics of science, we can better understand the workings of power and politics.

Following this logic, the community of political science will benefit from engaging in a broader conversation that expands the mainstream notion of the

political to include dimensions that go well beyond the so-called political system. This conversation not only entails turning our gaze beyond the political
system, but also requires looking inwards into the discipline itself, the site where
the very notion of a political system emerged. This operation of including epistemology into disciplinary critique is more productively disruptive than simply
expanding the political in topographic terms, because it problematizes the very
terms of the conversation about politics.

Chapter 1 delineated the study's approach, traced its conceptual paths and
assembled a set of critical vocabularies to navigate the politics of knowledge
and the epistemology of power. It showed how, among other radical approaches
and thinkers, Marx, Nietzsche, Sade, Freud, Gramsci, Foucault, the Frankfurt
School, postcolonial studies, queer theory, neo/post-Marxism, critical indigenous studies, and critical disability studies all shared the idea that *knowledge
and power are inseparable*. The acknowledgment of this inseparability, I argued,
meant that PS, including narratives of its identity, is not politically innocent.
This insight sustained the analysis of the politics of the discipline, which, in
turn, allowed us to interrogate the role played by its knowledge in broader social
and political relations of power. In other words, by interrogating the academic
field that names and studies the political, we expand our knowledge about the
political.

The list of contemporary scholars who have developed, in one way or another,
a self-reflexive critique of the uses and deployment (and also power effects) of
knowledge is extensive. For concluding purposes, the following are just a few
illustrative examples. Edward Said's *Orientalism* (1979) was devoted to unpacking a mainstream body of knowledge that informs (to this day) imperialist policies. The critical project of Enrique Dussel (1995) problematizes modernity and
science as well as the projects of civilizational superiority attached to them.
Gayatri Chakravorty Spivak's "Can the Subaltern Speak?" (1988) persuasively
shows, among others, the violences critical theory may incur when it avoids the
task of representation. Judith Butler (1990) has shown how knowledges about
sex are not neutral. Meanwhile, the connections between (American) political science and "one-dimensional" domination have been explicitly unpacked
by Herbert Marcuse (1991). Inspired by these and other voices where knowledge becomes the object of political critique,[4] I identified the politics of political science (PPS) as a *problématique* worth exploring, and engaged in a study
of political meta-epistemology, that is, the politics *of* the narratives *about* the
development of PS. In other words, not only self-reflection but also meta-self-
reflection was situated as a crucial procedure to capture the embeddedness of
our practices and categories of knowing in the complex relationality that shapes
personal and social experience.

One of the basic points mobilized in this study is that the emergence of a non-
oppressive knowledge requires critical introspection. For Marcuse (1991), "epistemology is in itself ethics, and ethics is epistemology" (p. 125).[5] Self-reflection

is, after all, fundamentally a strategy to avoid abuse. Hence, self-reflection is especially important for progressives and critical theorists in order to examine the consequences and implications of our ways of proceeding and theorizing, which go beyond the alleged good intentions of the doer, as I argue later on in this final chapter.

Chapter 2 focused on the circumstances of Chilean PS during Pinochet's dictatorship. The exploration analyzed authoritarian political science (APS), a notion I resorted to in order to show the interconnections between the regime and the discipline's trajectory, which was affected by the parameters set by the politics of authoritarianism. There is an indicative contrast with Chapter 1: the analysis of APS embodies a dry and *cold* moment of the book, obsessively focused on empirical reconstruction. Theory is, however, present here in the ways the story is told and in how the analytical artifacts were constructed. Conceived as both a quantitative and a qualitative exercise in critical theory, in the sense of Horkheimer (1978), APS carries theoretical implications for situating the politics of political science—in particular, for problematizing conventional views about the (ironclad) relationship between liberalism, democracy, and political science. Through its empirical idiom, the chapter took us to an ignored part of PS history which, when theoretically interrogated, denaturalizes the discipline's dominant self-image and questions the democratic *nature* of liberalism.[6]

The Uruguayan dictatorship did not foster the emergence of APS; the case study documented instead a different path toward the hegemony of liberalism within the discipline. Chapter 3 did not focus on a peculiar phenomenon (such as APS), offering instead a global reframing of the history of PS in Uruguay. It problematized the dominant narrative about the discipline's development, providing relatively extensive data and keeping a cautious comparative eye open *without* pretending to offer a "full" comparison. Despite the significant absence of APS in Uruguay, the trajectory of the academic left in Chile and Uruguay nonetheless share important similarities in terms of the *democratic learning* that manifested itself in the embrace of liberalism and modern academic practices. The peculiarity of Chapter 3 is that it expands the inquiry by pondering the role that subjectivity in general, and trauma in particular, has played within these epistemological and political transformations. Following the temperature metaphor, this was a *warm*er moment of the book in which memories and personal experiences became analytical material. Hence, the chapter took further steps toward radical introspection because it unfolded disciplinary self-reflection by linking discourse analysis to the exploration of the personal. The methodological procedure consisted in navigating the narratives of political scientists about PS' history and identity. Thus, with the analysis of Uruguay, another register of PPS was opened and engaged with by showing the important role that subjectivity plays in political and intellectual change.[7]

This chapter resembles, in some ways, Urvashi Butalia's (2000) research on the voices (and silences) of the victims of the partition of India, including in its limitations. Both studies focus on the discourse and subjectivity of others and keep the researcher relatively safe. However, though this safety may be warranted at times, in this instance I found it troubling; after all, the author is part of the discipline. Some further steps toward radical critique, then—*self*-critique—seemed to be in order. For how can I ask political scientists to think about their own position *vis-à-vis* power relations (Alexander, 2005; Ghosh, 1992; Grewal & Kaplan, 2001; Hall, 1990; Hasan, 2012; Mohanty, 1991; Said, 1979; Schafer, Haslam, & Beaudet, 2012; Spivak, 1988; Smith, 1999) without situating *myself* within the problem?

Chapter 4 has been the *hot* epistemological moment of the book. I entered the territory of autobiographical reflection starkly aware of two dire risks: I might either burn within the obscene fire of personal over-exposure or be burned by others' contempt for having broken the golden rules of science. Be that as it may, and inspired by the literature on narrative and auto-ethnography (Brigg & Bleiker, 2010; Dauphinee, 2013a, 2013b; Inayatullah, 2013; Hamati-Ataya, 2014; Löwenheim, 2010; Ravecca & Dauphinee, 2018) while providing my own Marxist twists to it, Chapter 4 began by delineating the intimate architecture of this research and concluded by digging deeper into its very auto*bio*graphical foundations.[8]

Offering an auto-ethnography is hardly an exercise about "me," however (Pin-Fat, 2016; Shepherd, 2016). It is about theory and politics. If, as Morgan Brigg and Roland Bleiker (2010) suggest, knowledge potentiates itself by rigorously engaging with the author's personal circumstances, then one's own subjectivity, materiality and lived experience may serve, through critical introspection, to better grasp the politics of political science. This reflexive exercise may open up a number of interesting questions for the reader to keep exploring if she chooses to do so. These range from the role of personal experience in scholarship to the multiple sites where knowledge, power, and trauma operate and meet; from how to account for the integrity of the socially concrete (Bannerji, 2005) to the liberating powers of self-reflection.

This book has gone through stages of cold, warm, and hot. Temperature—or more accurately, the experience of temperature—translates intensity levels in the engagement with the interplay between subject (i.e. subjectivity), knowledge, and power.[9] The recognition of the subject as a social being whose knowledge is part of power (and, more generally, part of life) is the starting point of the critical awareness that sustains the conditions of possibility for projecting change.[10] The aim of this book to dismantle exteriorities and find relations between the arenas of subjectivity, knowledge, and politics (which are actively and ideologically detached by mainstream PS) goes in such a critical direction. Through this process, the subjectivity of the author became a tool for grasping PS' involvement(s) in power.

The temperature metaphor may function as a useful conceptual infrastructure for (self-)reflection as long as it does not reinsert linearity into the project. In other words: so long as hot does not overcome cold. In the same way that in capitalist societies, original accumulation, production, and exchange are all always synchronically happening (Barlow, 2007; De Angelis, 2004; Harvey, 2003, 2010; Ferguson & McNally, 2015), the kind of cold gaze and ideological analysis offered by Chapter 2 is just as needed as the other epistemologically warmer moments of this book. Subjectivity may operate as a weapon of mass simplification if we do not pay attention to the objective determinations that affect it: the personal is political, but the personal can also depoliticize the public.[11] In other words, subjectivism is counterproductive (Hamati-Ataya, 2014) and thus subjectivity has to be—temporarily and precariously—objectified if the aim is to unpack its role within power dynamics. Similarly, language itself, devoid of the materiality of bodies, cannot grasp power; in effect, analytical "over-linguistification" can conceal injustice (McNally, 2002).[12] Reification and oppression come from unexpected places. Every theory has its own economy of conceptual violence and simplification. This is why dialogue and friction is needed between them (Ravecca & Upadhyay, 2013). In order to grasp the complex relations engulfing PS, PPS needs *all* of the different temperatures of epistemology and theory. Therefore, detached analysis is also a moment of the plurality and multilayeredness of knowing: put crudely, critique requires quantification.

In aphoristic terms, statistics and narrative go together. There is porosity, fluidity, and mixing between cold, warm, and hot. The complexity of PS as a socially concrete phenomenon makes traditional epistemic thermostats and tendencies toward simplification collapse. If voices, registers, and methods are mutually constitutive, then the notion of intersectionality seems somehow wanting in being able to capture this fullness; I propose instead the notion of complex relationality.[13] It is precisely by taking this notion as a premise that "cold," "warm," and "hot" do not displace each other. Through these lenses, the very notion of cold *requires* the other thermal states to be intelligible, and vice versa, which means that there is a conceptual, experiential, and dialectical relationship between them. In other words, they are already happening in each other, just as for Hegel (1977), falsity is a part of Truth. The motion in circulation through every thermal moment of this journey into the politics of political science is always the same: the attempt to know; which, in order to be fully unlocked, demands mobility and diversity. The meanings produced by human practices, including the practices of PS, are flexible and unstable. Therefore, they require a theoretically guided flexibility of thinking. Chapters 2 and 4 belong to the same architecture and to the same urge of trying to understand PPS.

Power and knowledge are about social relations (Marx, 1978a). In Marxist terms, political science itself may be understood as a bundle of relations (Ollman, 1971). Defining PS in this way is a gesture toward its historicization and de-reification, which can be read as a queer intervention *vis-à-vis* the very identity of the discipline. This book took some steps in the direction of looking at PS itself as a *problématique*, mobilizing vocabularies that tend to be thought of as belonging to disconnected theoretical universes (and epistemological temperatures). The encounter between Marxism and queer theory queered conceptual boundaries (Ravecca & Upadhyay, 2013) between subjectivity, discourse, culture, and political economy, opening the possibility for a complex relationality of the subject—in this case, the collective subject of PS.

This discontinuous and multiple reflection unfolded a unitary exercise that we may rename as a problematizing re-inscription of PS. Through a reinterpretation (Geertz, 1997) and a problematizing re-description (Shapiro, 2005) of PS' trajectory in two concrete cases, and by showing the complex relationality of factors and registers that shape this discipline, I have attempted to re-inscribe PS into social reality and *as* a social reality (which is, of course, also personal). In other words, I explored PS as a human activity (Marx, 1978b) from the point of view of different critical theories, in particular (neo-)Marxist and post-structuralist approaches. Human activities are political because they are social (Leftwich, 1986; Menéndez-Carrión, 2015), because they involve people and power, and because they affect—and are affected by—other human activities. Knowledge is political because it is about power on many levels, some of which were explored by this research.

This exercise of reflection on the politics of political science has been a study of politics as such. If we are going to confront the critical task of deeply understanding the political nature of our times in Latin America and beyond, we need to interrogate the mechanisms through which liberal democracy, and implicitly, capitalism, became uncontestable and somehow unthinkable (a process that at moments seems to go beyond a Gramscian hegemony). The market economy and electoral democracy have become a dogma imposed by economic and political elites of the left and right, sanctioned by scientists (sometimes in the name of science, including political science) (Alexander, 2005; Marcuse, 1991). This is something new, historically speaking. The task for critical theorists and social scientists is now to denaturalize such a narrative and to show how radically historical and arbitrary the categories with which we think of the world are (Butler, Laclau, & Zizek, 2003; Buck-Morss, 2009; Said, 1979). Regionally, we can only grasp the discursive shift toward the fetishization of liberal democracy (Borón, 2007; Rico, 2005) in light of the tragic times of the dictatorships of the Southern Cone and how they were processed by society and academia alike. In this book, I have attempted to unpack PS as a nodal point in this set of complex, multidimensional, and interrelated political dynamics that has shaped the reality of Chile, Uruguay, and beyond.

By identifying the political conditions that had an impact on PS' trajectory and by exposing the arbitrary foundations of the political framework taken for granted by the disciplinary mainstream in Latin America, this book has endeavored to de-reify and confront dominant powers. The next section summarizes some of the main findings of PPS on a more concrete level.

Liberal Unthinking and the Epistemological *Desaparecidos* of 1990s Latin America

> We might see in shifting conceptions of democracy over time within political science a telling register of changes in the character of the liberal visions it articulates.
>
> —Robert Adcock (2014, p. 146)

Today, many Chilean political scientists dismiss the experience of APS. In their view, "that was not science: that was academic crap" (CHL17). Their Uruguayan colleagues do not have the chance to say the same, for the simple historical reason that PS did not experience a process of institutionalization during the authoritarian regime in their country. Instead, most Uruguayans firmly reject those "radical theories," Marxism in particular, which polarized politics and contributed to the breakdown of democracy. This view is shared by most Chilean scholars as well.[14] Thus, current mainstream PS dismisses both left-wing radicalism and authoritarian scholarship, representing them, with epistemological and moral disgust, as regrettable chapters of a past that should be overcome. This operation mimics the narrative of "the two demons" (Rico, 2005; Rossal, 2005; Marchesi, 2017), held by a significant segment of the political elites in Uruguay, where both the radical left and the far right are equated as regressive anti-democratic forces that belong to the past and do not have a role to play in the bright, *liberal* future of the country.[15]

After the democratic transition, order, stability, moderation, and reasonability became virtually uncontested values in both countries (the acceptance of liberal capitalism being part of the package of Reason).[16] Neopositivist and liberal PS took active part in this process and came to occupy a doubly privileged space of the *center*, getting political credit for being democratic as well as epistemological credit for being objective—a rare mix of conveniences! This study tried to unpack such an (ideological) operation.[17] To understand these transformations, PPS interpretively assembled so-called external factors (i.e., the dictatorship and its effects, the transition to democracy, and the hegemony of the US) with internal aspects (i.e., the separation from sociology and the need for institutionalization) of the discipline. In this sense, using the notion of complex relationality and engaging the (non-linear) lenses of different temperatures of politics and theories, I attempted to capture these multiple and interlocking registers of change.

There is an issue of time, memory, and power here. Marxism and APS have been actively forgotten by Chilean and Uruguayan political science. For that reason, both Marxism and authoritarian political science may be thought of as the epistemological *desaparecidos* [the disappeared] of democracy.[18] These *desaparecidos*, however, have different roles in contemporary power relations.

Turning to Chile, the legacy of APS remains invisibilized; yet mainstream PS takes advantage of APS' absence in today's most prestigious departments to avoid talking about the historical significance of this neoconservative discursive formation at both policy and intellectual levels. What is conveniently erased is that APS participated in a broader project that reshaped Chile, its power structures, and its social sciences.

Gramsci (2008) taught us that where there is hegemony, there is knowledge. Pinochet's regime[19] operated through the production of infrastructures for knowledge production, gaining legitimacy in Weberian terms, and becoming hegemonic in Gramscian ones. This is why, even today, one might encounter youth in a supermarket in Santiago proudly wearing pins with the dictator's face, while any analogous situation in Uruguay would be almost unthinkable. This smart regime, at least in relative terms, was successful in moderating a transition to a governable democracy that secured the dictatorship's legacy (Lechner, 1990; Moulián, 2002; Mayol, 2012). PS' development (i.e., APS) was a relevant component of this political process. PS was one of the devices that transformed power relations in the country and conditioned future scholarship, including the mainstream PS that today ignores APS' existence! In Chile, the hegemony of liberalism was crafted by *neoconservative* liberalism, which reshaped the terrain of ideology, even for leftists. Later, the modernization of the discipline and its "objective" perspective naturalized this status quo.

While the story of the Chicago Boys in economics has been extensively told (Biglasier, 2001; Camou, 1997; Markoff & Montecinos, 1994; McNally, 2011; Munck, 2005, among others), the story of APS is just as relevant, but less well-known.[20] APS was perhaps one of the most intriguing findings of this study. Several of my Chilean interviewees seemed to be unaware that some of the most important elements of the infrastructure of the discipline were put in place during the authoritarian period and by educational authorities complicit with the Pinochet regime. At the time of the interviews, there was resistance, both in plain and psychoanalytic terms, to face this reality in the PS community. This gesture of negation erases what current mainstream PS has in common with APS—an obsession with order and stability, and suspicion toward the grassroots as a potential political subject.

The imposition of the logic of "order and stability first; democracy afterward" was a victory of the right-wing dictatorships in the Southern Cone that shaped the 1990s. The durability of this legacy has had different levels of solidity in each country, but has been reinforced by post-transition liberalism in general, and, in particular, by mainstream PS. The political operations of liberalism put into motion through academic knowledge have been crafted by the defeat of the left.

Chile and Uruguay: Traces of a Comparative Politics of Political Science

The experiences of disciplinary political transformation explored in this study are, first of all, of theoretical interest to the subfield of the history of political science, which has seen a rapid expansion in Latin America (Bulcourf, Krzy-wicka, & Ravecca, 2017). Additionally, they can offer insights into broader conversations about the politics of the social sciences, and even the role of knowledge production in politics.

In answer to the scholarship on PS' trajectory and development, APS specifically showcases, in very literal terms, that the discipline does not always operate as the knowledge of freedom and democracy. APS is a modern social science that, in its search for methodological progress, the assertion of a specific scientific model of research, the emphasis on institution building, and the establishment of international connections (with the United States in particular, but also with apartheid South Africa and others) actually supported, by action or omission, an authoritarian regime. In short, and we are already getting into broader debates here, a type of PS that can be identified as liberal in many relevant respects was instrumental to an authoritarian regime.

In my view, this has consequences for the political interpretation of the operations and practices of liberalism in the region. In line with other critical projects such as Losurdo (2011), this book takes us very far from liberal hagiographies: in the Southern Cone, particularly in the 1990s, liberal discourse in the academy and beyond (as disciplined by the neoliberal turn) was entrenched with the defense of the capitalist order and the power of elites. And it still does: in Chile, but also in Uruguay, as we will see below, current mainstream PS reinforces the naturalization of capitalism.

At first sight, the power-knowledge regime of Uruguayan PS stands in stark contrast with the Chilean. Uruguayan PS was institutionalized *after* the democratic transition. This fits in quite well with the mainstream account of the development of PS (Altman, 2005; Filgueira, 1974; Garcé, 2005; Pérez Antón, 1986, 1992), a narrative that positively associates disciplinary and democratic developments. This differential timing is related to the divergent ways the two dictatorships engaged with knowledge production. As documented in Chapter 3, Uruguay's social scientists were censored and persecuted during the dictatorship. At best, the military only tolerated the practice of social science at private research centers. This repressive proclivity was also reflected in its engagement with Marxism. Whereas in Chile Marxism was obsessively talked about throughout the dictatorship, in Uruguay it was "buried."

In the cultural legacy of the Uruguayan dictatorship, a *negative* moment seems to predominate. The brutality and anti-intellectualism of this dictatorship might have paradoxically protected the country from a more articulated or hegemonic advancement of the neoliberal logic—which proved to be devastating for Latin America and beyond (Akram-Lodhi, 2013; Bello, 2008; Borón, 2007; Leiva, 2008; McNally, 2011; Morelli, 2008; Saad-Filho & Johnston, 2005; Panitch & Gindin, 2004; Felder & Patroni, 2011; Patroni & Poitras, 2002; Rothstein, 2007; Sears, 2014)—as well as from other regressive transformations in the cultural terrain, including the reinforcement of conservatism and social hierarchies.[21]

Even though the dynamics of trauma and resistance gave birth to cultural changes in Uruguay and, in this sense, it is clear that the dictatorship did have significant impacts on the future life of the country, the Chilean dictatorship's articulation of policy-knowledge-discourse was more solid and effective. Pinochet's regime proved that *positive* power is superior to repression. Its institutional innovations in the terrain of the economy and politics are related to its productive articulation with knowledge(s). I am not suggesting, of course, that the Chilean dictatorship was not traumatic, and that repression and oppression did not have a significant role there. Nor am I implying that in Uruguay the dictatorship did not have policy plans. The noted contrast is a question of analytical emphasis.

The lack of APS in Uruguay corresponded with a negative engagement with the academic community that traumatized scholarship in the sense of producing ideological guilt in its practitioners for having supported anti-democratic, radical projects that allegedly led to the dictatorship. As a consequence, Uruguayan PS was forged *against* both authoritarianism and radicalism, and *as* a liberal-democratic enterprise. PS was itself a product of democratic learning—an unexpected effect of authoritarianism. It is in this regard that the two cases can be summed-up nicely with a title like: "two contrasting dictatorships, two knowledge regimes." Yet a question mark needs to be added to such a title, considering what follows.

Besides these disparities, there are some crucial major commonalities between the two disciplinary experiences. Two of them are the following. First, major international events such as the collapse of the USSR and the rise of US hegemony in the region are obviously shared by both Chile and Uruguay. Second, the academic opposition to the Pinochet dictatorship went through a similar process of democratic learning (Puryear, 1994); it is not a minor detail that at the end of the day, Marxism was buried in both countries. The experience of the dictatorships changed how *any* form of left radicalism is perceived by right *and left* alike. The tense triad capitalism-socialism-democracy was completely re-arranged with the *disappearance* of the term in the middle. Capitalism became the new unquestionable basis of democracy for mainstream politicians and academics (even though one of the fathers of mainstream PS, Robert Dahl, argued the opposite: in his account, private property is not a necessary condition of polyarchy). Although neoliberalism has not been popular among political scientists in Uruguay, since the 1990s, both academic communities have a shared rejection of anti-capitalist politics and embraced elitism along with a fear for "the many" (Rancière, 2005),[22] which more recently has found expression in the rejection of populism and disruptive grass-roots movements (Castañeda, 2006; Lazarte, 2008; Ramírez Gallegos, 2006; Varnoux Garay, 2005; Traversa, 2008).[23] In this narrative, democracy was recuperated and remained viable *because* it was severed from (socialist) politics. Democracy has been reduced to a Schumpeterian game of compromises between elites (Schumpeter, 1985).

In simpler terms, the right-wing dictatorships and the American-led global capitalist project that they represented, won the battle in the region (McNally, 2011; Munck, 2005). They reshaped power relations in these societies, re-delineating the realm of the politically thinkable. Stability as a desirable object displaced other values, removing from democracy its radical and creative dimensions. In other words, there are radically different ways of thinking about democracy, something that mainstream PS usually forgets. In this sense, for US foreign policy in 1973, Pinochet's and by extension the other dictatorships of the Southern Cone were in transition to democracy. Latin America was, from this perspective, a battlefield for (capitalist) freedom in the world. Democracy would become possible only after the left had "disappeared" and politics were disciplined. In the end, that is exactly what happened.

The ways democracy, ideology, time, and reason are discussed and connected in the mainstream imagination show how context and power shape academia. Today, Chile and Uruguay are both stable and orderly liberal democracies where socialism is no more than a name with some social and anti-poverty policies attached. The discussions about formal and substantive democracy, so important in the 1960s, sound prehistoric or mad (Rico, 2005).[24]

In Uruguay, the dictatorship may have been less successful in projecting a new development path for the country. However, its effects were enormous at all registers: political, economic, social, and cultural. One example suffices: in post-transition democratic times, Uruguayans accepted not to judge human rights violations during the dictatorship and instead protected its perpetrators. Liberalism undoes itself: the Expiry Law, or Ley de Caducidad, violated the liberal principle of the division of powers, severely distorting the rule of law, as we saw in Chapters 3 and 4. Liberal democracy internalized unequal power dynamics into its institutions, legitimizing the interests of both the ruling class and the military, which operated as the arm of the former. The discipline did not problematize this.

Up until 2012, not a single critical article was published by the *Revista Uruguaya de Ciencia Política*, the main PS journal in Uruguay, questioning the quality of democracy in the country in light of the Expiry Law. Political scientists were too busy celebrating traditional political parties (the authors of this shameful law), dismissing Marxism as dated and anti-political, and teaching reductive versions of this school of thought to their students. To entirely dismiss the leftist critique of liberal democracy was usually perceived as the smart and critical thing to do in PS circles.[25]

As the innovative literature on auto-ethnography in the field of international relations shows, knowledge is also biographical and experiential: guardianship of the identity of the discipline has been performed, among others, by ex-communists trying to escape "the Marxist Church." In order to cross the ideological border, the new converts needed to show their liberal democratic credentials. Conversion meant new forms of dogmatism and reification that placed capitalism and other fundamental structures of power far away from democratic scrutiny and critical analysis.

This study has revealed how, in specific yet interconnected ways, the trajectories of political science in Chile and Uruguay are heavily political; our exploration has shed light on politics and power dynamics in the cases under scrutiny from the point of view of the political regimes' engagement with knowledge and its institutions. The following segment presents, in a systematic fashion, an alternative narrative, anchored in complex relationality, of PS and its circumstances. Even though the exercise is focused on Chile and Uruguay, I believe it offers analytical tools and empirical observations that are relevant for the experience of Latin America and beyond.

Complex Relationality at Work: A Radical Alternative to Mainstream Tales

This section presents a condensed version of the mainstream narrative on the development of the discipline and proposes complex relationality as an alternative to it. The dominant tale, as illustrated by Figure 5.1, was delineated by interpretively weaving together the 58 interviews, participatory observation in multiple academic settings, and a critical reading of the literature on the history

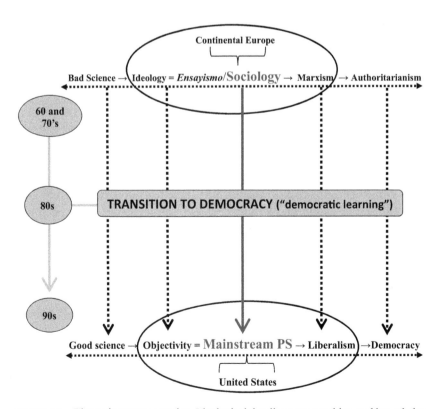

FIGURE 5.1   The mainstream narrative: Ideological timelines, geographies, and knowledge

of PS. Even though the focus is again on Chile and Uruguay, the story, which reads as follows, does circulate beyond their borders, irradiating and involving Latin America as a whole:

> Latin America has traditionally been intellectually influenced by conti-
> nental Europe, France in particular. This French style of writing translated
> into ensayismo, a vernacular, anti-methodological, and anti-scientific
> form of thinking. Thus, a kind of useless rhetorical verbosity character-
> ized intellectuals in the region.
>
> In the 1960s, the era of the Cold War, political polarization took over
> the continent. Sociology, the most developed social science then, was
> dominated by Marxism and radicalism infected academia. Ideologi-
> cal radicalization among scholars not only obliterated objectivity and
> neutrality—essential features of science—but also contributed to the esca-
> lation of political tensions. In those years, democracy and the rule of law
> were not priorities for leftist activists and scholars. They were searching
> for a new world, which in their (erroneous) view, would only be achiev-
> able through social revolution. Instead of socialism, what their messianic
> adventure brought about were *coups d'état* all over the Southern Cone.
>
> The combination of all of these factors prevented the emergence of
> political science. First, the legitimacy of ensayismo prevented the devel-
> opment of proper social and political science. Second, Marxism, along
> with other socio-centric approaches in vogue in the 1960s and 1970s, con-
> ceptualized politics as an epiphenomenon. It was ideological, and some-
> times even partisan.[26] Third, the right-wing dictatorships that followed,
> particularly in the Southern Cone, were hostile toward academia. Where
> PS could emerge was against, or in spite of, the authoritarian governments.
>
> However, the brutality of state terror, repression, and censorship pushed
> the left and scholars in Chile and Uruguay (but also in Argentina and Bra-
> zil) to rethink their positions. Paradoxically, the dictatorships led to a posi-
> tive reevaluation of democracy. Those were years of democratic learning.
> In the meantime, private research centers professionalized research and
> the academic career, making both institutional and methodological pro-
> gress. As a consequence of these developments, both during and after the
> democratic transition, society and academia changed for the better: both
> embraced liberal democracy while the latter (slowly) started to abandon
> ensayismo.
>
> Liberalism and objectivity were markers of the new times. With democ-
> racy, PS flourished and became an established profession, while improv-
> ing political analysis with methods and theories imported from the best
> universities in the world (i.e., top-ranked American schools). The fight is
> not over, however. Latin American social sciences, and even PS, are still
> too influenced by dated theories and over-theoretical approaches imported

from continental Europe. There are still shadows of radicalism within academia and beyond. Ensayismo has not been completely eradicated. The very much needed methodological improvement requires PS to strictly emulate the natural sciences. Within the social sciences, economics is the model to follow.[27] Luckily, the younger generations are fully committed to modernizing and improving PS' methods and theory. The United States of America are home to the best universities and the best PS in the world, and therefore we, in Latin America, have everything to learn from them. The irrational resistance against an imaginary "academic American imperialism" must disappear.

Mainstream Latin American political scientists dismiss modernization theory (see Harrison, 2008; Ibister, 2006; Lipset, 1959; Rostow, 1956) as being sociocentric, and probably dated at this point. Yet the very logic of such a perspective, in particular its linear conception of development, structures their narrative on academic progress, which became dominant in the 1990s and 2000s. Put bluntly, the North was ahead, and we needed to follow it. It was rather common to hear that we, in the South, were academically underdeveloped and in order to escape this condition, we needed to move in the direction of the United States both epistemologically and politically. In other words, the adoption of liberalism (capitalism goes without saying) and positivism was not debatable. Good institutions and rules of the game had to be put in place for politics as well as for science.[28] According to this self-evident mantra, Latin American academia was already too far behind to allow dissidence regarding such obvious truths. The narrative fused democracy, objectivity, and liberalism, imposing them as uncontestable. This operation has had enormous consequences for academia and for politics. However, given the current situation of the United States, it can likely no longer function as a political model anymore. Nonetheless, there are still significant aspects of the tale, such as the welding of neopositivism and liberal democracy, that continue to persist. Let us turn now to PPS' critique.

According to the mainstream narrative, one period of time, i.e., the 1960s, was more ideological than others, in particular the 1990s when both society and the academy allegedly adopted forms of updated rationality. Similarly, whereas one ideology (i.e., Marxism) is posed as political even if it does not acknowledge the autonomy of politics (or so we are told), another one (i.e., liberalism) is thought of as objective even though it supposedly embraces the independence of politics. Furthermore, in this narrative, there are countries (i.e., the United States and England) that are better homes for science than other regions (i.e., continental Europe and, clearly, Latin America). These fictions, timelines, and cartographies of places and theories are absurd. The 1960s were no more (or less) ideological than the 1990s; Marxism is not more (or less) ideological than liberalism.

Ideology operates in all periods of time; the exercise of comparing the ideological intensity of different ideologies seems a rather awkward enterprise.

Quite debatable is also the attempt to linearly link science to a specific country for many reasons, be it the transnational dimension of change, diversity within countries and regions, or the complexity of so-called globalization (Akram-Lodhi, 2013; Beaudet, Haslam, & Schafer, 2012; Grewal & Kaplan, 2001; Rothstein, 2007; Shilliam, 2009). Indeed, these kinds of political beliefs and narratives about periods of times, ideologies, countries, and events are supposed to be the *objects* of scholarly inquiry. However, in this case, these beliefs and narratives *are* scholarship; as such, academia itself necessarily becomes the object of study when attempting to understand the politics of political science.

How did these bizarre ideas become dominant among scholars dedicated to studying the complexity of politics, that is, among a community of canny people? One possible answer, as I have argued in this book, can be found in the transformations of context and power relations. Chapters 2, 3, and 4 have empirically shown situated interplays between objects of inquiry (political processes, regimes, discourses, etc.) and the knowing subject (the scientist and the discipline). Political scientists, political science, as well as tales about progress are affected by and affect politics. Positivism alone does not work if the aim is to understand the complexities of science and power.

The Politics of Political Science

This project has theoretically conceived of power dynamics as a complex relationality between knowledge, identity, subjectivity, political economy, conventional politics, and the transnational dimension of the political. From this standpoint, all of these aspects affect each other; knowledge is part of broader social relations and thus it is not exterior to power. How does this perspective translate into an analysis of the politics of political science? Figure 5.2 and Table 5.1 attempt to summarize this for the cases of Chile and Uruguay. In the process, the analysis provides us with some useful pieces to assemble the Latin American disciplinary puzzle.

In the Latin American academia of the 1960s, the presence of Marxism, structuralism, dependency theory, and other radical perspectives was prominent (Garcé, 2005). Those were also times of political polarization. In this period, the whole region experienced intense clashes between different ideological and political forces. The Cold War and international politics played a significant role in framing these disputes. The US backed the Southern Cone's right-wing dictatorships of the 1970s and 1980s and anti-leftist activities all over the continent (McSherry, 2005).

In Chile and Uruguay in particular, these regimes brutally repressed the opposition, including the intellectual. A specificity of the Chilean dictatorship was the mobilization of knowledge for policy and cultural change. Besides this difference, they had the aim—shared with far right-wing movements populating the

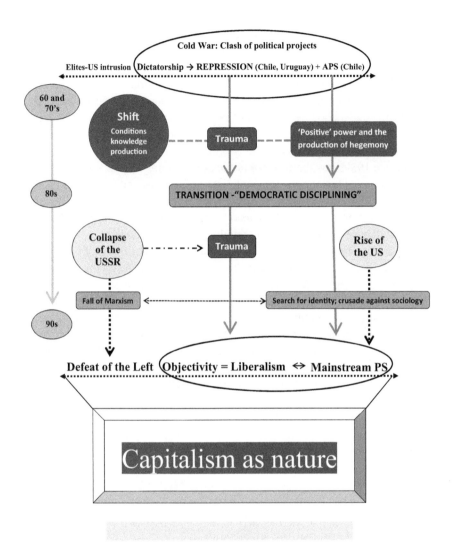

FIGURE 5.2 PPS critique and complex relationality at work

TABLE 5.1 The theoretical intervention of PPS

The mainstream narrative	*PPS critique*
Liberalism—Democracy	Liberalism—Order and stability
Political Science—Democracy	Political Science—Order and stability
US foreign policy— Democracy	US foreign policy—Order and stability

region at the time—of extirpating the so-called communist threat and securing capitalism. They were, in this regard, successful. To begin with, Chile became the first neoliberal experiment (Leiva, 2008; MacEwan, 2005; Munck, 2005; Saad-Filho & Johnston, 2005; Sears, 2014). Furthermore, one of the legacies of the specific form of democratic transition in both countries has been the push of socialism—understood as a project of radical transformation of human society, not just as a rubric of a political group—to the margins, not only of the political system but also of the academy.

The late 1980s saw the collapse of the Soviet Union and the consolidation of US hegemony in the region. The bankruptcy of Marxism added to the experiential and political defeats an intellectual one. In this context, the genuine desire for democracy was historically marshaled toward the victory of liberal capitalism as well as to a discourse of moderation, order, and stability.

Political economy and politics were not the only characters in this plot about ideological change in society and academia. Subjectivity and trauma played starring roles. The dictatorships imprinted extraordinary amounts of suffering into these societies, especially on the left. Social scientists, the majority associated with the left in both countries, "learned" what the absence of democracy meant: torture, disappearances, censorship, and continuous surveillance. Authoritarianism had dramatically affected their lives, sometimes leaving indelible marks on their loved ones, careers, and bodies.

Conflict and radical politics were perceived as the main causes of these tragic episodes. The notion of having contributed (as a collective) to the conditions that harmed their country haunted several of my interviewees. The loss of democracy fueled a sense of ideological liability. In this sense, the repressive activities deployed by the dictatorships, including physical and psychological torture, can be thought of as sites of political theory. The body of the tortured was a site of political and ideological battles. The trauma generated by the dictatorships was itself an ideological transformation—personal and collective trauma is a political phenomenon with profound impacts on what is and what is not thinkable. The rejection of Marxism and embrace of liberalism also have their intimate motions.

The internal dynamics of academia also played their part in this story. In the beginning, political science in Latin America was usually subsumed either under law or sociology (Artiga-González, 2005; Azpuru, 2005; Barrientos del Monte, 2015; Bejarano & Wills, 2005; Bulcourf, 2012; Cálix & Sierra, 2005; Filgueira, 1974; Heiss, 2015; Mejía Acosta, Freidenberg, & Pachano, 2005; Rojas Silva & Baquero, 2017; Sánchez González, 2005; Tanaka, 2005; Varnoux Garay, 2005). The democratic transitions of the Southern Cone created a window of opportunity for disciplinary independence, particularly in the case of Uruguay, where PS' institutionalization was a late process. In order to gain legitimacy, an institutional and conceptual crusade was fought. The shift from European to American influence and the international decay of Marxism were internalized into the development of PS. This was also an opportunity to push sociology away from political analysis. Indeed, the emergent PS narrative merged sociology with Marxism and other socio-centric theories and dismissed the "old" type of intellectual who engaged in politics. It is interesting to note that the ideological fight or shift, in some cases, happened within the same individual (see Chapter 3).[29]

The different pieces analytically identified by this alternative account appear, though with significant nuances, across the continent. Many scholars adopted institutions and institutionalisms as a new *ism*,[30] while PS, in some cases taking advantage of the transitional democratic effervescence, advanced into public space as a relevant—and safe, *vis-à-vis* the political establishment—form of knowledge. PS became the academic script for the re-emergent democracies.

In the 1990s, American positivism was acritically imported, and American academia was narrated as a homogeneous space where mainstream theories and methods were not contested.

As we saw in Chapter 3, through participatory observation, I registered how, in Latin America, this image of the US is mobilized by groups of scholars heavily identified with *the mainstream of the mainstream*—i.e., rational choice institutionalism (Monroe, 2005)—in their strategies to dominate the PS scientific field (Bourdieu, 1984). Part and parcel of such a strategy is to sometimes rhetorically exaggerate their ties to the US (and, in some cases, their command of the English language).

The US is thus instrumentalized for academic differentiation and to narrate scales of superiority and inferiority. This narrow-minded disciplining of the discipline has been confronted by reactions that range from calls for pluralism (Garcé & Rocha, 2015) to premature death sentences (Cansino, 2008). However, there has been less resistance to the equivalence between objectivity and good science. Paradoxically, this apparent epistemological neutrality is attached to liberalism and democracy. In the mainstream narrative, an ideology becomes non-ideological while, in the silent background, capitalism disappears as a topic of conversation. Liberalism is objective, and capitalism becomes nature.

During the 1990s, neoliberal discourse consolidated with more (Chile) or less (Uruguay) success. In this new ideological climate that enveloped PS, the discipline focused on the transition to democracy and electoral politics, and actively ignored issues of political economy, inequality, and manifestations of power transcending formally institutionalized arenas. At most, disciplinary attention went as far as including public policy from a procedural perspective. This type of knowledge conformed to the system (in the sense used by Herbert Marcuse) and, therefore, was elite-friendly. These circumstances require theorization: while Marxism and structuralism conceptually articulate society, politics, and the economy, liberalism analytically isolates these aspects of social reality (Bannerji, 2005). According to the liberal logic—which is still predominant, the recent growing interest in political economy within regional PS notwithstanding—PS' primary object of study, liberal democracy, belongs exclusively to politics and the institutional realm. In other words, this non-relational conception of politics implies a conception of democracy divorced from material equality. However, this divorce goes only one way: the combination of neoliberal discourse, political liberalism, and economic liberalism meant that political freedom could not interfere with the market economy; it is an operation that confines the powers of democracy—it *de*-democratizes democracy.

The dictatorships of the 1970s had prepared the terrain for the acceptance of this new set of "truths." Force and violence were the necessary conditions for neoliberal hegemony in Latin America (Leiva, 2008). The conceptual disconnect between the political and the socio-economic helps to produce the (illusory) compatibility between neoliberalism and democracy as well as the domestication of democratic politics. In general, PS did not analyze neoliberalism (Amadae, 2016; Brown, 2015) in critical terms: political scientists criticized specific policies and programs, but not *neoliberalism as such*. They did not have the language to do so.

The artificial isolation of the political realm (politics = elections) and the subsequent academic depoliticization of the economy, in other words, the theoretical obliteration of the political economy perspective within democratic discourse, is supplemented by the acritical incorporation of neoclassical economics' methodological repertoire into PS as *the* legitimate approach to politics. This double movement has huge political implications: as PS' possibilities become regulated by the narrow, rationalist premises and tools of economics, the economy and class relations become unthinkable and unreachable by the discipline. This ideological transformation has been adopted in the name of scientific objectivity. This is the neopositivist epistemological dimension that was referred to above: political science is allegedly objective; in turn, neopositivism sanctions capitalism as a realm of neutrality that lies outside the purview of political science, which is, of course, a great ideological operation.

Contemporary liberalism, mainstream PS, and US imperialism have something in common: all of them claim to speak in the name of democracy. But what kind of democracy? S.M. Amadae (2016) has shown how game theory changed "our vision of citizenship and sovereignty" (p. xiii). She disentangles the node between the transformation of the notion of democracy, game theory, and nuclear weapons: "the first rational actor was the thermonuclear/armed national security" (p. 287). Wendy Brown (2015) explored the detrimental implications of neoliberalism for democracy and humanity as such—what she calls a moment of "civilizational despair" (p. 222). From the Latin American context, Amparo Menéndez-Carrión (2015) has also theorized and explored the operations of global capitalism and the effects of the neoliberal logic, particularly in its destruction of public space. But not only critical scholars see these problems: political theorists of different stripes complain about PS' reductionist treatment of democracy. The examples suffice, then, to make the point about what kind of democracy can exist in the US-dominated neoliberal era.

Order and stability seem to have been the priority of the academic and the political establishment. Order and stability first—once democracy has been cleansed of its ungovernable intensity and energy, then this regime becomes a treasure in custody. Anyone who dares to question it shall be put into the symbolic bonfire, will be persecuted by so-called social-democratic governments, will not be published, will be not be heard: because they are perceived as crazy. The pathologization of dissent is an effective constraining move (Marcuse, 1991). Something that becomes clear when we unpack the mainstream narrative is that power does not go away from science after democracy arrives. Politics and power dynamics still affect us, political scientists. The question of how PPS operates in current democracies is worth exploring. How can we think of the relationship between PS and power within liberal democracies when market-based governmentality (Foucault, 2006) adopts invisible forms of power? The issue will be, I hope, explored in the future.

"The language of the conquerors soon came to supplant the other languages," writes Amitav Ghosh in *In an Antique Land* (1992). The quote above refers to the seventh century, when Judæo-Arabic was transformed by the conquest of the Middle East by Muslim armies (p. 101). In isolation, however, the statement could have been written by Nietzsche or Foucault. It is a statement about language and power, or perhaps more accurately, about discourse. Discourse transcends language, and it refers to the regulation of truth that is embedded within extra-linguistic mechanisms (Foucault, 1992). In present day global academia, English has displaced other tongues, while the Marxist "language" (with its own imperial aspirations in the past) has been displaced by liberal positivism, the epistemological idiom of conquest. These shifts are embedded within the materiality of imperialism and power.

As mentioned above, trauma and the defeat of the left shaped the return to democracy in the Southern Cone. These traumatized democracies prioritized order and stability over social justice. In Chile and Uruguay, order and stability were considered "objective" values whereas "justice" was a risky aim that may threaten the former.[31] PS did not critically analyze this process, and indeed, it has been an integral part of this political and intellectual transformation. Consequently, we simply cannot ignore power when we write the history of PS.

History, language, ideology, epistemology, and *power* are intertwined: if we, political scientists, ignore how political history (i.e., context) shapes academia and scholarship when narrating the history of our own discipline, we erase the political history of PS and naturalize its current language, exercising power in an oppressive way.[32] Re-writing the history of a discipline, as this study has tried to do, is always a way of framing knowledge: it is in itself a political act. Given that challenging neopositivism implies challenging objectivity, if we wish to look at ourselves in non-positivistic terms, we need to *politicize* our understanding of PS. In this way, epistemology becomes a subversive knowledge, especially when informed by critical theory. Political self-reflection may stop us from automatically reproducing the dominant languages and power relations of our times. In this theoretical framework, I wonder whether the mainstream (liberal) narrative about the development of PS (and about liberalism in general) may be totalitarian in the way Eichmann was (Guilhot, 2001), in the sense of obliterating critique where it is needed the most. What kind of violence and power is being deployed through objectivity, institutionalization, and quantification? What are the workings of the category of democracy, when unreflectively and undialectically deployed?

Having unpacked the discourse of PS in Chile and Uruguay, I hope its final implication becomes clear: capitalism, along with other social relations of oppression, has become the hidden and uncontested structure that disciplines democracy. If we are going to reflect deeply about both PS and the political reality in which the discipline is located, we need to seriously engage with this.

The emphasis on institutions and institutionalization—other words for order and stability—has permeated the way most political scientists in Latin America have thought about both democracy *and* their own discipline's development. This is a consequence of the acritical adoption of the tenets of the American mainstream, whose formalistic logic resembles the priority that exchange value has over use value in capitalist societies (McNally, 2011; Nicolaus, 1968; Pilling, 1980; Stallybrass, 1998): what matters is that certain (formal) institutions are in place, i.e., free elections for democracies, indexations, and clear rules for PS. What is lost is the *experience* that those institutions cannot grasp. The *lived experience* of both democracy and our discipline relates respectively to the concrete fabric of public life (Menéndez-Carrión, 2015) and the kind of knowledge that is created (validated or not through indexations and other market mechanisms).

Thus, in terms of the development of PS, *we*, the Latin American PS community, have a lot to gain from moving away from the obsession with institutionalization and opening up the question of power as well as listening to the political scientists who, outside the mainstream, have persisted in looking at politics from alternative lenses, even though the forces of prestige and hierarchy constantly suffocate and diminish their efforts.

The very constitution of PS is linked to technologies of social and political regulation. Hence, by exploring how power is both woven into and institutionalized as part of the consolidation of the discipline, history and epistemology operate as powerful self-reflexive tools. Through disciplinary self-reflection, political analysis gets refined and another dimension is added to important conversations about the usefulness of the discipline (Trent, 2009). On a more *self-centered* note, introspection and the widening of PS' use value (in the sense of Stallybrass, 1998) can improve the texture and quality (to appropriate an expression of Amparo Menéndez-Carrión) of our discipline's fabric, making it a more welcoming home for both scholars and the general public. More attention to PS' concrete trajectories and power dynamics may improve the lived experience of the discipline on many fronts. This observation goes in the same direction as the Perestroika movement (Monroe, 2005) and other more recent calls for ending different forms of discrimination and exclusion within our community (Breuning & Sanders, 2007; Trent, 2009, 2012; Brettschneider, 2011; Smith, 2011).

Last, but not least, the inclusion of pleasure, intellectual joy, and imagination (Trent, 2012) in the conversation about PS is also very much needed. In contrast to the dominant common sense and its celebration of the "sovereignty of competition" (Nicolaus, 1968, p. 45), represented so well by Kelsky (2012), for many of us, scholarship is more than just a job (Brown, 2017). It is a calling related to our personal and collective existential tragedies. It is a space we want to enjoy, where we can expand, reflect, connect, explore, and create. It is not written in stone that "science" has to be a boring and intimidating place where people are terrified of not using the right method. . . . Chapter 4 of this book is a contribution toward imagining academia as a place where we are not trained to abuse or fight abuse through asshole-type peer-reviewing, diminishing alternative views, or policing students' thinking. Again, narrative approaches seem to have a lot of potential to ask the questions we are trained not to ask.

Critical theory is right: "objective" knowledges are not actually objective. In the language of PS: "value-free politics is an oxymoron" (Trent, 2012, p. 170). We *are* political because, as Nietzsche taught Foucault, power is not exterior to knowledge. This has implications for the role of epistemology and self-reflection in knowledge production. In this particular case, through the critical analysis of PS, we can better understand politics. *Knowing the ways of knowing is a powerful way of knowing the object known.* Through this meta-navigation of the mediations performed by official knowledges, by dismantling their positivities and unpacking their silences, one can better understand power itself. This has been, in fact, the point of departure for all critical theories—Marxism, psychoanalysis, the Frankfurt School, queer theory, and postcolonial studies, among others. *All of them* critically engage with established forms of knowledge that reproduce oppression in its varied forms (capitalism, neurosis, homonormativity, colonialism, imperialism, etc.). Relations of oppression *are* knowledge; there is no emancipation without the critique of knowledge. PPS belongs to the saga of emancipatory self-reflection.

Does all of this mean that PS is not scientific? Or—even worse—is there no science at all? No. But it *does* mean that there is no science untouched by the life that it studies and within which it unfolds (again, science is a human activity). Having said this, I am not persuaded by a position, common in some circles of critical scholars and activists in North America, that collapses the distinction between social science, activism, and other (alternative) forms of knowledge (Alexander, 2005; Corntassel, 2012; Smith, 1999).[33] Science is, in a very particular sense, not political by definition. In a Weberian tone, the scientist and the politician (or the activist) embody incompatible identities, spaces, moments, and logics. At the same time, given that my work comes from a critical theory perspective, it seeks to go beyond the empirical accuracy of neopositivism. My main interest shares the concerns of critical intellectuals of different stripes: (re)thinking the connection between modes of (historical) analysis and forms of mapping the possible. What is "the possible" for political science is an open question.

How can we account for the role of thinking in politics, then? This project has been, in this regard, profoundly Nietzschean. By this I mean that the awareness that oppression can come from unexpected places is at the basis of my thinking (see Chapter 4).[34] Furthermore, thinking implies risks: I am not interested in concealing the violence that critique may convey. Critical thinking is disruptive and divisive; crashing common sense (Bourdieu, 1973) is indeed cruel. We have to cope with that. Additionally, there is something in the very nature of knowledge that expels the naïveté of good intentions (Nietzsche, 1990). There is no completely just knowledge: "Pity," says Nietzsche, "has an almost ludicrous effect on a man of knowledge, like tender hands on a Cyclops" (1990, p. 105). We do not need to go as far to get the point.

There is another, perhaps darker, misery regarding the art of critique: even if under attack by neoliberal policies (Borón, 2006, 2007; Giroux, 1999; McNally, 2011), it is still an industry sustained by power structures. If PS' discourses and practices are part of politics, a critical analysis of PS, the present study included, *is* political, and it is embedded in ongoing inequalities. Somehow, the winners in politics always speak through us, academics. We are involved in a process that justifies inequality. We are moments of its reproduction.

That this study was written *by* a Latin American based in an Anglo-Saxon institution *in* the English language is not a minor irony, for it makes this project belong to the problematic dynamics of knowledge and power that it tries to unpack. This text is part of the global political economy of knowledge in which language, geography, and fictions of prestige are the markers of hierarchy. Nietzsche and Foucault showed us that innocence in knowledge is a tragedy and a farce (even the first time it shows up). Postmodern and Marxist books are commodities too. Progressive scholars are critical illusions in (neo)liberal structures. Critical scholars also know about hierarchies and seniorities, dubious quotation practices, social capital reproduction, "interest group" dynamics and so on (not to mention narcissism and the conflation between the center of the world and our armchairs). Critical scholars and progressives also have their "star" system of gods and goddesses who only travel first class to deliver talks about the revolution and who come, mostly, from American universities. The brown scholar with an American-Canadian-UK passport and impeccable English profits from the communities that she claims to represent. *All* of this is knowledge and power too. There is no innocence.

Yet, their critique of mainstream knowledges and the contemporary society that they justify *remains valid*. Mainstream PS *is* functional to conventional democracy. The apolitical account of the history of PS and the idealization of our discipline as a pristine, neutral entity that was ruined by evils such as radical politics or dictatorships erases a simple fact: being political is not a matter of choice.

In sum, during the 1990s and early 2000s, mainstream PS was normatively focused on order and stability. This concern was introduced into the discipline by the political reality of the time and its power relations; other values (equality, justice, and to some extent even the liberal rule of law) were sent to the waiting room of history. PS became the knowledge of the status quo, which meant to be on the side of the elites and the powerful. Liberalism made democracy possible at the cost of weakening the democratic experience to the edge of its own (in)existence. This is about history and theory at the same time. With self-critique and more theory, we can resist becoming servants of the dominant powers of the day, be they from the left or right.

Whose Theory? Sustaining Thinking, Protecting (Self-)Reflection

A few months ago, I was pleasantly walking in downtown Toronto with headphones, listening (once again) to my interviewees talk about dictatorship, democracy, and the discipline. While looking around, I felt the incommensurable distance between peoples, circumstances, and sceneries: time, geography, even what most likely was in the heads of the people around me . . . every single thing spoke of an apparent separation between my research and my immediate experience. I wondered once more about the relevance of this study. Not only is PS a minor fragment of the social, but moreover, neither Uruguay nor Chile constitute big players in world politics. Even Latin America as a whole is not at the center of the stage anymore. These days, the so-called Islamic State seems to have become the new favorite evil-other of the racist and imperialist forces that shape the global arena. These thoughts remind me of a night of good wine and conversation when Constanza Moreira, one of the most well-known political scientists in Uruguay,[35] told me that there is no point in studying the politics of academia. After all, our job is to study reality, not ourselves. I want to close this book with a reflection on this question of self-reflection, periphery, and relevance—is the practice of introspection from the margins relevant at all?

In multiple scenarios, situations, and ways, this study has attempted to mobilize a fundamental insight of canonic philosophy, from Socrates to Kant: there is no freedom without reflection and critique. Sustaining the very possibility of thinking against the reifications that power structures, both within and beyond academia, push on us is a fundamental task of theory. Domination and abuse undermine and narrow the space for thinking; in this sense, critical theory, in its fight against both, can be seen as a genuine extension of philosophy. But the problem is that we all participate, in one way or another, in naturalized structures of oppression. Thus, *self*-reflection is crucial as its task is sensing our own positionality and investments *vis-à-vis* these reifications (i.e., dominations and abuses). Self-critique safeguards critical thinking, preventing us from harming ourselves and others in the name of democracy, socialism, or . . . critical theory. It is also about becoming less oppressive, freer, and keeping Socrates and Kant alive.

In more concrete terms, this book sought to unveil the regressive political nature of mainstream PS' narratives about democracy and about itself. Objectivity is a discreet epistemic courtier of domination (Horowitz, 1977; Marcuse, 1991). Self-reflection may challenge such a banality of academic evil, to use the powerful formula of Hannah Arendt (1999). However, this observation includes leftists. As Nietzsche showed us, the interrelations between knowledge and power are uneven and more intricate than moralist views are able to handle. Ideologies, isms, and good intentions do not account for the complexity of life and politics. As a matter of fact, they sometimes become excuses for obliterating reflection. Democracy or social justice can be the locus of harm. Constanza Moreira had a point—our task is to understand reality—but she also missed an important one: that we are *also* part of reality and that the worst thing that we may do to politics is to (re)present ourselves (and the academic enterprise) as transparent (Spivak, 1988). Let me go back to the economy of conceptual and material violence of academia. I will now focus on those who appear to be the most innocent side of academia: graduate students.

Neither power nor capitalism are (just) about bad people. As this study has shown on several occasions, the *mechanics* of academia are shaped by dynamics out of our control. Graduate research displays violence in mundane ways, such that the United States and Europe—even Canada—export thousands of students and experts to explore and assist the so-called Global South, while not many Uruguayans or Bolivians go *there* to study Canadian rituals and sexualities, the backwardness of monarchic loyalties in the country, the roughness of hockey, or the barbaric experience of residential schools. Furthermore, while Canadian mining companies are involved in very questionable practices in countries like Colombia and Guatemala, among others (Keenan, 2012; Gómez-Rojas & Velásquez Ruiz, 2012; Bradley, 2012; Sreeniva, 2012),[36] progressive Canadian students travel to those same places to critically study "Canadian imperialism." In both cases, even if in different ways, Latin America becomes—mistakenly!—transparent to Canada, yet Canada remains unreachable for Latin America. Taking for granted two rather naïve categories for a second, we can observe that oppressors and critical scholars (white or otherwise) share the same passport, and we should at least acknowledge the irony of this situation. Can imperialism also be critical? What does this mean for critical political thinking? Self-reflection may open up mainstream as well as critical eyes to the violence that scholarship unfolds.

This is perhaps an opportunity to recognize that academic prestige is sometimes more related to power than to quality (Gramsci, 2008; Kristof, 2014; Holt,

2003; Monroe, 2005).[37] It is not by chance that *all* the big philosophers of the (critical) political theory core course I took at York University were European men, while PS' big names and prestigious departments are mostly American (Hix, 2004; King, Lehman, & Nie, 2009). It seems that, according to North American PS academia and its southern acolytes, the rest of the world does not think. At this point, a few words on political theory *vis-à-vis* Latin America are needed. I did not want this study to reproduce widespread problematic assumptions (sadly shared by many progressive colleagues) around who can study whom (Hasan, 2012); nor did I wish to be a native informant reporting about Latin America or a recycled scholar from the South who, once re-educated in North America, is now able to theorize. I did not want to, but I am not sure about my abilities to navigate these dynamics. Such forces are, after all, far beyond my control.

The identity of this book is unclear: is it theoretical or empirical? Does it belong to Latin American studies, epistemology, comparative politics, or political theory? I hope that this study goes in the direction of problematizing such partitions. My purpose here has been to engage with human experiences usually underestimated or addressed in problematic ways by mainstream social science (i.e., power and knowledge relations within PS). The location of the analysis is multiple in terms of geography and other registers: it is precisely these instances of porosity and the encounters between different knowledges, spaces, and experiences that I find promising. While focusing on Chile and Uruguay, and occasionally looking more broadly to Latin America, I engaged their "outside" (in particular, the US and its academic and political role in the region and beyond);[38] while looking at political science, I examined broader political processes. Again, critical scrutiny of knowledge production is a way of engaging with the object that it is being known, produced, and enacted through that knowledge.

PS has been an unexpected but productive site to examine assemblages (Puar, 2007) between political economy, subjectivity, geopolitics, and academia/epistemology. In order to avoid and confront liberal reifications, this study has pushed for a conversation between Marxism and cultural (de)constructivisms.[39] In other words, I did not seek to focus on countries but rather on power relations taking place at different, yet interconnected, levels. This study, however, did not deny the need for sites of observation as well as for the delineation of specific spaces where we can see these dynamics in operation. Places matter because the local has its own density (Menéndez-Carrión, 2015). We saw, for instance, Chile and Uruguay's different experiences *vis-à-vis* neoliberalism. Furthermore, note that the places I have studied here do not represent for me three months of fieldwork during the Northern summer in an exotic place. No: they have been sites of my political commitments, my affects, and my life.

Power makes some voices and experiences more important than others, and the academy and its theories are no exceptions (Manalansan, 1995; Mohanty, 1991; Smith, 1999). Marginalized locations, in this case the academia(s) of the

Global South, may assist us in challenging naturalized conceptions of the origins and the very definition of the universal (de Sousa Santos, Arriscado Nunes, & Meneses, 2008; Laclau & Mouffe, 2004; Butler et al., 2003; Buck-Morss, 2009). Localizing marginal experiences in mainstream and critical academic markets— where some cases are sexier than others, where scholars project their desires for revolution or look for exoticism and redemption—is about, precisely, disputing the universal. My multiple references to the "ungraspable" thinker (Mallo, 2011), Carlos Real de Azúa, who happened to be Uruguayan, speaks of this desire. Latin America, for me, is not only fieldwork but also theory. *Here*, as in *any* other place, people not *only* organize themselves in "communities"; they also happen to think and write (and *luckily*, read "dead white men" *too*).[40] This is also a call for my colleagues of the North to listen to us, to read us as well, as what we are: your peers.

Geographic essentialism, however, shall not colonize these pages. Those among us who are from the so-called Global South not only face, but usually *embody* the constant tendency to undervalue academic contributions from countries that are not perceived as rich or white. Furthermore, scholars from the South trained in the North like me both take advantage of and struggle with this liminal position, given that it situates them as privileged in their countries of origin *and* as a second-class, native informant academic in global academia. Where is theory located and whose knowledge counts? Are there limits that we cannot trespass? What are those limits? I go through these contradictions and limits in my academic life and, given that human beings desperately struggle for survival and want to be appreciated by others in this unequal world, the threat of becoming a sort of subordinated oppressor or a subaltern that oppresses, engulfs academic experience.

Subjective transformation in the direction of emancipation seems to always be interrupted even after significant achievements have been gained. After the impression that we—let me refer to a "we" for present purposes—finally "get it," after going through significant internal transformation, we arrive at our workplace or interact with people, perhaps in politics or in simple everyday situations, with a family member or with police, and "reality" pulls us back: you have not changed; you cannot change. Löwenheim (2014) asks: "Can one lead a non-violent life in a violent space and society, and at what price?" (p. 51). The answer is no. And academia is, again, not exceptional. In the meantime, the critical academics' star system keeps moving in the unreachable sky of privilege (and relative wealth). Conceptual revolutions circulate through five-star hotels and first-class flights.

Sometimes I observe the pettiness of academia, which I have always tried to resist, subtly displayed in my own behavior. How is it possible to shut down the voices and narratives of rankings, impact factors, and even the number of likes? Is spiritual delinking possible? Being completely untouched by this institutionally induced anxiety is, for sure, impossible. Remaining focused on the ideas—and ideals—while stress, the mandate for productivity, and the subjective and objective experience of being at risk is pervasive is an enormous challenge. Preaching the revolution is easier for tenured scholars from prestigious US universities: we read them, we quote them, they build their careers on the inequalities they teach us about. Marxist and post-structuralist PhD students struggle to make it, dreaming of becoming the new Judith Butler or Slavoj Zizek, which sometimes requires submission to their Marxist or post-structuralist (perhaps postcolonial) supervisors. Fame and self-promotion are neoliberal traps that ruin the genuine desire to understand and to change. If the subjectivity and praxis of the critical scholar (and sometimes the activist) becomes subtly neoliberalized, what can be done? The landscape is, however, usually simpler and even more ludicrous than the one just described: plain anti-intellectualism, crass professionalism, and in Latin America, objective and subjective conditions that obstruct the creation of something new and beautiful shape scholarship on a daily basis.

If teaching is the most important academic task, if it is, perhaps, the most important *political* task for academics (Brown, 2013), these days is also a rescuing force for me. The students *rescue* me from the unhappiness and emptiness of my life at school. In the classroom I forget about myself—my career, my publications, my anxieties—because it is others I care for at that moment. It is collective thinking, creativity, and (their) future that matters in that space. I just came from a student conference in Popayán, Colombia:[41] the energy, the care for knowledge, and the thirst for change was a pedagogical reminder, *for us*, the international professors, of the meaning of our task. The educators need to be educated. . . .

Conversation with colleagues that elude calculation, competition, and the other treats of neoliberal rationality is also a form of resistance—and it is always there. Even though I agree with Marxists that resistance is not enough, it is, for now, all that we have. According to Ivan Manokha, depoliticization and de-intellectualization calls for parrhesia. The costs of rebellion are high and might imply academic death. After all, "there is lack of reflexivity involved if one thinks there is no price to pay for parrhesia" (Neumann, 2016, p. 274). Injustice will have a long life within and outside academia: our tenured heroes, like Superman, Wonder Woman, or Black Panther live comfortably in our quotes and in their privilege. This brings to mind a thought of Judith Shklar (1989): "I do not like disciples. And I fear that the students who so readily attach themselves to idols lose their education along with their independence" (p. 19). The very logic of the famous academic is a trap.

In a presentation, Himani Bannerji has convincingly argued for the need to challenge the reification of subjects and society, and to reform our "structures of feeling."[42] Both require boundless and radical introspection and dialogue (i.e., putting the critique there, where it hurts) and, in that sense, I foresee potential in narrative approaches (Ravecca & Dauphinee, 2018). Epistemology, political economy, and subjectivity need to work together for such a de-reification to take place. Granted, separation is needed in order to organize perception; in scholarship we separate, for instance, families from nation-states. The problem lies in the ideological belief that this separation is a property of the social itself, which precludes the possibility of seeing the relations between what has been artificially separated. Neoliberalism's motions (Amadae, 2016; Brown, 2015; Menéndez-Carrión, 2015), one of the global forces that shape our lives today, both inside and outside of classrooms, simply do not respect those separations. They are being applied, in keeping with our example, indiscriminately from dating services to state services. The conceptual disconnection between politics, subjectivity, and economy fetishizes the neoliberal enterprise that we are supposed to critically analyze by situating it beyond our sight. Only by showing the circulations of power through human life and its different spheres might scholarship contribute to better understanding what is going on. In short: subtracting politics from the social, the economic, and the personal is a mechanism to conceal how power operates. This book has critiqued this separation as the chief epistemological procedure.

This critique has, explicitly or implicitly, already been done by the critical theorists and theories that have guided this exercise. Yet this encounter between subjectivity, politics, the economy, and so on, including between the critical theories that name them, is always demanding to be fully unfolded. For sure, "it is not a question of achieving the perfect all-inclusive theory once and forever but rather of an ongoing commitment to understanding the partiality of each of our own frames of reference and seeking to extend them through listening, learning, and taking responsibility to ensure that oppressions and erasures are addressed" (Sears, 2014, p. 110). In my view, however, the infrastructures of dissent and integrative liberation politics that Sears refers to do include, or may include, academia. Granted, in order to participate in this political task, scholarship needs to be questioned—and reformed. It is not only science, but also epistemology (i.e., how we think about knowledge) that requires scrutiny.

In this theoretical context, this book critically addressed PS' narratives about its history and identity. The exercise problematized the ways in which PS' introspection has been practiced in Chile, Uruguay, and in the Americas more generally, drawing attention to how power and politics permeates scholarship. In the process, the limitations of mainstream conceptions of PS and its development were unveiled, and alternative conceptualizations were suggested. Reframing how we think and talk *about* knowledge may lead to broadening analytical and political possibilities within academia and beyond. Certainly, this type of meta-epistemological reflection needs to (critically) engage with political projects of emancipation to be completed and materialized.

In the end, however, there is complexity. I cannot give up the engagement with complexity in the name of any political rationale or self-celebratory social justice rhetoric (Real de Azúa, 1973). Power dynamics do not respect comfortable binaries, be it the left-right continuum, the East-West dichotomy, or the opposition between positivism and reflexivity. Critical reflection opposes *any* form of slavery. Domination is unpredictable because, among other things, the hypothetically oppressed (critical scholars, qualitative researchers, women, gays, queers, indigenous peoples, workers, the South, and so on) are not inherently better than the oppressors. In contrast with many Marxists and anti-racist scholars, I simply cannot believe in the purity of *any* space of enunciation or political view, including mine. Complex relationality as a theoretical perspective means abandoning the illusion of pure exteriorities and discrete uncontaminated identities. There is no unpolluted space. If we were going to talk about geography again, I would say: there is no academic hero coming from the North; there is no magic illumination coming from the South. What is "there," then? Perhaps the humbler task for us little human beings who choose to practice *and think about* political science and its politics, wherever we are, is to protect reflection.

If the power-knowledge dynamics scrutinized in this study are indicative, the politics of political science suggest a challenge for both widespread forms of Marxism and significant renditions of post-structuralism. The first dilemma refers to the political status of thinking and theory. Marx showed that interpretation alone cannot change history. Theory indeed *needs* to reach the masses and be realized through their action to actually have historical significance (Marx, 1978a, p. 145). To remain itself, however, critical thinking *needs*, in my view, independence from partial liberations—i.e., activism and politics (Real de Azúa, 1973). Democracy may oppress, while communism and communists may rape. Reflection needs protection from *any* political project that restrains, or may restrain, its conditions of possibility. This means that the two basic components of emancipation (collective action and reflection) oppose each other. This seems, to me, an unsolvable and painful contradiction, a tension that we have to live with because it is not going anywhere soon.

In the case of post-structuralism, and in particular the *oeuvre* of Michel Foucault, the conundrum refers to the meaning of knowledge. Power-knowledge goes beyond Foucault because reflection overcomes canons and authors: knowledge production is a collective activity and therefore will always be somehow related to power, but it does not have to be on the side of abuse and domination. Abuse reproduces itself at the level of thinking. I refuse to abuse others through my writing, and I assume that most people, including political scientists, share such a commitment. Confronting power within thinking and knowledge (i.e., political introspection) may unleash the powers of reflection. Reflection is also richer than resistance. Reflection is at the core of the political project of becoming autonomous, fulfilled, and emancipated human beings. Is it the start of historical change?

"Knowledge is a battlefield" was the very first statement of Chapter 1. The last sentence will be slightly different: *knowledge is not just a battlefield*; it is also a shelter that does not want to collapse—after all, reflection has always been changing history.

Notes

1. Lieber was "the first American academic to have 'Political Scientist' in his title" (Adcock, 2014, p. 67).
2. See the Introduction for an explanation of what I mean by mainstream PS. I follow Sartori (2004) in his characterization. In Latin America, the fixation with quantitative methods is less prominent than in the US, though it is on the rise. In previous chapters, I mapped out the mainstream landscape in this way: the older generation embraces liberalism, political parties, and liberal democracy; the younger generation follows them on these points, but claims that there should be methodological improvement in quantitative methods of analysis. The issue requires more exploration, but I have the impression that American political scientists whose focus is on Latin America tend to be very conventional in Sartori's terms. Thus, they study democracies and elections from the perspective of an institutionalism "on steroids," which has had an impact on their Latin American students.
3. In her studies on citizenship in Latin America, Amparo Menéndez-Carrión (2002, 2003), following Smith (1995), rejects "mindless eclecticism." As with Menéndez-Carrión (2015), this book is both modern and postmodern; consistency is provided by the problem under study.
4. For example: Alexander (2005); Buck-Morss (2009); Butler, Laclau, and Zizek (2003); de Sousa Santos, Arriscado Nunes, and Meneses (2008); Escobar (2004); Leiva (2008); and Smith (1999).
5. Thus, any scientific analyst that is not committed to the possibility of emancipation is pledged not to reason, but to the reason of established domination (Horowitz, 1977).
6. My obsession with critically confronting liberalism and its self-representation as the champion of freedom is shared with, and inspired by, Losurdo (2011).
7. I could have paid attention to these aspects in the case of Chile, where there were also many progressive academics traumatized by the dictatorship and by the feeling of guilt for not having held democratic convictions in the past. I opted to focus on what I thought was the most intriguing and singular thing in that case: APS.
8. In this regard, even though Chapters 2 and 4 are intellectual siblings, born from the exact same questions, I foresee different destinies for them. I cannot imagine the latter comfortably navigating the sea of the mainstream PS readership as a previous version of the former has already been doing (Ravecca, 2015). However, both the cold and warm temperatures were risky in their own ways—the former may freeze you while the latter is too comfortable a temperature to complete the important task at hand.
9. I keep in mind the risks implied in mobilizing metaphors taken from the natural world to understand social dynamics. In this case, however, I chose to work with the ideas of cold, warm, and hot only *after* doing the research and the theoretical reflection. They serve the analytical process without limiting it, I hope, in unwanted ways.
10. Marx's *Capital, Volume I*, and psychoanalysis share a similar structure. The former looks at the surface of exchange first, but in the process discovers capitalist production and its hidden and violent origin of primitive accumulation, located in a past that still is happening (Harvey, 2003; see also Harvey, 2010, pp. 304–313). The latter unpacks symptoms that, like exchange, are always representing *something else* and *another time* (Castoriadis, 1990; Fleming, 2005; Freud, 1986a; Horowitz, 1977; Marcuse, 1974; Robert, 2006). Both, of course, are theories against oppression and for emancipation; they denaturalize power relations by dismantling both immediate experience and time. Similarly, Nietzsche and his genealogical efforts complicated the seemingly obvious division between good and evil, and showed the profoundly intertwined roots of self-evident morals and power (Nietzsche, 1989, 1999a, 1999b). For all of them, thinking is profoundly political, which means that it either reproduces or confronts reification (domination). This book dug into experience and time,

opening up PS' multiplicity of meaning and temporality. By challenging common sense, objectivity, and apparently politically neutral knowledge and its reifications, it belongs to this saga of critical theories (see Chapter 1).

11. Being able to grasp the political seems unlikely if the subjective and the emotional are ignored (Greco & Stenner, 2013). Conversely, we are not well equipped to apprehend the subjective, the emotional, culture, sexuality, or identity while ignoring political economy (Floyd, 2009; Ahmad, 1992; Hennessy, 2000; Brown, 2002). Not everyone deserves to be loved, as Freud says somewhere, and I do not assume that the other has to care about my emotions. If this is a text of social science, it is because its goal is exploring power and knowledge dynamics, which is the basic background of PPS. Our biographies are personal and social at the same time and thus the personal may shed light on the social. Introspective narrative is, or it may be, personally healthy, socially productive, and politically relevant. From a social science perspective, it helps us to unpack the social dynamics of oppression in which our lives are embedded and in which we participate.

12. Following McNally, those theories that forget the genitals, the laboring body, and the pain of real people have undesirable political implications. If the textual world has no exteriority, then there is no exteriority to the commodity form, and capitalism cannot have an end (a factual exteriority, a concrete limit): the linguistic turn in political philosophy can be seen, as McNally does, as a revival of the classical idealism, but with even worse ideological effects. Thus, I basically agree with McNally on his ideological critique of (some forms of) post-structuralism: reality is not just a bunch of texts.

13. The term *intersectionality* does not capture the complexity of the register I am talking about here, which includes the psychoanalytical and temporal dimension of social experience. I agree with Puar (2007, p. 212) in that the "intersectional model of identity . . . presumes that components—race, class, gender, sexuality, nation, age, religion—are separable analytics and can thus [be] disassembled." My analysis is close to Puar's notion of assemblage in terms of looking at "interwoven forces that merge and dissipate time, space, and body against linearity, coherency, and permanency" (p. 212). The past *is* in the present, and there is an underground below the surface; but the surface is *also* in the underground and the present is in the past too. Amid this mobility, complex relationality acknowledges durabilities and structures because it is enough of a Marxist project.

14. This statement is supported by 35 interviews done in more than 10 PS Chilean institutions. In Argentina, mainstream political scientists also hold such perspective, but there seems to be more resistance to it (A1).

15. Radicals of both sides of the spectrum have some relevant things in common, i.e., they talk about power and share an adversarial conception of politics.

16. The label *transitología* [the study of transitions] refers to PS' fixation with the transition from authoritarianism to democracy. This literature is a good example of the ideological stance that privileges stability and tends to identify conflict as a problem (not only of inquiry but also in political terms) (Przeworski, 1991; O'Donnell & Schmitter, 1986). Lesgart (2003) is an extensive study of this literature.

17. Its effects are experienced today when a supposedly progressive Uruguayan government rhetorically equates dissident left-wing groups with fascism because they are "anti-democratic"—both in Chile and Uruguay, the left arrived in office only after being ideologically defeated (Menéndez-Carrión, 2015). While I write this conclusion, the "leftist" government of the Broad Front, in the voice of the Head of Interior, Eduardo Bonomi, claims that groups such as the Plenary of Memory and Justice wear "Taliban scarves."

18. The right-wing dictatorships of the 1970s systematically tortured and killed their political adversaries and people potentially affiliated with groups considered suspicious by the authorities, partisan or not. In many cases of murder performed by state

forces, the crime was perpetuated by hiding the victims' bodies, which, repeatedly, have not yet been found. These are *los desaparecidos* [the disappeared], a powerful and hurtful notion and reality that remains in the Southern Cone's politics today. By talking about Marxism and APS as the *desaparecidos* of democracy, a move that can understandably be shocking for many, I am arguing that without these two pieces, the historical intellectual puzzle will remain incomplete. I also think that the disappearance of authoritarian knowledges from the conversation produces a nice feeling of difference and contrast between "these" and "those" times, erasing the multiple *academic and political continuities* between the democratic and the authoritarian period. If the tradition of all dead generations weighs like a nightmare on the brains of the living, as Karl Marx says, in Chile APS domesticated the spirit of mainstream PS.

19. I use the expression "Pinochet's regime" for descriptive purposes only. It is not a statement about the centrality of the person of Augusto Pinochet in Chile's recent history. I am aware that the nature of this dictatorship is the product of the accumulation and interaction of many historical and sociological factors. This research does not pretend to account for the contrasts between Chile's and Uruguay's authoritarian experiences. It just describes their different interactions with knowledge and knowing as well as their implications.

20. The fate of Marxism and mainstream economics, even though both were involved in the "anti-democratic" politics of the 1970s, has been very different, especially within the dominant narratives of the 1990s. Interestingly enough, even though the discipline of economics was heavily involved in the dictatorship's policies, few question its democratic nature (McNally, 2011), perhaps because of the clear continuities between Pinochet's hardcore neoliberalism and the adjusted one of the democratic governments that followed (Leiva, 2008). It is also strange that neoclassical economics, the knowledge of the dictatorship, is actually the methodological model for mainstream political science today in Latin America and beyond (Sartori, 2004; Monroe, 2005). As Razmig Keucheyan (2013, p. 53) argues, "of all academic disciplines, economics is doubtless the one subject to most pressure from the dominant ideology. This is explained by its proximity to power."

21. Menéndez-Carrión (2015) offers an alternative interpretation: in her analysis, the dictatorship, and its civilian authoritarian prelude, operate as decisive enablers in settling the process of neoliberal creative-destruction in Uruguay.

22. The French philosopher Jacques Ranciére has said in an interview (n.d.) in this regard: "*La démocratie n'est ni la forme du gouvernement représentatif ni le type de société fondé sur le libre marché capitaliste. Il faut rendre à ce mot sa puissance de scandale. Il a d'abord été une insulte: la démocratie, pour ceux qui ne la supportent pas, est le gouvernement de la canaille, de la multitude, de ceux qui n'ont pas de titres à gouverner.*" [Democracy is neither representative government nor a kind of society founded on the capitalist free market. We must return to the word the power of scandal. It used to be an insult: democracy, for those who did not support it, was the government of the vulgar, of the multitude, of those who do not have the titles to govern.]

23. The closing roundtable of the First Uruguayan Congress of Political Science (October 30–31, 2006) was titled "*Gobiernos de Izquierda en América Latina: Populismo vs. Socialdemocracia*" [Leftist Governments in Latin America: Populism vs. Social Democracy]. Note that the sentence is *not* formulated in interrogative terms: the dichotomy in question functioned as a premise that shaped what was thinkable and arguable in this event. With the exception of Constanza Moreira's intervention that problematized this assumption, self-reflection around the political effects of rubrics such as populism, so obviously ideologically charged in this context, was totally absent. It was clear that in the opposition between social democracy and populism, it was implied that the latter was worse than the former—what a "scientific" fact!

Also note that in many analyses, Chile, a clearly neoliberalized country, is included among the social democracies (Lanzaro, 2007).

24. In an informal conversation (May 1, 2012), Viviana Patroni compellingly elaborated on how the ideas debated by the left in the 1960s and 1970s have been constructed as "mad theories," being ultimately erased by mainstream academic and political narratives.

25. Paradoxically, at this time, liberal democracy proved to be as fake as it could be. The Expiry Law shows that elections mean little for human rights and effective equality.

26. When asked about the role of Marxist approaches within academia, my 58 interviewees from both countries tended to link the approach to "political theory," "philosophy," or even "*ensayismo*." The exclusion of Marxism from empirical research is in itself revealing.

27. This view has become globally dominant (Andrews, 2010; Bennett, Barth, & Rutherford, 2003; McGovern, 2010; Monroe, 2005; Luke & McGovern, 2010; Sartori, 2004; Trent, 2014), even in France (Corcuf, 2008, p. 15).

28. This case was made strongly in most of the conferences, seminars, and meetings about the discipline's development that I attended during these years. The argument was also present in the 58 interviews with Chilean and Uruguayan colleagues, especially those who belong to the mainstream of the discipline.

29. The complexity of discursive and cultural transformations is precisely that they constantly challenge the way we represent change.

30. The repertoire of new institutionalisms—historical, sociological, and rational choice (Immergut, 1998; March & Olsen, 1983; Evans, Skocpol, & Rueschemeyer, 1985; Hall & Taylor, 1996)—has been recently expanded by the "discovery" that ideas and discourses matter (Schmidt, 2008). Political scientists seem to be determined to rescue institutionalism from its narrow scope by appropriating ideas developed by other schools of thought.

31. The displacement, destruction, or appropriation of "native" knowledges has been named "epistemicide" (De Sousa Santos, 2008). Similarly, neoliberalism has produced its own knowledge dynamics: economics is the most prestigious social discipline in many environments, even after the incredibly dire consequences of implementing this scientific dogma (Bello, 2008; McNally, 2011; Morelli, 2008).

32. The short but substantial summary of Stein (2012) on the discussions around the development of PS shows that political scientists tend to avoid talking about power. I agree with Kaymak (2001) and his critique of the Perestroika movement that the invigoration of the qualitative side of the methodological spectrum does nothing to the epistemology informing PS and that "conformity" should be interrogated in more nuanced ways. It is not just about opening new theoretical horizons to graduate students, but also about questioning the kind of tools we use to explore ourselves. The Perestroika movement lacked politics (Rudolph, 2005), and it is indeed quite colonial: they did not confront imbalances at the transnational level.

33. The postcolonial critique of science as a Western construct misses the point that Europe does not actually have a monopoly on Reason. In fact, Dussel (2000) shows the fluidity of the notion of Europe itself (which implies, of course, recognizing the fluidity of the notion of the West as a whole) and how even Aristotle was, in the Middle Ages, considered closer to the Orient than to the West. Hobson (2004) also shows how Eastern technological advances were incorporated into Western societies and vice versa, while Pomeranz (2000) criticizes Eurocentrism because it assumes "Western superiority" from the outset (a non-empirical assumption) and because, in this framework, the West, as the Nietzschean Master, is conceived as a totally independent agent/space. Paradoxically, Said, as Ahmad (1992) argues, falls in the same "Eurocentric iron logic of immanence," to use Hobson's formulation. The West is a fetish (Lazarus, 2002) that prevents a materialist and profound exploration

of orientalist logics. What kind of analytical *and political* work the term "Western" does remains an open question: the antimodern discourses seem to reproduce the idea that modernity is the monopoly of Europe, instead of showing the complexity and multiple locations of the making of modernity and science. In this sense, academic practices that take for granted "Europe" as a reified subject or space are ideological. Science is not European. Complex relationality attempts to neutralize the pitfalls of the different critical theories that it mobilizes.

34. Nietzsche's entire work deals with the dark side of moral reification.
35. Moreira is both a leading voice of the alternative left and one of the most well-known political scientists in Uruguay. Currently, she is an MP and leader of Casa Grande [Large House], a new political organization within the Frente Amplio [Broad Front], the political party in office today. She ran for the presidential candidacy in 2013.
36. In 2012, York University's Centre for Research on Latin America and the Caribbean (CERLAC) and Centre for Refugee Studies (CRS) hosted the "Workshop on Trade and Investment-Induced Population Displacement in Latin America," which brought together more than 30 academics, researchers, NGO practitioners, and graduate students from Colombia and Canada to systematize and critically engage with current knowledge on the ways trade and investment are connected to forcible migration in the region. A summary of the activity is available at http://www20.iadb.org/intal/catalogo/PE/2012/10335.pdf. The Extractive Industries Research Group (EIRG) at York University has also extensively researched Canadian mining initiatives as well as other extractive industries and their questionable implications.
37. Uruguayan scholar Federico Traversa (n.d.) recently uploaded to academia.edu a playful but bitter essay about the peer review process, which is worth reading.
38. The academic hegemony of the US affects political analysis. In fact, globally dominant analytical perspectives tend to idealize the liberal democracies of the "North" and to depict political regimes of the "South" in ways that are functional to the dominance of the former. In particular, my overall perception is that the literature on democratization is largely dominated by a narrative that tends to enact and reproduce international asymmetries and to essentialize political regimes, cultures, and countries. As a consequence, "Southern" institutions are often seen as late and defective copies of the corresponding structures that are allegedly observed in Western Europe and North America. These "others" are then conceptualized as imperfect democracies or failed states that are often characterized by low-intensity citizenship. This is a form of orientalization (Said, 1979) of the "South" in the realm of politics— exercised from different spaces, *including of course Latin America itself*—and therefore a manifestation of power relations within knowledge production (Torres-Ruiz & Ravecca, 2014).
39. Although Marxism or cultural (de)constructivism, when isolated from other critical perspectives, may not be liberal as such, they can become part of a liberal academic mechanism of territorialization of different fields, perspectives, and canons that, critical or not, do not speak to each other. This lack of dialogue is very productive: it produces the radical obscurity of power relations (at times, it "does liberalism" in the name of its opposite). Himani Bannerji (2005, p. 18) explains that "the epistemology which ruptures the integrity of the socially concrete at a conceptual level and posits this as a property of the social is identified by Marx in the *German ideology* as 'ideology.'" To fully unfold this insight, Marxism needs to go beyond Marxism.
40. This is an expression that I have heard many times in graduate courses and other "critical" spaces. I consider the refusal to acknowledge the importance of reading and learning from "the canon" the most unproductive and anti-intellectual way possible of dealing with global inequality within academia. Furthermore, in Latin America, scholars and activists do actually engage with such a canon.
41. www.unicauca.edu.co/versionP/eventos/encuentro/ii-encuentro-internacional-de-ciencia-politica

42. This is precisely why Bannerji's essentialization and impoverishing reduction of postmodernism has to be questioned: reifying bodies of theory is as problematic as freezing subjects. It *is actually another way of reifying society* (see Chapter 4).

Works Cited

Adcock, R. (2014). *Liberalism and the emergence of American political science: A trans-atlantic tale*. Oxford: Oxford University Press.

Ahmad, A. (1992). Orientalism and after. In A. Ahmad (Ed.), *In theory: Classes, nations, literatures* (pp. 159–220). London: Verso.

Akram-Lodhi, A. (2013). *Hungry for change: Farmers, food justice and the agrarian question*. Halifax: Fernwood Publishing.

Alexander, J. M. (2005). *Pedagogies of crossing: Meditations on feminism, sexual politics, memory, and the sacred*. Durham, NC: Duke University Press.

Altman, D. (2005). La institucionalización de la ciencia política en Chile y América Latina: Una mirada desde el sur. *Revista de Ciencia Política, 25*(1), 3–15.

Amadae, S. M. (2016). *Prisoners of reason: Game theory and neoliberal political economy*. New York: Cambridge University Press.

Andrews, C. W. (2010). Esboço de uma disciplina em crisa: A disputa metodológica na ciência política norte-americana. *Perspectivas: Revista de Ciências Sociais, 38*, 171–194.

Arendt, H. (1999). *Eichmann en Jerusalén: Un estudio sobre la banalidad del mal*. Barcelona: Lumen.

Artiga-González, Á. (2005). La ciencia política en El Salvador: Sus primeros pasos. *Revista de Ciencia Política, 25*(1), 162–170.

Azpuru, D. (2005). La ciencia política en Guatemala: El reto de la consolidación como disciplina independiente. *Revista de Ciencia Política, 25*(1), 171–181.

Bannerji, H. (2005). *Building from Marx: Reflections on "race," gender and class*. Retrieved from http://davidmcnally.org/wp-content/uploads/2011/01/bannerji.build ingfrommarx.pdf

Barlow, M. (2007). *Blue covenant: The global water crisis and the coming battle for the right to water*. Toronto: McClelland & Stewart.

Barrientos del Monte, F. (2015). Crecimiento e institucionalización de la ciencia política en México. *Revista de Ciencia Política, 35*(1), 95–120.

Beaudet, P., Haslam, P. A., & Schafer, J. (2012). *Introduction to international development: Approaches, actors and issues*. New York: Oxford University Press.

Bejarano, A. M., & Wills, M. E. (2005). La ciencia política en Colombia: De vocación a disciplina. *Revista de Ciencia Política, 25*(1), 111–123.

Bello, W. (2008, May 16). *How to manufacture a global food crisis: Lessons from the World Bank, IMF and WTO*. Transnational Institute. Retrieved from www.tni.org/en/article/how-to-manufacture-a-global-food-crisis-lessons-from-the-world-bank-imf-and-wto

Bennett, A., Barth, A., & Rutherford, K. R. (2003). Do we preach what we practice? A survey of methods in political science journals and curricula. *PS: Political Science & Politics, 36*(3), 373–378.

Biglasier, G. (2001). The internationalization of Chicago's economics in Latin America. *Economic Development and Cultural Change, 50*, 269–286.

Borón, A. (2006). Las ciencias sociales en la era neoliberal: Entre la academia y el pensmaiento crítico. *Tareas, 122*. Retrieved from http://bibliotecavirtual.clacso.org.ar/ar/libros/panama/cela/tareas/tar122/03boron.pdf

Borón, A. (2007). Aristóteles en Macondo: Notas sobre el fetichismo democrático en América Latina. In G. Hoyos Vázquez (Ed.), *Filosofía y teorías políticas entre la crítica y la utopía* (pp. 49–67). Buenos Aires: CLACSO.

Bourdieu, P. (1973). *El oficio del sociólogo*. Buenos Aires: Siglo Ventiuno.

Bourdieu, P. (1984). *Homo academicus*. Stanford, CA: Stanford University Press.

Bradley, M. (2012). Resolving 'investment-induced' displacement in Latin America: Rethinking durable solutions. In W. Payne & P. Ravecca (Eds.), *Trade and investment-induced population displacement in Latin America: A workshop organized by The Centre for Research on Latin America and the Caribbean (CERLAC) and the Centre for Refugee Studies (CRS)* (pp. 33–34). Toronto: York University. Retrieved from http://www20.iadb.org/intal/catalogo/PE/2012/10335.pdf

Brettschneider, M. (2011). Heterosexual political science. *PS: Political Science & Politics, 44*(1), 23–26.

Breuning, M., & Sanders, K. (2007). Gender and journal authorship in eight prestigious political science journals. *PS: Political Science & Politics, 40*(2), 347–351.

Brigg, M., & Bleiker, R. (2010). Autoethnographic international relations: Exploring the self as a source of knowledge. *Review of International Studies, 36*, 779–798.

Brown, W. (2002). At the edge. *Political Theory, 30*(4), 556–576.

Brown, W. (2013, January 30). Reclaiming democracy: An interview with Wendy Brown on occupy, sovereignty, and secularism (R. Celikates & Y. Jansen, Interviewers). *Critical Legal Thinking: The Law and the Political*. Retrieved from http://criticallegalthinking.com/2013/01/30/reclaiming-democracy-an-interview-with-wendy-brown-on-occupy-sovereignty-and-secularism/

Brown, W. (2015). *Undoing the demos: Neoliberalism's stealth revolution*. New York: Zone Books.

Brown, W. (2017, April 25). Interview—Wendy Brown (A. Hoffmann, Interviewer). *E-International Relations*. Retrieved from www.e-ir.info/2017/04/25/interview/

Buck-Morss, S. (2009). *Hegel, Haiti and universal history*. Pittsburgh: University of Pittsburgh Press.

Bulcourf, P. (2012). El desarrollo de la ciencia política en Argentina. *Política, 50*(1), 59–92.

Bulcourf, P., Krzywicka, K., & Ravecca, P. (2017). Reconstruyendo la ciencia política en América Latina. *Anuario Latinoamericano—Ciencias Políticas y Relaciones Internacionales, 5*, 17–31.

Butalia, U. (2000). *The other side of silence: Voices from the partition of India*. Durham, NC: Duke University Press.

Butler, J. (1990). *Gender trouble: Feminism and the subversion of identity*. New York: Routledge.

Butler, J., Laclau, E., & Zizek, S. (2003). *Contingencia, hegemonía, universalidad: Diálogos contemporáneos en la izquierda*. Buenos Aires: Fondo de Cultura Económica.

Cálix, Á., & Sierra, R. (2005). Una mirada a la ciencia política en Honduras: La necesidad de sentar bases para su institucionalización. *Revista de Ciencia Política, 25*(1), 182–191.

Camou, A. (1997). Los consejeros del príncipe: Saber técnico y política en los procesos de reforma económica en América Latina. *Nueva Sociedad, 152*, 54–67.

Cansino, C. (2008). *La muerte de la ciencia política*. Rosario: Espacios políticos.

Castañeda, J. G. (2006). Latin America's left turn. *Foreign Affairs, 85*(3), 28–43.

Castoriadis, C. (1990). *El mundo fragmentado*. Montevideo: Editorial Nordam-Comunidad.

Corcuff, P. (2008). Figuras de la individualidad: De Marx a las sociologías contemporáneas: Entre clarificaciones científicas y antropologías filosóficas. *Cultura y Representaciones Sociales, 2*(4), 9–41.

Corntassel, J. (2012). Re-envisioning resurgence: Indigenous pathways to decolonization and sustainable self-determination. *Decolonization: Indigeneity, Education, and Society, 1*(1), 86–101.

Dauphinee, E. (2013a). *The politics of exile.* New York: Routledge.

Dauphinee, E. (2013b). Writing as hope: Reflections on the politics of exile. *Security Dialogue, 44*(4), 347–361.

De Angelis, M. (2004). Separating the doing and the deed: Capital and the continuous character of enclosures. *Historical Materialism, 12*(2), 57–87.

De Sousa Santos, B. (Ed.). (2008). *Another knowledge is possible: Beyond northern epistemologies.* London: Verso.

De Sousa Santos, B., Arriscado Nunes, J., & Meneses, M. P. (2008). Introduction: Opening up the canon of knowledge and recognition of difference. In B. de Sousa Santos (Ed.), *Another knowledge is possible: Beyond northern epistemologies* (pp. xix–lxii). New York: Verso.

Dussel, E. (1995). *The invention of the Americas: Eclipse of 'the other' and the myth of modernity.* New York: Continuum Intl Pub Group.

Dussel, E. (2000). Europe, modernity and eurocentrism. *Nepantla: Views from the South, 1*(3), 465–478.

Escobar, A. (2004). Beyond the third world: Imperial globality, global coloniality and anti-globalisation social movements. *Third World Quarterly, 25*(1), 207–230.

Evans, P., Skocpol, T., & Rueschemeyer, D. (1985). *Bringing the state back in.* New York: Cambridge University Press.

Felder, R., & Patroni, V. (2011). Austerity and its aftermath: Neoliberalism and labour in Argentina. *Socialist Studies/Études socialistes, 7*(1–2), 259–281.

Ferguson, S., & McNally, D. (2015). Precarious migrants: Gender, race and the social reproduction of a global working class. *Socialist Register, 51,* 1–23.

Filgueira, C. H. (1974). *25 años de sociología uruguaya.* Montevideo: Centro de Investigaciones y Estudios Sociales del Uruguay (CIESU).

Fleming, P. (2005, July). *Marcuse, memory and the psychoanalysis of workplace resistance.* Paper presented at the meeting of Critical Management Studies, Cambridge, UK. Retrieved from www.mngt.waikato.ac.nz/ejrot/cmsconference/2005/proceedings/psychoanalytic/Fleming.pdf

Floyd, K. (2009). *The reification of desire: Toward a queer marxism.* Minneapolis: University of Minnesota Press.

Foucault, M. (1992). *Microfísica del poder.* Madrid: Ediciones La Piqueta.

Foucault, M. (2006). *Seguridad, territorio, población: Curso en el Collège de France (1977–1978).* Buenos Aires: Fondo de Cultura Económica.

Freud, S. (1986a). El malestar en la cultura. In J. Stratchey (Ed.) & J. L. Etcheverry (Trans.), *Obras completas, volumen XXI (1927–1931)* (pp. 57–140). Buenos Aires: Amorrortu Editores.

Garcé, A. (2005). La ciencia política en Uruguay: Un desarrollo tardío, intenso y asimétrico. *Revista de Ciencia Política, 25*(1), 232–244.

Garcé, A., & Rocha C. (2015). La ciencia política en Uruguay: Entre la profesionalización, la partidización y el fantasma del 'movimiento perestroika.' *Revista Ciencia Política, 35*(1), 121–144.

Geertz, C. (1997). *La interpretación de las culturas*. Barcelona: Gedisa.

Ghosh, A. (1992). *In an antique land*. New York: Vintage books.

Giroux, H. A. (1999). Rethinking cultural politics and radical pedagogy in the work of Antonio Gramsci. *Educational Theory, 49*(1), 1–19.

Gómez-Rojas, J. F., & Velazco Ruiz, M. A. (2012). The relation between economic globalization and human rights in the context of the Canada-Colombia free trade agreement: Some notes on balance and responsibility. In W. Payne & P. Ravecca (Eds.), *Trade and investment-induced population displacement in Latin America. A workshop organized by The Centre for Research on Latin America and the Caribbean (CERLAC) and the Centre for Refugee Studies (CRS)* (pp. 30–31). Toronto: York University. Retrieved from http://www20.iadb.org/intal/catalogo/PE/2012/10335.pdf

Gramsci, A. (2008). *Selections from the prison notebooks* (Q. Hoare & G. Nowell, Trans. & Eds.). New York: International Publishers.

Greco, M., & Stenner, P. (2013). *Emotions and social theory: A social science reader*. London: Routledge.

Grewal, I., & Kaplan, C. (2001). Global identities: Theorizing transnational studies of sexuality. *GLQ: A Journal of Lesbian and Gay Studies, 7*(4), 663–679.

Guilhot, N. (2001). Les professionnels de la démocratie: Logiques militantes et logiques savants. *Actes de la recherche en sciences sociales, 139*, 53–65.

Hall, S. (1990). Cultural identity and diaspora. In J. Rutherford (Ed.), *Identity: Community, culture, difference* (pp. 2–27). London: Lawrence & Wishart.

Hall, P., & Taylor, R. (1996). Political science and the three new institutionalisms. *Political Studies, 44*(5), 936–957.

Hamati-Ataya, I. (2014). Transcending objectivism, subjectivism, and the knowledge in-between: The subject in/of 'strong reflexivity.' *Review of International Studies, 40*(1), 153–175.

Harrison, L. (2008). Underdevelopment is a state of mind. In M. Seligson & J. Passe-Smith (Eds.), *Development and underdevelopment: The political economy of global inequality* (pp. 227–235). Boulder, CO: Lynne Riener.

Harvey, D. (2003). *The new imperialism*. Oxford: Oxford University Press.

Harvey, D. (2010). *A companion to Marx's Capital*. New York: Verso.

Hasan, N. Z. (2012, February 16). *Containing fieldwork: Locating the 'field' in academic knowledge production*. Paper presented at CERLAC seminar "Problematizing 'fieldwork': Seminar on knowledge, power and self-reflection," York University, Toronto, Canada.

Hegel, G. W. F. (1977). *Phenomenology of spirit*. Oxford: Oxford University Press.

Heiss, C. (2015). Ciencia política en Chile: ¿Una disciplina consolidada? *Revista de Ciencia Política, 35*(1), 47–70.

Hennessy, R. (2000). *Profit and pleasure: Sexual identities in late capitalism*. London: Routledge.

Hix, S. (2004). A global ranking of political science departments. *American Political Studies Review, 2*(3), 293–313.

Hobson, M. J. (2004). *The eastern origins of western civilization*. Cambridge: Cambridge University Press.

Holt, N. L. (2003). Representation, legitimation, and autoethnography: An autoethnographic writing story. *International Journal of Qualitative Methods, 2*(1), 18–58.

Horkheimer, M. (1978). *Théorie critique*. Paris: Payot.

Horowitz, G. (1977). *Basic and surplus repression in psychoanalytic theory: Freud, Reich and Marcuse*. Toronto: University of Toronto Press.

Ibister, J. (2006). *Promises not kept*. Bloomfield, CT: Kumarian Press.

Immergut, E. (1998). The theoretical core of the new institutionalism. *Politics and Society, 26*, 5–34.

Inayatullah, N. (2013). Pulling threads: Intimate systematicity in the politics of exile. *Security Dialogue, 44*(4), 331–345.

Kaymak, E. (2001). Defeat narrowmindedness, not 'hard science.' *PS: Political Science & Politics, 34*(4), 768–769.

Keenan, K. (2012). Partners in crime? Extractive companies and the Canadian government. In W. Payne & P. Ravecca (Eds.), *Trade and investment-induced population displacement in Latin America. A workshop organized by The Centre for Research on Latin America and the Caribbean (CERLAC) and the Centre for Refugee Studies (CRS)* (pp. 37–40). Toronto: York University. Retrieved from http://www20.iadb.org/intal/catalogo/PE/2012/10335.pdf

Kelsky, K. (2012, March 27). Graduate school is a means to a job. *The Chronicle of Higher Education*. Retrieved from http://chronicle.com/article/Graduate-School-Is-a-Means-to/131316/

Keucheyan, R. (2013). *The left hemisphere: Mapping critical theory today*. New York: Verso.

King, G., Lehman Schlozman, K., & Nie, N. (2009). *The future of political science: 100 perspectives*. New York: Routledge.

Kristof, N. (2014, February 15). Professors, we need you! *The New York Times*. Retrieved from www.nytimes.com/2014/02/16/opinion/sunday/kristof-professors-we-need-you.html?nytmobile=0

Laclau, E., & Mouffe, C. (2004). *Hegemonía y estrategia socialista: Hacia una radicalización de la democracia*. Buenos Aires: Fondo de Cultura Económica.

Lanzaro, J. (2007). La 'tercera ola' de las izquierdas latinoamericanas: Entre el populismo y la social-democracia. *Encuentros Latinoamericanos, 1*(1), 20–57.

Lazarte, J. (2008). *¿Multiculturalismo o multinacionalismo? Crítica a la propuesta del Movimiento al Socialismo*. Unpublished manuscript.

Lazarus, N. (2002). The fetish of 'the west' in postcolonial theory. In C. Bartolovich & N. Lazarus (Eds.), *Marxism, modernity and postcolonial studies* (pp. 43–64). Cambridge: Cambridge University Press.

Lechner, N. (1990). *Las condiciones políticas de la ciencia política en Chile* (FLACSO-Chile Working Paper No. 453). Santiago de Chile: FLACSO-Chile. Retrieved from http://flacsochile.org/biblioteca/pub/memoria/1990/000219.pdf

Leftwich, A. (1986). *¿Qué es la política?* Mexico City: Fondo de Cultura Económica.

Leiva, F. I. (2008). *Latin American neostructuralism: The contradictions of post-neoliberal development*. Minneapolis: University of Minnesota Press.

Lesgart, C. (2003). *Usos de la transición a la democracia: Ensayo, ciencia y política en la década del '80*. Rosario: HomoSapiens.

Lieber, F. (2003). Manual of political ethics, designed chiefly for the use of colleges and students at law (2nd ed., Vol. 1). In T. D. Woolsey (Ed.). Reprint Clark, NJ: The Lawbook Exchange. (Original work published 1890)

Lipset, M. S. (1959). Some social requisites of democracy: Economic development and political legitimacy. *The American Political Science Review, 53*(1), 69–105.

Losurdo, D. (2011). *Liberalism: Counter-history*. New York: Verso Books.

Löwenheim, O. (2010). The "I" in IR: An autoethnographic account. *Review of International Studies, 36*(4), 1023–1045.

Löwenheim, O. (2014). *The politics of the trail*. Ann Arbor, MI: University of Michigan Press.

Luke, T. W., & McGovern, P. J. (2010). The rebels' yell: Mr. Perestroika and the causes of this rebellion in context. *PS: Political Science & Politics, 43*(4), 729–731.

MacEwan, A. (2005). Neoliberalism and democracy: Market power versus democratic power. In A. Saad-Filho & D. Johnston (Eds.), *Neoliberalism: A critical reader* (pp. 170–176). London: Pluto Press.

Mallo, S. (2011). *Carlos Real de Azúa: Un intelectual inasible. El papel de los intelectuales, la política y los vaivenes del Uruguay y la región en la segunda mitad del Siglo XX*. Montevideo: Banda Oriental.

Manalansan, M. F. (1995). In the shadows of Stonewall: Examining gay transnational politics and the diasporic dilemma. *GLQ: A Journal of Lesbian and Gay Studies, 2*(4), 425–438.

March, J. G., & Olsen, J. P. (1983). The new institutionalism: Organizational factors in political life. *American Political Science Review, 78*(3), 734–749.

Marchesi, A. (2017). *Latin America's radical left: Rebellion and cold war in the global 1960s*. New York: Cambridge University Press.

Marcuse, H. (1974). *Eros and civilization: A philosophical inquiry into Freud*. Boston: Beacon Press.

Marcuse, H. (1991). *One-dimensional man: Studies in the ideology of advanced industrial society*. Boston: Beacon Press.

Markoff, J., & Montecinos, V. (1994). El irresistible ascenso de los economistas. *Desarrollo Económico, 133*(34), 3–29.

Marx, K. (1978a). Theses on Feuerbach. In R. C. Tucker (Ed.), *The Marx-Engels reader* (pp. 143–145). New York: W.W. Norton & Company.

Marx, K. (1978b). Economic and philosophic manuscripts of 1844. In R. C. Tucker (Ed.), *The Marx-Engels reader* (pp. 66–125). New York: W.W. Norton & Company.

Mayol, A. (2012). *El derrumbe del modelo: La crisis de la economía de mercado en el Chile contemporáneo*. Santiago de Chile: LOM Ediciones.

McGovern, P. J. (2010). Perestroika in political science: Past, present, and future—Editor's introduction. *PS: Political Science & Politics, 43*(4), 725–727.

McNally, D. (2002). *Bodies of meaning: Studies on language, labor, and liberation*. New York: State University of New York Press.

McNally, D. (2011). *Global slump: The economics and politics of crisis and resistance*. Oakland: PM Press.

McSherry, P. (2005). *Predatory states: Operation condor and covert war in Latin America*. New York: Rowman and Littlefield.

Mejía Acosta, A., Freidenberg, F., & Pachano, S. (2005). La ciencia política en Ecuador: Un reflejo de su fragilidad democrática (1978–2005). *Revista de Ciencia Política, 25*(1), 147–161.

Menéndez-Carrión, A. (2002). Pero dónde y para qué hay cabida: El lugar de la ciudadanía en América Latina, algunas consideraciones para situar el problema. *Ecuador Debate, 57*, 199–219.

Menéndez-Carrión, A. (2003). El lugar de la ciudadanía en los entornos de hoy: Una mirada desde América Latina. *Ecuador Debate, 58*, 181–215.

Menéndez-Carrión, A. (2015). *Memorias de ciudadanía: Los avatares de una polis golpeada. La experiencia uruguaya*. Montevideo: Fin de Siglo.

Mohanty, C. T. (1991). Introduction: Cartographies of struggle: Third world women and the politics of feminism. In C. Mohanty, A. Russo, & L. Torres (Eds.), *Third world women and the politics of feminism* (pp. 1–41). Bloomington: Indiana University Press.

Monroe, K. R. (Ed.). (2005). *Perestroika! The raucous rebellion in political science*. New Haven, CT: Yale University Press.

Morelli, C. (2008). Behind the world food crisis. *International Socialism, 119*. Retrieved from www.isj.org.uk/index.php4?id=455&issue=119

Moulián, T. (2002). *Chile actual: Anatomía de un mito*. Santiago de Chile: LOM editores.

Munck, R. (2005). Neoliberalism and politics, and the politics of neoliberalism. In A. Saad-Filho & D. Johnston (Eds.), *Neoliberalism: A critical reader* (pp. 60–69). London: Pluto Press.

Neumann, I. B. (2016). Conclusion. In J. L. Amoureux & B. J. Steele (Eds.), *Reflexivity and international relations: Positionality, critique, and practice* (pp. 272–274). New York: Routledge.

Nicolaus, M. (1968). The unknown Marx. *New Left Review, I/48*(March-April), 41–61.

Nietzsche, F. (1989). *Genealogy of morals*. New York: Vintage Books.

Nietzsche, F. (1990). *Beyond good and evil*. London: Penguin Books.

Nietzsche, F. (1999a). *Ecce Homo*. Madrid: Edimat Libros.

Nietzsche, F. (1999b). *El caminante y su sombra*. Madrid: Edimat Libros.

O'Donnell, G., & Schmitter, P. (1986). *Transiciones desde un gobierno autoritario: Conclusiones tentativas sobre las democracias inciertas*. Buenos Aires: Ediciones Paidós.

Ollman, B. (1971). *Alienation: Marx's conception of man in capitalist society*. New York: Cambridge University Press.

Panitch, L., & Gindin, S. (2004). Global capitalism and American empire. *Socialist Register, 40*, 1–42.

Patroni, V., & Poitras, M. (2002). Labour in neoliberal Latin America: An introduction. *Labour, Capital and Society/Travail, capital et société, 35*(2), 207–220.

Pérez Antón, R. (1986). Ciencia política. In *Ciencia y tecnología en el Uruguay* (pp. 223–233). Montevideo: Centro de Investigaciones Económicas (CINVE).

Pérez Antón, R. (1992). Ciencia política. In G. Caetano, P. Mieres, R. Pérez, & J. Rilla (Eds.), *Partidos y electores: Centralidad y cambios* (pp. 41–62). Montevideo: Centro Latinoamericano de Economía Humana (CLAEH).

Pilling, G. (1980). *Marx's Capital, philosophy and political economy*. New York: Routledge & Keagan Paul.

Pin-fat, V. (2016). Dissolutions of the self. In E. Dauphinee & N. Inayatullah (Eds.), *Narrative global politics* (pp. 25–34). London: Routledge.

Pomeranz, K. (2000). *The great divergence: China, Europe, and the making of the modern world*. Princeton, NJ: Princeton University Press.

Przeworski, A. (1991). *Democracy and the market*. Cambridge: Cambridge University Press.

Puar, J. (2007). *Terrorist assemblages: Homonationalism in queer times*. Durham, NC: Duke University Press.

Puryear, J. (1994). *Thinking politics: Intellectuals and democracy in Chile, 1973–1988*. Baltimore: Johns Hopkins University Press.

Ramírez Gallegos, F. (2006). Mucho más que dos izquierdas. *Nueva Sociedad, 205*, 30–44.

Rancière, J. (2005). *La haine de la démocratie*. Paris: La Fabrique éditions.

Rancière, J. (n.d.). La haine de la démocratie: Chroniques des temps consensuels (J. B. Marongiu, Interviewer). *Multitudes: Revue politique, artistique, philosophique*. Retrieved from www.multitudes.net/La-Haine-de-la-democratie/

Ravecca, P. (2015). Our discipline and its politics. Authoritarian political science: Chile 1979–1989. *Revista de Ciencia Política, 35*(1), 145–178.

Ravecca, P., & Dauphinee, E. (2018). Narrative and the possibilities for scholarship. *International Political Sociology, 12*(2), 125–138.

Ravecca, P., & Upadhyay, N. (2013). Queering conceptual boundaries: Assembling indigenous, marxist, postcolonial and queer perspectives. *Jindal Global Law Review, 4*(2), 357–378.

Real de Azúa, C. (1973). *La teoría política latinoamericana: Una actividad cuestionada.* Retrieved from www.autoresdeluruguay.uy/biblioteca/Carlos_Real_De_Azua/lib/exe/fetch.php?media=teoriayetica.pdf

Rico, A. (2005). *Cómo nos domina la clase gobernante: Orden político y obediencia social en la democracia posdictadura, 1985–2005.* Montevideo: Ediciones Trilce.

Robert, J. (2006). Herbert Marcuse: Sexualidad y psicoanálisis. *Revista de Filosofía de la Universidad de Costa Rica, 44*(111–112), 153–163.

Rojas Silva, N., & Baquero, S. Á. (2017). 'Estancamiento paradójico': La ciencia política en los tiempos de la Revolución Bolivariana. *Anuario Latinoamericano—Ciencias Políticas y Relaciones Internacionales, 5*, 157.

Rossal, M. (2005). *Ritos y mitos políticos: Una mirada antropológica del campo político uruguayo.* Montevideo: Lapzus.

Rostow, W. W. (1956). The take-off into self-sustained growth. *The Economic Journal, 66*(261), 25–48.

Rothstein, F. A. (2007). *Globalization in rural Mexico: Three decades of change.* Austin: University of Texas Press.

Rudolph, S. H. (2005). Perestroika and its other. In K. R. Monroe (Ed.), *Perestroika! The raucous rebellion in political science* (pp. 12–20). New Haven, CT: Yale University Press.

Saad-Filho, A., & Johnston, D. (Eds.). (2005). *Neoliberalism: A critical reader.* London: Pluto Press.

Said, E. (1979). *Orientalism.* New York: Vintage Books.

Sánchez González, S. (2005). La ciencia política en Panamá: Un nuevo punto de partida. *Revista de Ciencia Política, 25*(1), 204–221.

Sartori, G. (2004). Where is political science going? *PS: Political Science & Politics, 34*(4), 785–789.

Schafer, J., Haslam, P. A., & Beaudet, P. (2012). Meaning, measurement, and morality in international development. In J. Schafer, P. A. Haslam, & P. Beaudet (Eds.), *Introduction to international development: Approaches, actors and issues* (pp. 3–27). New York: Oxford University Press.

Schmidt, V. A. (2008). Discursive institutionalism: The explanatory power of ideas and discourse. *Annual Review of Political Science, 11*, 303–326.

Schumpeter, J. (1985). *Capitalismo, socialismo y democracia.* Barcelona: Folio.

Sears, A. (2014). *The next new left: A history of the future.* Winnipeg: Fernwood Publishing.

Shapiro, I. (2005). Problems, methods, and theories in the study of politics or what's wrong with political science and what to do about it. In K. R. Monroe (Ed.), *Perestroika! The raucous rebellion in political science* (pp. 66–86). New Haven, CT: Yale University Press.

Shepherd, L. J. (2016). Research as gendered intervention: Feminist research ethics and the self in the research encounter. *Crítica Contemporánea: Revista de Teoría Política, 6*, 1–15.

Shilliam, R. (2009). *German thought and international relations: The rise and fall of a liberal project.* Hampshire: Palgrave McMillan.

Shklar, J. N. (1989, April 6). *A life of learning* (Charles Homer Haskins Lecture, American Council of Learned Societies (ACLS) Occasional Paper 9). Washington, DC: ACLS. Retrieved from www.acls.org/uploadedFiles/Publications/OP/Haskins/1989_JudithNShklar.pdf

Smith, C. A. (2011). Gay, straight, or questioning? Sexuality and political science. *PS: Political Science & Politics, 44*(1), 35–38.

Smith, P. H. (1995). The changing agenda for social science research on Latin America. In P. H. Smith (Ed.), *Latin America in comparative perspective: New approaches to methods and analysis* (pp. 1–30). Boulder, CO: Westview Press.

Smith, T. (1999). *Decolonizing methodologies: Research and indigenous peoples*. London: Zed Press.

Spivak, G. C. (1988). Can the subaltern speak? In C. Nelson & L. Grossberg (Eds.), *Marxism and the interpretations of culture* (pp. 271–313). Basingstoke: Macmillan Education.

Sreeniva, G. (2012). Managing multiple accountabilities: State obligations, trade regimes and human rights. In W. Payne & P. Ravecca (Eds.), *Trade and investment-induced population displacement in Latin America. A workshop organized by The Centre for Research on Latin America and the Caribbean (CERLAC) and the Centre for Refugee Studies (CRS)* (pp. 34–35). Toronto: York University. Retrieved from http://www20.iadb.org/intal/catalogo/PE/2012/10335.pdf

SSEX BBOX. [SSEXBBOX]. (2017, May 22). *On inequality: Angela Davis and Judith Butler in conversation.* [Video file]. Retrieved from www.youtube.com/watch?v=-MzmifPGk94

Stallybrass, P. (1998). Marx's coat. In P. Speyer (Ed.), *Border fetishism: Material objects in unstable spaces* (pp. 183–207). New York: Routledge.

Stein, M. B. (2012). Is there a genuinely international political science discipline? An overview and assessment of recent views on disciplinary historical trends. In J. Trent & M. Stein (Eds.), *The world of political science: A critical overview of the development of political studies around the globe: 1990–2012* (pp. 67–89). Toronto: Barbara Budrich Publishers.

Tanaka, M. (2005). Los estudios políticos en Perú: Ausencias, desconexión de la realidad y la necesidad de la ciencia política como disciplina. *Revista de Ciencia Política, 25*(1), 222–231.

Torres-Ruiz, A., & Ravecca, P. (2014). The politics of political science and toxic democracies: A hemispheric perspective. *Crítica Contemporánea: Revista de Teoría Política, 4*, 107–136.

Traversa, F. (2008). Democracia y redistribución en América Latina. *Stockholm Review of Latin American Studies, 3*, 65–79.

Traversa, F. (n.d.). *Maquiavelo y el arbitraje doble-ciego (especulación inédita).* Retrieved from www.academia.edu/10735317/Maquiavelo_y_el_arbitraje_doble_ciego_especulaci%C3%B3n_in%C3%A9dita_

Trent, J. E. (2009, July). *Political science 2010: Out of step with the world? Empirical evidence and commentary.* Paper presented at the 21st International Political Science World Congress, Santiago, Chile. Retrieved from www.johntrent.ca/published-writings/IPSAIsPolSci-0709.html

Trent, J. (2012). Issues and trends in political science at the beginning of the 21st century: Perspectives from the world of political science book series. In J. Trent & M. Stein (Eds.), *The world of political science: A critical overview of the development of political studies around the globe: 1990–2012* (pp. 91–153). Toronto: Barbara Budrich Publishers.

Trent, J. (2014, July). *The state of political studies in the world: Thinking about new paradigms*. Paper presented at the World Congress of the International Political Science Association, Montréal, Canada.

Varnoux Garay, M. (2005). La ciencia política en Bolivia: Entre la reforma política y la crisis de la democracia. *Revista de Ciencia Política, 25*(1), 92–100.

APPENDIX A

The Academic Articles Database

This appendix lists and briefly explains a few of the most relevant variables used in the articles database (out of a total of 89) along with the labels used to classify them. It focuses on conceptual variables that require explanation. It does not include descriptive ones (such as the title of the article, keywords, and so on) or biographic information about the authors (such as nationality, institutional affiliation, etc.). Each variable will be provided in bold and evaluative labels in italics.

Spatial Conception of the Political

This variable attempts to classify the articles in terms of how much "ground" is covered by their conception of the political. Following Giovanni Sartori's notion of politics, a *narrow* perspective on politics was used to label articles that only look at objects located inside the "political system" (with a focus on political parties and the state in particular). An *intermediate* perspective was used to label articles that have objects of study located on the border between politics, as traditionally defined, and the social (for example, interest groups, corporations, trade unions, social movements, etc.). An article labeled as *expansive* addresses issues that are conventionally considered to be nonpolitical (i.e., cultural production, the family, the arts, the dynamics of everyday life, subjectivity, etc.). A last label, *unclear*, was used for articles that did not clearly fit into the above categories.

Type of Democracy Promoted or Assumed

This variable was not among the original set, since it has typically been assumed that political science promotes polyarchy. However, the experience of APS in Chile showed that the relationship between democracy and the discipline is more

complex. This category addresses the type of democracy that articles either promote or assume in their analysis:

- *Polyarchy*. This is the natural(ized) realm inhabited by the political scientist. Thus, if there were no signs in the opposite direction, it was assumed
  that the author held polyarchic beliefs.
- *Protected*. Articles falling into this category argue that democracy needs to
  be protected from the communist threat. Thus, democracy should be "protected" by the military.
- *Expansive or Radical*. The authors propose conceptions of democracy that
  transcend the institutional realm and include society, the economy, and/or
  subjectivity.

Presence of Marxism as a Topic (or View of Marxism)

This variable classifies articles according to whether or not Marxism was present as an issue or topic, and if so, whether they held positive or negative views
toward it. *None* was used to label articles that did not address Marxism at all.
Articles that addressed Marxism but held a negative view were labeled *negative*,
whereas articles that favorably addressed Marxism were labeled *postive*. Articles that did address Marxism but did not clearly promote a positive or negative
view of it were classified as *unclear*.

Marxism and Neo-Marxism as an Analytical Perspective

This variable tried to distinguish between articles in which Marxism was present
as a topic from those that actually adopted it as a theoretical perspective. The
labels here were straightforward, either *yes* or *no*. A similar exercise was done for
other critical theories such as feminism, postmodernism, and post-structuralism.

View of Communism (as a Historical Reality)

This variable measures the presence of, including the articles' view of, communist regimes and movements. Those with a clear orientation were labeled as
either *anti-communist* or *pro-communist*. Those articles without a clear orientation were labeled *neutral*. Those articles that did not discuss communist regimes
and movements at all were given the label *none*.

Theoretical Perspective

This variable examines theoretical variation over time. An interesting finding
(absent in this book's analytical corpus) is that in the first issues of the journals, it
is extremely hard to identify the articles' theoretical perspective. Today, it seems
easier to perform the classification. This is a sign of the institutionalization of

the discipline, given that the adoption of a clear theoretical framework is one of the hallmarks of professionalism expected from an academic article today. The labels used to classify the theoretical perspectives adopted by the articles were: *neo-institutionalism; political culture and social capital; pluralism and neo-pluralism; rational choice and game theory; Marxism or neo-Marxism; post-structuralism, post-Marxism and postmodernism; geopolitical approach; law-centered approach; governance and networks; unclear;* and *other.*

In a September 2013 panel on the development of PS in Uruguay ("The Study of Public Policy in Uruguay: Evolution, Assessment and Perspectives," XII Research Conference of the School of Social Sciences, University of the Republic), colleagues doing a similar kind of typology of articles (by theoretical framework) reported comparable difficulties in assigning concrete values.

Alternative Topics

In Chapter 3 I argued that Uruguayan PS did not address human rights violations perpetrated by the dictatorship from 1973 to 1985. This is the variable that allowed me to measure this. This variable classifies articles that address alternative topics (*vis-à-vis* mainstream PS in Latin America); in some cases these topics were considered new. Alternative topics included: *human rights; gender and sexual diversity; social movements; sustainable development; intellectuals and power; the environment; art and politics; race and racism; other;* and *none* (i.e., the article did not address any alternative topic).

View of Globalization

Articles were classified as either: *aligned; opposed; neutral* or *unclear;* or *unaddressed.*

View of the United States

Articles were classified as either: *aligned; opposed; neutral* or *unclear;* or *unaddressed.*

View of the Soviet Union

Articles were classified as either: *aligned; opposed; neutral* or *unclear;* or *unaddressed.*

View of *Tercerismo* [Third-Worldism/Third-Wayism]

The notion of *tercerismo* refers to a third position that challenged both super-powers during the Cold War. It was a Third-Worldist as well as leftist perspective. Again, articles were classified as *aligned; opposed; neutral or unclear;* or *unaddressed.*

View of MERCOSUR and Latin American Integration

Articles were classified as either: *aligned; opposed; neutral* or *unclear;* or *unaddressed.*

View of Bilateralism

Articles were classified as either: *aligned; opposed; neutral* or *unclear;* or *unaddressed.*

View of Neoliberal Reforms

It was particularly surprising to find numerous articles that support neoliberalism in *Política* and *RCP*. Articles were labeled as either having a *positive* view of neoliberalism, a *negative* view of neoliberalism, or as *neutral/unaddressed.*

The West and Christianity

This variable was added after considering the findings of my fieldwork in Chile (see Chapter 2). Coming from a highly secularized society such as Uruguay, it was shocking for me to discover that Chilean political scientists writing in both *Política* and *RCP* frequently referred to the West as a cultural or civilizational entity as well as a spiritual space marked by Christianity that should be protected from its others/enemies (communism, other cultures, etc.). The following labels were applied to the articles for this variable: *defense/celebration; critical; neutral;* or *unaddressed.*

APPENDIX B

The Interviews

List of Interviewees (in Alphabetical Order, by First Name)

Adolfo Garcé
Alberto Mayol
Alfonso Donoso
Alfredo Joignant
Alfredo Rehren
Álvaro Rico
Andreas Feldmann
Anthony Pezzola
Carlos Durán
Carlos Fortín
Carlos Huneeus
Carmen Midaglia
Claudia Heiss
Claudio Fuentes
Daniel Buquet
Daniel Chasquetti
David Altman
Diego Rossello
Eugenio Guzmán
Francisca Quiroga
Francisco Díaz
Gerardo Caetano
Hugo Frühling
Jacques Ginesta
Jaime Baeza

Jaime Yaffé
Javier Gallardo
Jorge Landinelli
Jorge Lanzaro
José Miguel Busquets
José Viacava
Juan Andrés Moraes
Juan Carlos Gómez Leyton
Julián González Guyer
Julieta Suárez
Laura Gioscia
Leonardo Letelier
Lorena Oyarzún
Lucía Selios
Luis Senatore
Marcelo Mella
Ma. de los Ángeles Fernández Ramil
María Ester Mancebo
Marisa von Bülow
Mónica Tagle
Nicolás Bentancur
Niki Johnson
Óscar Landerretche
Pablo Bulcourf
Patricio Navia
Pedro Narbondo
Roberto Durán
Rodrigo Egaña
Romeo Pérez Antón
Rossana Castiglioni
Stéphanie Alenda
Tomás Chuaqui
Umut Aydin

Interview Questions

1. *¿Podría contarme sobre sus comienzos en la ciencia política? ¿Por qué eligió esta disciplina?* [Can you tell me about your beginnings in political science? Why did you choose this discipline?]
2. *De acuerdo a su experiencia, ¿qué tipo de cambios institucionales, teóricos y metodológicos ha experimentado la ciencia política desde su surgimiento hasta hoy en la región? ¿Cómo ha sido la evolución de la relación entre la academia latinoamericana y las academias europeas y estadounidense en el terreno de las ciencias sociales?* [What kind of institutional, theoretical, and

methodological changes has political science gone through since its inception in the region? What has the relationship of Latin American academia
with European and American social sciences been like in the past decades?]

3. *¿Cómo han cambiado sus perspectivas a nivel teórico, conceptual y metodológico con el pasar del tiempo? Y estos cambios, ¿han tenido alguna relación con eventos políticos concretos? Por ejemplo, ¿hizo la última dictadura que usted reconsiderada sus posturas en torno a la democracia, el estado de derecho, el socialismo u otros temas importantes? ¿De qué forma?* [How have your perspectives on theoretical, conceptual, and methodological issues changed over the past years? And have these changes been informed by concrete political events? For instance, did the dictatorship of the 1970s make you reconsider your views on themes such as democracy, rule of law, socialism, and others? How?]

4. *¿De qué formas, todo lo ocurrido a nivel político, social y económico durante los años 60s y 70s afectó a las ciencias sociales en la región y su propia experiencia profesional?* [How did the political, social, and economic events of the 1960s and 1970s affect the social sciences in the region? Did they affect your own professional experience?]

5. *¿Qué tipo de transformaciones institucionales han experimentado las ciencias sociales, especialmente la ciencia política, en la región durante los últimos años? ¿Cómo han afectado su carrera?* [What kind of institutional transformations have social sciences in the region gone through in the last years? Did these transformations affect or shape your career?]

6. *Chile es visto por muchos colegas como un país que ha logrado modernizarse y profesionalizarse en muy diversas áreas. ¿Piensa usted que esta observación aplica también a las ciencias sociales? ¿Son las ciencias sociales chilenas particularmente avanzadas en el contexto de la academia latinoamericana?* [Chile is seen by many colleagues as a country that has been successful in going through a process of modernization in many areas. Do you think that this is the case also for social sciences? Are Chilean social sciences particularly advanced within the context of Latin American academia?]

7. *¿Cuál ha sido la trayectoria del debate regional sobre el socialismo desde los 1950s a la fecha y cómo pueden explicarse estos cambios? ¿Cuál es el lugar o el rol del marxismo en la ciencia política latinoamericana en la actualidad?* [What has the trajectory of the regional debate about socialism from the 1950s to the 2000s been, and how can these changes be explained? What is the place of Marxism within political science today?]

8. *¿Cree usted que el abandono generalizado del marxismo por los cientistas sociales ha representado un progreso para la ciencia política latinoamericana?* [Do you think that the generalized rejection of Marxism has represented a progress for Latin American political science?]

9. *¿Cree usted que el debate "democracia formal-democracia sustantiva" ha sido superado en la región? ¿Podría explayarse un poco sobre esto?* [Do you think that the debate between substantive and formal democracy has been overcome in Latin America? Could you please elaborate on this?]

10. *Algunos colegas han señalado que la comunidad politológica no ha sido lo suficientemente crítica con las políticas y el discurso neoliberal. ¿Qué piensa de esto?* [Some colleagues think that political science has not been critical enough with neoliberal policies and neoliberal discourse in general. What do you think about this?]

11. *Desde siempre los cientistas sociales hemos debatido la cuestión de la obje- tividad en nuestras disciplinas. ¿Puede y debe la investigación politológica ser objetiva? ¿Cuál estima es la mirada predominante hoy entre nuestros colegas sobre este punto?* [Social scientists have always debated about the question of objectivity in our disciplines. Can and should research be neutral? What do you think is the predominant view among political scientists today?]

12. *¿Debe la ciencia política encarar el problema del colonialismo de algún modo? ¿En qué sentido?* [Should political science address the issue of colo- nialism in some way? How?]

13. *¿Está al tanto del debate planteado por el movimiento de la Perestroika en el seno de la Asociación Americana de Ciencia Política? ¿Cree usted que la (supuesta) hegemonía de enfoques asociados a la elección racional y la exten- dida aplicación de técnicas cuantitativas es positivo para la disciplina?* [Are you familiar with the debate opened up by the Perestroika movement at the Ameri- can Political Science Association? Do you think that the alleged hegemony of rational choice and quantitative approaches is good or bad for the discipline?]

14. *En el último congreso de LASA (2012) se debatieron los casos de Ecuador y Venezuela, entre otros, a la luz de la categoría de "autoritarismo competi- tivo." ¿Piensa usted que los gobiernos de izquierda populista representan una amenaza o un retroceso para la democracia en América Latina? ¿En qué sentido?* [In the last LASA conference, the cases of Ecuador and Ven- ezuela were debated in light of the category of "competitive authoritarian- ism"? Do you think that these leftist populist governments represent a threat or a setback to democracy in the region today? How?]

15. *¿Ha sido la ciencia política exitosa en afirmar una identidad propia en el marco de las ciencias sociales? ¿Hay acuerdo hoy entre los colegas en que existe una distinción clara entre ciencia política y sociología política?* [Has political science been successful in affirming its identity among the social sciences? How are we different from sociologists?]

16. *¿Cómo ve el futuro de nuestra disciplina en la región?* [How do you envi- sion the future of political science in the region?]

17. *¿Cuál de las siguientes categorías mejor describe su trabajo académico?* [Which of the following categories best describes your academic work?]

    a.   partidos políticos y gobierno [political parties and government]
    b.   estado y políticas publicas [the state and public policy]
    c.   teoría política [political theory]
    d.   política y género [politics and gender]
    e.   relaciones internacionales [international relations]
    f.   otro [other]

Descriptive Tables

TABLE B1 Interviews by country*

Country	Number
Argentina	1
Chile	35
Uruguay	22
Total	58

* **Important note:** As shown by B5, nine (9) colleagues that, during the fieldwork, were based in Chilean institutions have academic histories in the United States, Europe, Argentina, Brazil, and other locations. Thus, the research covers several other Latin American countries and beyond.

TABLE B2 Average length of interview, by country

Country	Minutes
Argentina	105
Chile	79
Uruguay	106
General average	96.81

TABLE B3 Maximum length of interview, by country

Country	Minutes
Argentina	105 (A1)
Chile	166 (CHL10)
Uruguay	271 (U10)

TABLE B4 Minimum length of interview, by country

Country	Minutes
Argentina	105 (A1)
Chile	37 (CHL26)
Uruguay	42 (U9)

TABLE B5 Number of foreign interviewees, by country

Country	Foreigners
Argentina	0
Chile	9
Uruguay	1

APPENDIX C

Situated Understanding(s) of the Terms "Quantitative" and "Quantification"

Sartori's (2004) harshly critical piece on American PS sparked controversy in Latin America (see Introduction). To a lesser extent, the Perestroika movement within the APSA (Monroe, 2005) also reached the Latin American conversation (see also Introduction, especially the passages on my conception of "the mainstream"). Cecilia Rocha (2014) explores to what extent mainstream American PS is being imported into or imposed on the region, and concludes that there is enough empirical evidence of a shift in that direction. Indeed, the growth of quantitativism is clear to any informed observer. However, and this is perhaps even more significant, *the very notion* of what constitutes quantitative research varies across geographies and academic cultures: while in many academic conversations in Latin America, descriptive statistics or even the mere presence of tables with numerical data are considered markers of a quantitative identity, within American debates only statistical techniques of analysis such as regression or correlation are the doorbell to the world of quantification.

For instance, if we use the American concept of quantitative research, the research of Uruguayan political scientists are actually *extremely* qualitative. Following the typology of academic articles by methods used by Pion-Berlin and Cleary (2005) and Kasza (2005) (see Figure C1), between 1991 and 2000, 74% of *APSR* articles used "statistics" or "mathematical modeling" (Pion-Berlin & Cleary, 2005, p. 307), while, according to my own analysis, that is the case for only a tiny minority of articles in *RUCP* (around 5%). Figure C2 shows that even in the more recent period of 2001–2012, only 17% of *RUCP* articles fall into the category of using statistical methods. This is an expression of the situated condition of science; again, knowledge has its political circumstances.

- **Statistics:** articles that analyze empirical, numerical data sets using statistical techniques such as regression or correlation.
- **Mathematical or formal modeling:** articles that use deductive reasoning to develop formal models.
- **Philosophy or theory:** articles on philosophers such as Plato and articles that explore questions such as "What is political culture?" without examining specific empirical cases.
- **Qualitative empirical research:** articles that explore empirical subjects without using statistical techniques.

FIGURE C1 Typology of academic articles by methods

(Pion-Berlin & Cleary, 2005; Kasza, 2005)

TABLE C1 Typology of articles by methods, AJPS and APSR

Typology of articles	American Journal of Political Science	American Political Science Review
Statistics + Modeling (%)	90.3 (2000–2001)	79.4 (only 2000)

(Pion-Berlin and Cleary (2005, p. 307))

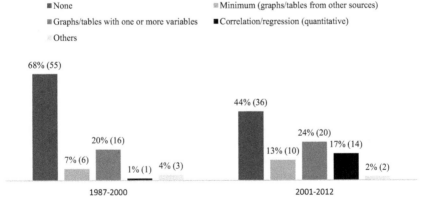

FIGURE C2 "Quantitative" articles in *RUCP* (1987–2012).

APPENDIX D

An Example of the Acritical Relationship with the Elites? PS and Mining

On February 27, 2014, at 6:00 p.m., the ICP hosted a roundtable titled "Mega-Mining and the Environment," where only mining-friendly individuals were invited to speak. Moreover, one of them was actively involved in the Aratirí project.[1] The activity was disrupted by a group called Asamblea Pachamama Uruguay [Mother Earth Assembly Uruguay] with accusatory shouts.[2] The activists asked to participate in the event as speakers, a possibility that was denied by the organizers who argued that there would be another roundtable including critical voices later on. Thus, they made their contribution to the debate in the only way available—by protesting. There was a second round-table hosted by the ICP on March 7, where a mea culpa was made in terms of the unbalanced view presented by the first event. Indeed, this event included panelists critical of the Aratirí project. However, Asamblea Pachamama was again excluded; groups that were perceived as more moderate were instead invited.

The disorganized and heated way in which both conversations took place shows the lack of dialogue and symbolic violence that official voices exercise over dissent (to the point that a trade-union leader prevented one member of the public from speaking). In an email interview with one of the leaders of Asamblea Pachamama Uruguay, it was mentioned that they are systematically invisibilized by the mass media and by academia. According to a study, 25% of the Uruguayan population have never heard of the Aratirí project, which is going to be the biggest foreign direct investment in Uruguayan history.[3]

Notes

1. Minera Aratirí, the Uruguayan subsidiary of Anglo-Swiss group Zamin Ferrous, is engaged in the prospecting, exploration, mining, processing, and export of iron ore in Uruguay. The company is developing the greenfield Valentines iron ore extraction project.
2. This is the website of the organization: www.pachamama.org/.
3. More information can be found in the following links: www.subrayado.com.uy/Site/noticia/31457/paridad-entre-quienes-estan-a-favor-y-en-contra-de-aratiri; www.elobservador.com.uy/noticia/273459/charla-sobre-mineria-casi-termina-a-los-golpes/.

INDEX

Note: page numbers in *italics* indicate figures and page numbers in **bold** indicate tables on the corresponding pages.

231, 238n2, 238n6, 242n39; critique
of 19; democratic 130; dogmatic 123,
178–179; economic 73, 190, 226;
hegemony of 2, 4, 112, 136, 149, 210,
215; neoconservative 215; objectivist
148; political 73, 190, 226; post-
transition 215; transatlantic 194n18; *see
also* neoliberalism
liberal unthinking 145–151, 214–219
liberation theology 5, 75
Locke, John 67, 69, 117

Machado, Antonio 1
Machiavelli 124
Macri, Mauricio 196n31
Maduro, Nicolás 187
mainstream narrative 2, 6–7, 9, 33, 102,
127, 147, 219, *219*, 221, **223**, 225, 227
mainstream PS 2, 5–6, 10n2, 10–11n6,
21, 30, 62, 66, 120, 129, 131, 140,
174–175, 179, 195n24, 197–198n38,
211, 214–218, *219*, *223*, 226, 230–232,
238n2, 238n8, 239–240n18; narratives
of 25, 103; scholars 11n7, 128
Marcuse, Herbert 5, 21–23, 33,
38n5, 40n24, 87n2, 142–143,
153n25, 155n54, 168, 191, 209,
225; *Eros and Civilization* 21; *One-
Dimensional Man* 21
Mariátegui, José Carlos 10n2
market economy 67–71, 85, 213, 226
market utopias 141–144
Márquez, Gabriel García 10n2
Marx, Karl 16, 17–18, 19, 21, 58, 75,
117–118, 120, 148, 152n8, 165, 179,
182, 197n36, 209, 237, 239–240n18,
242n39; *Capital* 17, 37n1, 123,
148, 238–239n10; *Economic and
Philosophical Manuscripts* 21, 123,
156n59
Marxism 1–2, 5, 7, 9, 16–17, 20–21, 23,
26, 34, 37–38n1, 38n4, 40–41n28, 50,
58, 60, 62, 75, 83, 85, 98, 101–102,
106–107, 111–112, 115, 117–118,
120–126, 129–132, 145–150, 153n29,
170, 173–174, 176, 178, 180, 191,
194–195n21, 197n35, 213–214,
216–218, *219*, 220–222, *223*,
224–225, 229, 233, 237, 239–240n18,
240n20, 241n26, 242n39; neo- 26,
58, 117, 125, 130, 209; in *Política
60*; post- 118, 209; in *RCP* 58, *61*; in
RUCP 118

Marxism-Leninism 58, 150; *see also*
Marxism
"Marxist Church" 112, 178, 218
masculinity: positivist 172–177
materialism 20
McCarthyism 156n55, 195n25
Menéndez-Carrión, Amparo 151n, 153n3,
153n21, 155n44, 197–198n38, 226,
228, 238n3, 240n21
Mexico 87n4, 156n55
MLN-Tupamaros 152n16
Montesquieu 67
Montevideo 36–37, 168, 171, 177,
180–182, 193n9, 196n29

Narbondo, Pedro 37, 41n35
narrative: academic 20; activist 130;
alternative 219; anti-communist 118;
approaches 29, 31, 35, 191–192n1,
193n8, 199n53, 229, 236; APS 85;
auto-ethnographic 3; of collective self-
blaming 102; dominant 17, 25, 64, 121,
179, 210, 240n20; gradualism 155n44;
hegemonic 121; "I" 166, 182; meta-
131; political 241n24; post-dictatorship
97; pro-capitalist 180; of protected
democracy 63–64; PS 3, 5, 103, 114,
125, 134, 137, 139, 146, 225; on trauma
191; writing 182, 198n45; *see also*
mainstream narrative
nation-state 9, 125, 167–168, 181,
186, 236
neoliberalism 1, 8, 18, 26–27, 39n16,
50, 67, 69–70, 85, 110, 140–143,
151, 155n54, 156n55, 176, 178, 187,
197–198n38, 199n48, 217, 226, 233,
236, 240n20, 241n31; global 26;
hegemony of 5, 226
neoliberalization 109
neoliberal turn 216
Neruda, Pablo 10n2
Nietzsche, Friedrich 1, 18–19, 22–23,
38n3, 75, 169–170, 179, 182, 184–185,
192n6, 209, 227, 229–230, 232,
238–239n10, 241–242n33, 242n34;
ascetic ideal 18–19; *Beyond Good and
Evil* 19; and positivism 19
nihilism 75
North America 7, 24, 34, 37, 38n9, 85,
229, 233, 242n38

objectivism 108, 131
objectivist rationality 32

objectivity 2, 19–20, 31, 98, 108, 114,
129, 131, 147–148, 150, 176, *219*,
220–221, *223*, 225, 227–228, 232,
238–239n10; academic 81; hegemony
of 112; narratives of 208; positivist 146;
scientific 132, 226
oppression 16, 19, 23, 26–27, 31, 38n2,
40n22, 126, 166, 169–170, 175–177,
179–180, 183–184, 186–188,
196n31, 199n48, 212, 217, 229–230,
236, 238–239n10; social dynamics
of 239n11; social relations of 228;
structural 198n45; structures of 188,
231; unlearning 23, 37
orientalism 23–24, 38n8
other, the 122, 127, 145, 171, 186,
188, 235
othering 26, 167, 192n4, 194–195n21

Parra, Violeta 10n2
Partido Colorado (Colorado Party)
153n27
partidocracia (partyocracy) 132–139
Partido Nacional (National Party) 153n27
partyocracy: Uruguay as 132, 134, 147
patriarchy 27, 194n18; hetero- 198n47
Perestroika movement 6–7, 25, 30,
39n15, 130–131, 229, 241n32
Pérez Antón, Romeo 104, 112, 129, 150,
152n6, 152n10
Perú 86n, 151n, 186
Pinochet, Augusto 11n8, 51, *51*, 81,
83–84, 88n28, 240n19, 240n20;
dictatorship of 3, 8, 50, 79, 88n18, 210,
217–218; government 11n8, 69–70;
regime 48, 51, 54, 58, 70–71, 85, 87n3,
88n27, 98, 104, 215, 217, 240n19
PIT-CNT 187
pluralism 32, 61–62, 66, 120, 225;
limited 85; political 61
plurality 3, 18, 28, 116, 212;
epistemological 33
pluralization 3
Política (Politics) 33–34, 49–55, *51*, *52*,
57–58, 61, 64, 66–67, 74, 81, 83, 87n5,
87n9, 88n22, 88n25, 144; academic
training of contributors 75–76, 79,
79, *80*; anti-communism of *56*, 57;
contributors to *80*, 81; on Marxism
58; on neoliberal reforms 70, *70*; on
polyarchy 63; on protected democracy
63; on religion *79*; *Revista Política
79*, *80*; view toward US 56, *57*; view
toward USSR 56, *57*; on the West and
Christianity 77–79

political correctness 173, 177, 196n31
political economy 6, 17, 21, 24–28,
37–38n1, 49, 81, 97, 112, 132, 137,
147–149, 153n26, 154n40, 156n62, 167,
194–195n21, 213, 222, 224–226, 233,
235, 239n11; global 230; international
147, 167, 208; neoliberal 196n26
political parties 55, 58, 97, 112, 115–116,
122–123, 127, 129, 132–134, 136,
148, 150, 152n10, 153n27, 154n42,
154–155n43, 172, 238n2; leftist 103;
mainstream 147, 149; traditional 115,
123, 132–135, 137, 139, 147, 218
political polarization 101–102, 107, 115,
147, 172, 178, 220, 222
political science (PS): academics 105;
American 7, 10–11n6, 39n15, 87n2,
139, 143; Anglo-Saxon 65; birth of
114, 124, 129; Chilean 63, 81, 84, 98,
210; conformist 98; conventional 117;
development of 7–8, 10n1, 37, 41n34,
54, 120, 122, 129, 209, 216, 225,
228, 241n32; emergence of 99, 102,
123; identity 26, 114, 125, 132–133,
146–148; institutionalization of 48, 86,
133, 224; Latin American 6–7, 39n20,
40n21, 130, 228; liberal 39–40n20,
55, 72, 155n54, 178, 214; modern 124;
narrative 3, 5, 103, 114, 125, 134, 137,
139, 146, 225; neopositivist 178, 214;
North American 233; political role of
135; positivist 22; practitioners 11n7,
102, 155n45, 166; professionalization
of 79; scholars 128, 134; scholarship
135; "standard" *82*, 86; Uruguayan 4,
41n32, 97–98, 108, 117–118, 122, 124,
127–129, 131–133, 136, 138–139,
141, 145–148, 154n40, 154n41,
154n42, 177–178, 208, 216–217; *see
also* mainstream PS
politics: autonomy of 39–40n20; 120,
125, 128, 132, 134, 221
politics of political science (PPS) 2, 4, 6,
8–10, 10n4, 17–18, 21, 23–25, 28–35,
37, 39n17, 40n26, 41n34, 48, 50–51,
85, 96–99, 124, 150, 165–166, 182,
209–210, 212–214, 221, *223*, **223**, 227,
229, 239n11
Pontificia Universidad Católica de
Chile (Pontifical Catholic University
of Chile) 35
populism 217, 240–241n23
Portugal 76
positivism 2, 19, 21, 40n22, 199n48,
221–222, 237; American 225; liberal